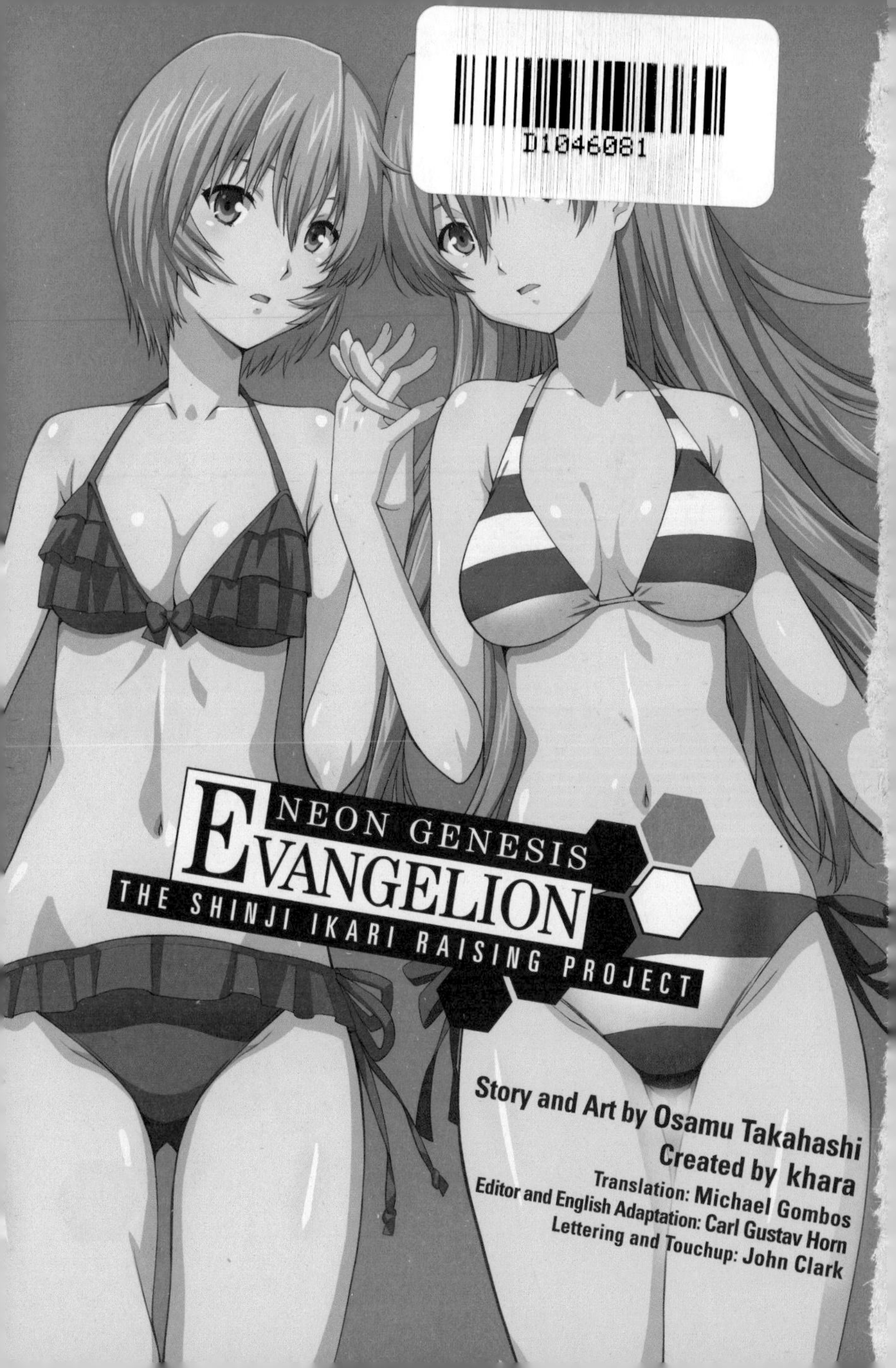
NEON GENESIS
EVANGELION
THE SHINJI IKARI RAISING PROJECT
Story and Art by Osamu Takahashi
Created by khara
Translation: Michael Gombos
Editor and English Adaptation: Carl Gustav Horn
Lettering and Touchup: John Clark

NEON GENESIS EVANGELION

THE SHINJI IKARI RAISING PROJECT

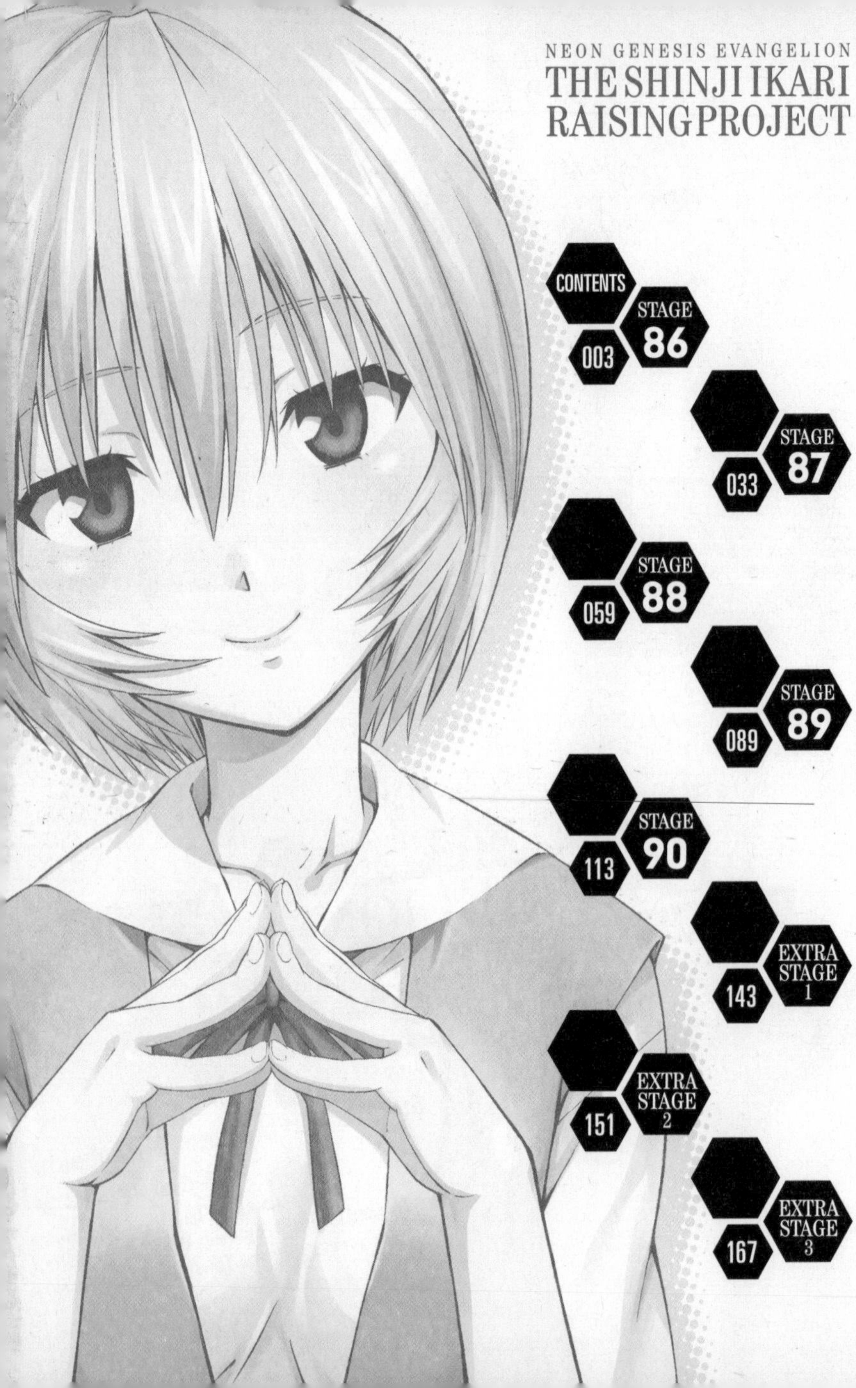

CONTENTS

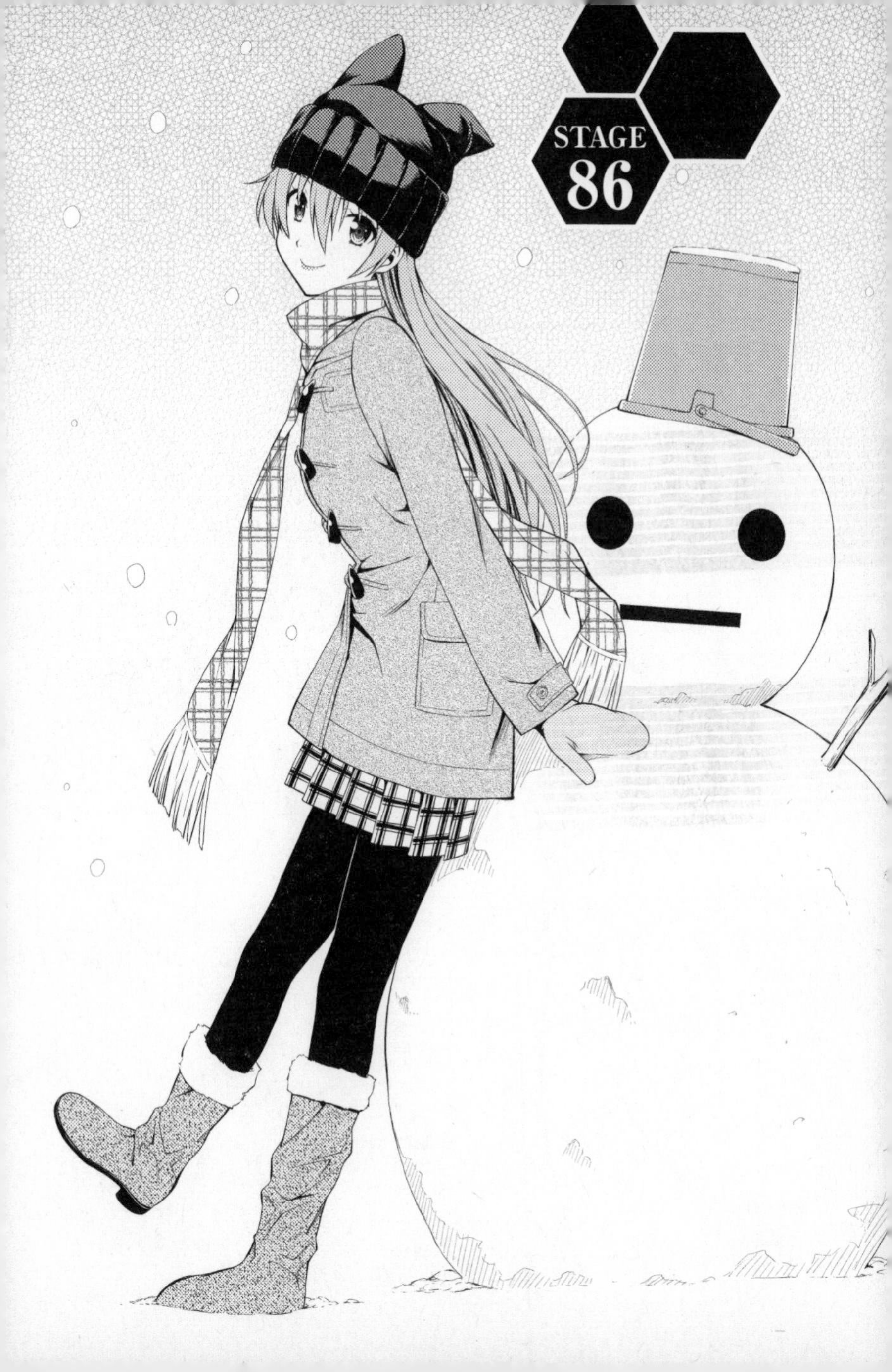
STAGE
86

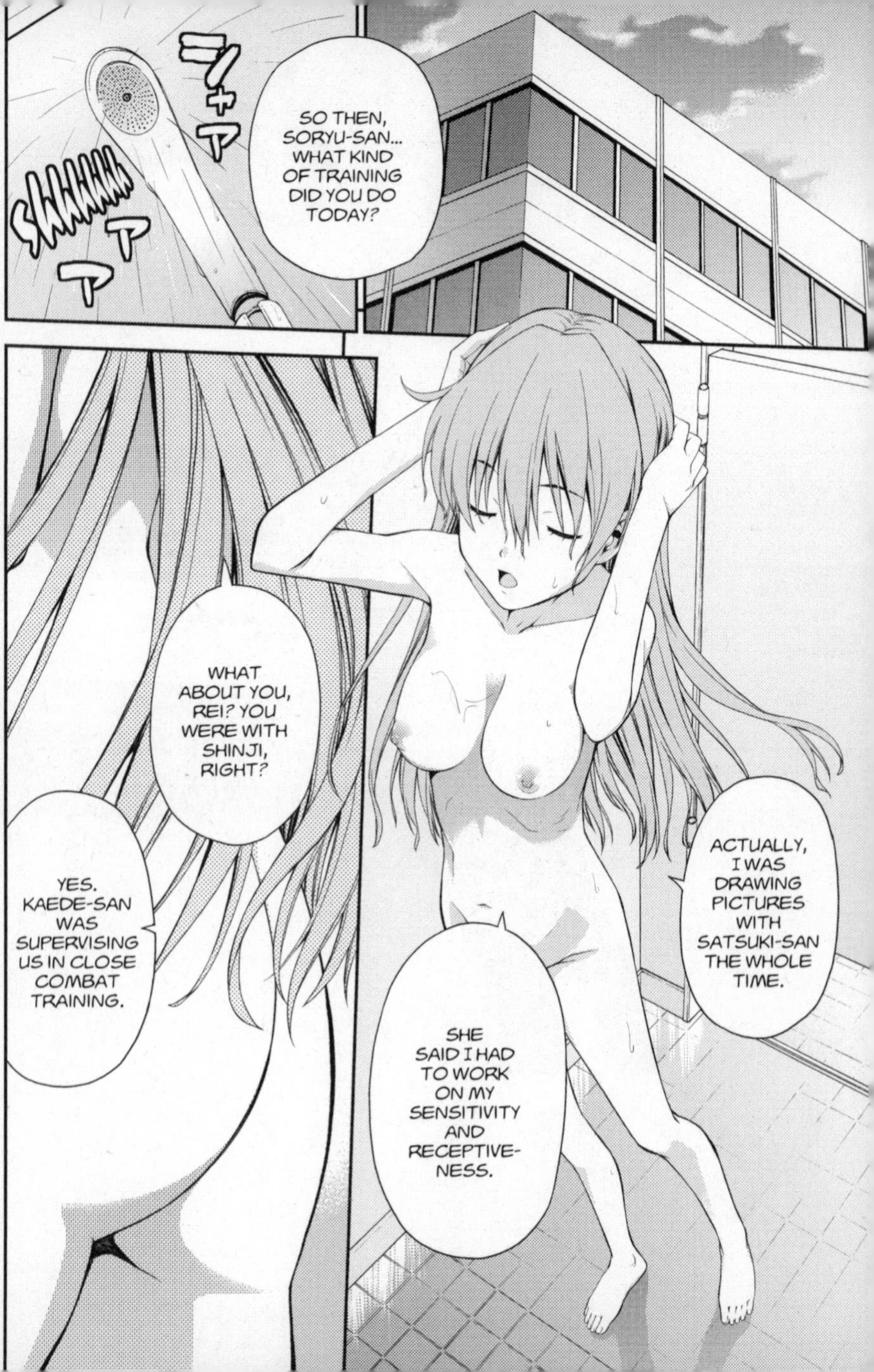
SO THEN, SORYU-SAN... WHAT KIND OF TRAINING DID YOU DO TODAY?
シャアアア
SHAAAAA
ACTUALLY, I WAS DRAWING PICTURES WITH SATSUKI-SAN THE WHOLE TIME.
SHE SAID I HAD TO WORK ON MY SENSITIVITY AND RECEPTIVE-NESS.
WHAT ABOUT YOU, REI? YOU WERE WITH SHINJI, RIGHT?
YES. KAEDE-SAN WAS SUPERVISING US IN CLOSE COMBAT TRAINING.

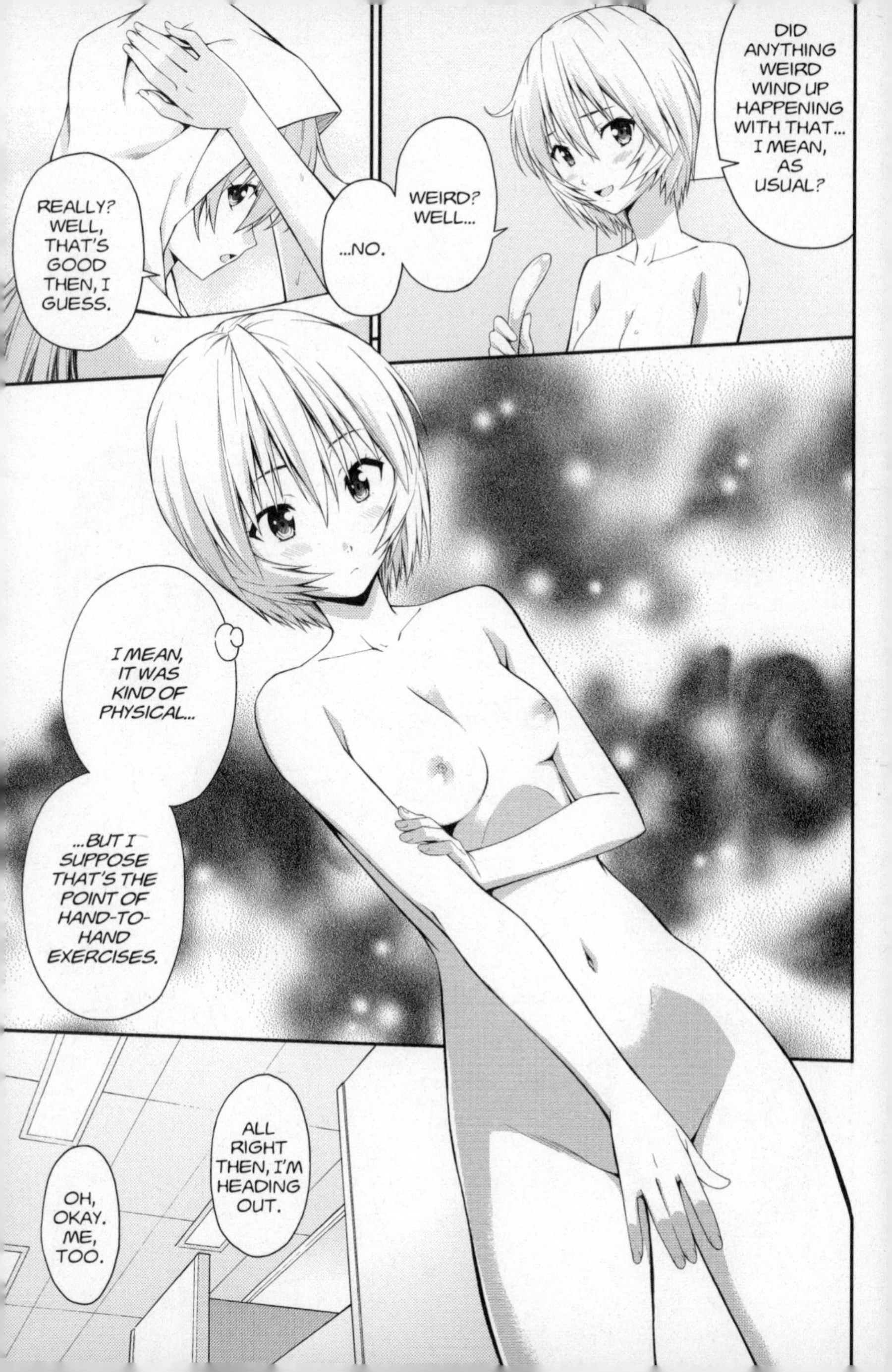
DID ANYTHING WEIRD WIND UP HAPPENING WITH THAT... I MEAN, AS USUAL?
WEIRD? WELL...
...NO.
REALLY? WELL, THAT'S GOOD THEN, I GUESS.
I MEAN, IT WAS KIND OF PHYSICAL...
...BUT I SUPPOSE THAT'S THE POINT OF HAND-TO-HAND EXERCISES.
ALL RIGHT THEN, I'M HEADING OUT.
OH, OKAY. ME, TOO.

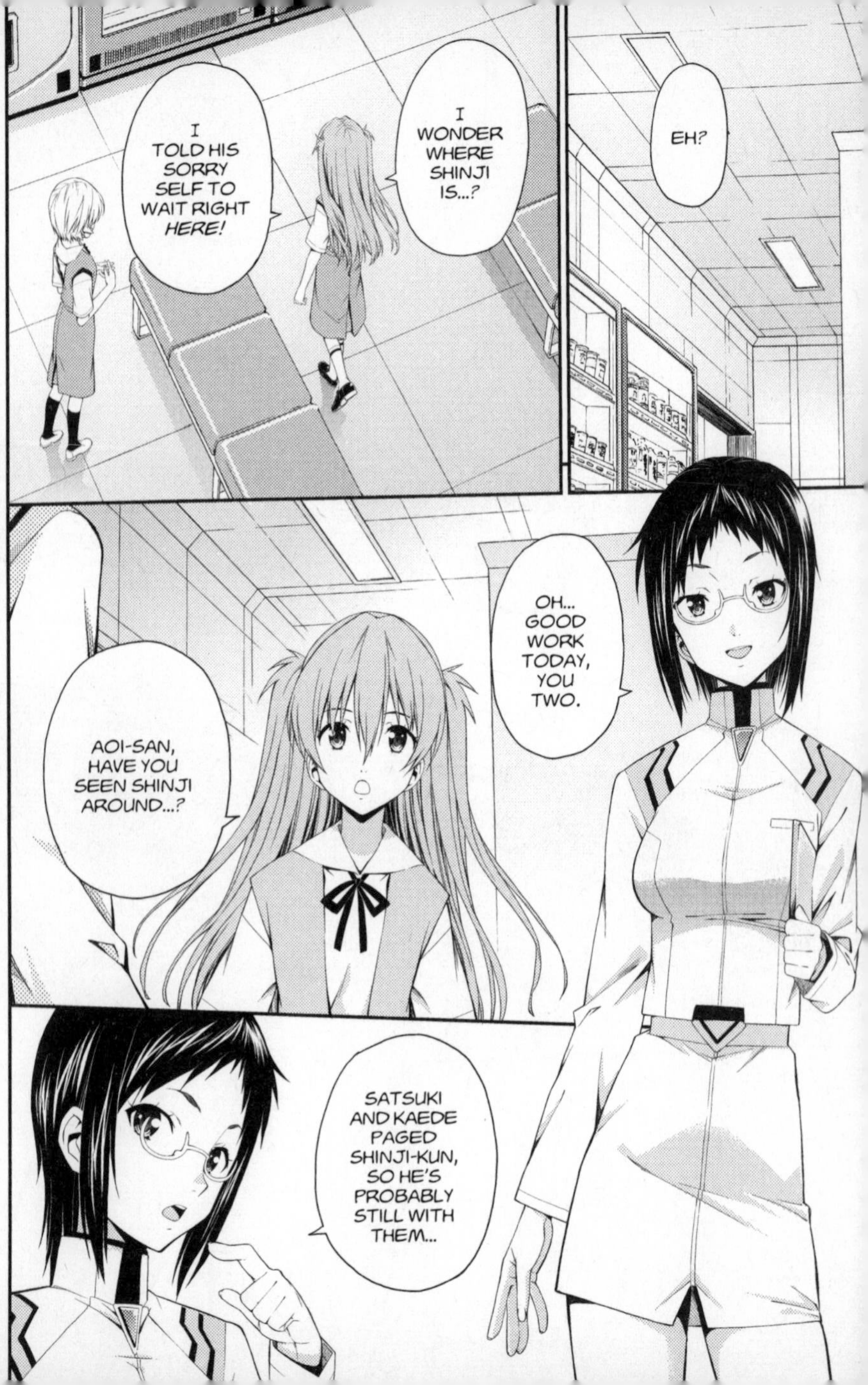
EH?
I WONDER WHERE SHINJI IS...?
I TOLD HIS SORRY SELF TO WAIT RIGHT *HERE!*
OH... GOOD WORK TODAY, YOU TWO.
AOI-SAN, HAVE YOU SEEN SHINJI AROUND...?
SATSUKI AND KAEDE PAGED SHINJI-KUN, SO HE'S PROBABLY STILL WITH THEM...

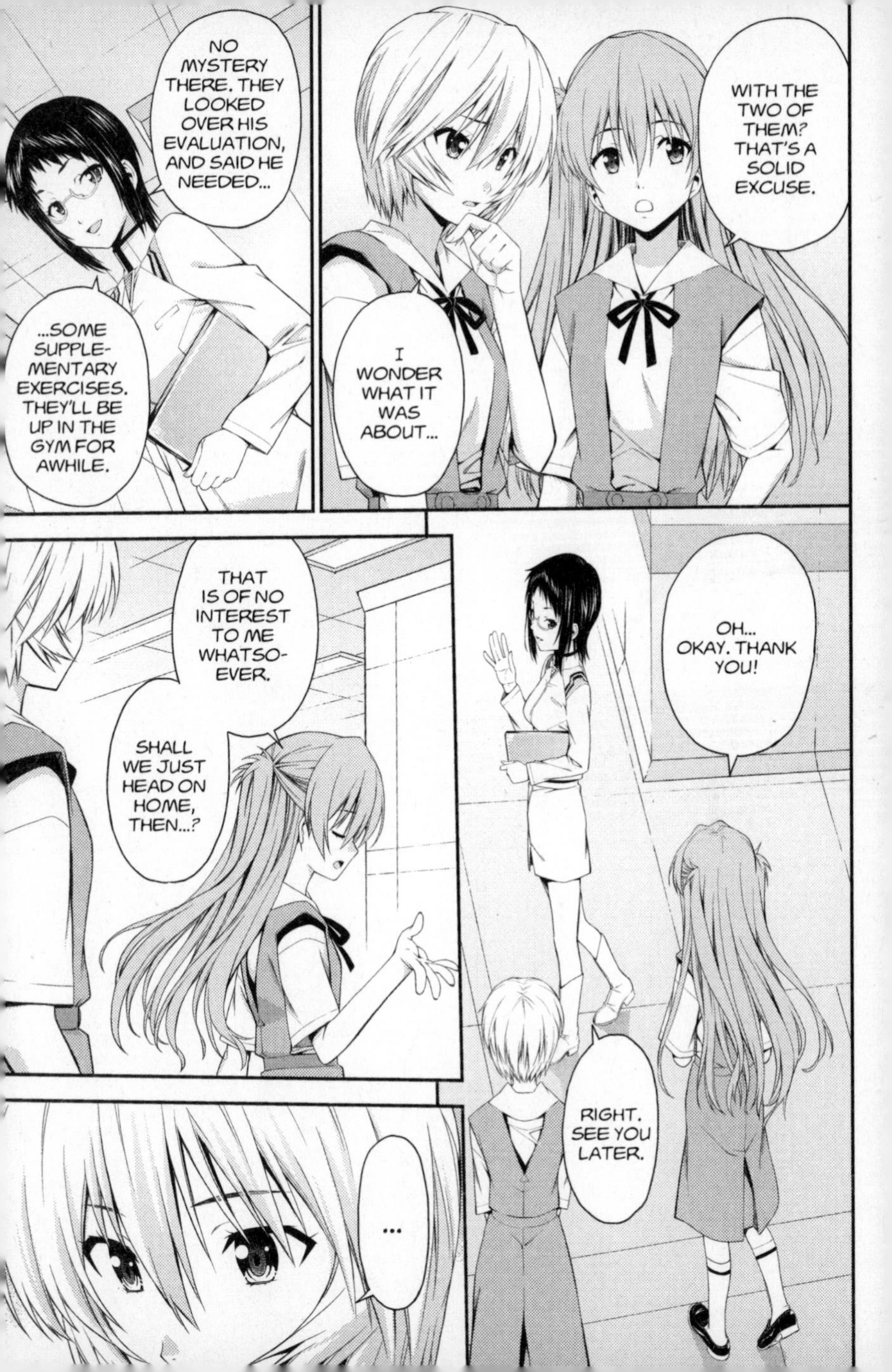
WITH THE TWO OF THEM? THAT'S A SOLID EXCUSE.
I WONDER WHAT IT WAS ABOUT...
NO MYSTERY THERE. THEY LOOKED OVER HIS EVALUATION, AND SAID HE NEEDED...
...SOME SUPPLE-MENTARY EXERCISES. THEY'LL BE UP IN THE GYM FOR AWHILE.
OH... OKAY. THANK YOU!
RIGHT. SEE YOU LATER.
THAT IS OF NO INTEREST TO ME WHATSO-EVER.
SHALL WE JUST HEAD ON HOME, THEN...?
...

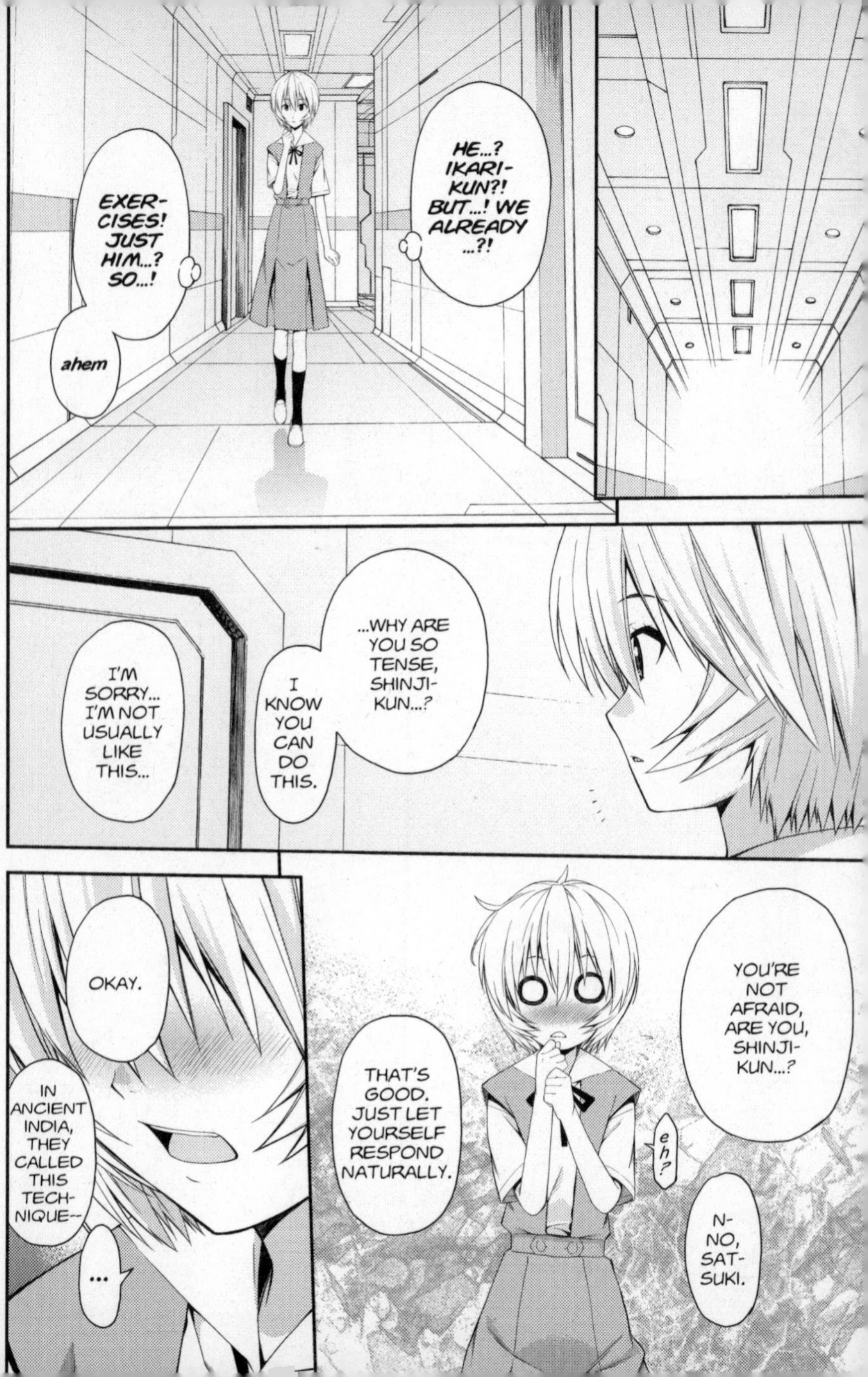
HE...? IKARI-KUN?! BUT...! WE ALREADY ...?!
EXER-CISES! JUST HIM...? SO...!
ahem
...WHY ARE YOU SO TENSE, SHINJI-KUN...?
I KNOW YOU CAN DO THIS.
I'M SORRY... I'M NOT USUALLY LIKE THIS...
YOU'RE NOT AFRAID, ARE YOU, SHINJI-KUN...?
eh?
N-NO, SAT-SUKI.
THAT'S GOOD. JUST LET YOURSELF RESPOND NATURALLY.
OKAY.
IN ANCIENT INDIA, THEY CALLED THIS TECH-NIQUE--
...

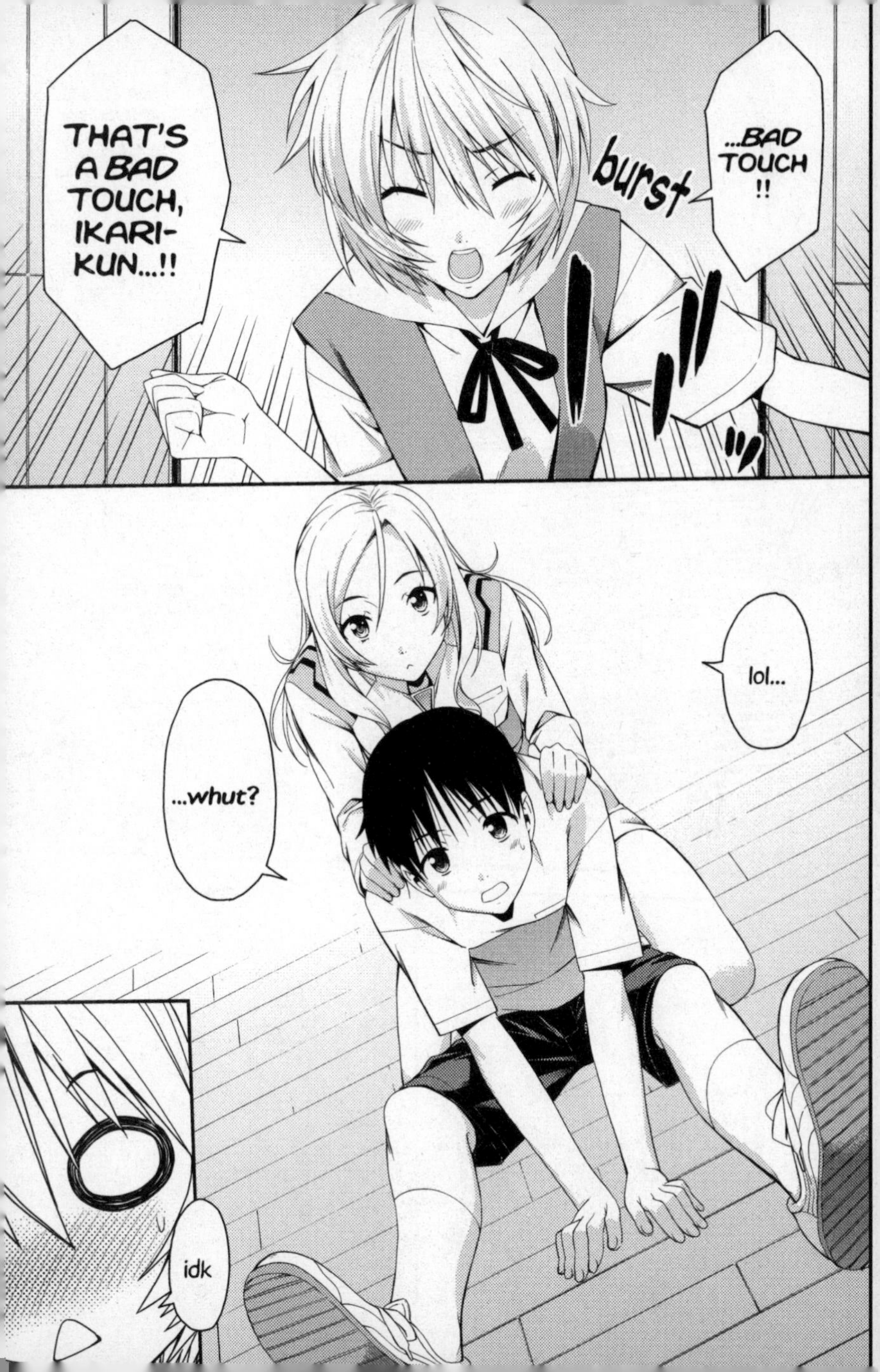
...BAD TOUCH !!
burst
THAT'S A BAD TOUCH, IKARI-KUN...!!
lol...
...whut?
idk

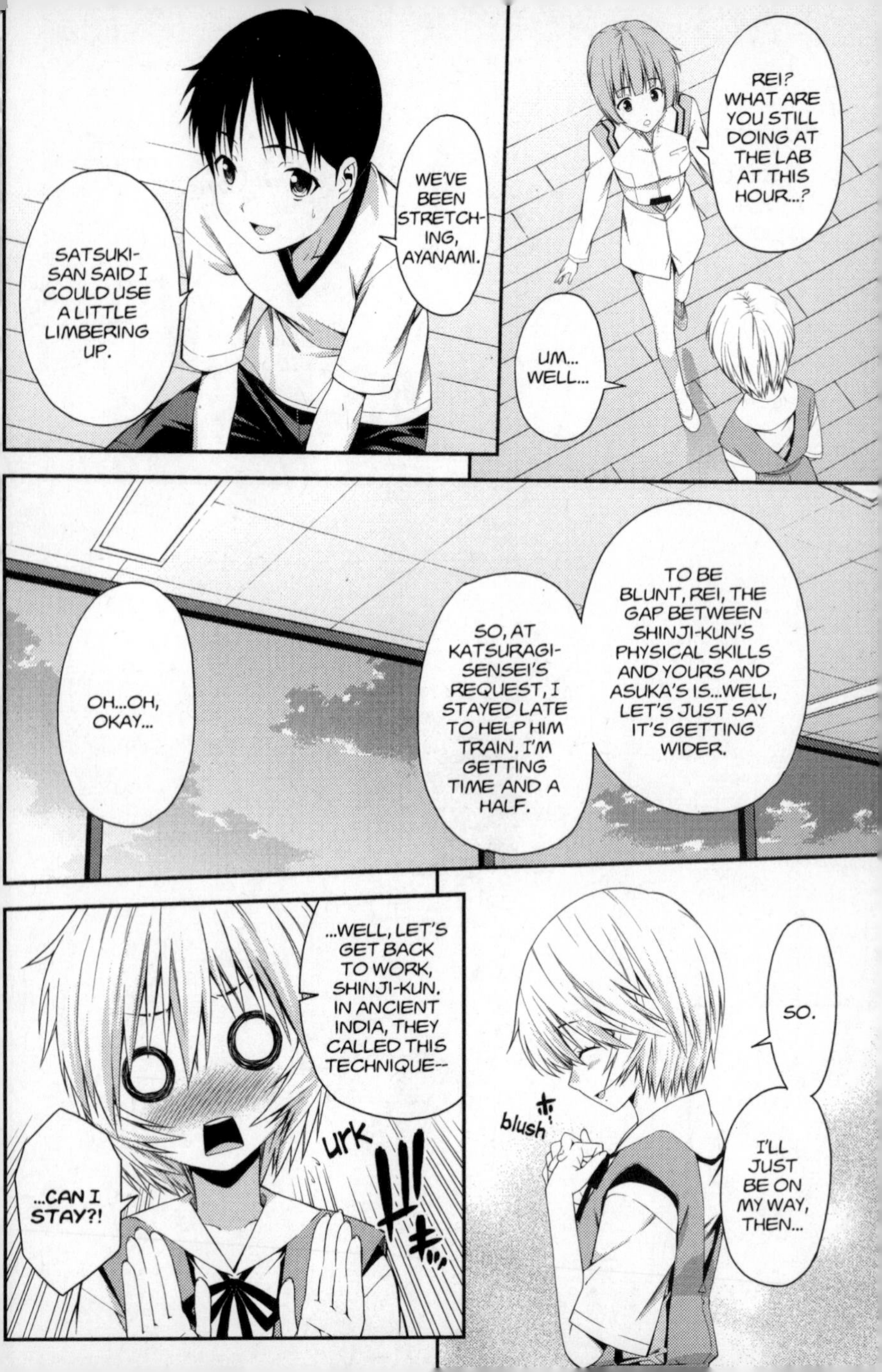
REI? WHAT ARE YOU STILL DOING AT THE LAB AT THIS HOUR...?
UM... WELL...
WE'VE BEEN STRETCH-ING, AYANAMI.
SATSUKI-SAN SAID I COULD USE A LITTLE LIMBERING UP.
TO BE BLUNT, REI, THE GAP BETWEEN SHINJI-KUN'S PHYSICAL SKILLS AND YOURS AND ASUKA'S IS...WELL, LET'S JUST SAY IT'S GETTING WIDER.
SO, AT KATSURAGI-SENSEI'S REQUEST, I STAYED LATE TO HELP HIM TRAIN. I'M GETTING TIME AND A HALF.
OH...OH, OKAY...
SO.
I'LL JUST BE ON MY WAY, THEN...
blush
...WELL, LET'S GET BACK TO WORK, SHINJI-KUN. IN ANCIENT INDIA, THEY CALLED THIS TECHNIQUE--
urk
...CAN I STAY?!

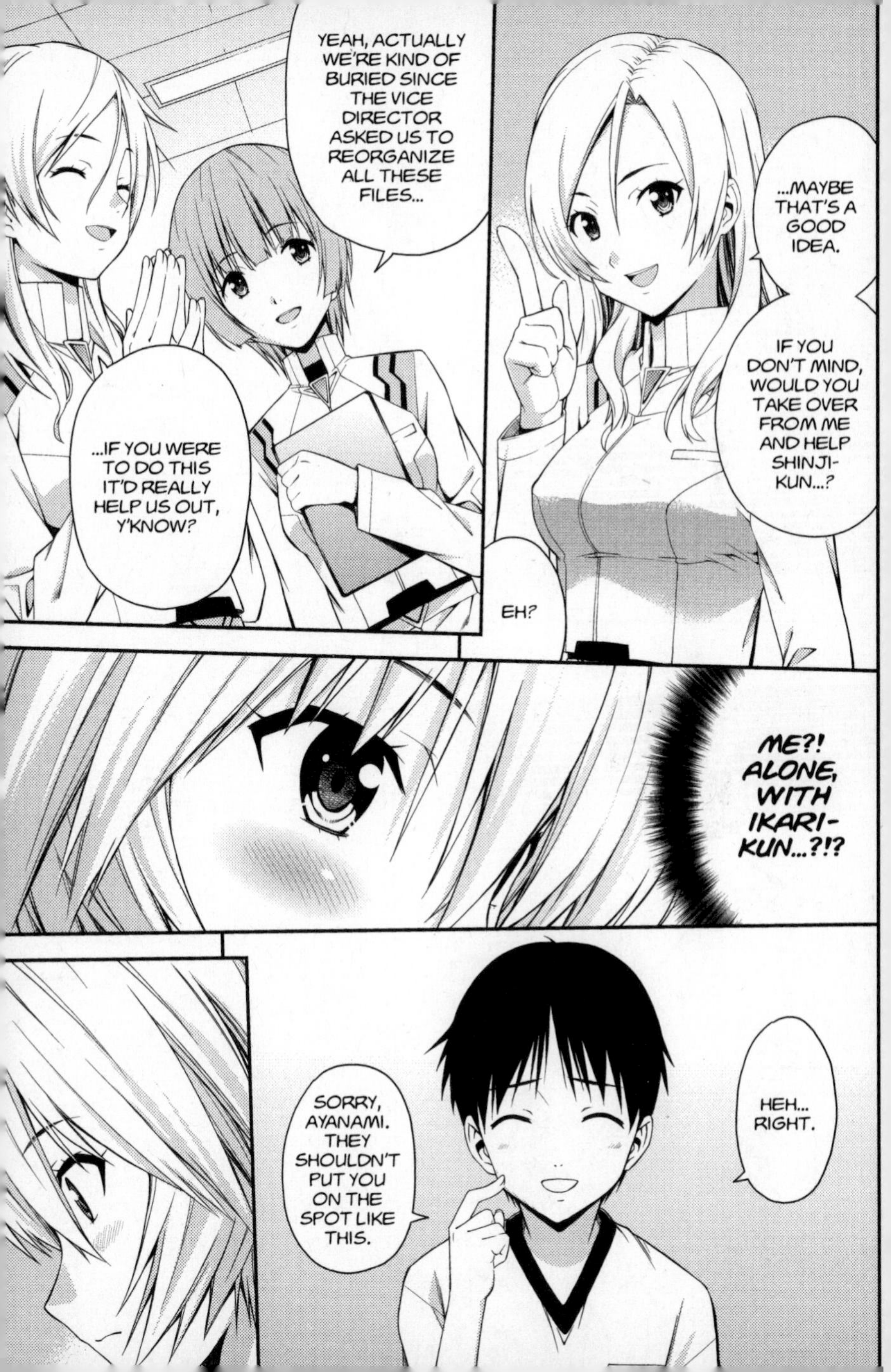
...MAYBE THAT'S A GOOD IDEA.
IF YOU DON'T MIND, WOULD YOU TAKE OVER FROM ME AND HELP SHINJI-KUN...?
EH?
YEAH, ACTUALLY WE'RE KIND OF BURIED SINCE THE VICE DIRECTOR ASKED US TO REORGANIZE ALL THESE FILES...
...IF YOU WERE TO DO THIS IT'D REALLY HELP US OUT, Y'KNOW?
ME?! ALONE, WITH IKARI-KUN...?!?
HEH... RIGHT.
SORRY, AYANAMI. THEY SHOULDN'T PUT YOU ON THE SPOT LIKE THIS.

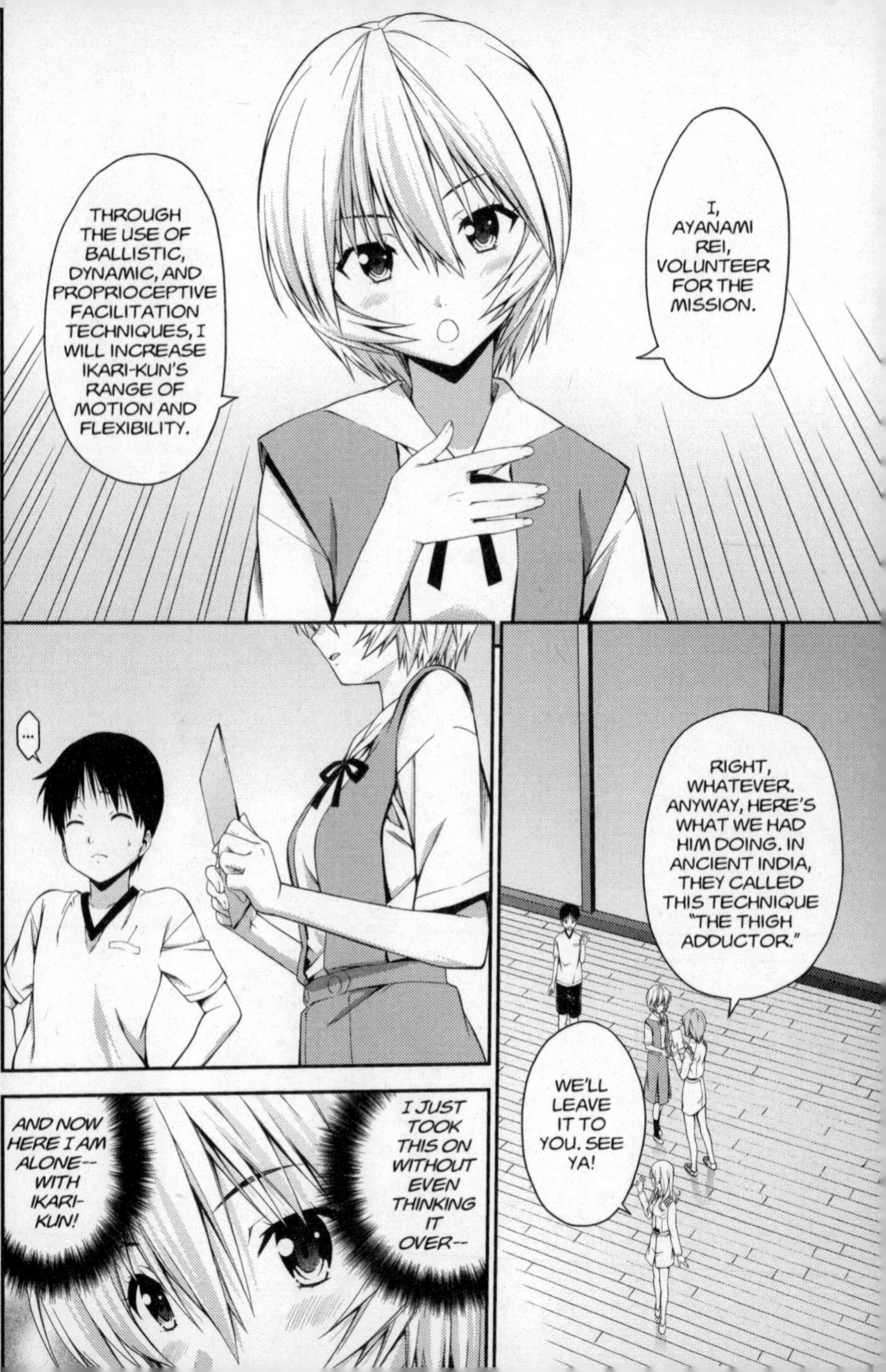
I, AYANAMI REI, VOLUNTEER FOR THE MISSION.
THROUGH THE USE OF BALLISTIC, DYNAMIC, AND PROPRIOCEPTIVE FACILITATION TECHNIQUES, I WILL INCREASE IKARI-KUN'S RANGE OF MOTION AND FLEXIBILITY.
RIGHT, WHATEVER. ANYWAY, HERE'S WHAT WE HAD HIM DOING. IN ANCIENT INDIA, THEY CALLED THIS TECHNIQUE "THE THIGH ADDUCTOR."
WE'LL LEAVE IT TO YOU. SEE YA!
...
I JUST TOOK THIS ON WITHOUT EVEN THINKING IT OVER--
AND NOW HERE I AM ALONE-- WITH IKARI-KUN!

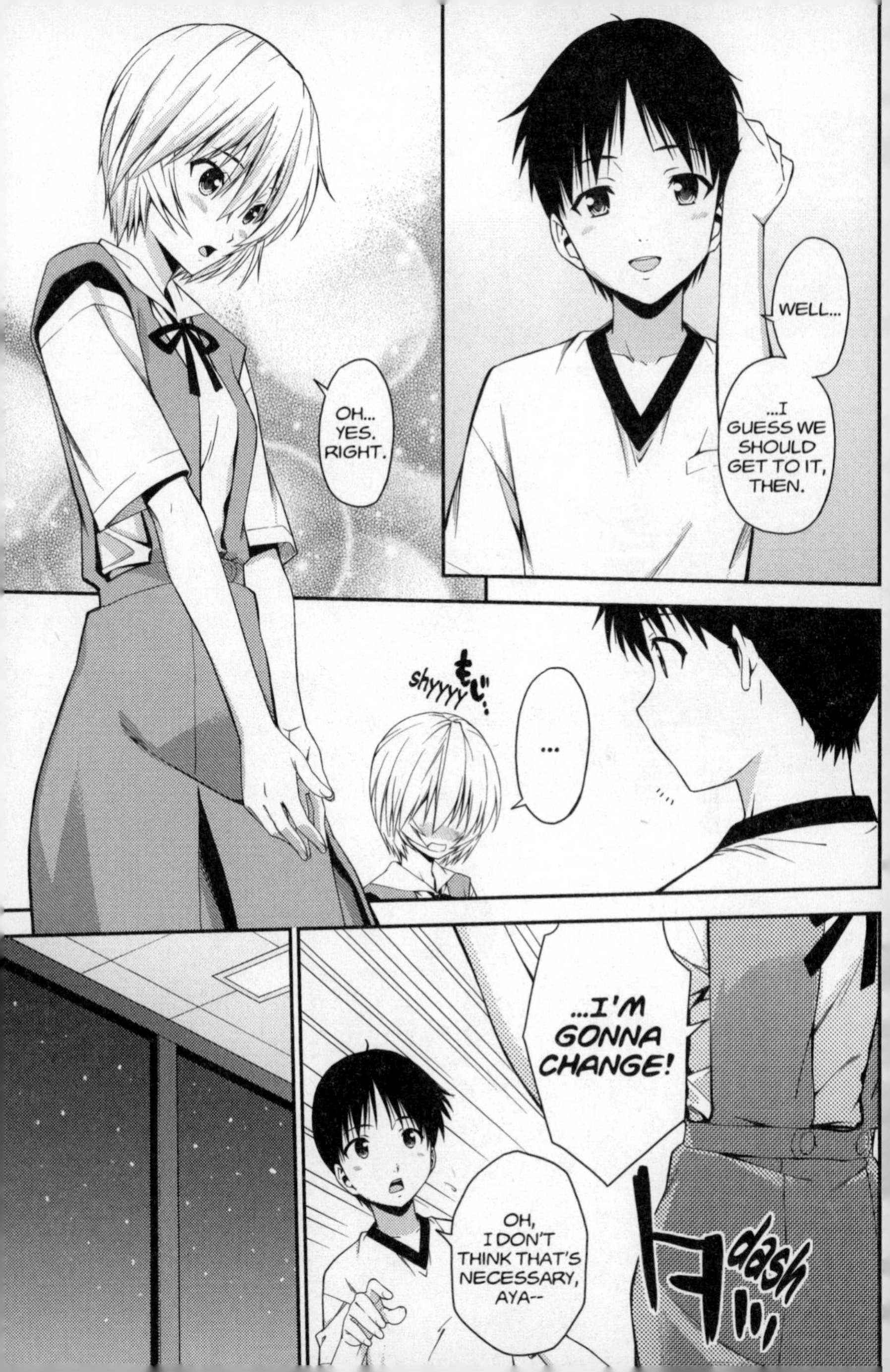

WELL...
...I GUESS WE SHOULD GET TO IT, THEN.
...
もじ
shyyyy
OH... YES. RIGHT.
...I'M GONNA CHANGE!
dash
OH, I DON'T THINK THAT'S NECESSARY, AYA--

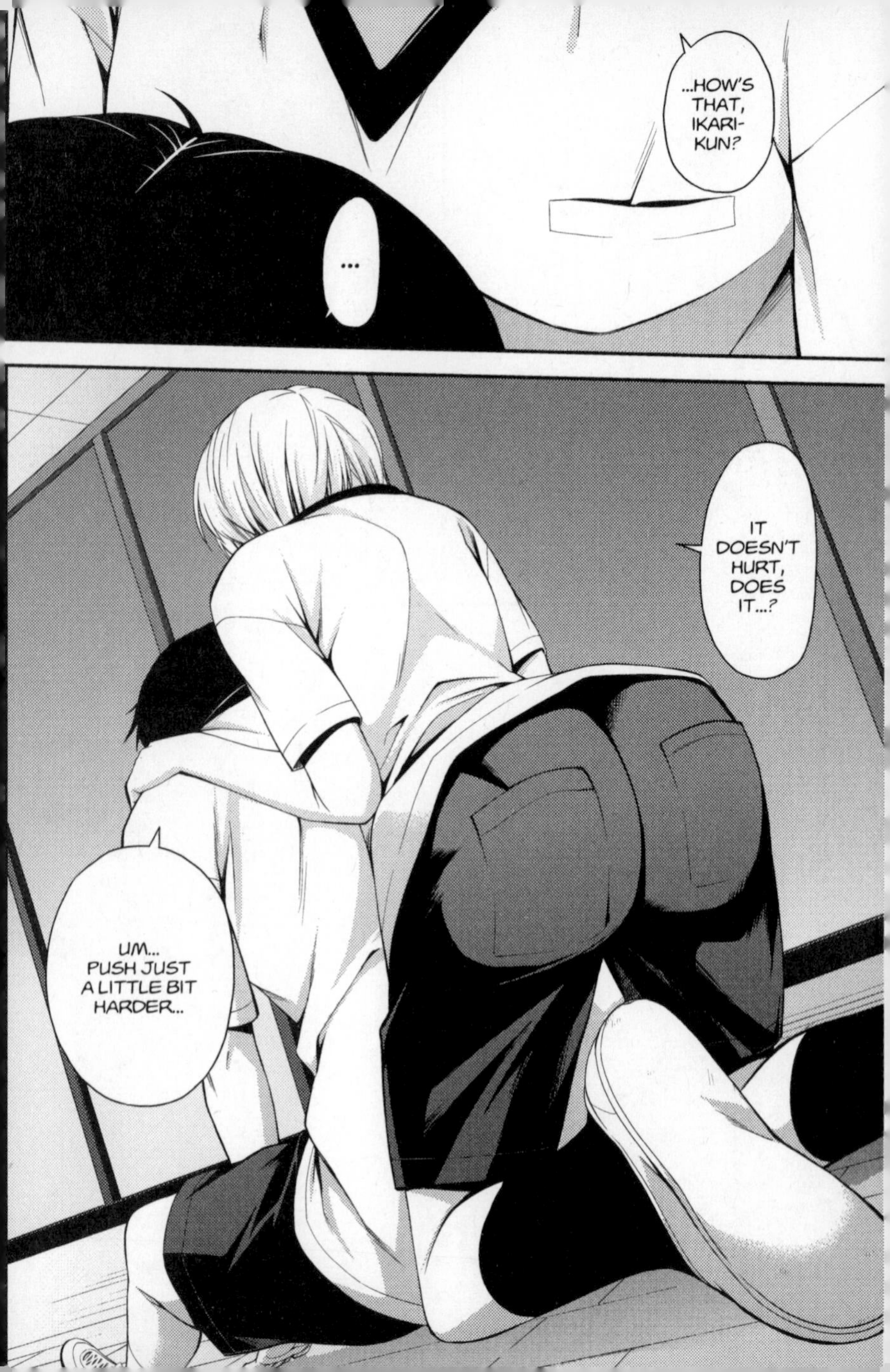
...HOW'S THAT, IKARI-KUN?
...
IT DOESN'T HURT, DOES IT...?
UM... PUSH JUST A LITTLE BIT HARDER...

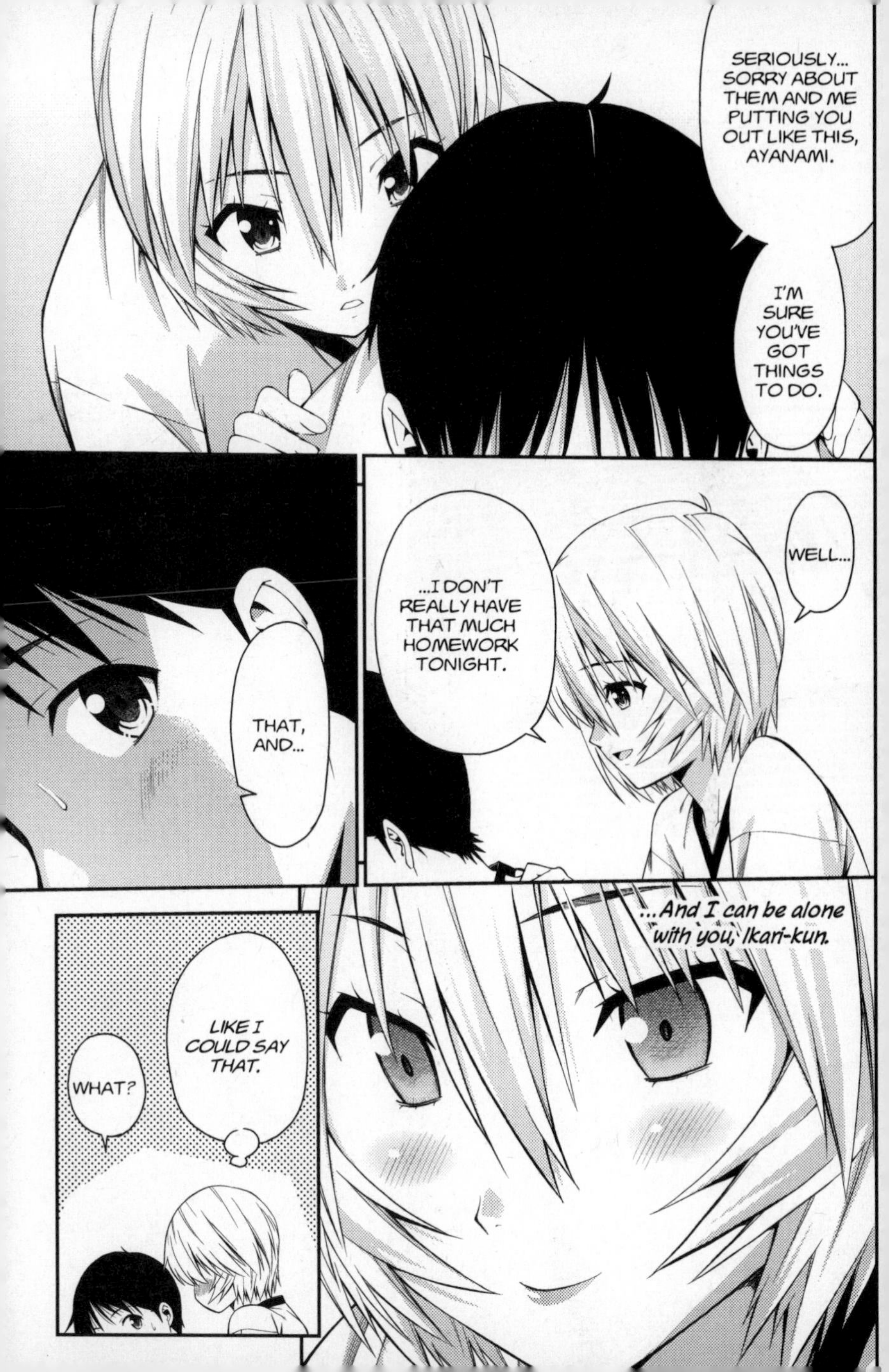
SERIOUSLY... SORRY ABOUT THEM AND ME PUTTING YOU OUT LIKE THIS, AYANAMI.
I'M SURE YOU'VE GOT THINGS TO DO.
WELL...
...I DON'T REALLY HAVE THAT MUCH HOMEWORK TONIGHT.
THAT, AND...
...And I can be alone with you, Ikari-kun.
LIKE I COULD SAY THAT.
WHAT?

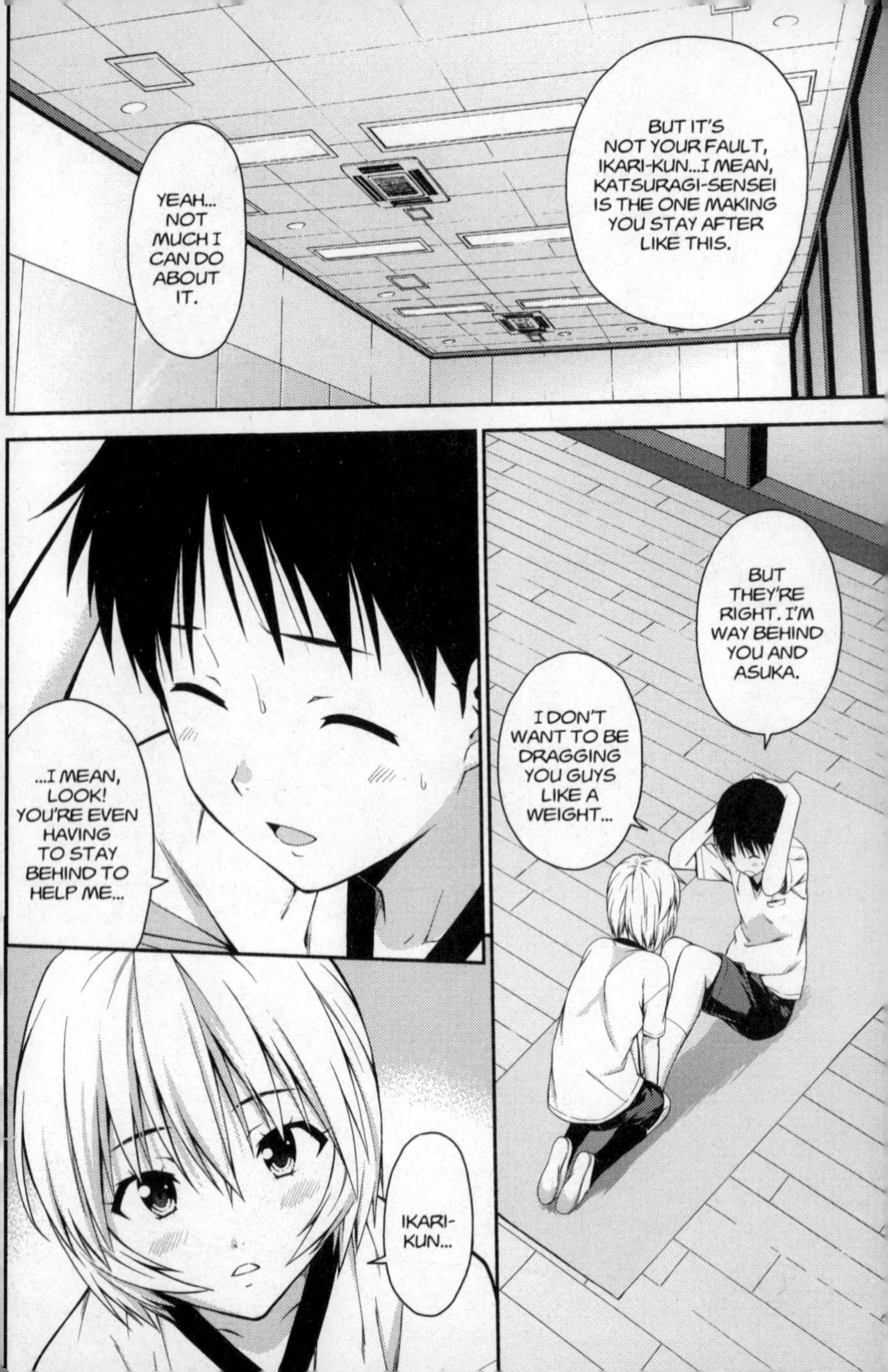
BUT IT'S NOT YOUR FAULT, IKARI-KUN...I MEAN, KATSURAGI-SENSEI IS THE ONE MAKING YOU STAY AFTER LIKE THIS.
YEAH... NOT MUCH I CAN DO ABOUT IT.
BUT THEY'RE RIGHT. I'M WAY BEHIND YOU AND ASUKA.
I DON'T WANT TO BE DRAGGING YOU GUYS LIKE A WEIGHT...
...I MEAN, LOOK! YOU'RE EVEN HAVING TO STAY BEHIND TO HELP ME...
IKARI-KUN...

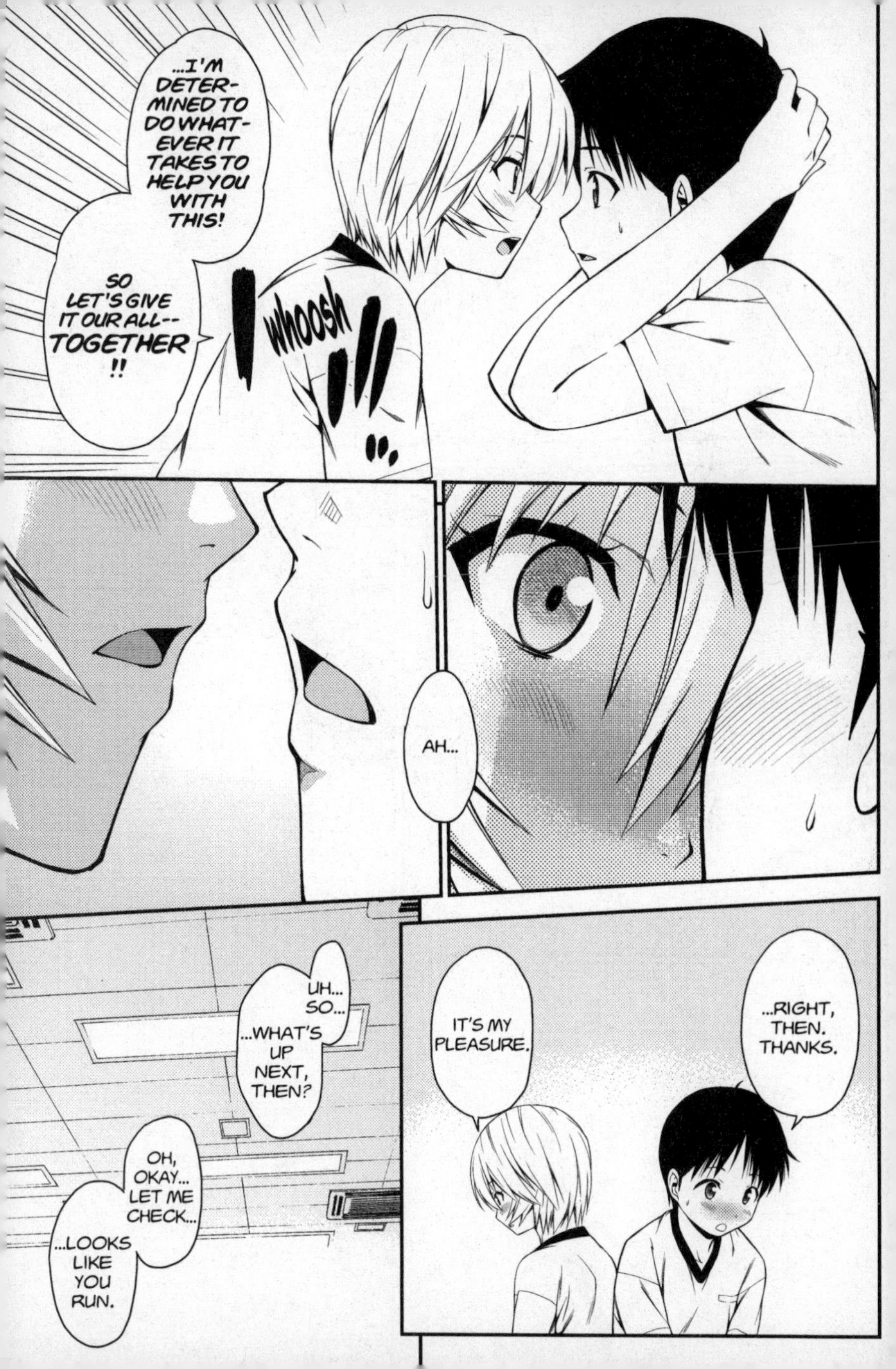
...I'M DETERMINED TO DO WHATEVER IT TAKES TO HELP YOU WITH THIS!
SO LET'S GIVE IT OUR ALL-- TOGETHER!!
whoosh
AH...
...RIGHT, THEN. THANKS.
IT'S MY PLEASURE.
UH... SO... ...WHAT'S UP NEXT, THEN?
OH, OKAY... LET ME CHECK... ...LOOKS LIKE YOU RUN.

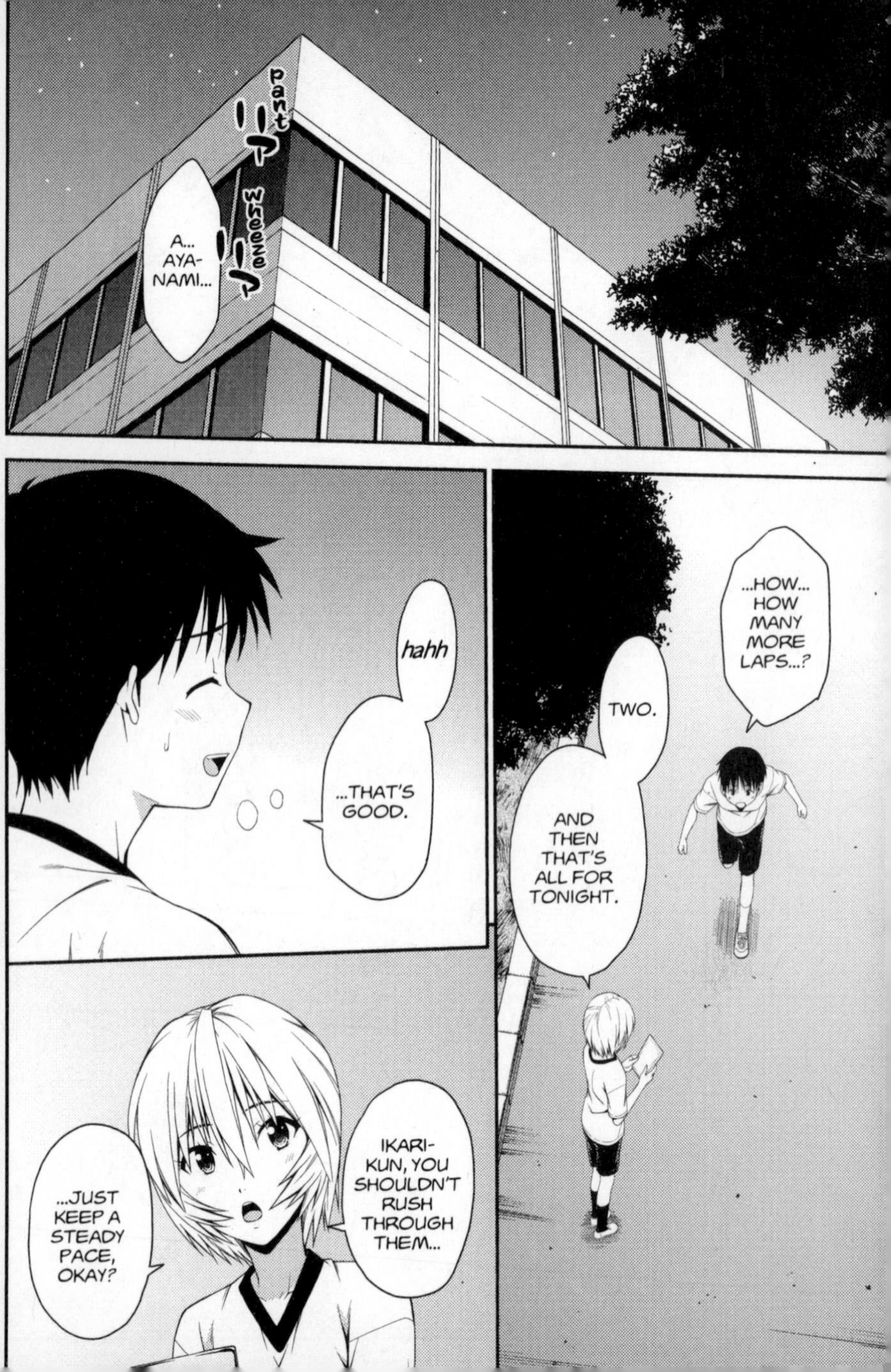
pant
wheeze
A... AYA-NAMI...
...HOW... HOW MANY MORE LAPS...?
TWO.
AND THEN THAT'S ALL FOR TONIGHT.
hahh
...THAT'S GOOD.
IKARI-KUN, YOU SHOULDN'T RUSH THROUGH THEM...
...JUST KEEP A STEADY PACE, OKAY?

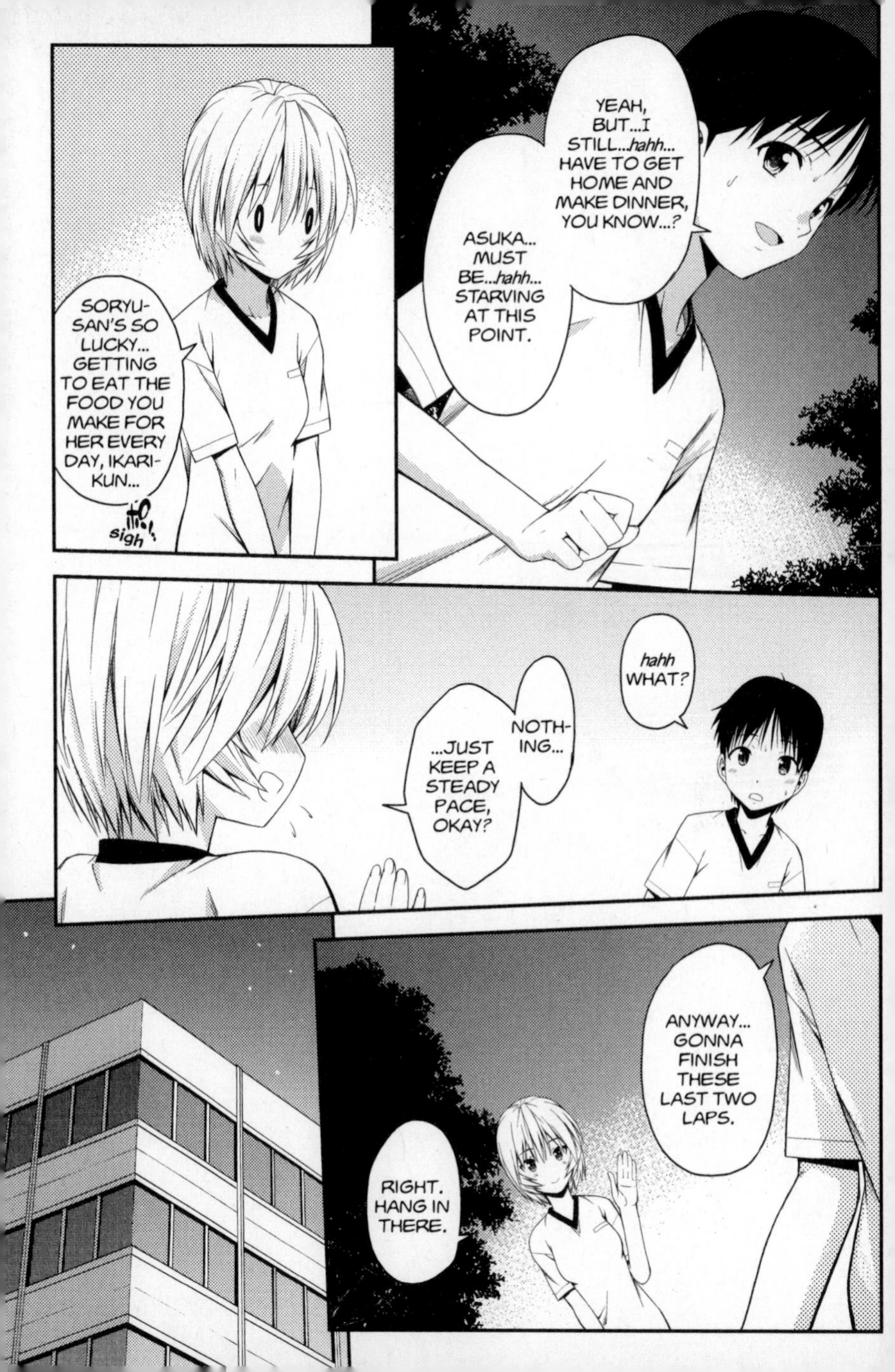
YEAH, BUT...I STILL...*hahh*... HAVE TO GET HOME AND MAKE DINNER, YOU KNOW...?
ASUKA... MUST BE...*hahh*... STARVING AT THIS POINT.
SORYU-SAN'S SO LUCKY... GETTING TO EAT THE FOOD YOU MAKE FOR HER EVERY DAY, IKARI-KUN...
sigh
hahh WHAT?
NOTHING...
...JUST KEEP A STEADY PACE, OKAY?
ANYWAY... GONNA FINISH THESE LAST TWO LAPS.
RIGHT. HANG IN THERE.

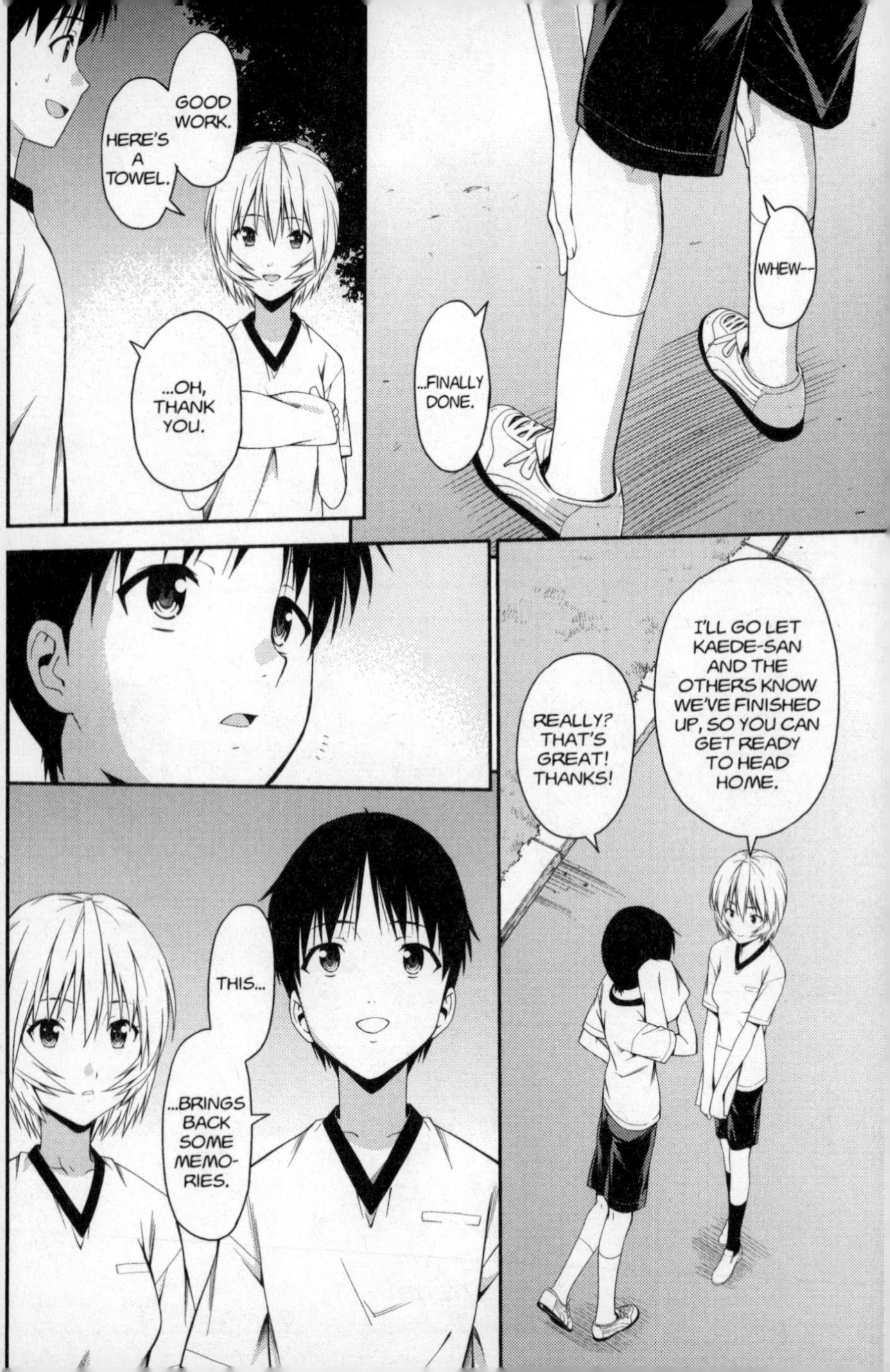
WHEW--
...FINALLY DONE.
GOOD WORK.
HERE'S A TOWEL.
...OH, THANK YOU.
I'LL GO LET KAEDE-SAN AND THE OTHERS KNOW WE'VE FINISHED UP, SO YOU CAN GET READY TO HEAD HOME.
REALLY? THAT'S GREAT! THANKS!
THIS...
...BRINGS BACK SOME MEMO-RIES.

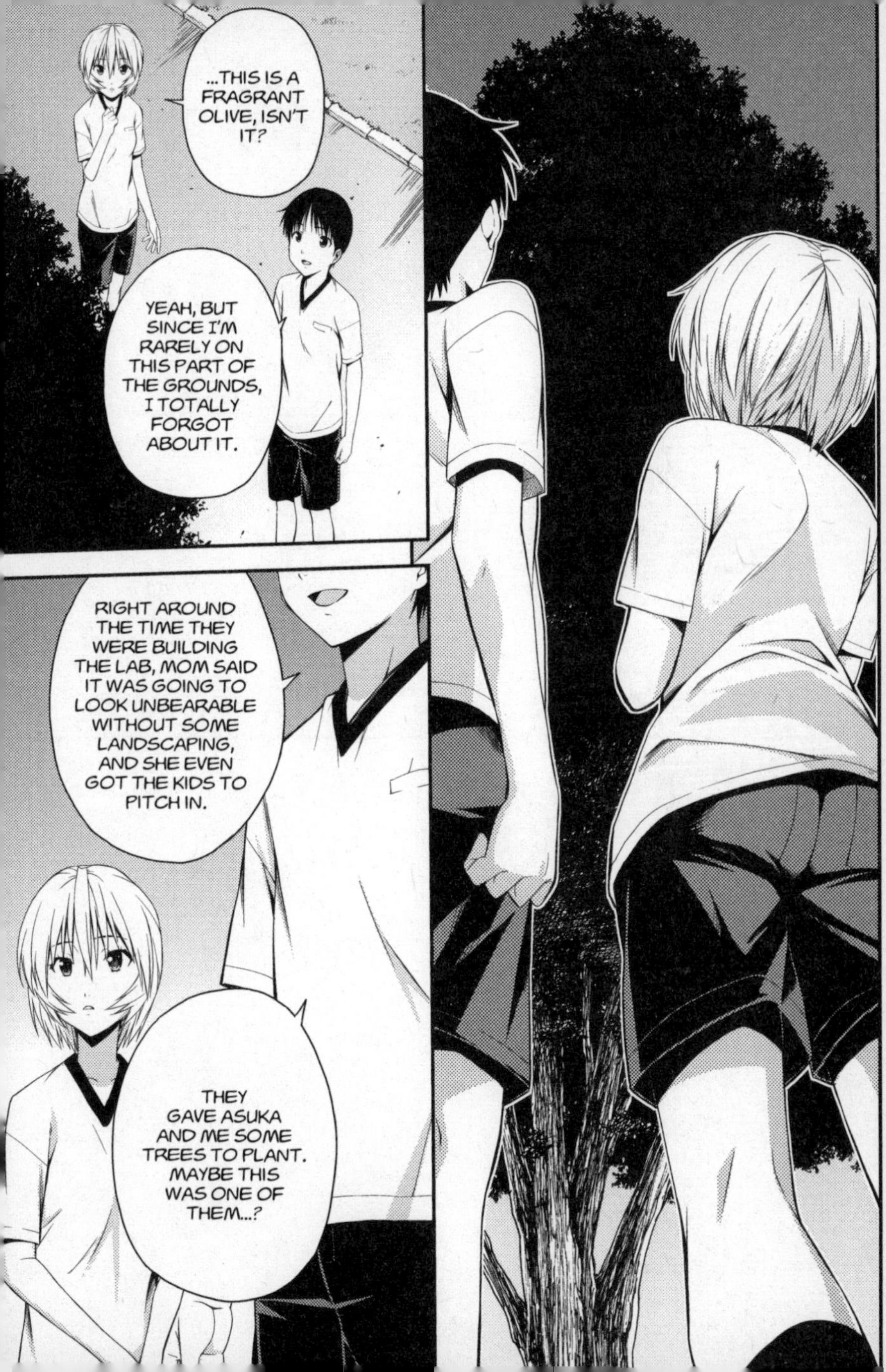
...THIS IS A FRAGRANT OLIVE, ISN'T IT?
YEAH, BUT SINCE I'M RARELY ON THIS PART OF THE GROUNDS, I TOTALLY FORGOT ABOUT IT.
RIGHT AROUND THE TIME THEY WERE BUILDING THE LAB, MOM SAID IT WAS GOING TO LOOK UNBEARABLE WITHOUT SOME LANDSCAPING, AND SHE EVEN GOT THE KIDS TO PITCH IN.
THEY GAVE ASUKA AND ME SOME TREES TO PLANT. MAYBE THIS WAS ONE OF THEM...?

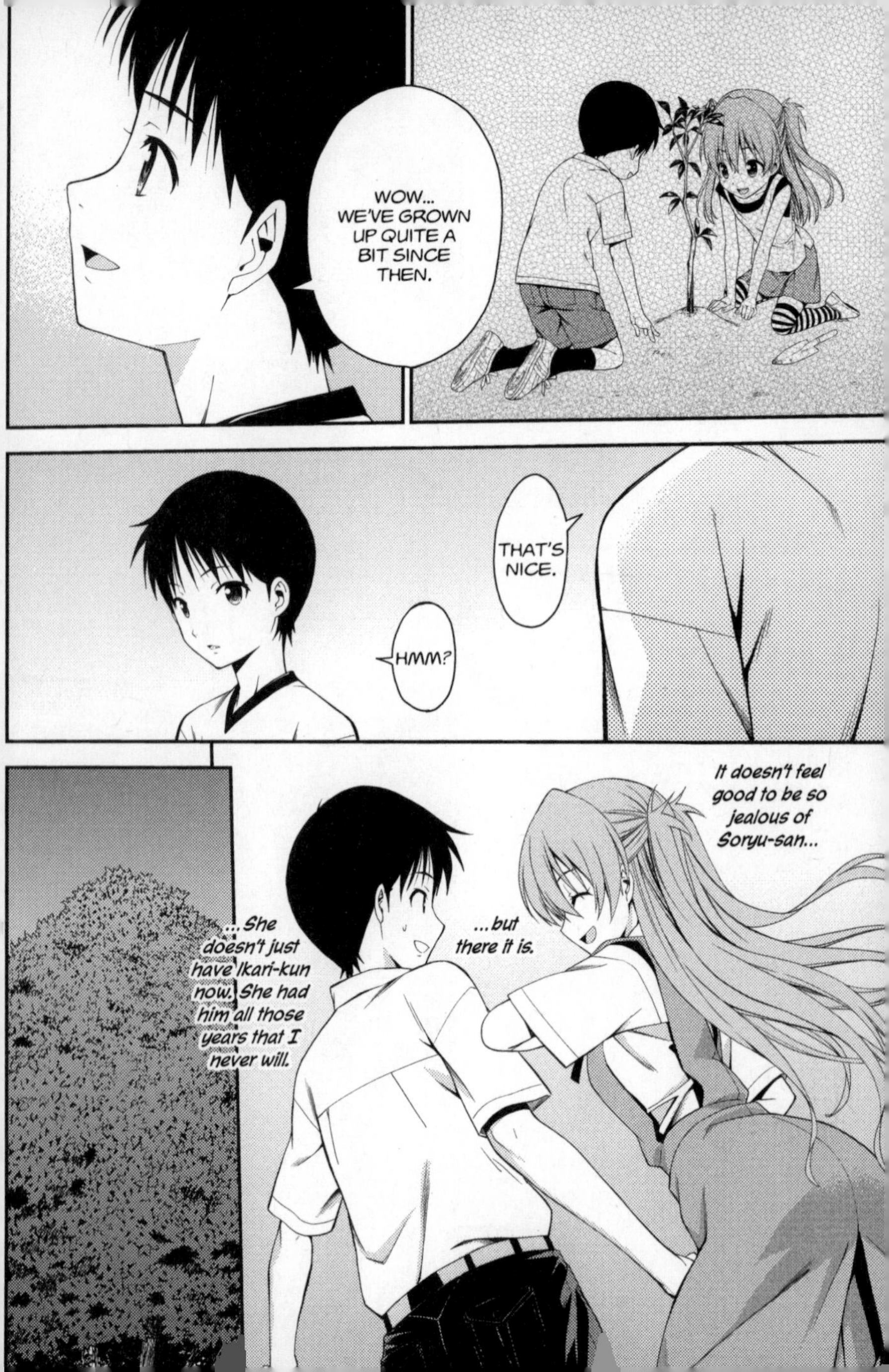
WOW... WE'VE GROWN UP QUITE A BIT SINCE THEN.
THAT'S NICE.
HMM?
It doesn't feel good to be so jealous of Soryu-san...
...but there it is.
...She doesn't just have Ikari-kun now. She had him all those years that I never will.

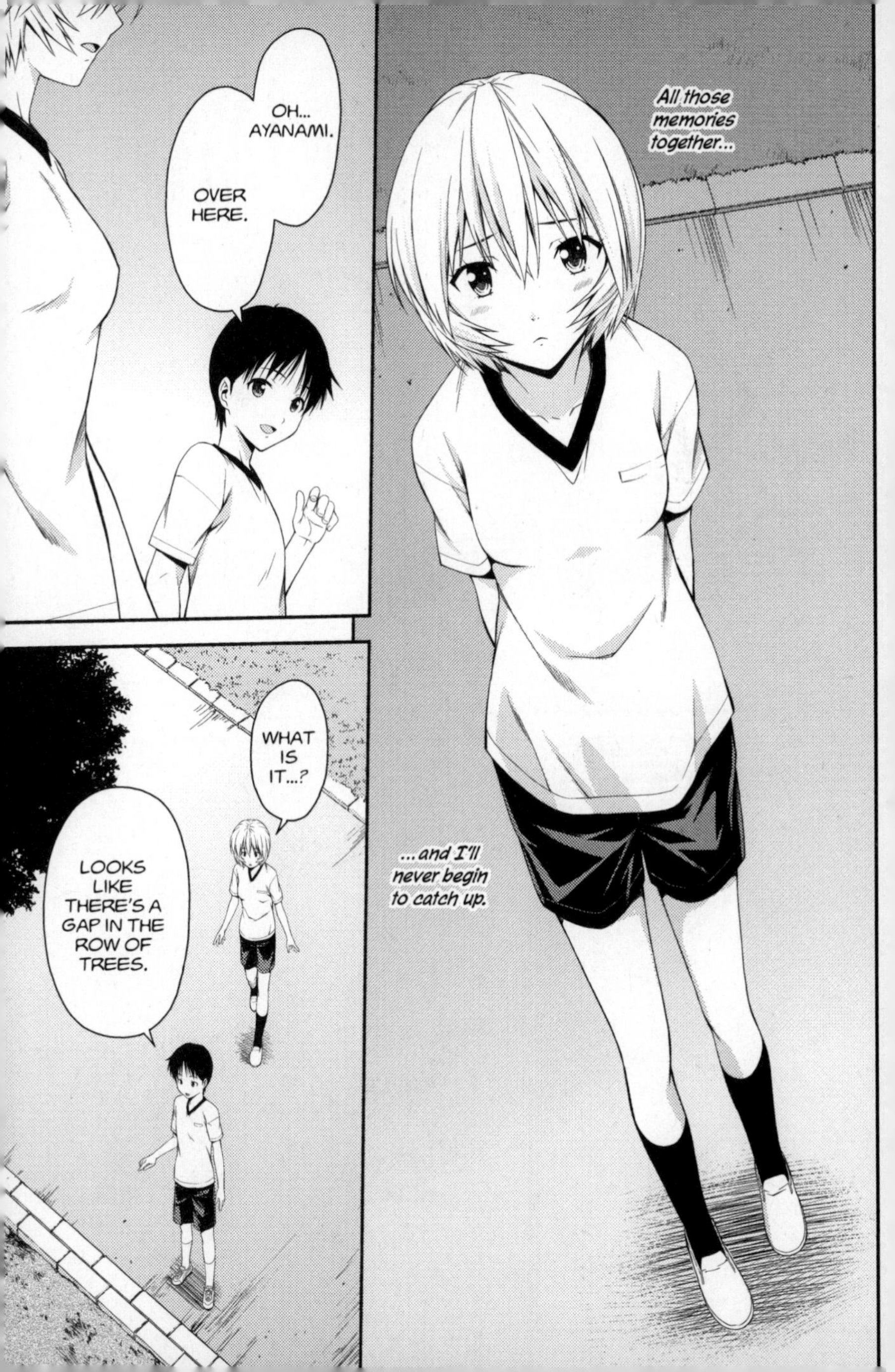
All those memories together...
...and I'll never begin to catch up.
OH... AYANAMI.
OVER HERE.
WHAT IS IT...?
LOOKS LIKE THERE'S A GAP IN THE ROW OF TREES.

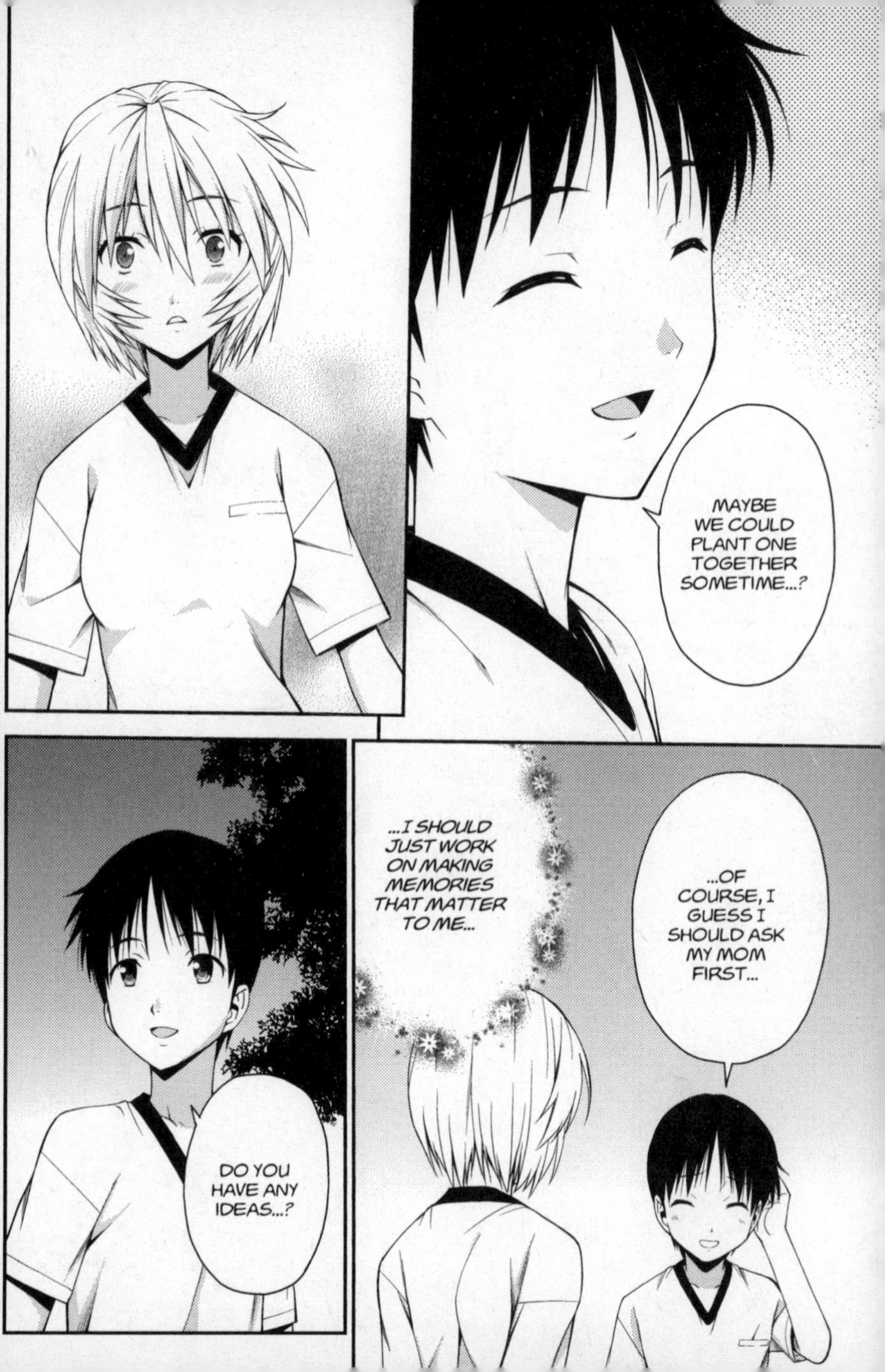
MAYBE WE COULD PLANT ONE TOGETHER SOMETIME...?
...OF COURSE, I GUESS I SHOULD ASK MY MOM FIRST...
...I SHOULD JUST WORK ON MAKING MEMORIES THAT MATTER TO ME...
DO YOU HAVE ANY IDEAS...?

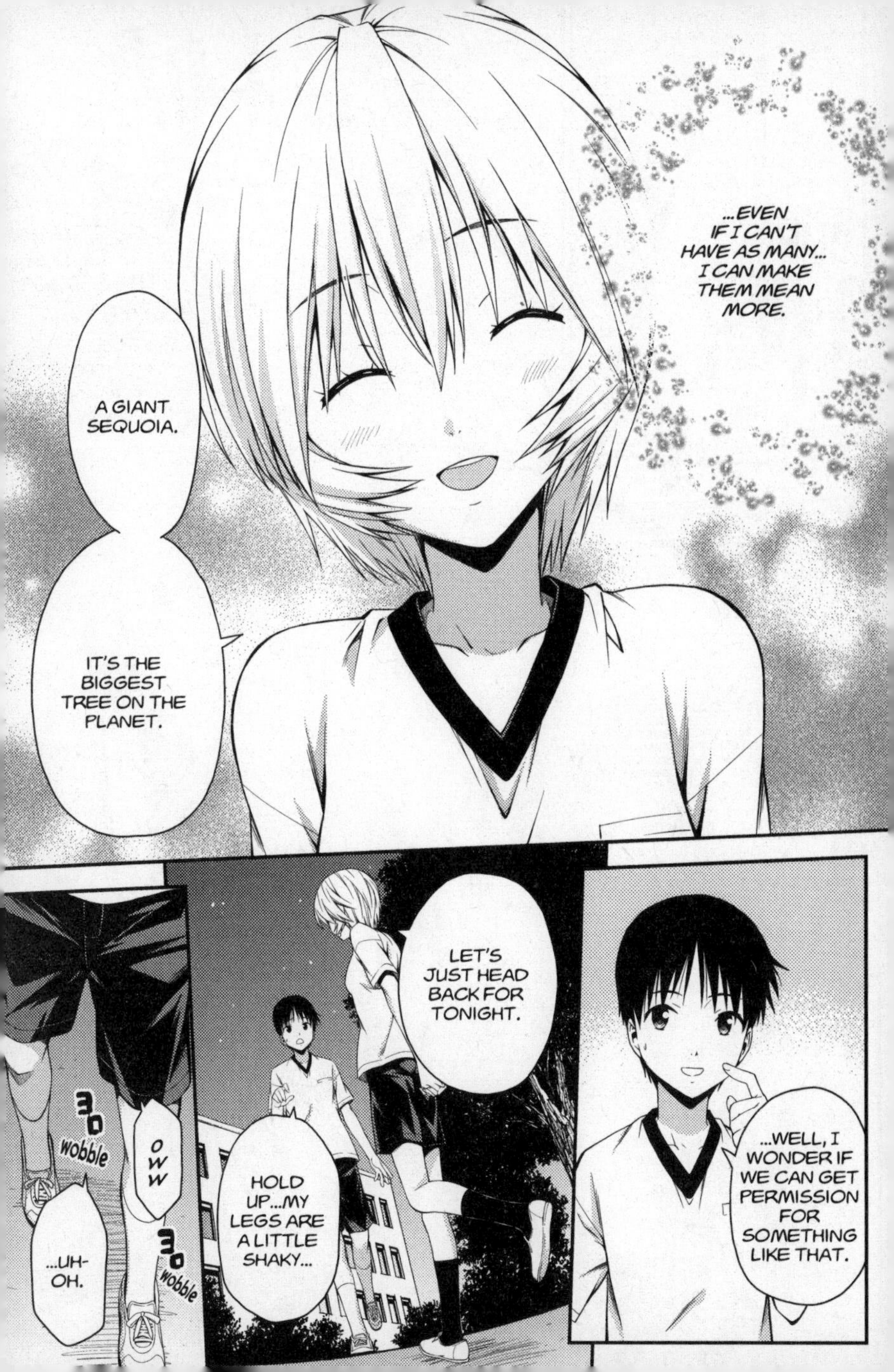
...EVEN IF I CAN'T HAVE AS MANY... I CAN MAKE THEM MEAN MORE.
A GIANT SEQUOIA.
IT'S THE BIGGEST TREE ON THE PLANET.
...WELL, I WONDER IF WE CAN GET PERMISSION FOR SOMETHING LIKE THAT.
LET'S JUST HEAD BACK FOR TONIGHT.
HOLD UP...MY LEGS ARE A LITTLE SHAKY...
OWW
wobble
...UH-OH.
wobble

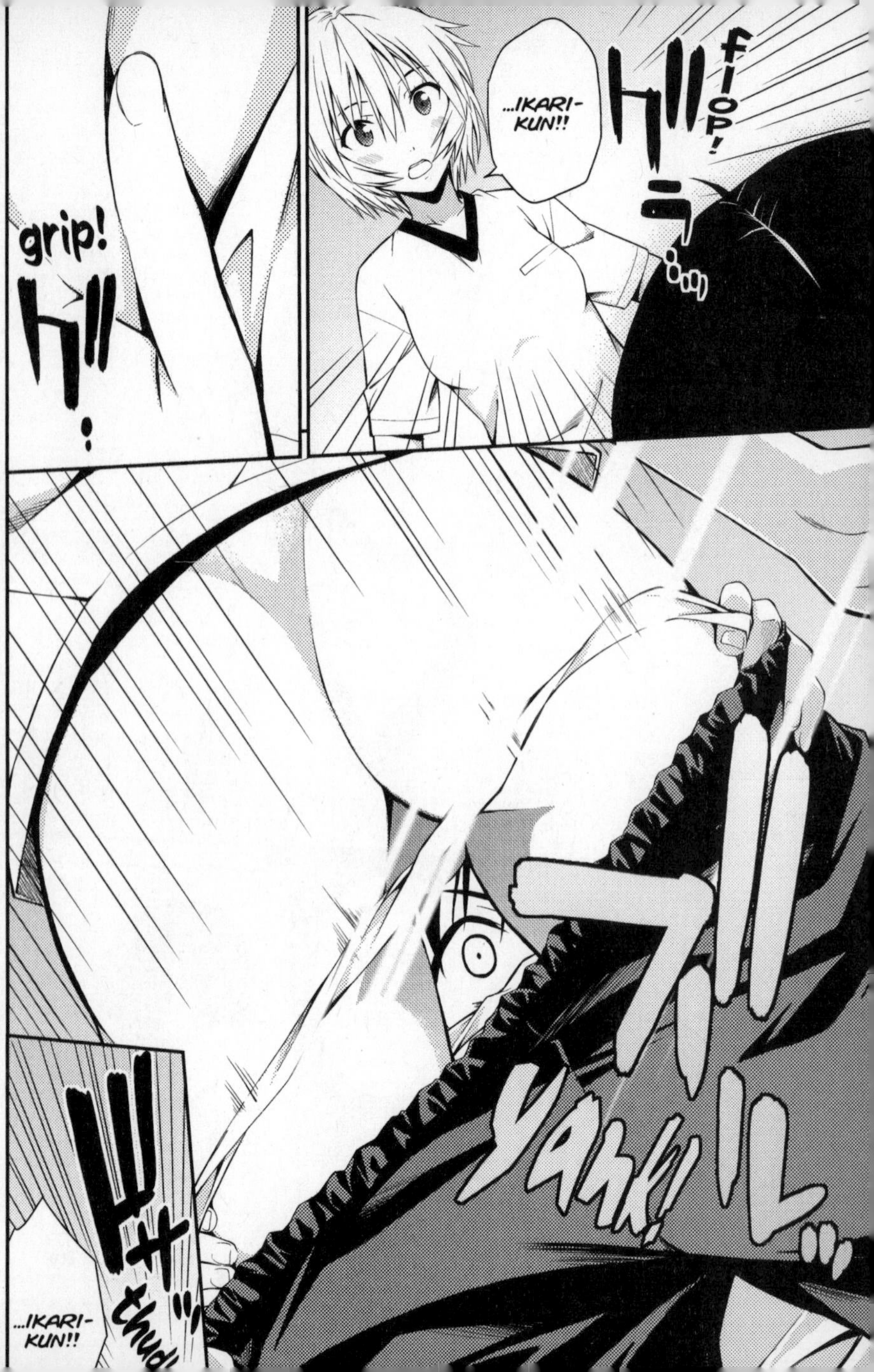
FLOP!
...IKARI-KUN!!
grip!
YANK!!
...IKARI-KUN!!
thud!

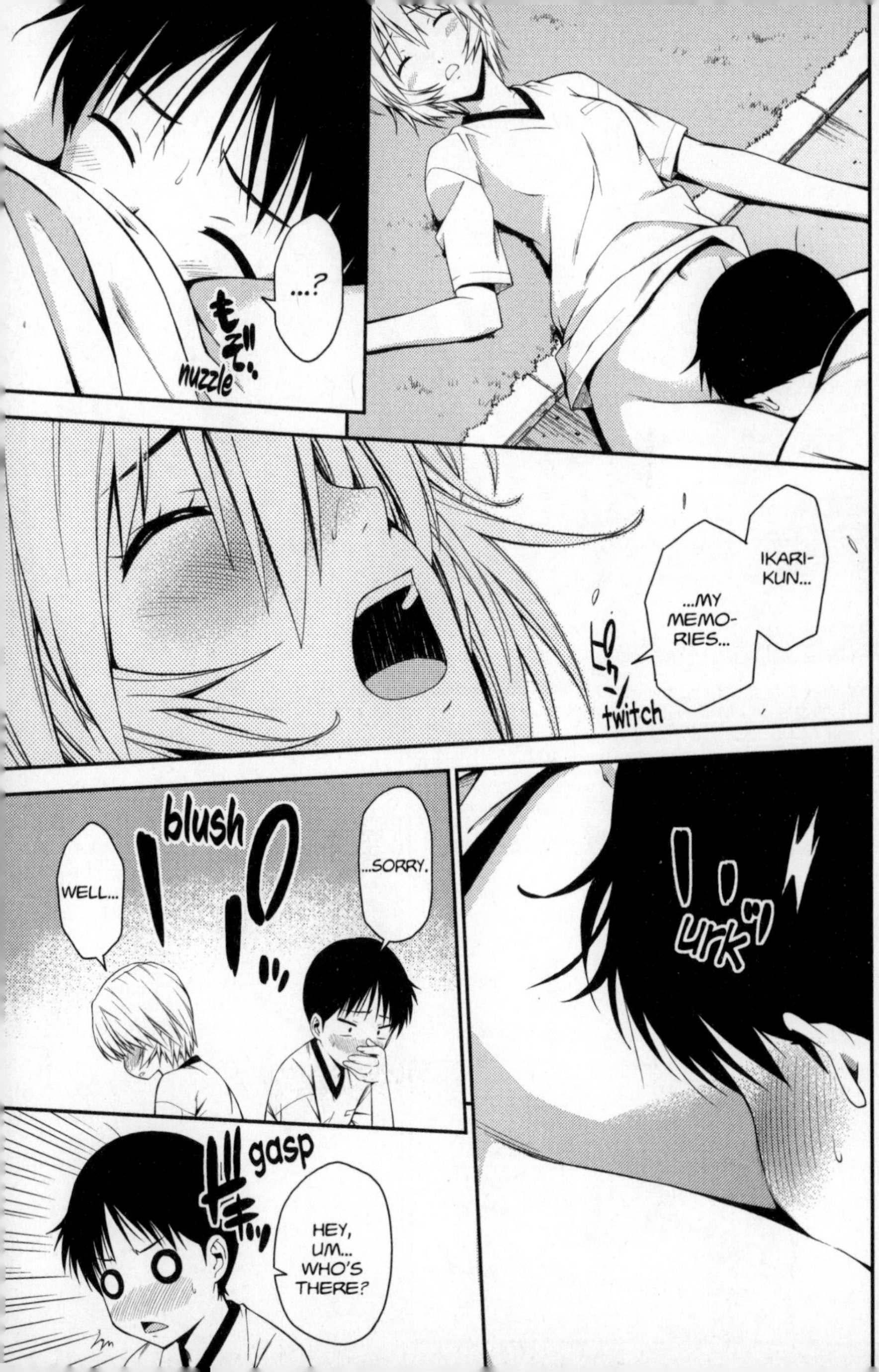
...?
もぞ..
nuzzle
IKARI-KUN...
...MY MEMORIES...
twitch
urk
...SORRY.
blush
WELL...
gasp
HEY, UM... WHO'S THERE?

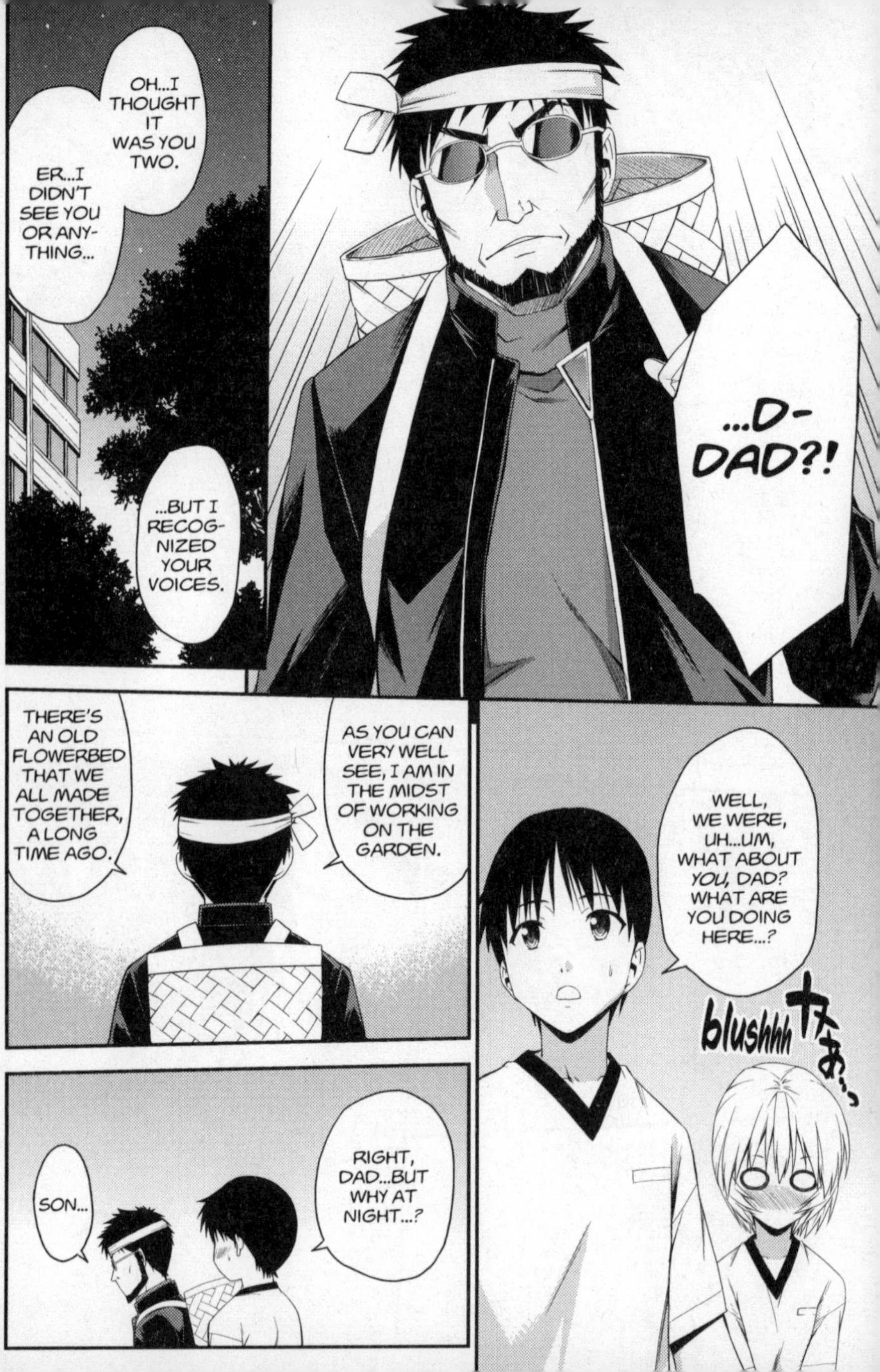
...D-DAD?!
OH...I THOUGHT IT WAS YOU TWO.
ER...I DIDN'T SEE YOU OR ANYTHING...
...BUT I RECOGNIZED YOUR VOICES.
WELL, WE WERE, UH...UM, WHAT ABOUT *YOU*, DAD? WHAT ARE YOU DOING HERE...?
blushhh
AS YOU CAN VERY WELL SEE, I AM IN THE MIDST OF WORKING ON THE GARDEN.
THERE'S AN OLD FLOWERBED THAT WE ALL MADE TOGETHER, A LONG TIME AGO.
RIGHT, DAD...BUT WHY AT NIGHT...?
SON...

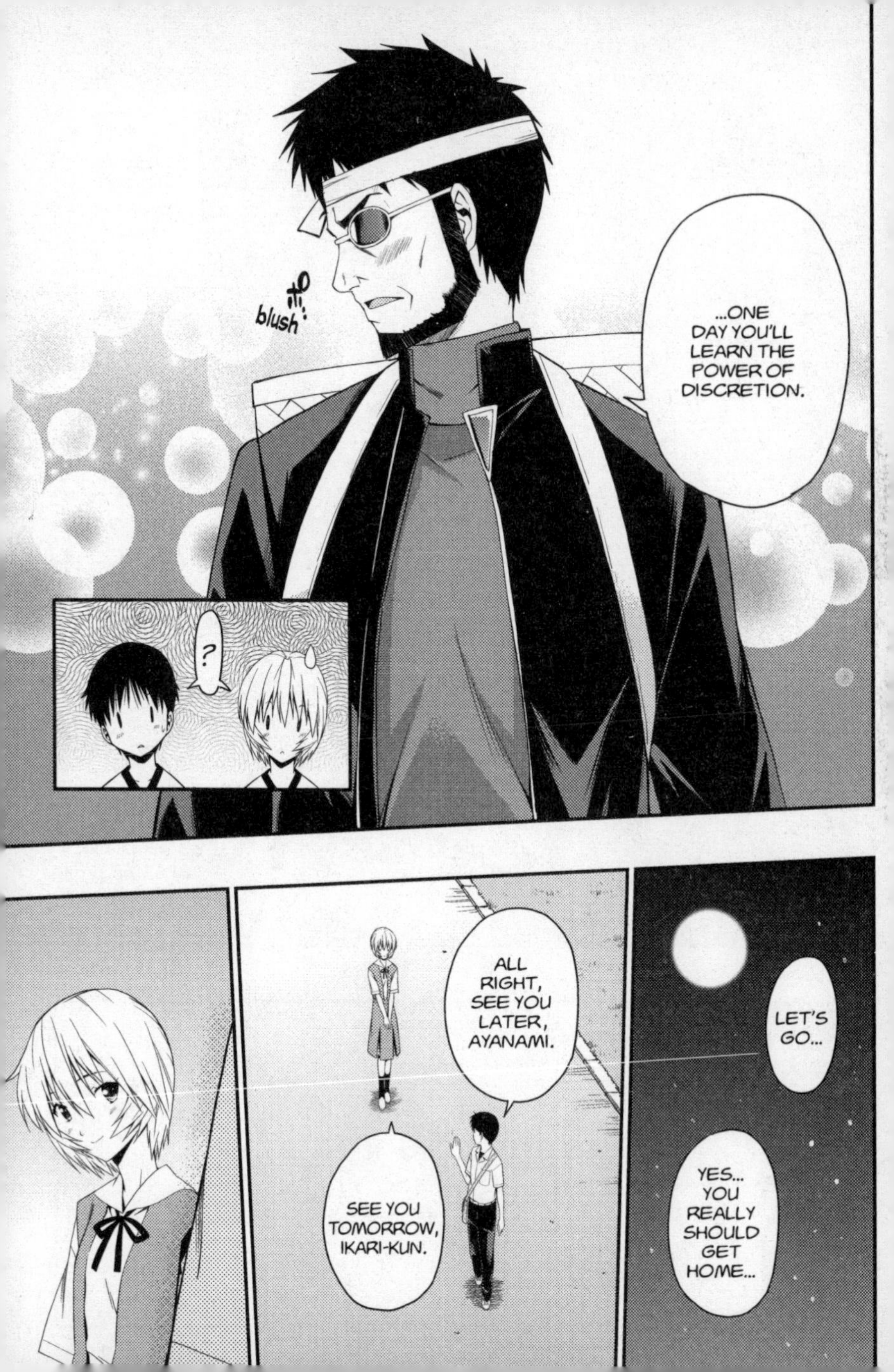
...ONE DAY YOU'LL LEARN THE POWER OF DISCRETION.
blush
?
LET'S GO...
YES... YOU REALLY SHOULD GET HOME...
ALL RIGHT, SEE YOU LATER, AYANAMI.
SEE YOU TOMORROW, IKARI-KUN.

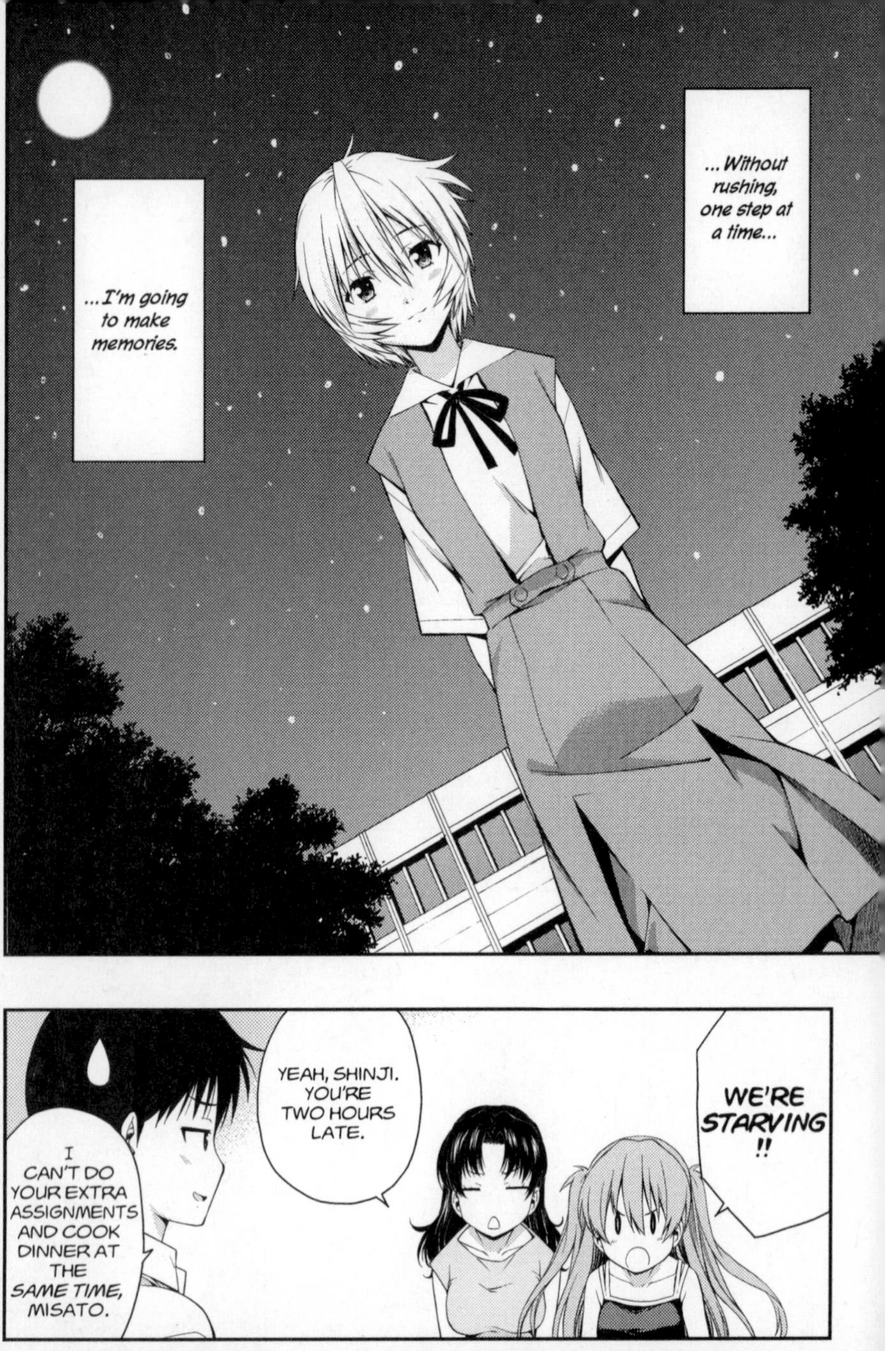
...Without rushing, one step at a time...
...I'm going to make memories.
WE'RE STARVING!!
YEAH, SHINJI. YOU'RE TWO HOURS LATE.
I CAN'T DO YOUR EXTRA ASSIGNMENTS AND COOK DINNER AT THE SAME TIME, MISATO.

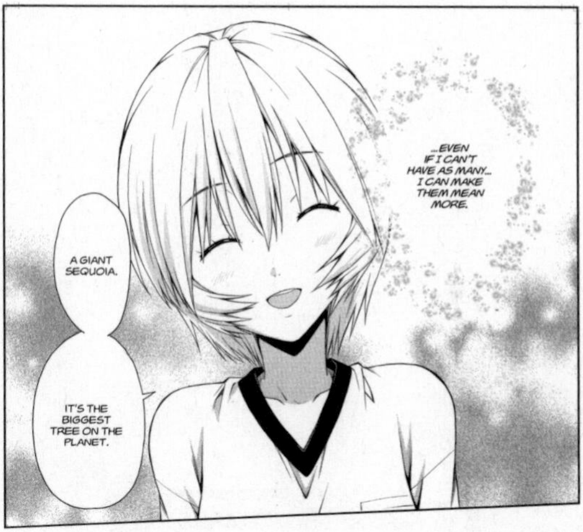
...EVEN IF I CAN'T HAVE AS MANY... I CAN MAKE THEM MEAN MORE.
A GIANT SEQUOIA.
IT'S THE BIGGEST TREE ON THE PLANET.

the shinji ikari raising project

NEON GENESIS EVANGELION

THE SHINJI IKARI RAISING PROJECT

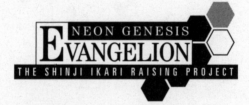

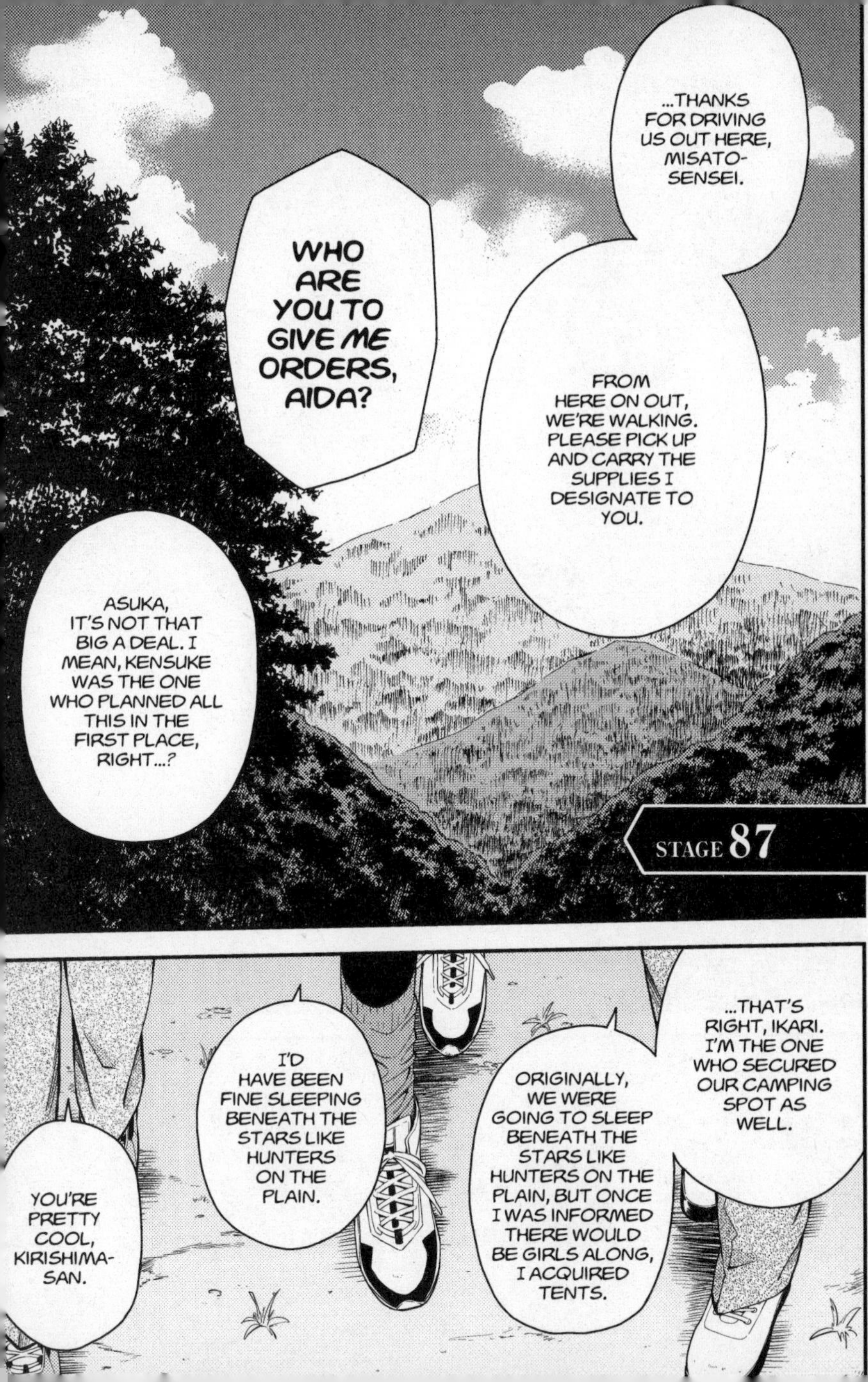
...THANKS FOR DRIVING US OUT HERE, MISATO-SENSEI.
FROM HERE ON OUT, WE'RE WALKING. PLEASE PICK UP AND CARRY THE SUPPLIES I DESIGNATE TO YOU.
WHO ARE YOU TO GIVE ME ORDERS, AIDA?
ASUKA, IT'S NOT THAT BIG A DEAL. I MEAN, KENSUKE WAS THE ONE WHO PLANNED ALL THIS IN THE FIRST PLACE, RIGHT...?
STAGE 87
...THAT'S RIGHT, IKARI. I'M THE ONE WHO SECURED OUR CAMPING SPOT AS WELL.
ORIGINALLY, WE WERE GOING TO SLEEP BENEATH THE STARS LIKE HUNTERS ON THE PLAIN, BUT ONCE I WAS INFORMED THERE WOULD BE GIRLS ALONG, I ACQUIRED TENTS.
I'D HAVE BEEN FINE SLEEPING BENEATH THE STARS LIKE HUNTERS ON THE PLAIN.
YOU'RE PRETTY COOL, KIRISHIMA-SAN.

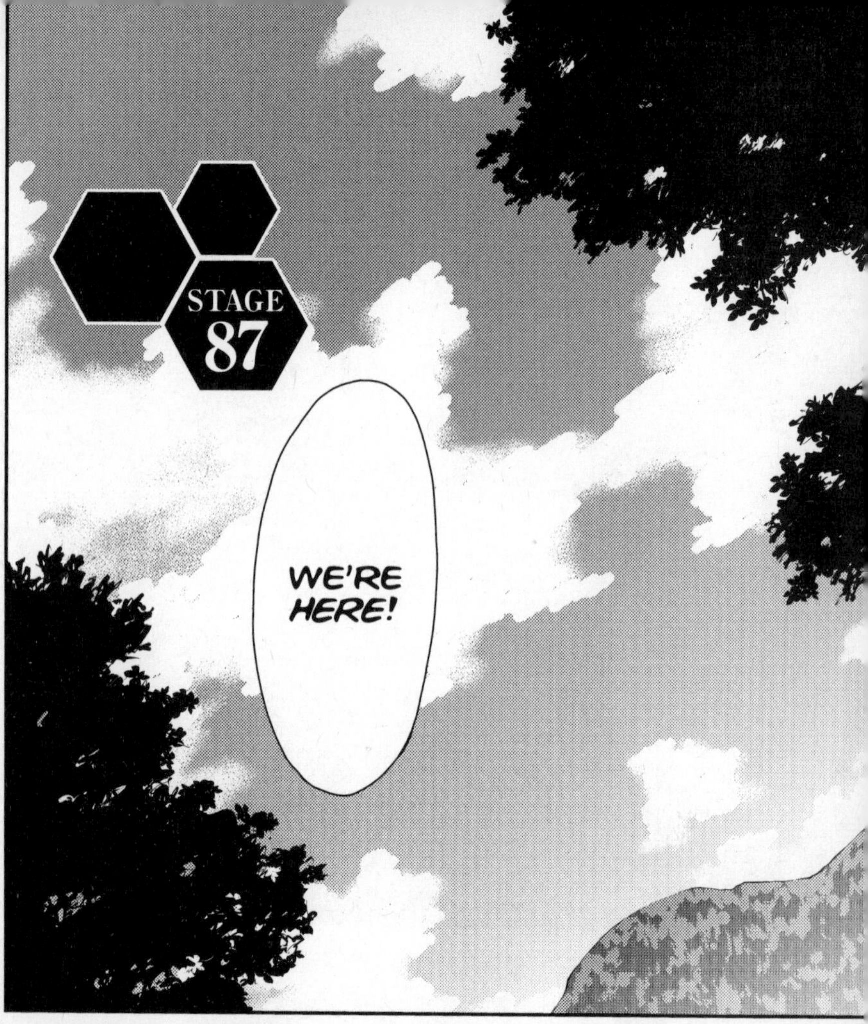
STAGE 87
WE'RE HERE!
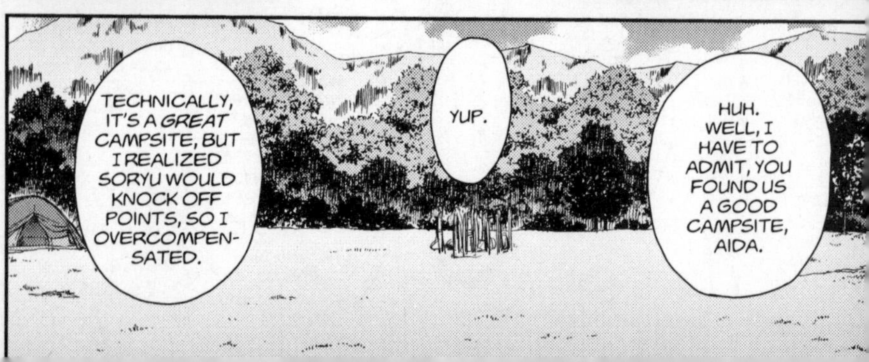
HUH. WELL, I HAVE TO ADMIT, YOU FOUND US A GOOD CAMPSITE, AIDA.
YUP.
TECHNICALLY, IT'S A *GREAT* CAMPSITE, BUT I REALIZED SORYU WOULD KNOCK OFF POINTS, SO I OVERCOMPEN-SATED.

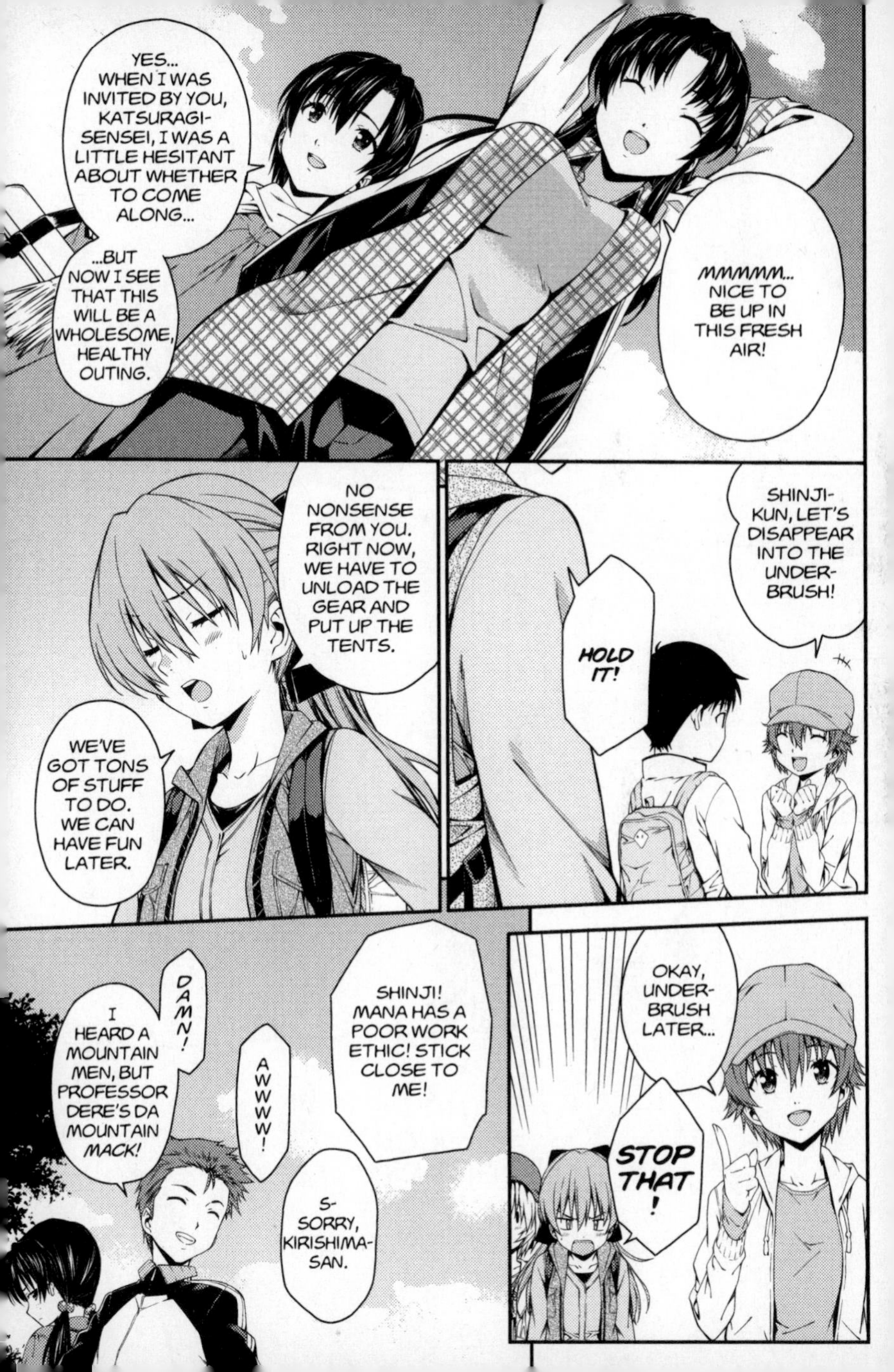
MMMMM... NICE TO BE UP IN THIS FRESH AIR!
YES... WHEN I WAS INVITED BY YOU, KATSURAGI-SENSEI, I WAS A LITTLE HESITANT ABOUT WHETHER TO COME ALONG...
...BUT NOW I SEE THAT THIS WILL BE A WHOLESOME, HEALTHY OUTING.
SHINJI-KUN, LET'S DISAPPEAR INTO THE UNDER-BRUSH!
HOLD IT!
NO NONSENSE FROM YOU. RIGHT NOW, WE HAVE TO UNLOAD THE GEAR AND PUT UP THE TENTS.
WE'VE GOT TONS OF STUFF TO DO. WE CAN HAVE FUN LATER.
OKAY, UNDER-BRUSH LATER...
STOP THAT!
SHINJI! MANA HAS A POOR WORK ETHIC! STICK CLOSE TO ME!
AWWWW!
S-SORRY, KIRISHIMA-SAN.
DAMN!
I HEARD A MOUNTAIN MEN, BUT PROFESSOR DERE'S DA MOUNTAIN MACK!

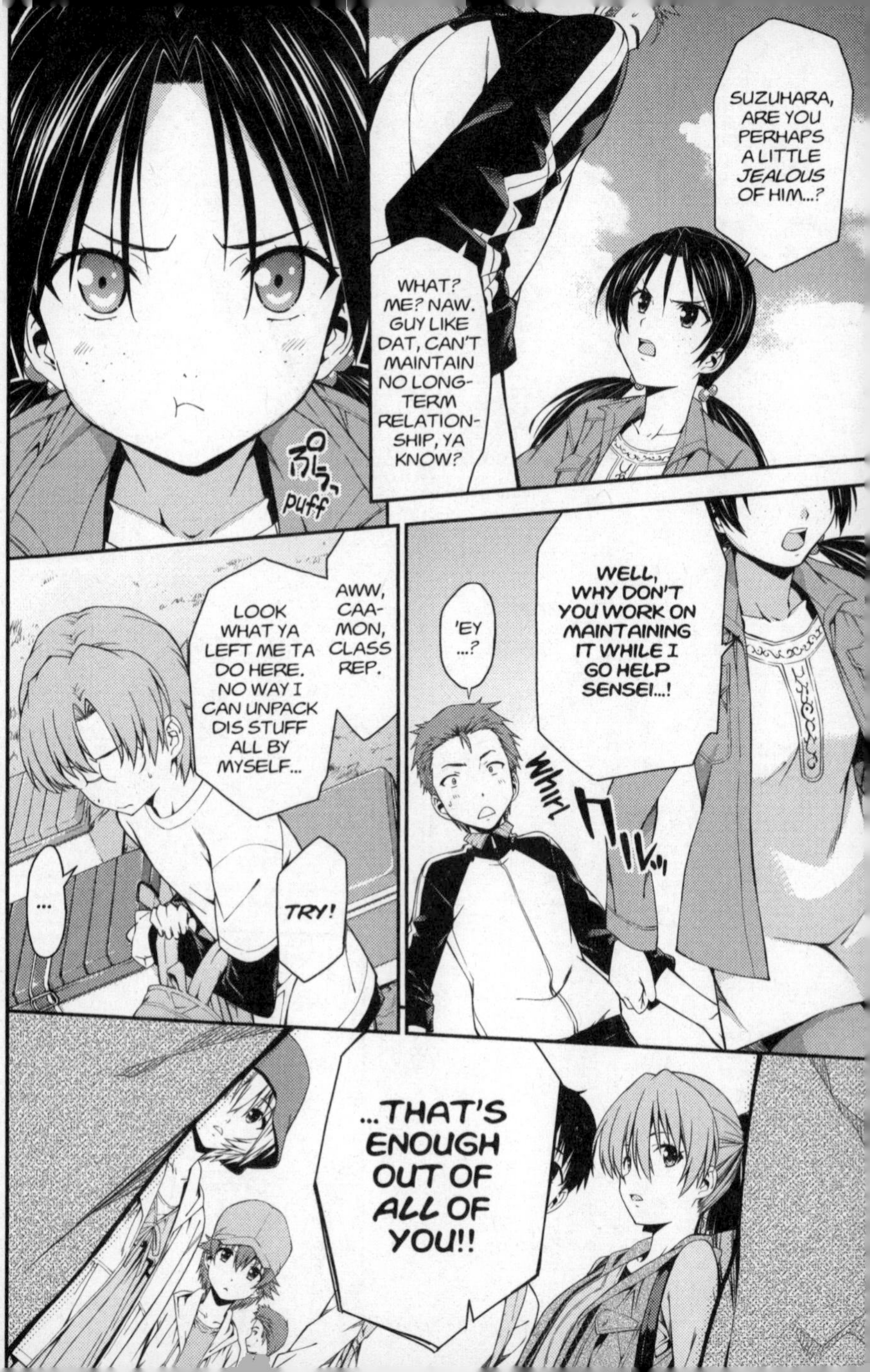
SUZUHARA, ARE YOU PERHAPS A LITTLE JEALOUS OF HIM...?
WHAT? ME? NAW. GUY LIKE DAT, CAN'T MAINTAIN NO LONG-TERM RELATION-SHIP, YA KNOW?
puff
WELL, WHY DON'T YOU WORK ON MAINTAINING IT WHILE I GO HELP SENSEI...!
'EY ...?
whirl
AWW, CAA-MON, CLASS REP.
LOOK WHAT YA LEFT ME TA DO HERE. NO WAY I CAN UNPACK DIS STUFF ALL BY MYSELF...
TRY!
...
...THAT'S ENOUGH OUT OF ALL OF YOU!!

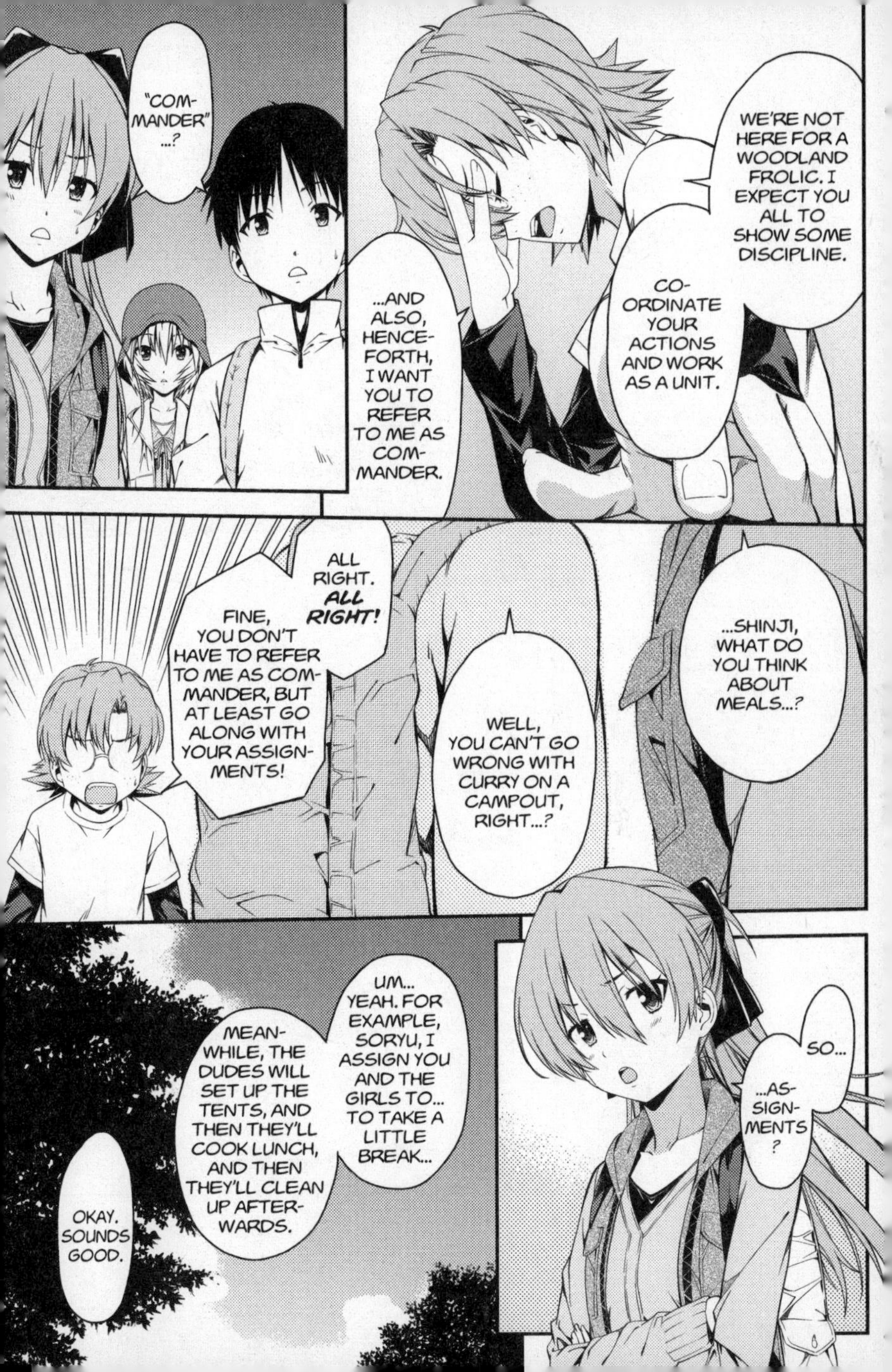
WE'RE NOT HERE FOR A WOODLAND FROLIC. I EXPECT YOU ALL TO SHOW SOME DISCIPLINE.
CO-ORDINATE YOUR ACTIONS AND WORK AS A UNIT.
...AND ALSO, HENCEFORTH, I WANT YOU TO REFER TO ME AS COMMANDER.
"COMMANDER" ...?
...SHINJI, WHAT DO YOU THINK ABOUT MEALS...?
WELL, YOU CAN'T GO WRONG WITH CURRY ON A CAMPOUT, RIGHT...?
ALL RIGHT. ***ALL RIGHT!***
FINE, YOU DON'T HAVE TO REFER TO ME AS COMMANDER, BUT AT LEAST GO ALONG WITH YOUR ASSIGNMENTS!
SO...
...ASSIGNMENTS?
UM... YEAH. FOR EXAMPLE, SORYU, I ASSIGN YOU AND THE GIRLS TO... TO TAKE A LITTLE BREAK...
MEANWHILE, THE DUDES WILL SET UP THE TENTS, AND THEN THEY'LL COOK LUNCH, AND THEN THEY'LL CLEAN UP AFTERWARDS.
OKAY. SOUNDS GOOD.

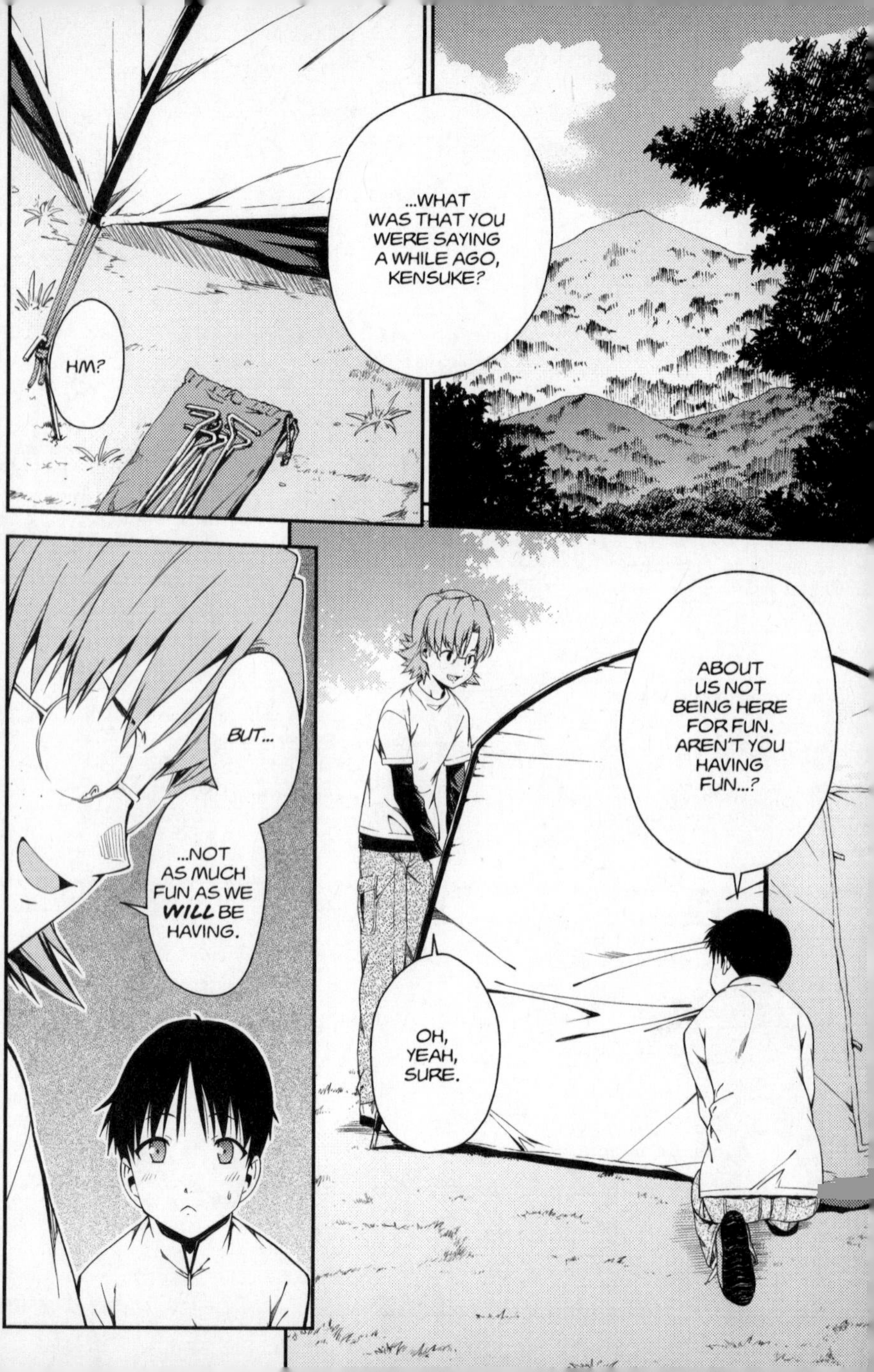
...WHAT WAS THAT YOU WERE SAYING A WHILE AGO, KENSUKE?
HM?
ABOUT US NOT BEING HERE FOR FUN. AREN'T YOU HAVING FUN...?
OH, YEAH, SURE.
BUT...
...NOT AS MUCH FUN AS WE **WILL** BE HAVING.

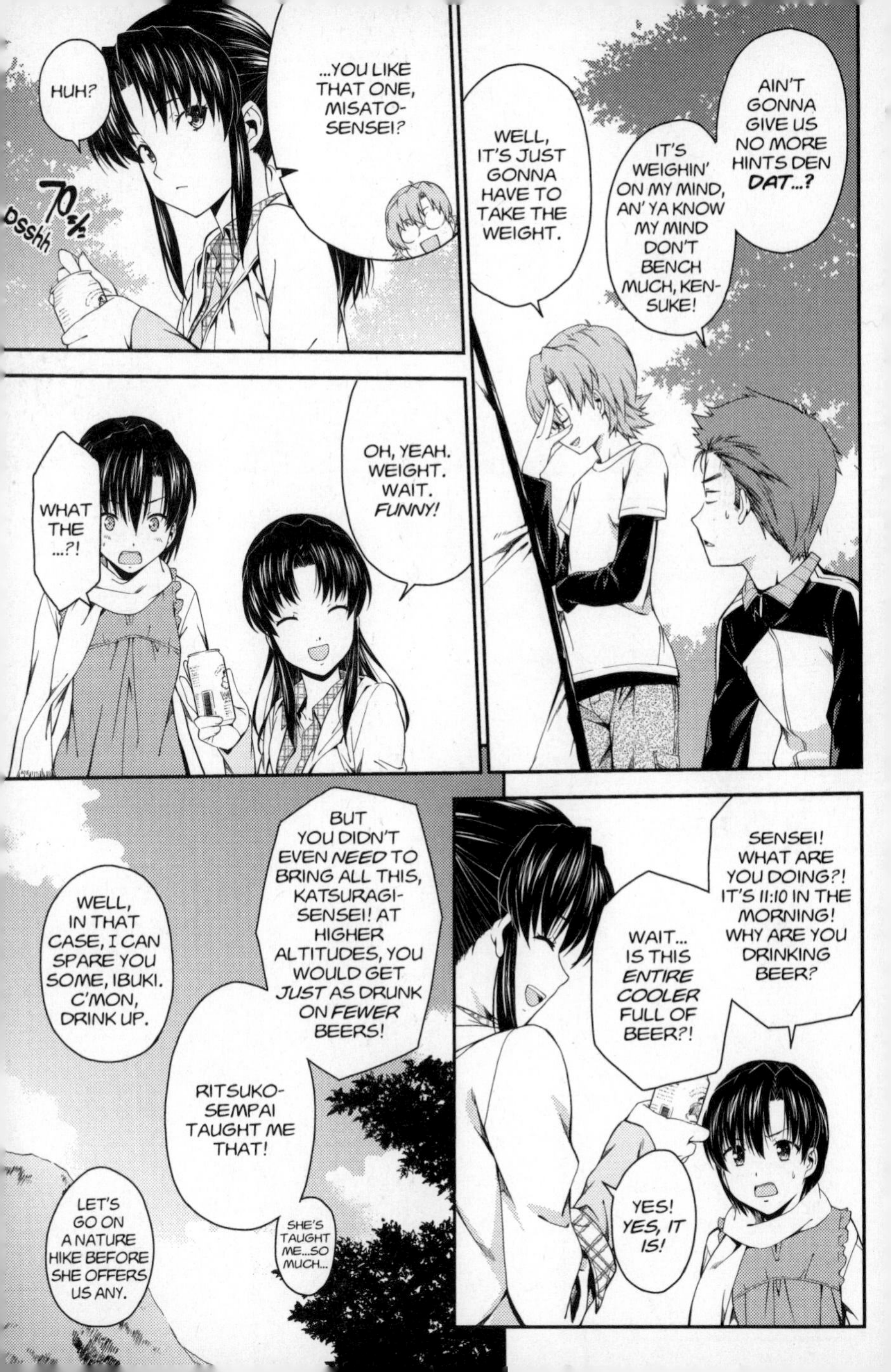
AIN'T GONNA GIVE US NO MORE HINTS DEN *DAT*...?
IT'S WEIGHIN' ON MY MIND, AN' YA KNOW MY MIND DON'T BENCH MUCH, KEN-SUKE!
WELL, IT'S JUST GONNA HAVE TO TAKE THE WEIGHT.
...YOU LIKE THAT ONE, MISATO-SENSEI?
HUH?
Dsshh
OH, YEAH. WEIGHT. WAIT. *FUNNY!*
WHAT THE ...?!
SENSEI! WHAT ARE YOU DOING?! IT'S 11:10 IN THE MORNING! WHY ARE YOU DRINKING BEER?
WAIT... IS THIS *ENTIRE COOLER* FULL OF BEER?!
YES! *YES, IT IS!*
BUT YOU DIDN'T EVEN *NEED* TO BRING ALL THIS, KATSURAGI-SENSEI! AT HIGHER ALTITUDES, YOU WOULD GET *JUST* AS DRUNK ON *FEWER* BEERS!
RITSUKO-SEMPAI TAUGHT ME THAT!
WELL, IN THAT CASE, I CAN SPARE YOU SOME, IBUKI. C'MON, DRINK UP.
SHE'S TAUGHT ME...SO MUCH...
LET'S GO ON A NATURE HIKE BEFORE SHE OFFERS US ANY.

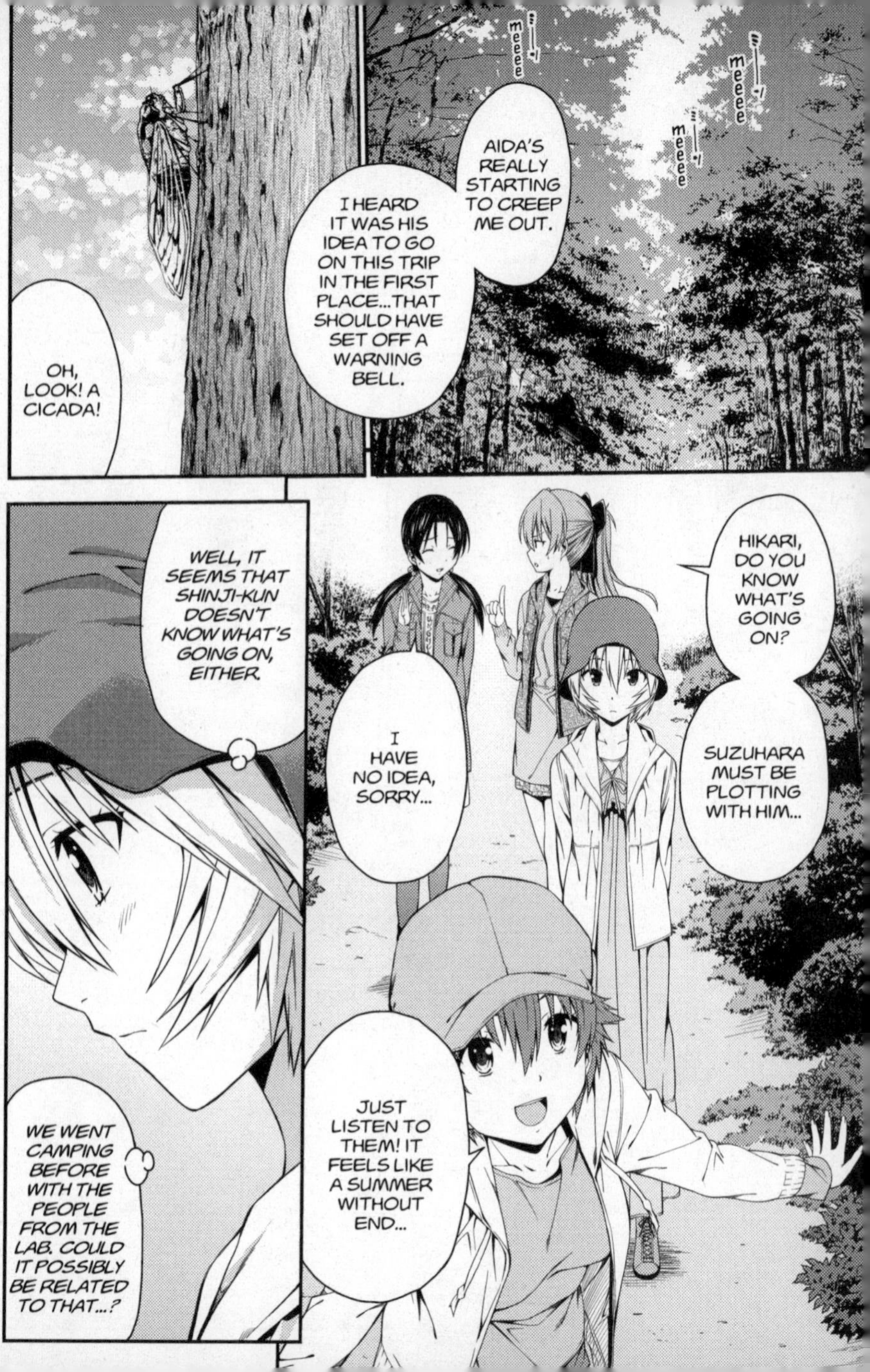
meeee
meeee
meeee
AIDA'S REALLY STARTING TO CREEP ME OUT.
I HEARD IT WAS HIS IDEA TO GO ON THIS TRIP IN THE FIRST PLACE...THAT SHOULD HAVE SET OFF A WARNING BELL.
OH, LOOK! A CICADA!
HIKARI, DO YOU KNOW WHAT'S GOING ON?
SUZUHARA MUST BE PLOTTING WITH HIM...
I HAVE NO IDEA, SORRY...
JUST LISTEN TO THEM! IT FEELS LIKE A SUMMER WITHOUT END...
WELL, IT SEEMS THAT SHINJI-KUN DOESN'T KNOW WHAT'S GOING ON, EITHER.
WE WENT CAMPING BEFORE WITH THE PEOPLE FROM THE LAB. COULD IT POSSIBLY BE RELATED TO THAT...?

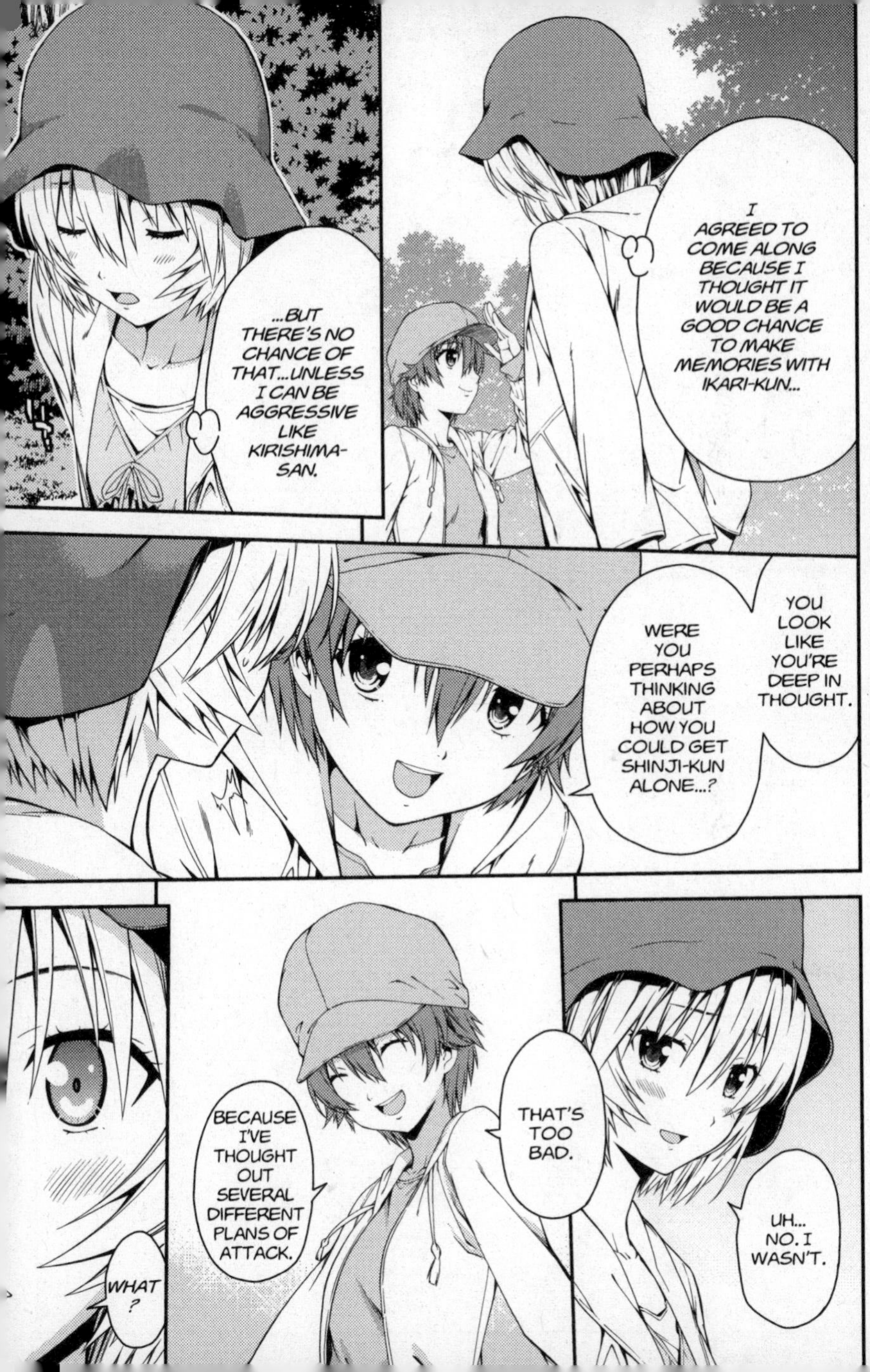
I AGREED TO COME ALONG BECAUSE I THOUGHT IT WOULD BE A GOOD CHANCE TO MAKE MEMORIES WITH IKARI-KUN...
...BUT THERE'S NO CHANCE OF THAT...UNLESS I CAN BE AGGRESSIVE LIKE KIRISHIMA-SAN.
YOU LOOK LIKE YOU'RE DEEP IN THOUGHT.
WERE YOU PERHAPS THINKING ABOUT HOW YOU COULD GET SHINJI-KUN ALONE...?
UH... NO. I WASN'T.
THAT'S TOO BAD.
BECAUSE I'VE THOUGHT OUT SEVERAL DIFFERENT PLANS OF ATTACK.
WHAT?

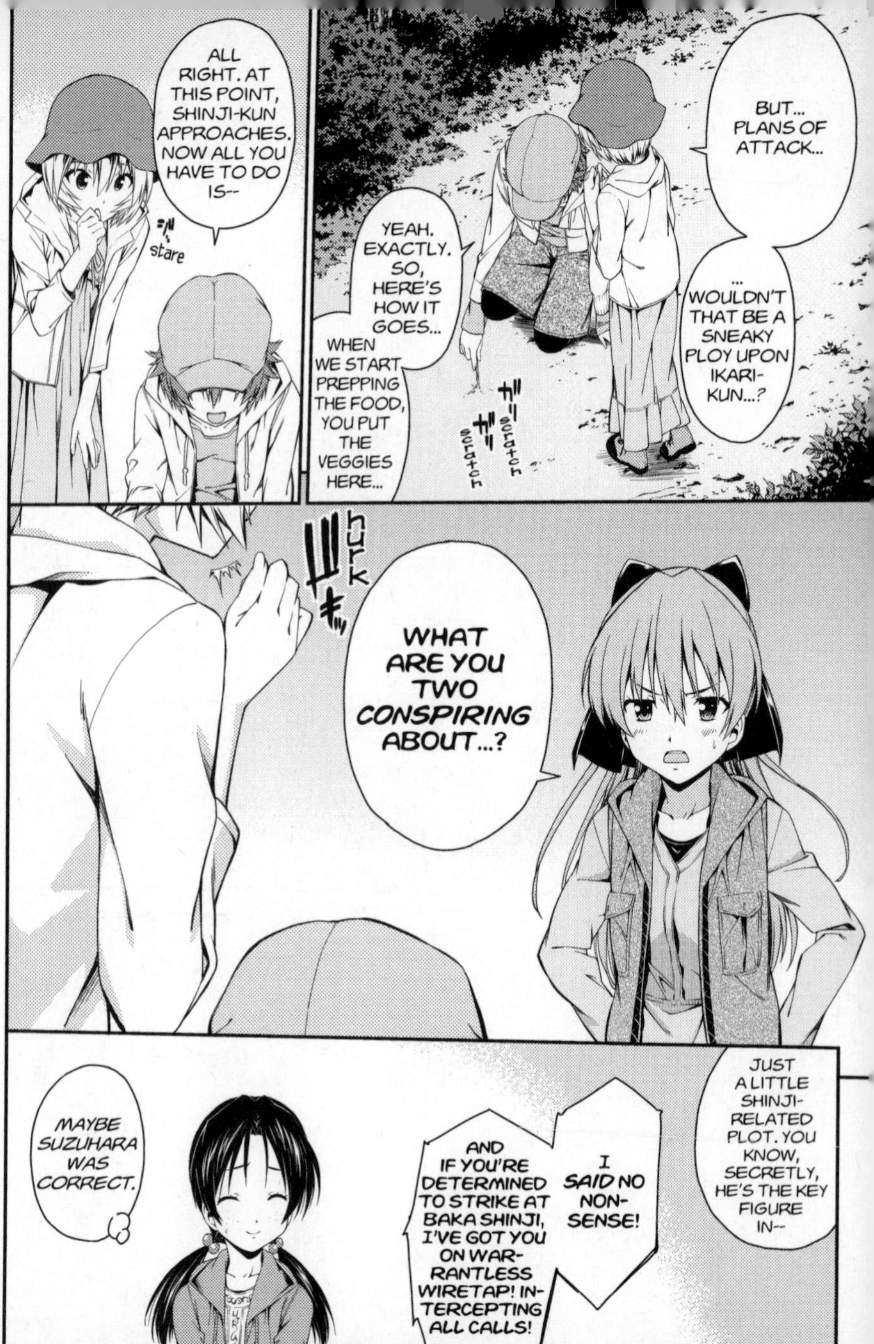
BUT... PLANS OF ATTACK...
... WOULDN'T THAT BE A SNEAKY PLOY UPON IKARI-KUN...?
YEAH. EXACTLY. SO, HERE'S HOW IT GOES...
WHEN WE START PREPPING THE FOOD, YOU PUT THE VEGGIES HERE...
ガリ scratch
ガリ scratch
ALL RIGHT. AT THIS POINT, SHINJI-KUN APPROACHES. NOW ALL YOU HAVE TO DO IS--
stare
ギッ hurk
WHAT ARE YOU TWO CONSPIRING ABOUT...?
JUST A LITTLE SHINJI-RELATED PLOT. YOU KNOW, SECRETLY, HE'S THE KEY FIGURE IN--
I SAID NO NONSENSE!
AND IF YOU'RE DETERMINED TO STRIKE AT BAKA SHINJI, I'VE GOT YOU ON WARRANTLESS WIRETAP! INTERCEPTING ALL CALLS!
MAYBE SUZUHARA WAS CORRECT.

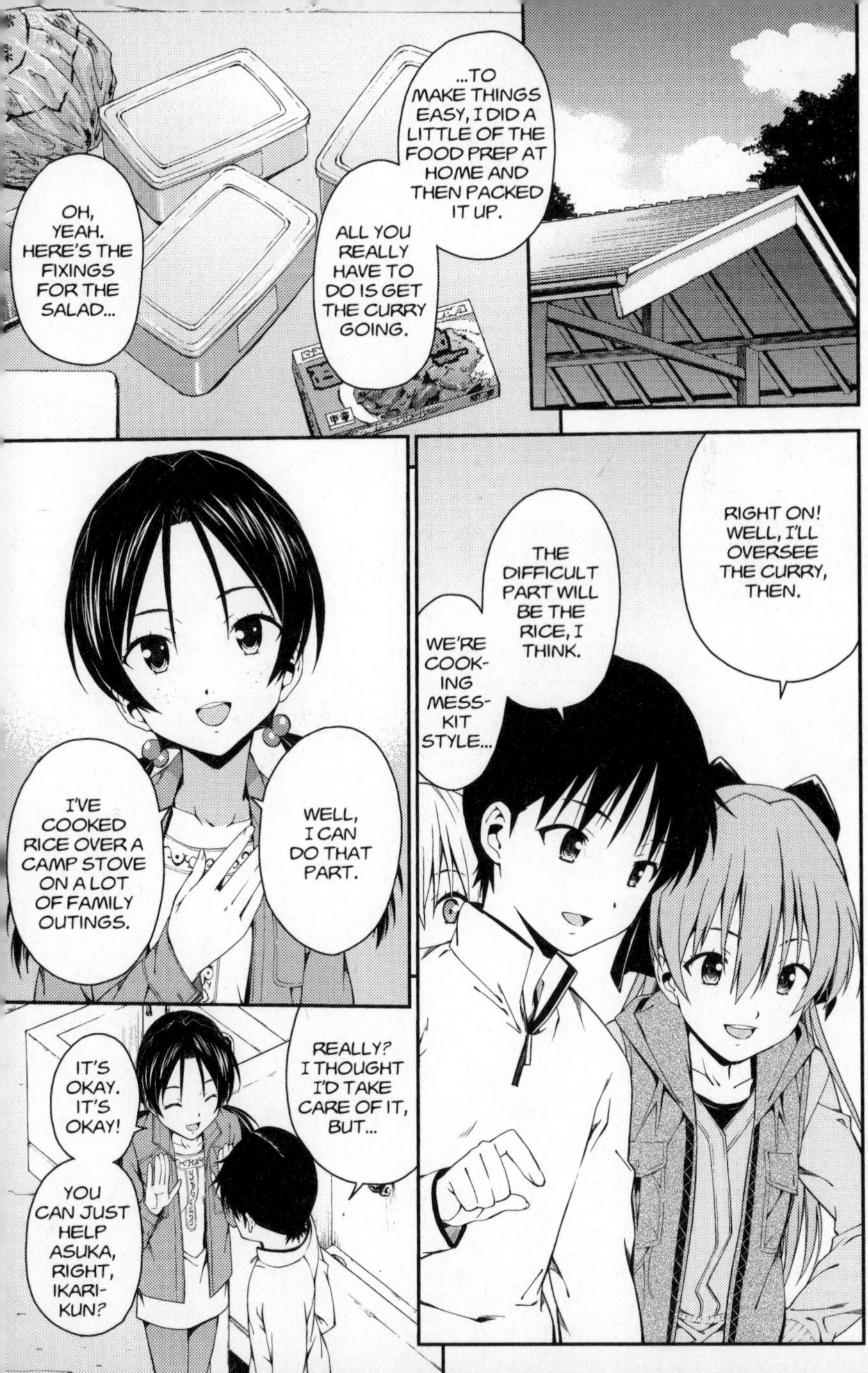
...TO MAKE THINGS EASY, I DID A LITTLE OF THE FOOD PREP AT HOME AND THEN PACKED IT UP.
ALL YOU REALLY HAVE TO DO IS GET THE CURRY GOING.
OH, YEAH. HERE'S THE FIXINGS FOR THE SALAD...
RIGHT ON! WELL, I'LL OVERSEE THE CURRY, THEN.
THE DIFFICULT PART WILL BE THE RICE, I THINK.
WE'RE COOKING MESS-KIT STYLE...
WELL, I CAN DO THAT PART.
I'VE COOKED RICE OVER A CAMP STOVE ON A LOT OF FAMILY OUTINGS.
REALLY? I THOUGHT I'D TAKE CARE OF IT, BUT...
IT'S OKAY. IT'S OKAY!
YOU CAN JUST HELP ASUKA, RIGHT, IKARI-KUN?

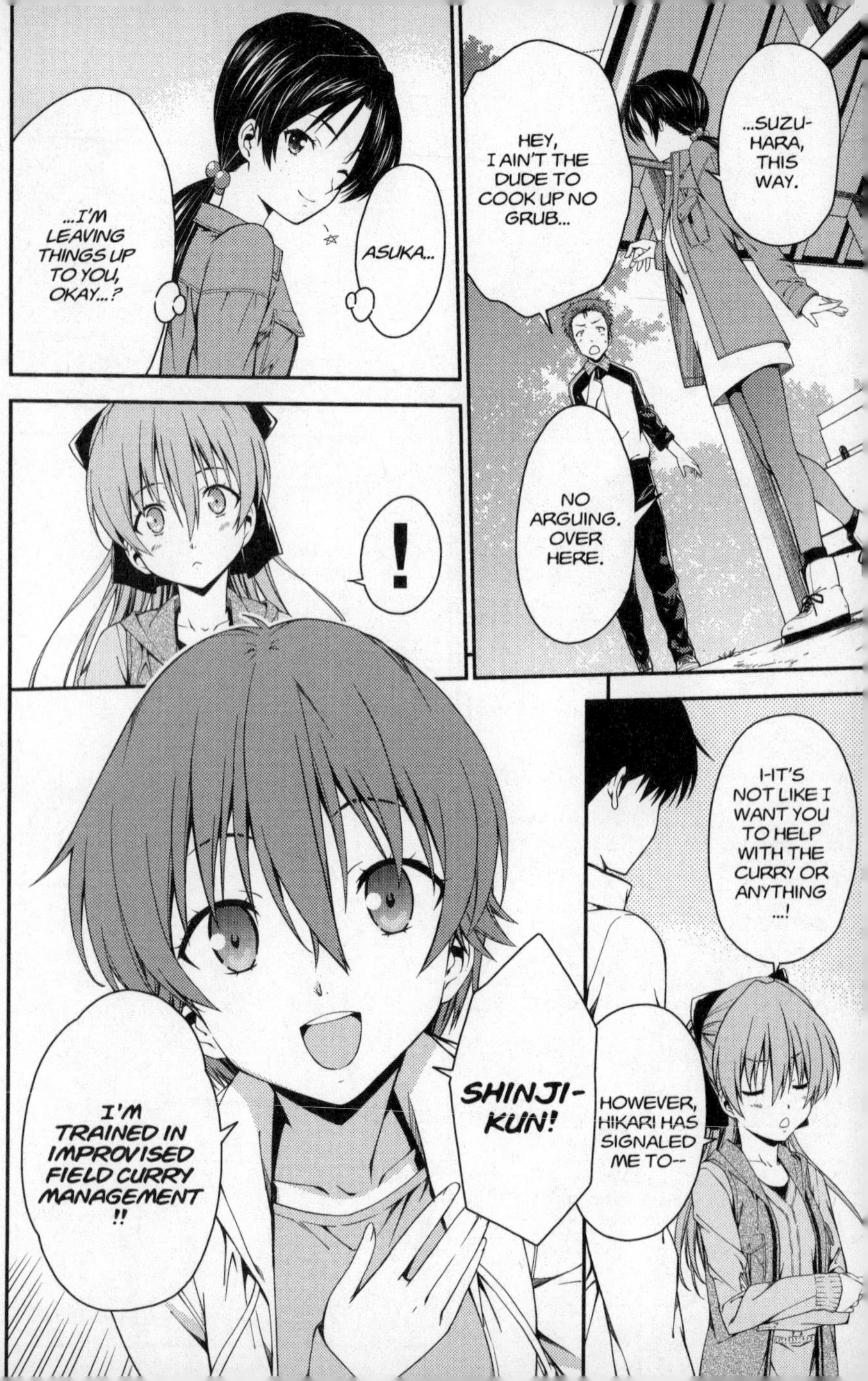
...SUZU-HARA, THIS WAY.
HEY, I AIN'T THE DUDE TO COOK UP NO GRUB...
NO ARGUING. OVER HERE.
ASUKA...
...I'M LEAVING THINGS UP TO YOU, OKAY...?
!
I-IT'S NOT LIKE I WANT YOU TO HELP WITH THE CURRY OR ANYTHING ...!
HOWEVER, HIKARI HAS SIGNALED ME TO--
SHINJI-KUN!
I'M TRAINED IN IMPROVISED FIELD CURRY MANAGEMENT !!

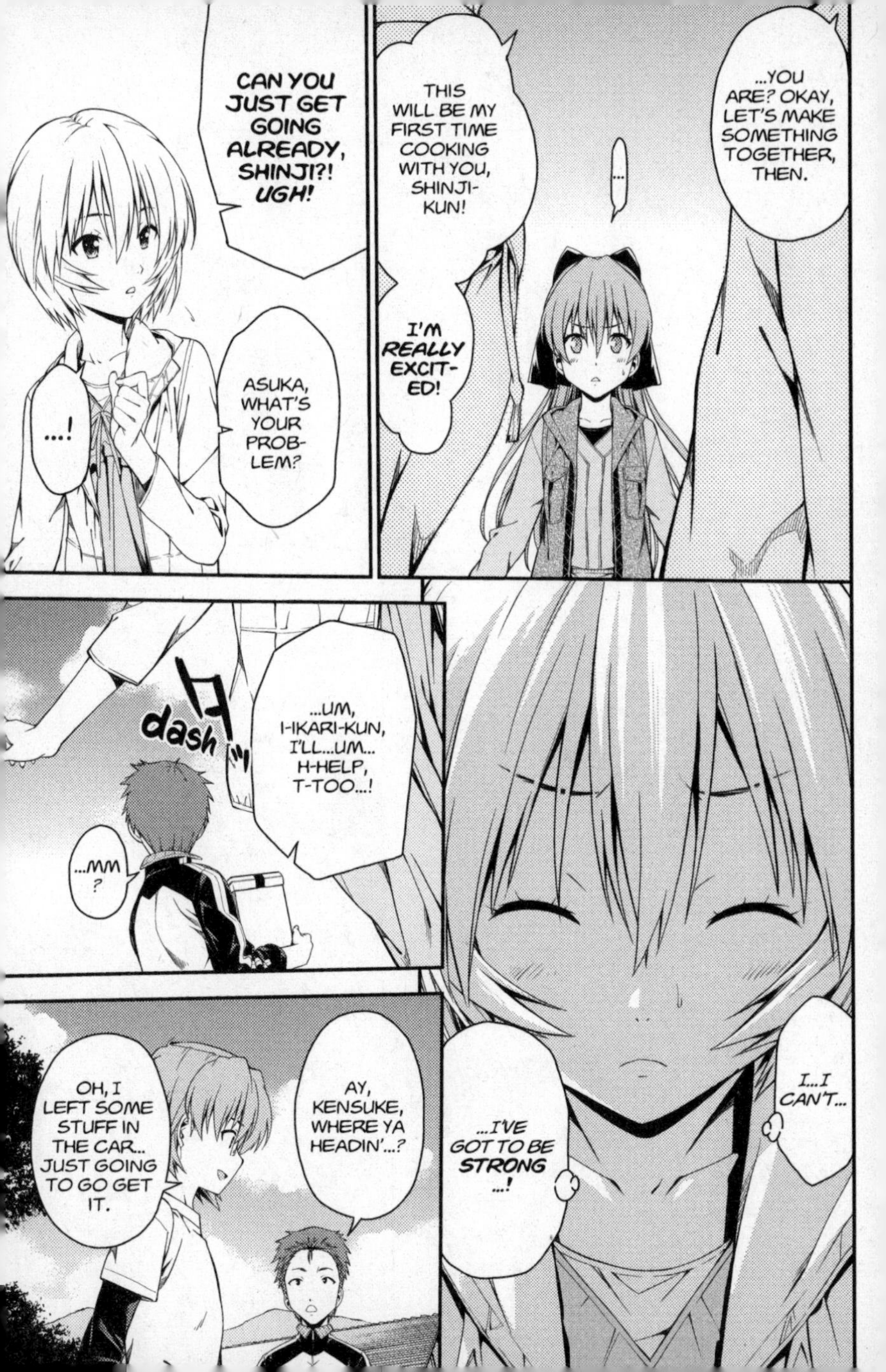
...YOU ARE? OKAY, LET'S MAKE SOMETHING TOGETHER, THEN.
...
THIS WILL BE MY FIRST TIME COOKING WITH YOU, SHINJI-KUN!
I'M REALLY EXCIT-ED!
CAN YOU JUST GET GOING ALREADY, SHINJI?! UGH!
ASUKA, WHAT'S YOUR PROB-LEM?
...!
I... I CAN'T...
...I'VE GOT TO BE STRONG...!
...UM, I-IKARI-KUN, I'LL...UM... H-HELP, T-TOO...!
dash
...MM?
AY, KENSUKE, WHERE YA HEADIN'...?
OH, I LEFT SOME STUFF IN THE CAR... JUST GOING TO GO GET IT.

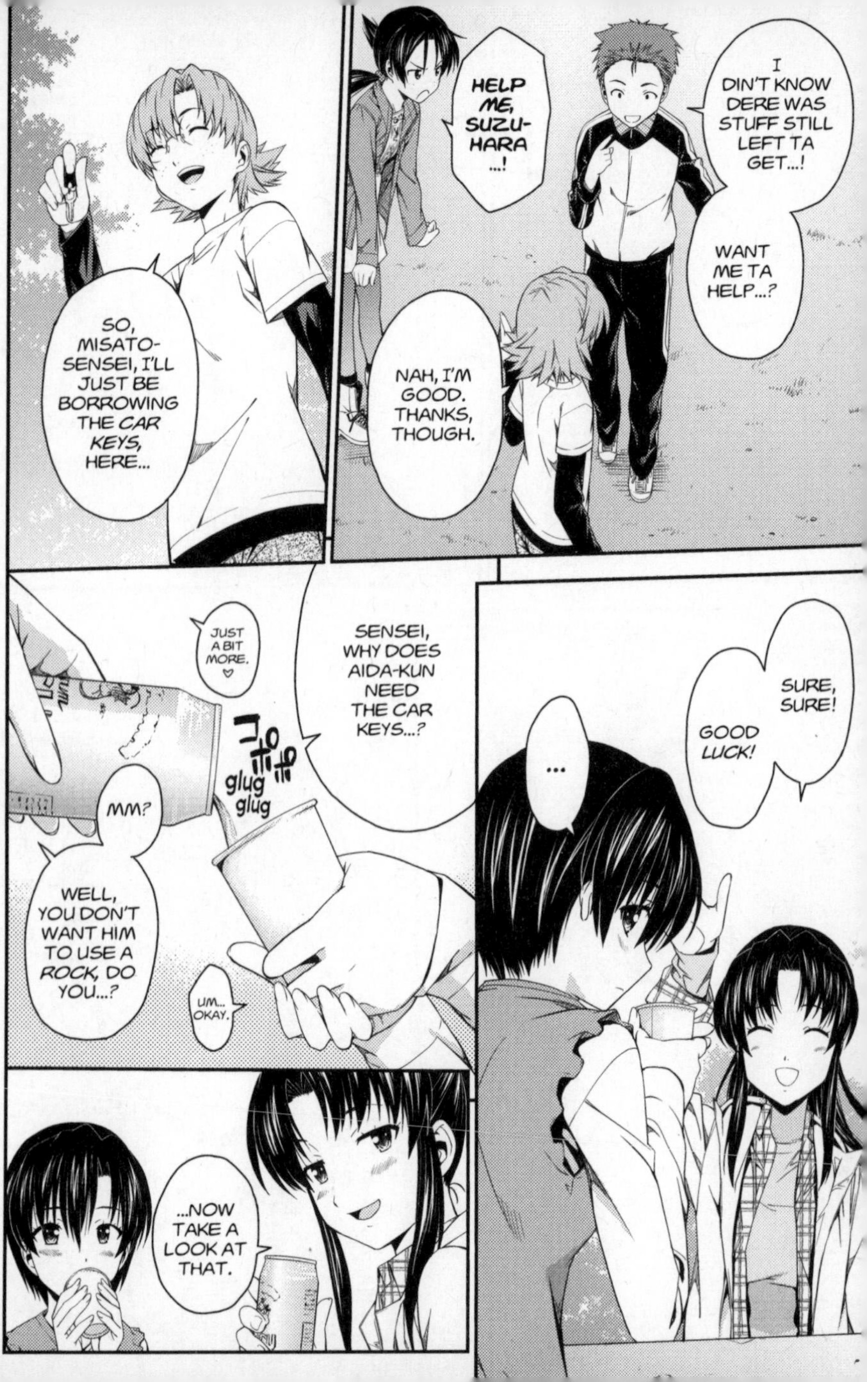
I DIN'T KNOW DERE WAS STUFF STILL LEFT TA GET...!
HELP *ME*, SUZUHARA...!
WANT ME TA HELP...?
NAH, I'M GOOD. THANKS, THOUGH.
SO, MISATO-SENSEI, I'LL JUST BE BORROWING THE *CAR KEYS*, HERE...
SURE, SURE!
GOOD *LUCK!*
...
SENSEI, WHY DOES AIDA-KUN NEED THE CAR KEYS...?
JUST A BIT MORE. ♥
コポポ
glug glug
MM?
WELL, YOU DON'T WANT HIM TO USE A *ROCK*, DO YOU...?
UM... OKAY.
...NOW TAKE A LOOK AT THAT.

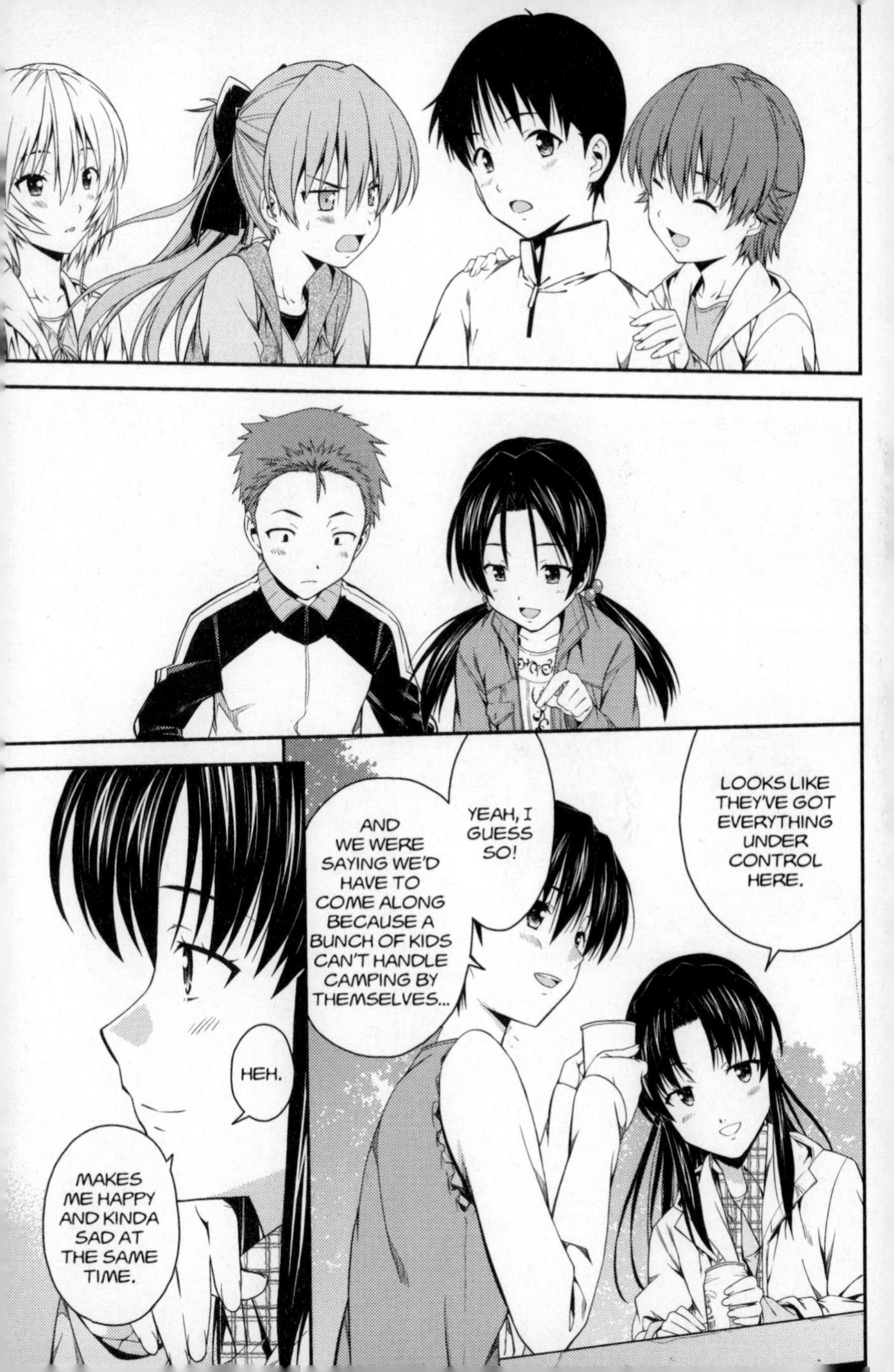
LOOKS LIKE THEY'VE GOT EVERYTHING UNDER CONTROL HERE.
YEAH, I GUESS SO!
AND WE WERE SAYING WE'D HAVE TO COME ALONG BECAUSE A BUNCH OF KIDS CAN'T HANDLE CAMPING BY THEMSELVES...
HEH.
MAKES ME HAPPY AND KINDA SAD AT THE SAME TIME.

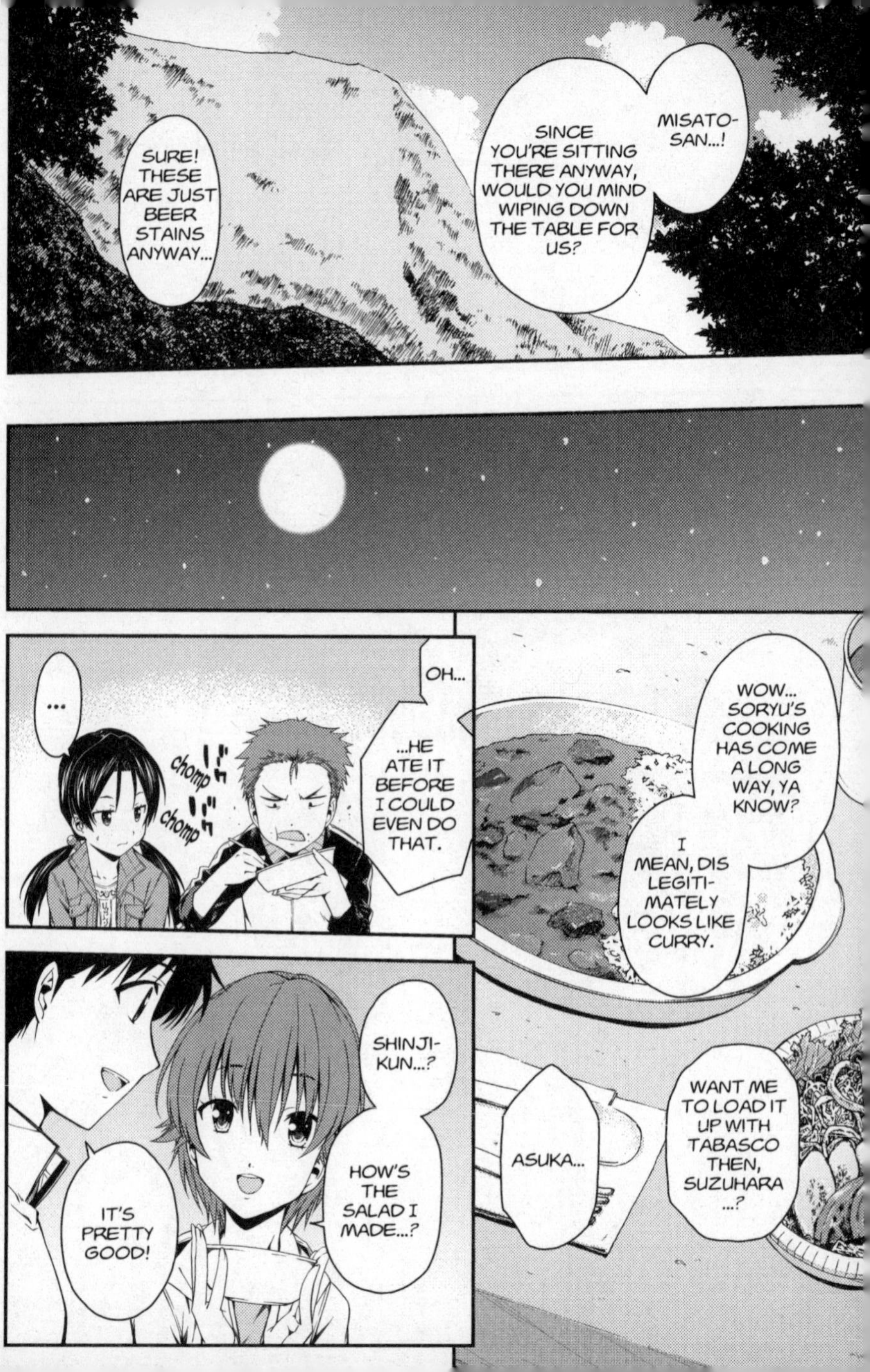
MISATO-SAN...!
SINCE YOU'RE SITTING THERE ANYWAY, WOULD YOU MIND WIPING DOWN THE TABLE FOR US?
SURE! THESE ARE JUST BEER STAINS ANYWAY...
WOW... SORYU'S COOKING HAS COME A LONG WAY, YA KNOW?
I MEAN, DIS LEGITI-MATELY LOOKS LIKE CURRY.
WANT ME TO LOAD IT UP WITH TABASCO THEN, SUZUHARA ...?
ASUKA...
OH...
...HE ATE IT BEFORE I COULD EVEN DO THAT.
chomp
chomp
...
SHINJI-KUN...?
HOW'S THE SALAD I MADE...?
IT'S PRETTY GOOD!

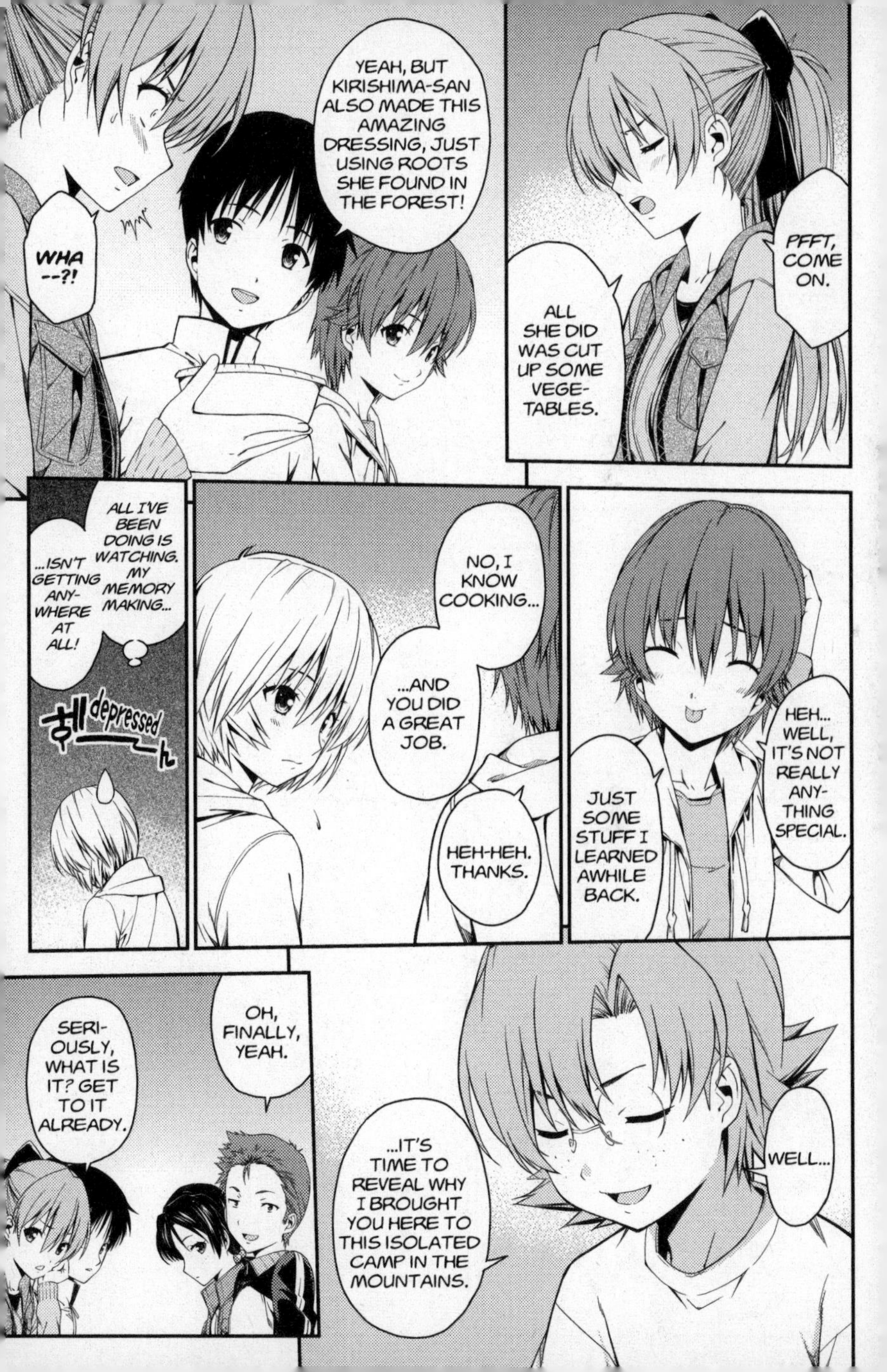
PFFT, COME ON.
ALL SHE DID WAS CUT UP SOME VEGE-TABLES.
YEAH, BUT KIRISHIMA-SAN ALSO MADE THIS AMAZING DRESSING, JUST USING ROOTS SHE FOUND IN THE FOREST!
WHA--?!
HEH... WELL, IT'S NOT REALLY ANY-THING SPECIAL.
JUST SOME STUFF I LEARNED AWHILE BACK.
NO, I KNOW COOKING...
...AND YOU DID A GREAT JOB.
HEH-HEH. THANKS.
ALL I'VE BEEN DOING IS WATCHING. MY MEMORY MAKING...
...ISN'T GETTING ANY-WHERE AT ALL!
depressed
WELL...
...IT'S TIME TO REVEAL WHY I BROUGHT YOU HERE TO THIS ISOLATED CAMP IN THE MOUNTAINS.
OH, FINALLY, YEAH.
SERI-OUSLY, WHAT IS IT? GET TO IT ALREADY.

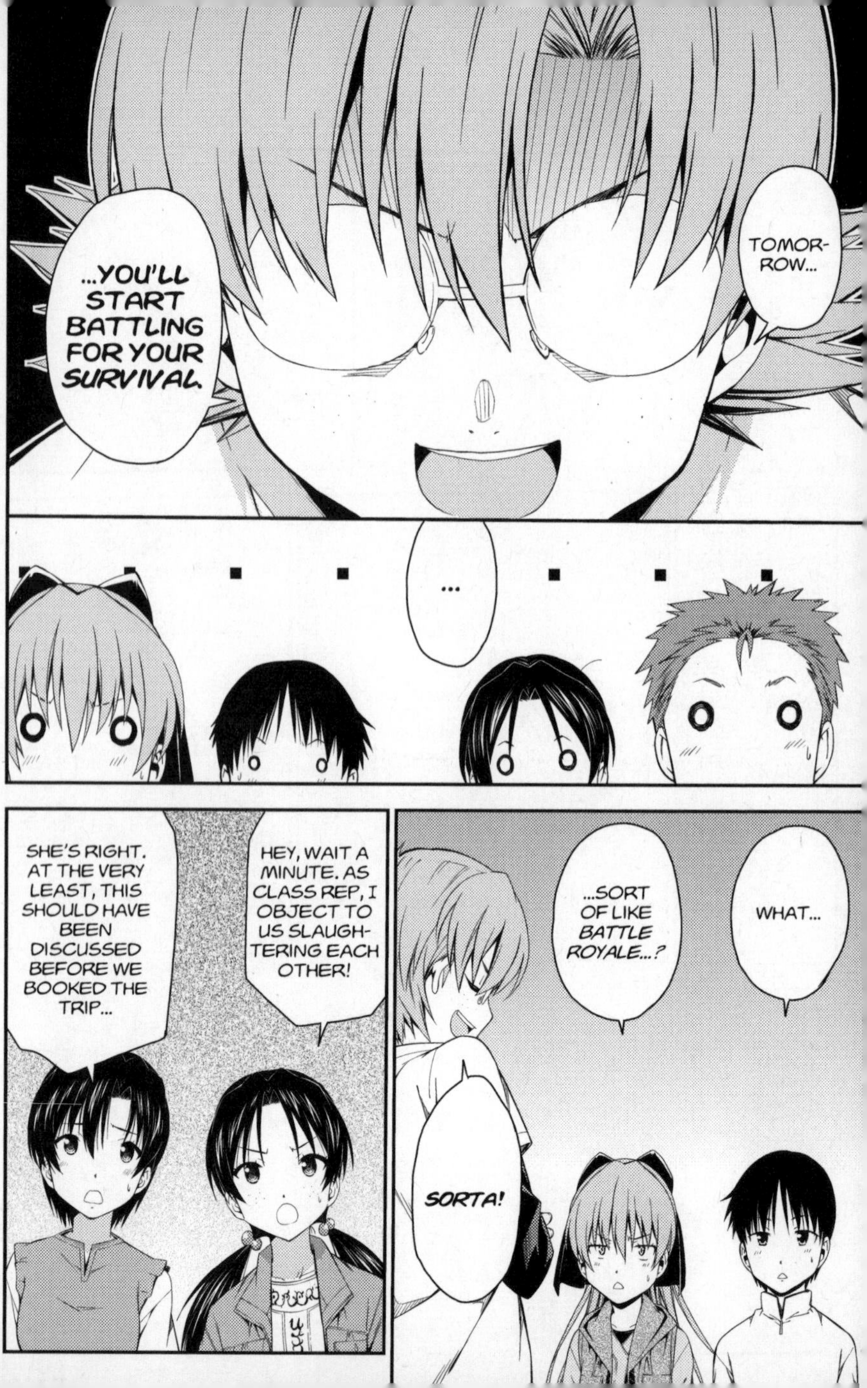
TOMOR-ROW...
...YOU'LL START BATTLING FOR YOUR SURVIVAL.
...
WHAT...
...SORT OF LIKE BATTLE ROYALE...?
SORTA!
HEY, WAIT A MINUTE. AS CLASS REP, I OBJECT TO US SLAUGH-TERING EACH OTHER!
SHE'S RIGHT. AT THE VERY LEAST, THIS SHOULD HAVE BEEN DISCUSSED BEFORE WE BOOKED THE TRIP...

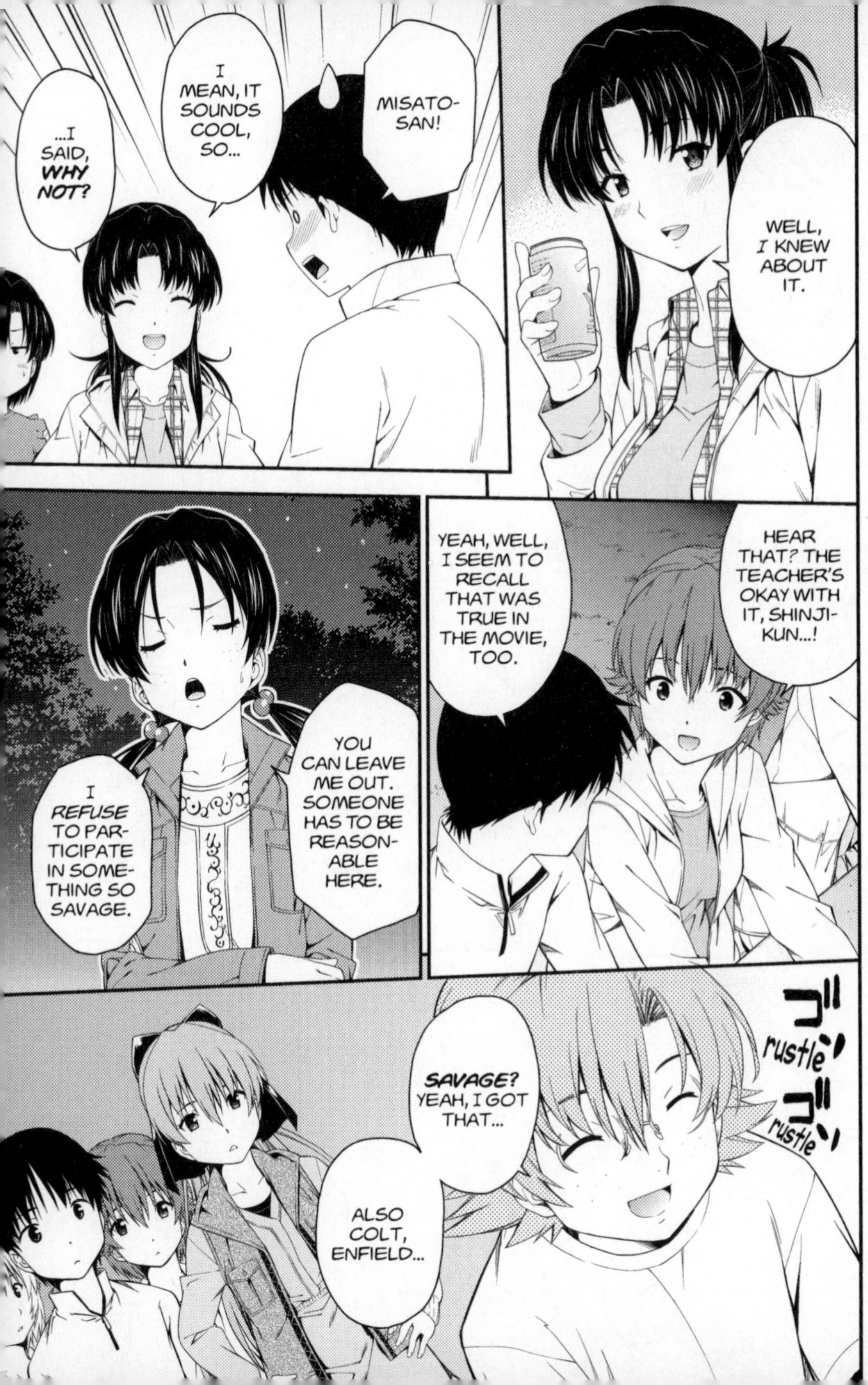
WELL, *I* KNEW ABOUT IT.
MISATO-SAN!
I MEAN, IT SOUNDS COOL, SO...
...I SAID, **WHY NOT?**
HEAR THAT? THE TEACHER'S OKAY WITH IT, SHINJI-KUN...!
YEAH, WELL, I SEEM TO RECALL THAT WAS TRUE IN THE MOVIE, TOO.
YOU CAN LEAVE ME OUT. SOMEONE HAS TO BE REASON-ABLE HERE.
I *REFUSE* TO PAR-TICIPATE IN SOME-THING SO SAVAGE.
ゴソ rustle
ゴソ rustle
SAVAGE? YEAH, I GOT THAT...
ALSO COLT, ENFIELD...

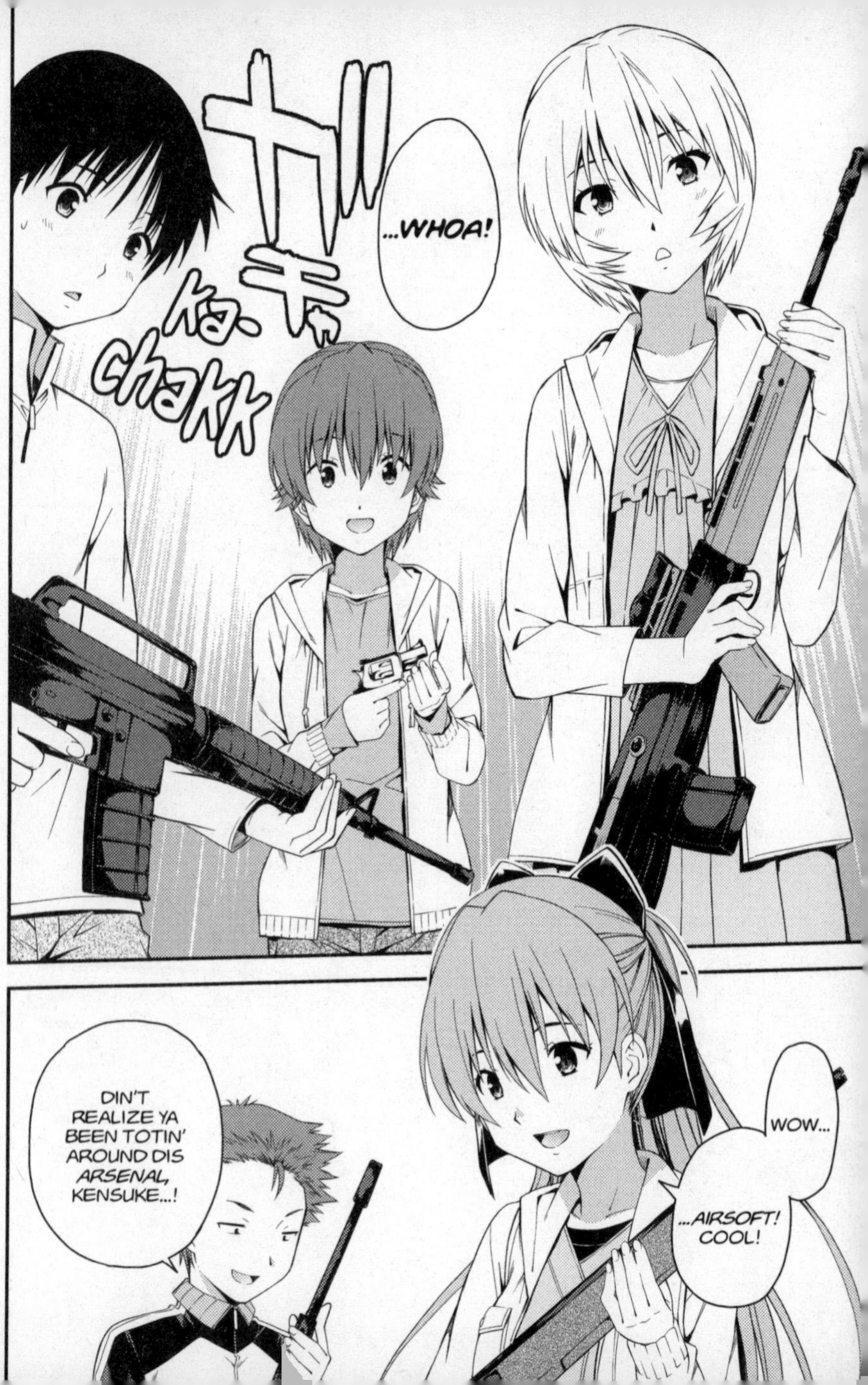
...WHOA!
ka-chakk
WOW...
...AIRSOFT! COOL!
DIN'T REALIZE YA BEEN TOTIN' AROUND DIS ARSENAL, KENSUKE...!

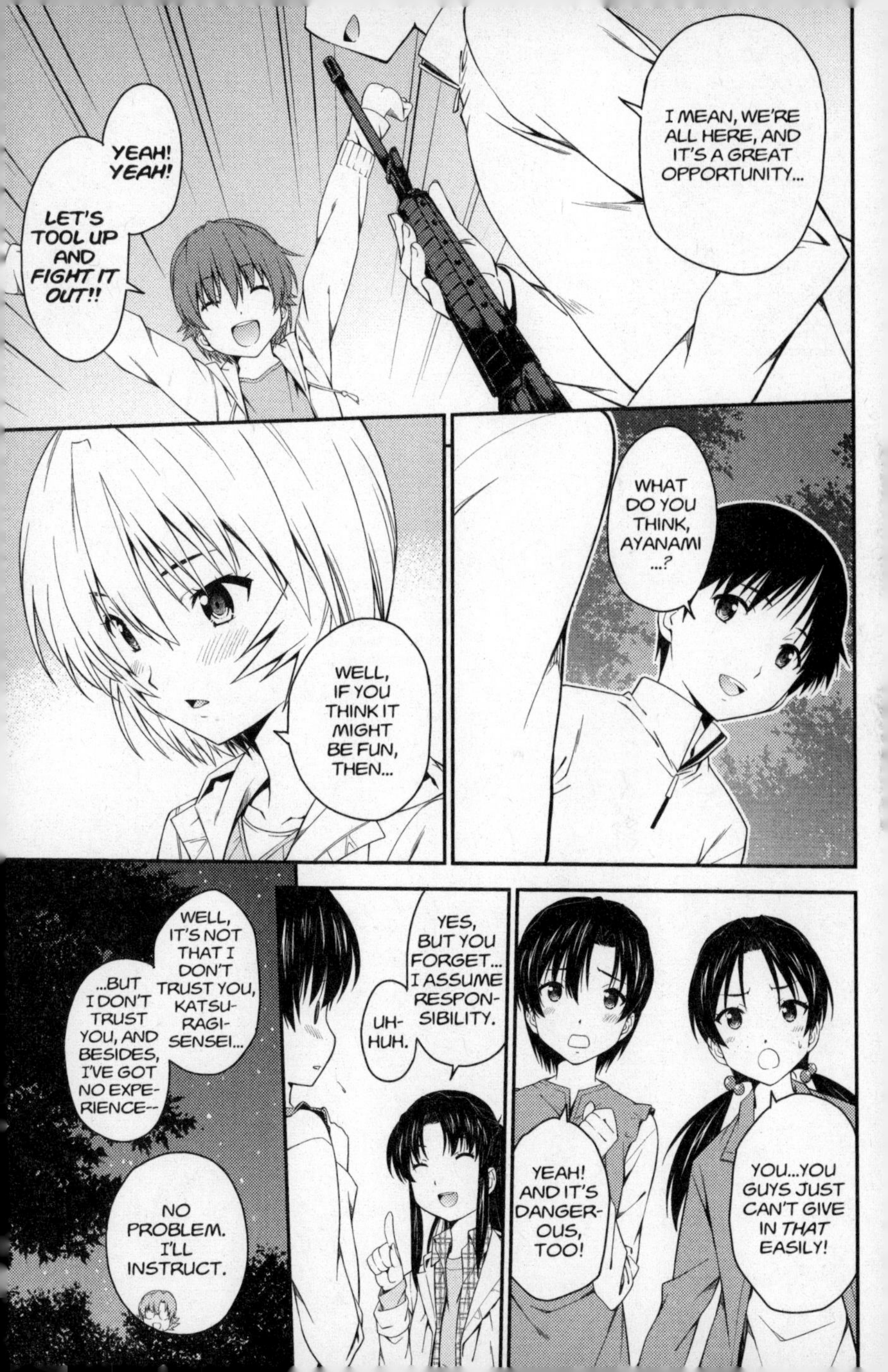
I MEAN, WE'RE ALL HERE, AND IT'S A GREAT OPPORTUNITY...
YEAH! YEAH!
LET'S TOOL UP AND FIGHT IT OUT!!
WHAT DO YOU THINK, AYANAMI...?
WELL, IF YOU THINK IT MIGHT BE FUN, THEN...
YOU...YOU GUYS JUST CAN'T GIVE IN *THAT* EASILY!
YEAH! AND IT'S DANGEROUS, TOO!
YES, BUT YOU FORGET... I ASSUME RESPONSIBILITY.
UH-HUH.
WELL, IT'S NOT THAT I DON'T TRUST YOU, KATSURAGI-SENSEI...
...BUT I DON'T TRUST YOU, AND BESIDES, I'VE GOT NO EXPERIENCE--
NO PROBLEM. I'LL INSTRUCT.

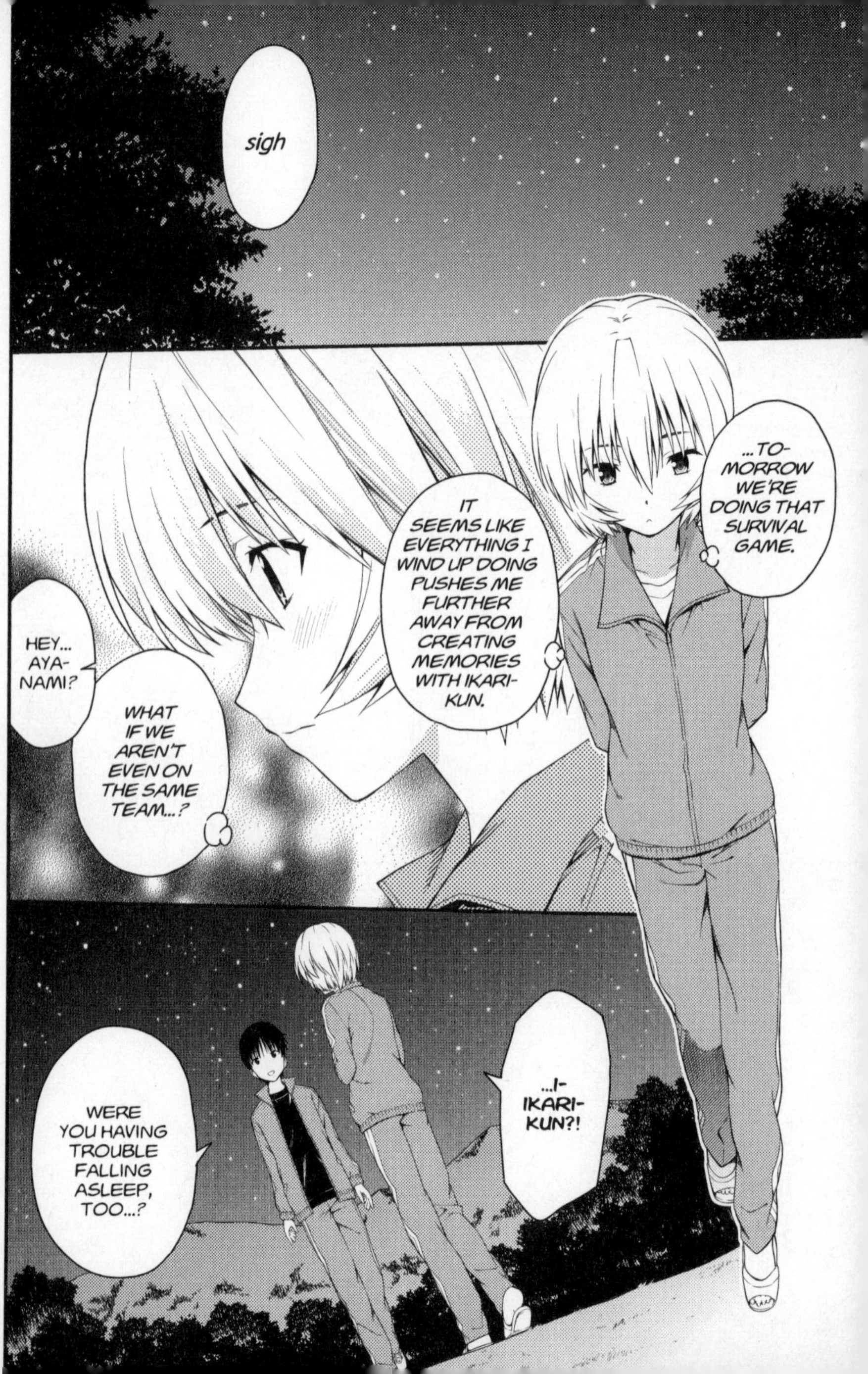
sigh
...TO-MORROW WE'RE DOING THAT SURVIVAL GAME.
IT SEEMS LIKE EVERYTHING I WIND UP DOING PUSHES ME FURTHER AWAY FROM CREATING MEMORIES WITH IKARI-KUN.
WHAT IF WE AREN'T EVEN ON THE SAME TEAM...?
HEY... AYA-NAMI?
...I-IKARI-KUN?!
WERE YOU HAVING TROUBLE FALLING ASLEEP, TOO...?

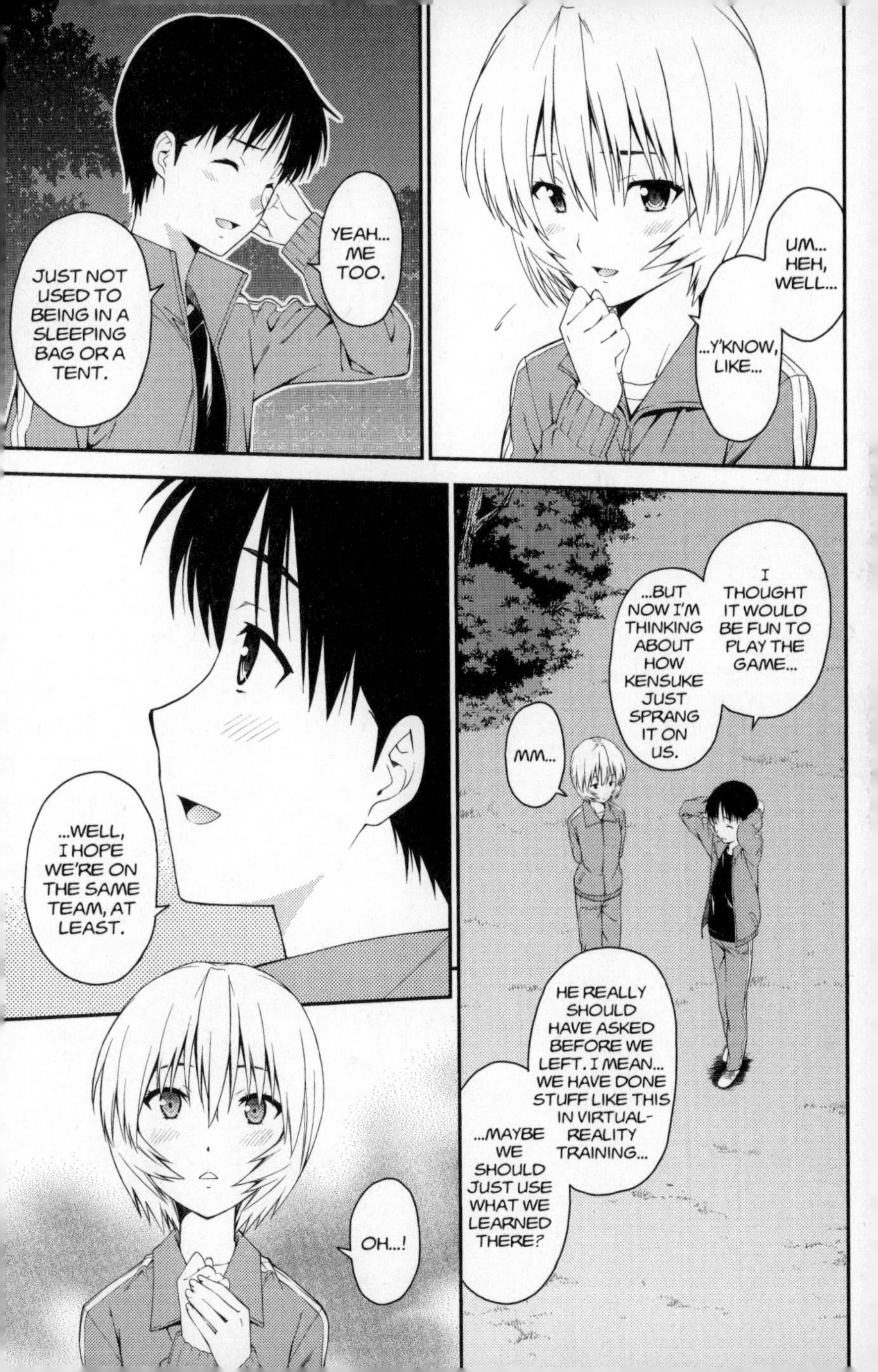
UM... HEH, WELL...
...Y'KNOW, LIKE...
YEAH... ME TOO.
JUST NOT USED TO BEING IN A SLEEPING BAG OR A TENT.
I THOUGHT IT WOULD BE FUN TO PLAY THE GAME...
...BUT NOW I'M THINKING ABOUT HOW KENSUKE JUST SPRANG IT ON US.
MM...
HE REALLY SHOULD HAVE ASKED BEFORE WE LEFT. I MEAN... WE HAVE DONE STUFF LIKE THIS IN VIRTUAL-REALITY TRAINING...
...MAYBE WE SHOULD JUST USE WHAT WE LEARNED THERE?
...WELL, I HOPE WE'RE ON THE SAME TEAM, AT LEAST.
OH...!

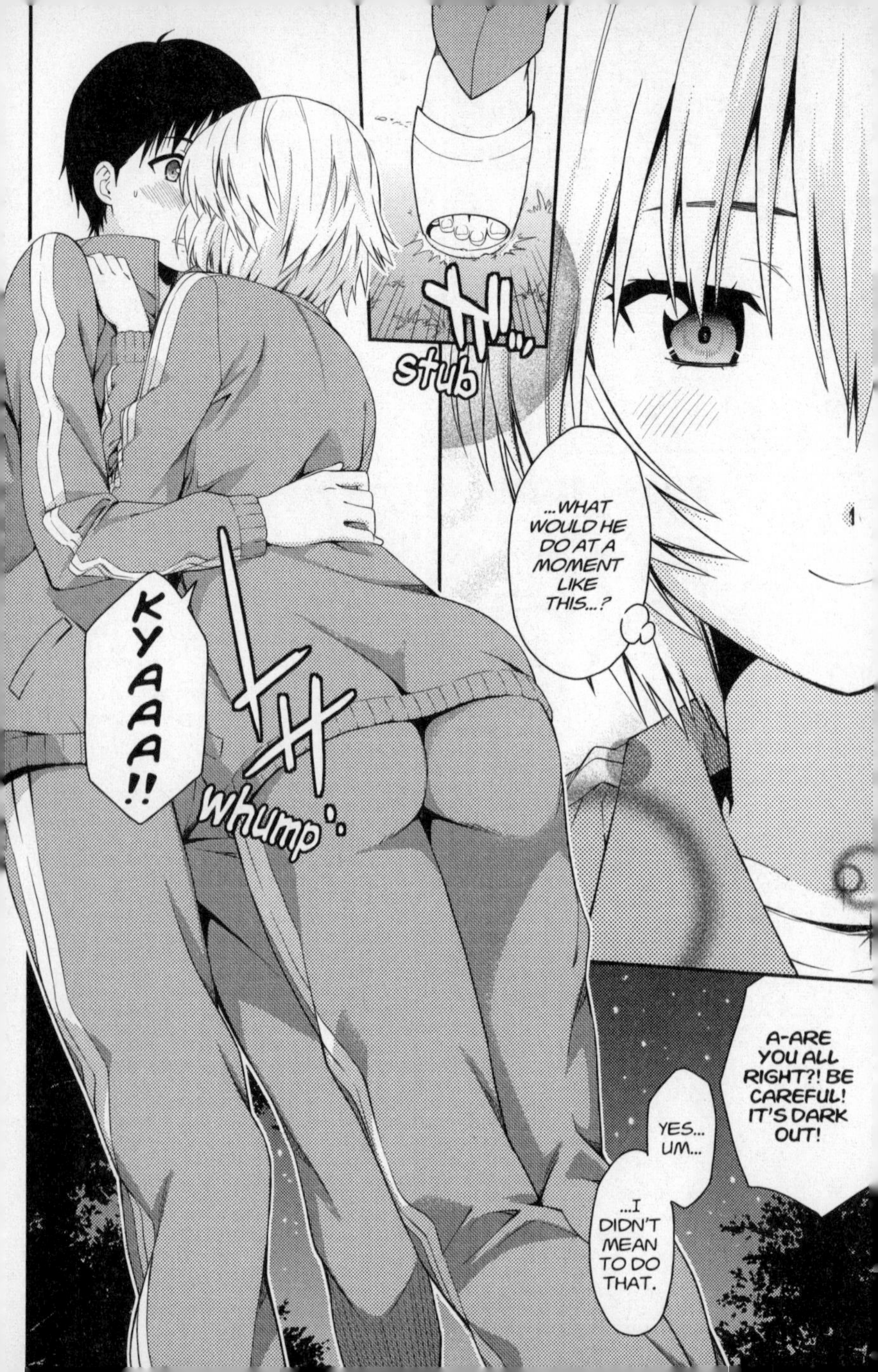
...WHAT WOULD HE DO AT A MOMENT LIKE THIS...?
stub
KYAAA!!
whump
A-ARE YOU ALL RIGHT?! BE CAREFUL! IT'S DARK OUT!
YES... UM...
...I DIDN'T MEAN TO DO THAT.

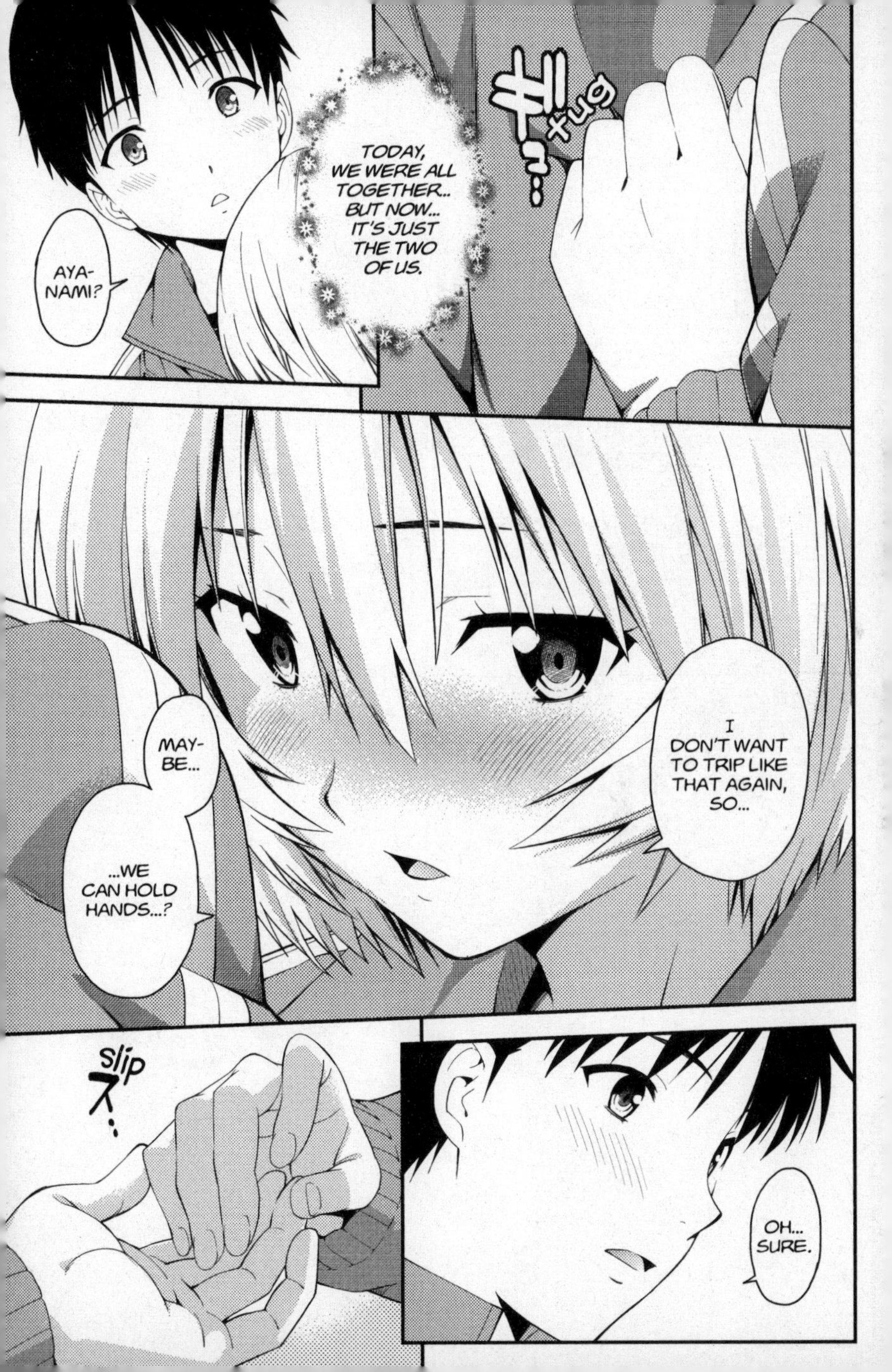
tug
TODAY, WE WERE ALL TOGETHER... BUT NOW... IT'S JUST THE TWO OF US.
AYA-NAMI?
I DON'T WANT TO TRIP LIKE THAT AGAIN, SO...
MAY-BE...
...WE CAN HOLD HANDS...?
OH... SURE.
slip

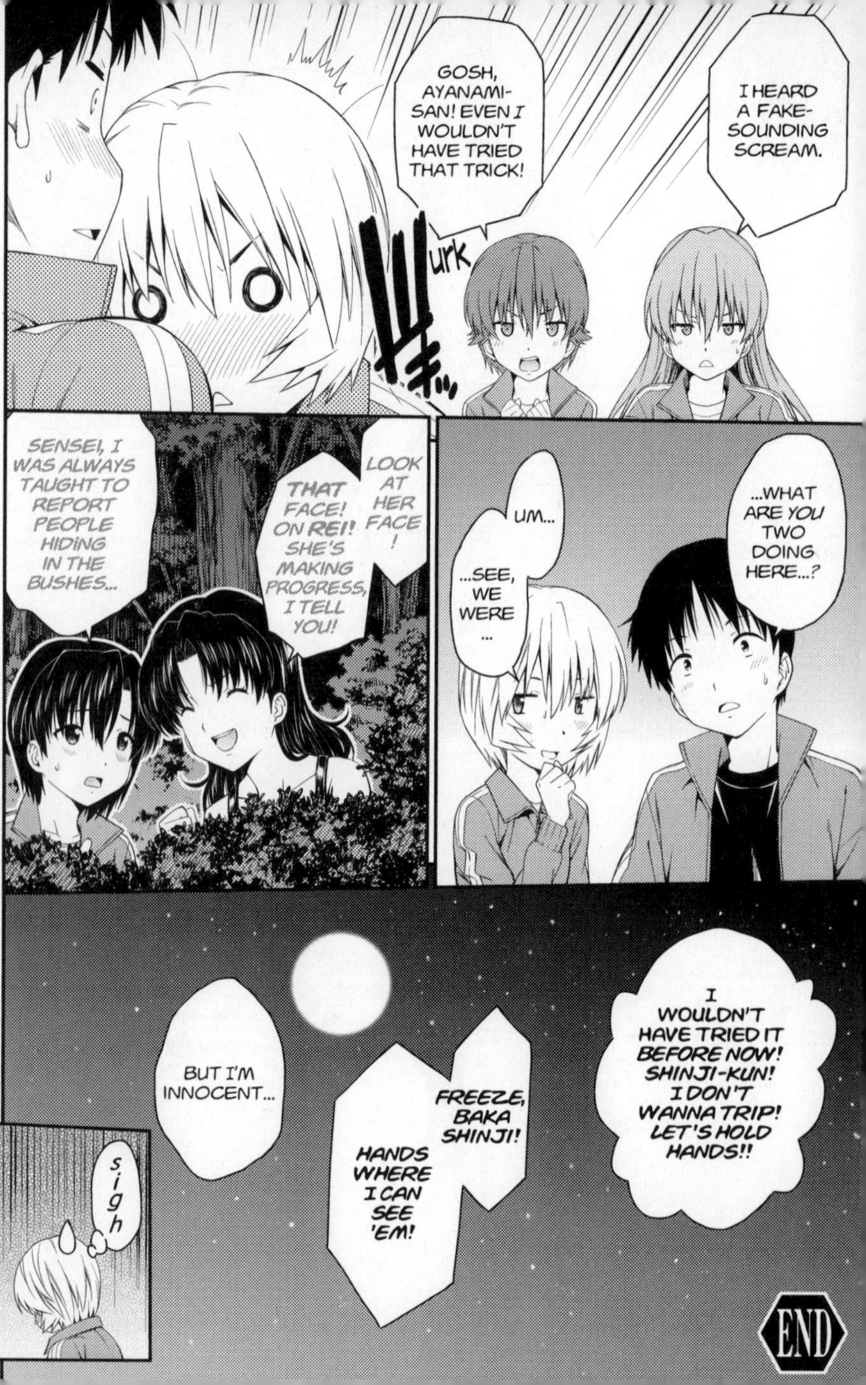
I HEARD A FAKE-SOUNDING SCREAM.
GOSH, AYANAMI-SAN! EVEN I WOULDN'T HAVE TRIED THAT TRICK!
urk
ギッ
...WHAT ARE YOU TWO DOING HERE...?
UM...
...SEE, WE WERE ...
LOOK AT HER FACE!
THAT FACE! ON REI! SHE'S MAKING PROGRESS, I TELL YOU!
SENSEI, I WAS ALWAYS TAUGHT TO REPORT PEOPLE HIDING IN THE BUSHES...
I WOULDN'T HAVE TRIED IT BEFORE NOW! SHINJI-KUN! I DON'T WANNA TRIP! LET'S HOLD HANDS!!
FREEZE, BAKA SHINJI!
HANDS WHERE I CAN SEE 'EM!
BUT I'M INNOCENT...
sigh
END

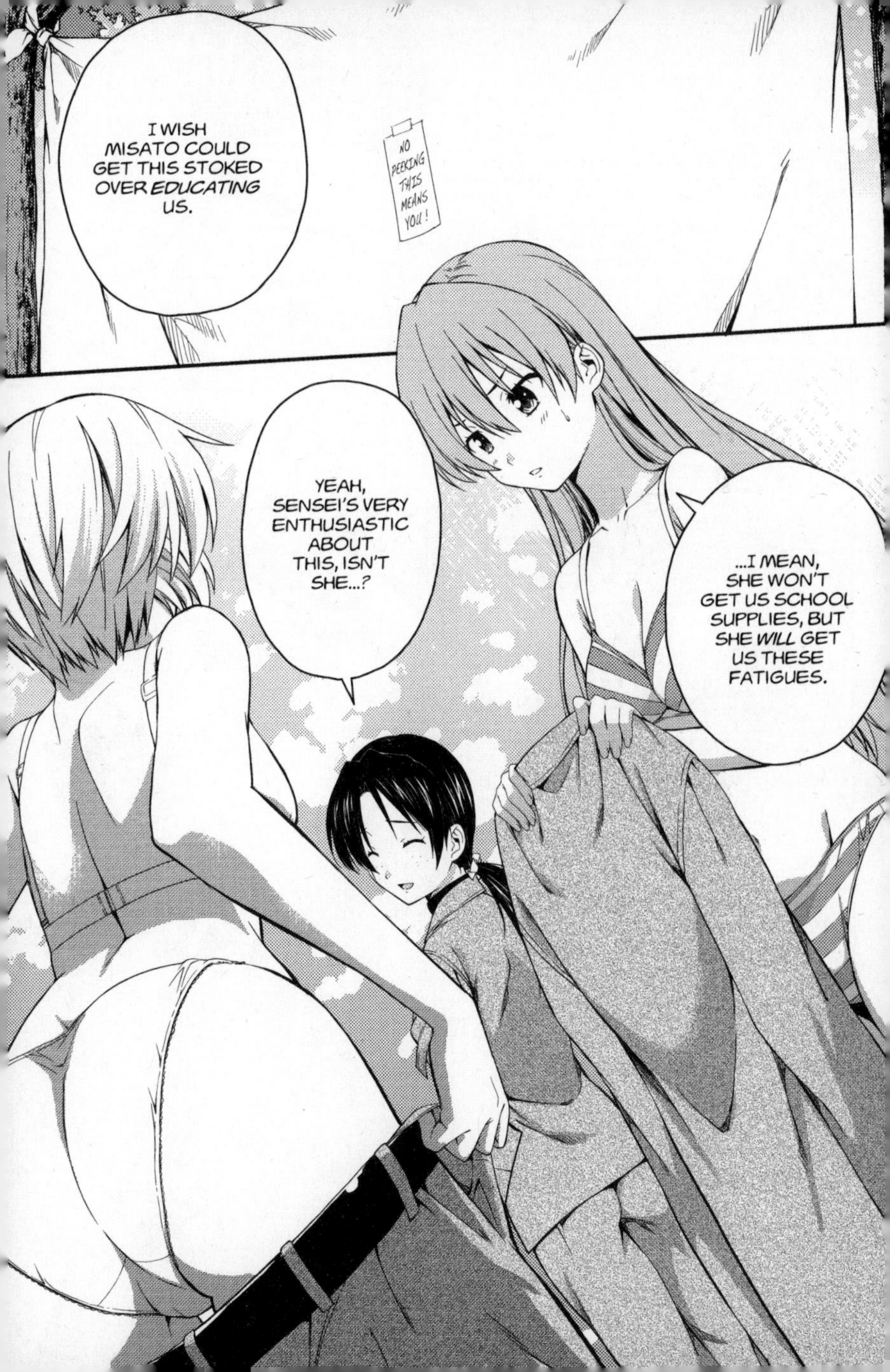
NO PEEKING THIS MEANS YOU!
I WISH MISATO COULD GET THIS STOKED OVER *EDUCATING* US.
...I MEAN, SHE WON'T GET US SCHOOL SUPPLIES, BUT SHE *WILL* GET US THESE FATIGUES.
YEAH, SENSEI'S VERY ENTHUSIASTIC ABOUT THIS, ISN'T SHE...?

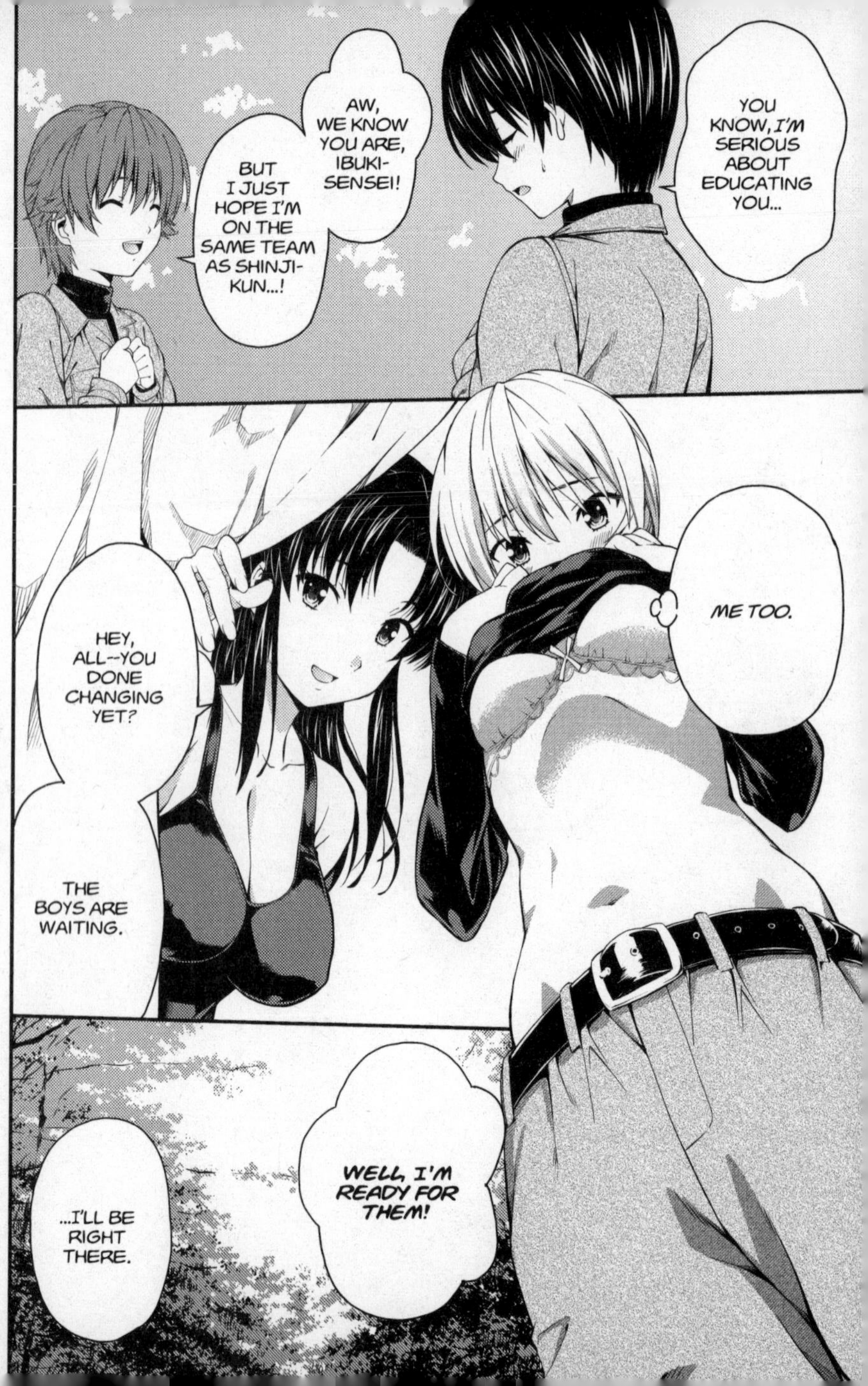
YOU KNOW, I'M SERIOUS ABOUT EDUCATING YOU...
AW, WE KNOW YOU ARE, IBUKI-SENSEI!
BUT I JUST HOPE I'M ON THE SAME TEAM AS SHINJI-KUN...!
ME TOO.
HEY, ALL--YOU DONE CHANGING YET?
THE BOYS ARE WAITING.
WELL, I'M READY FOR THEM!
...I'LL BE RIGHT THERE.

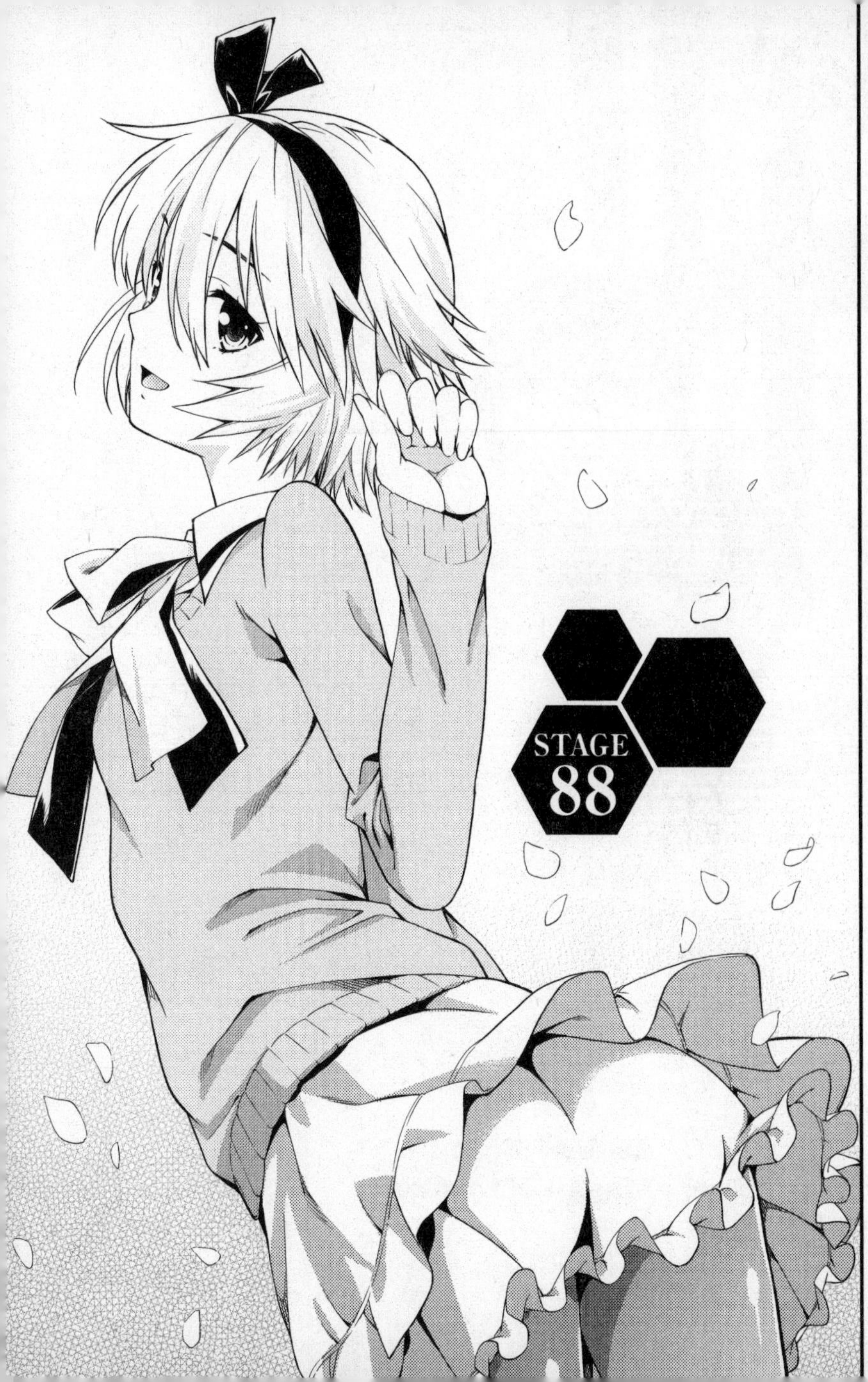
STAGE
88

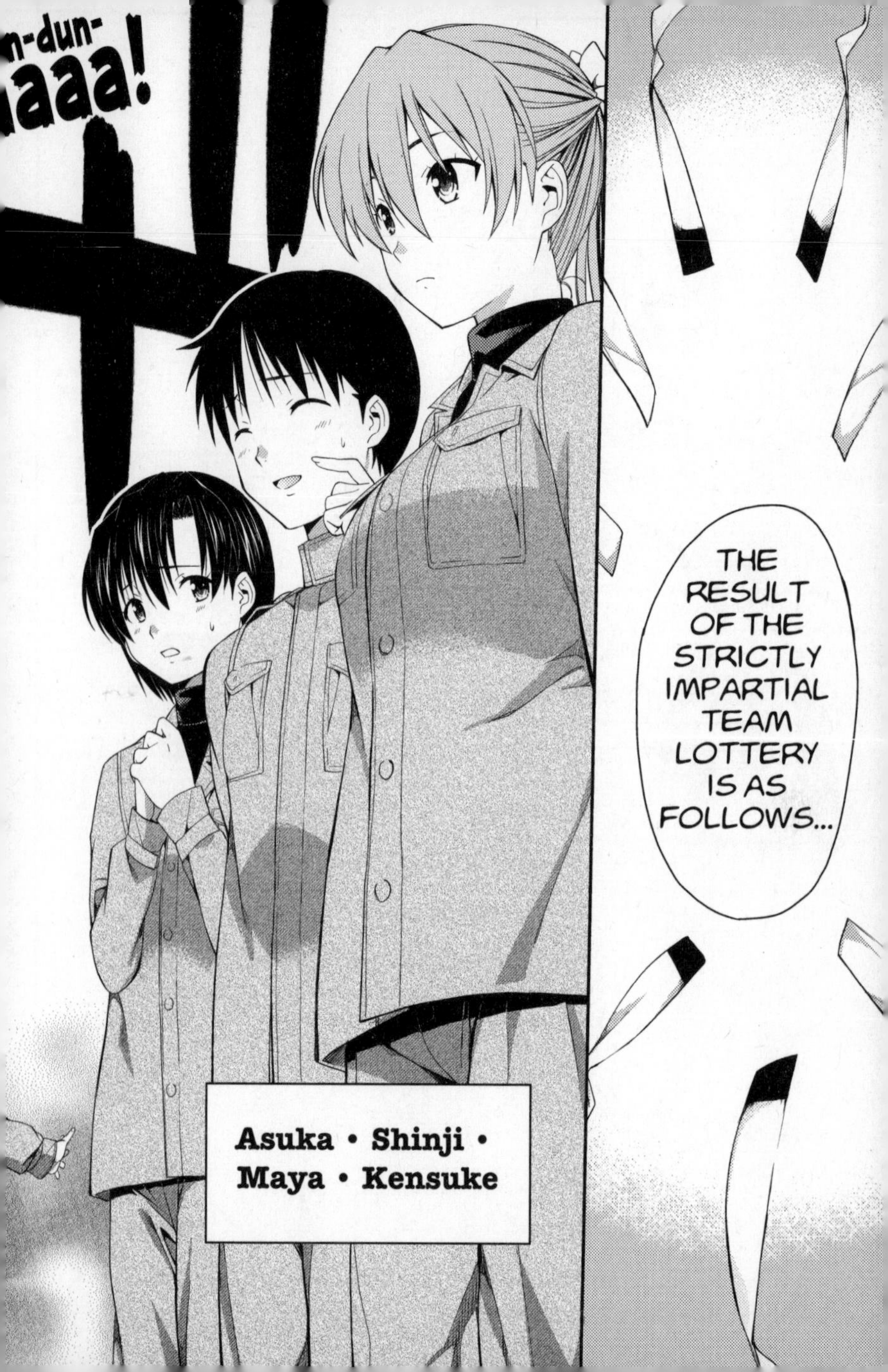
THE RESULT OF THE STRICTLY IMPARTIAL TEAM LOTTERY IS AS FOLLOWS...
n-dun-
aaa!
Asuka • Shinji • Maya • Kensuke

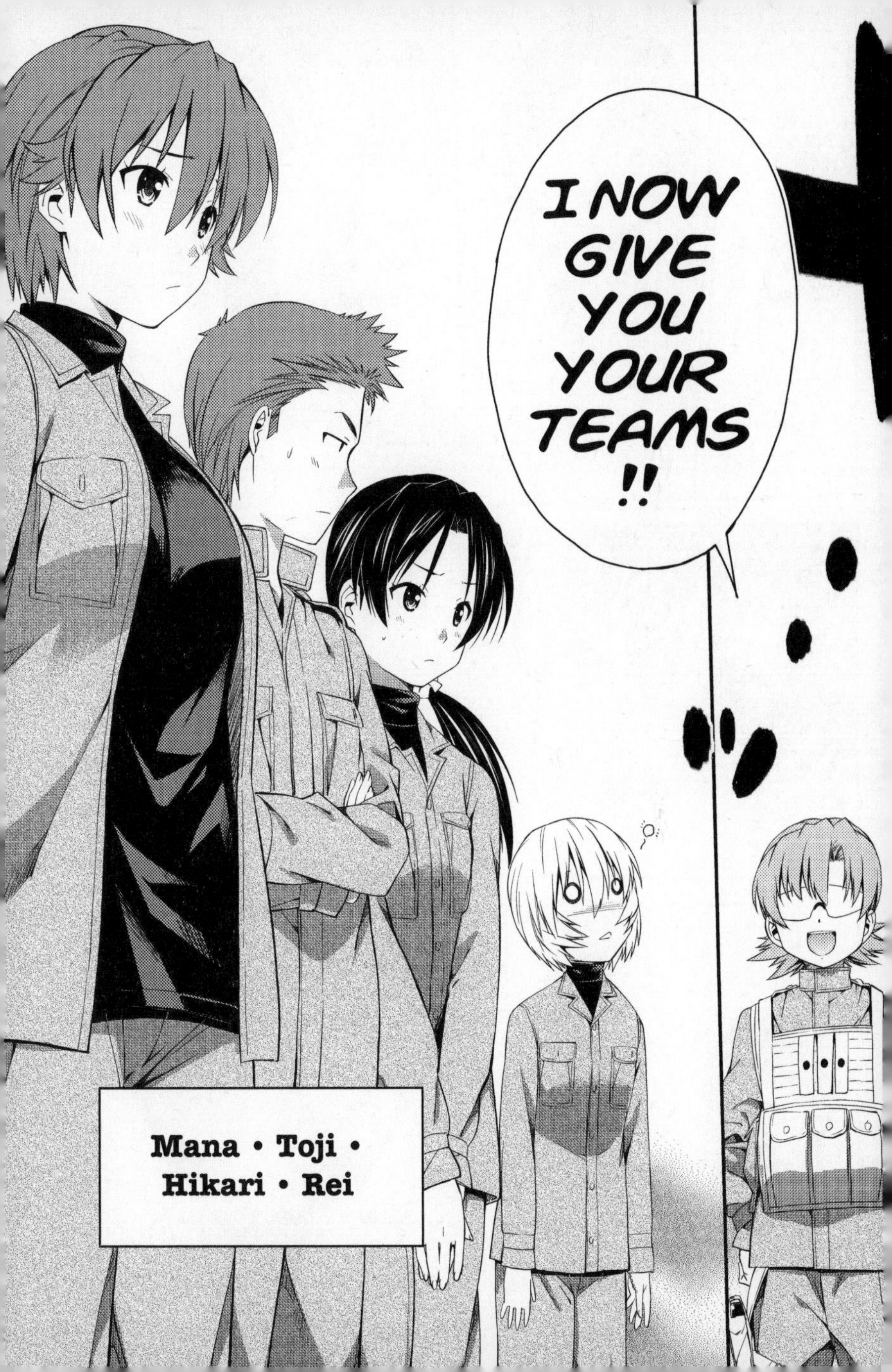
I NOW GIVE YOU YOUR TEAMS!!
Mana • Toji • Hikari • Rei

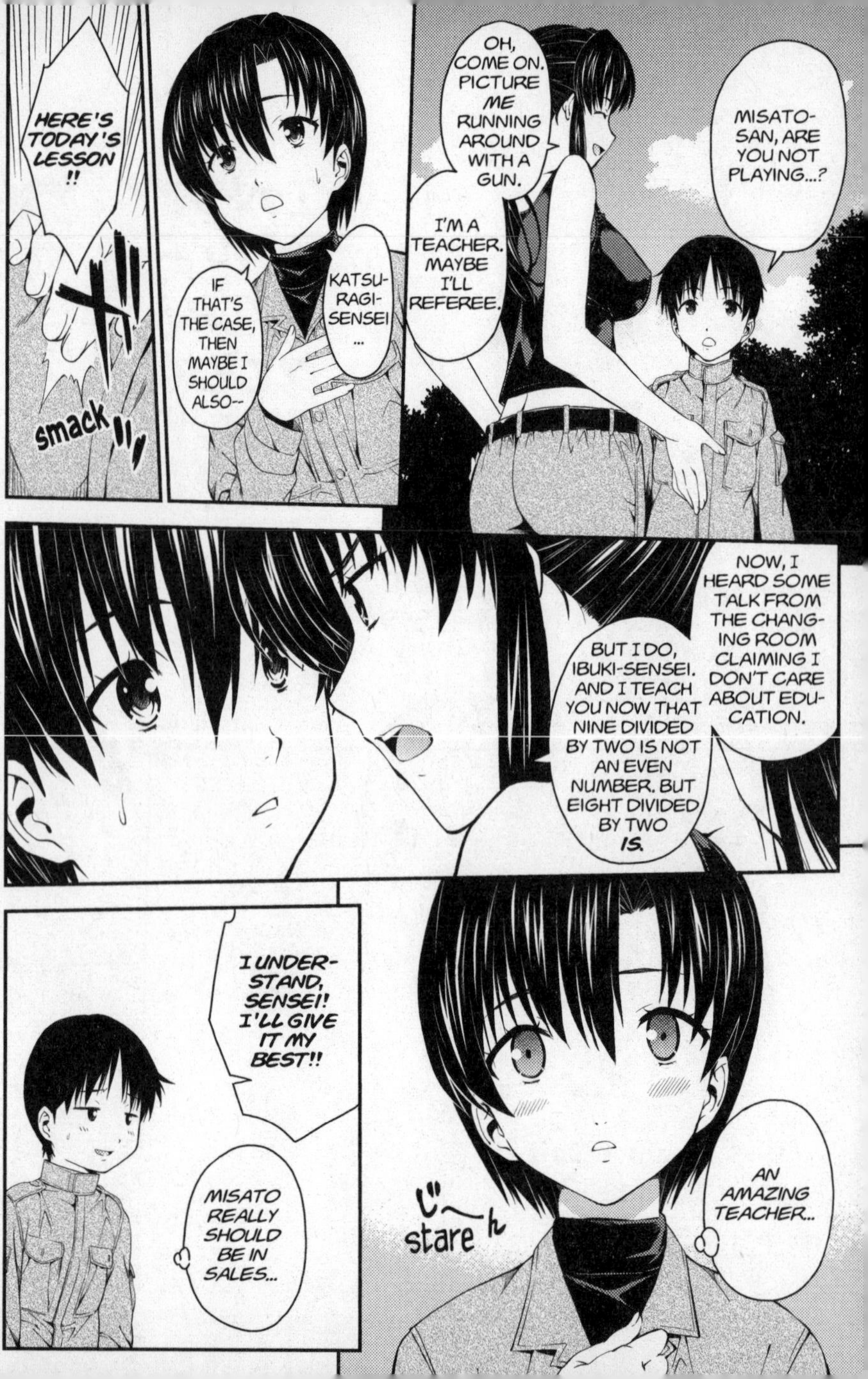
MISATO-SAN, ARE YOU NOT PLAYING...?
OH, COME ON. PICTURE *ME* RUNNING AROUND WITH A GUN.
I'M A TEACHER. MAYBE I'LL REFEREE.
KATSURAGI-SENSEI...
IF THAT'S THE CASE, THEN MAYBE I SHOULD ALSO--
HERE'S TODAY'S LESSON!!
smack
NOW, I HEARD SOME TALK FROM THE CHANGING ROOM CLAIMING I DON'T CARE ABOUT EDUCATION.
BUT I DO, IBUKI-SENSEI. AND I TEACH YOU NOW THAT NINE DIVIDED BY TWO IS NOT AN EVEN NUMBER. BUT EIGHT DIVIDED BY TWO *IS*.
AN AMAZING TEACHER...
じ〜ん
stare
I UNDERSTAND, SENSEI! I'LL GIVE IT MY BEST!!
MISATO REALLY SHOULD BE IN SALES...

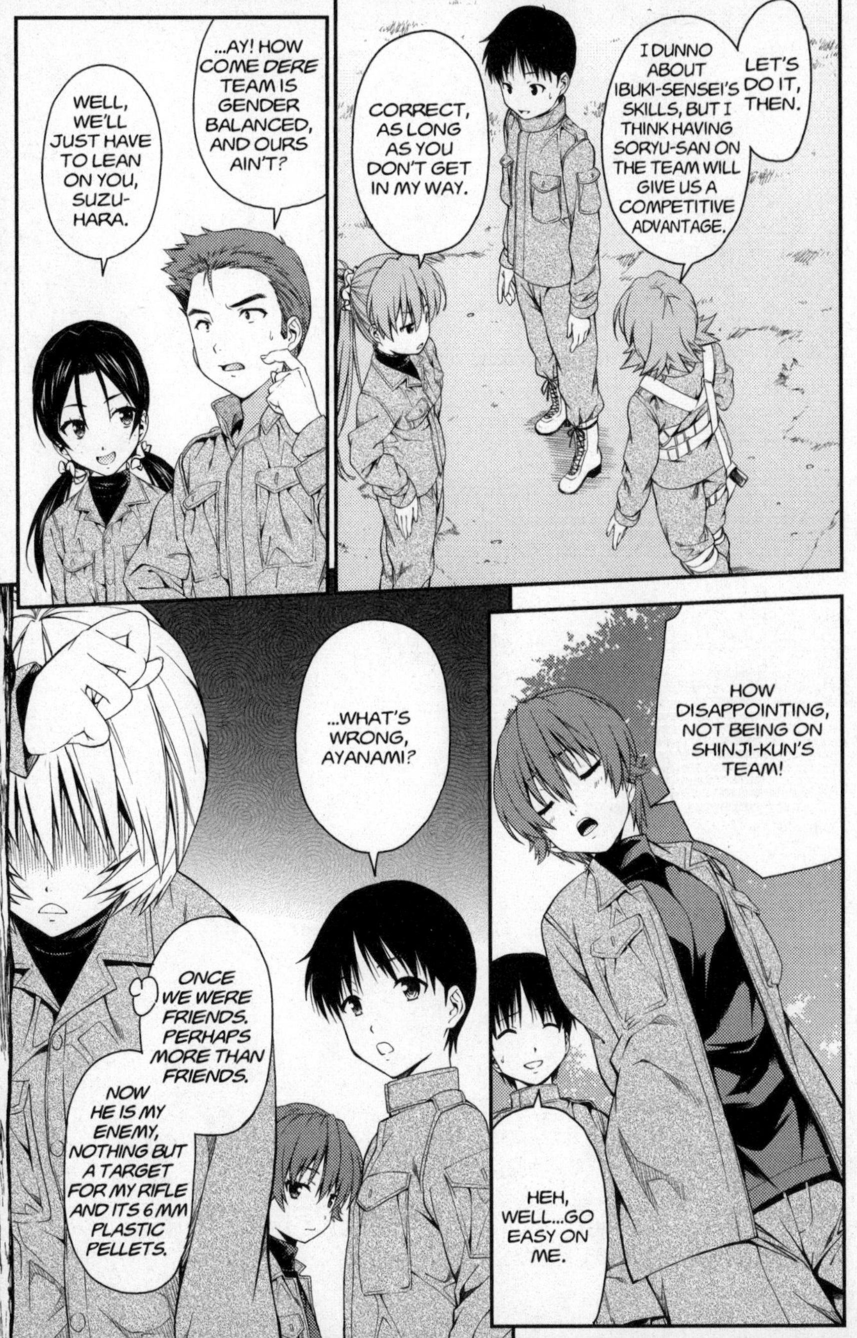
I DUNNO ABOUT IBUKI-SENSEI'S SKILLS, BUT I THINK HAVING SORYU-SAN ON THE TEAM WILL GIVE US A COMPETITIVE ADVANTAGE.
LET'S DO IT, THEN.
CORRECT, AS LONG AS YOU DON'T GET IN MY WAY.
...AY! HOW COME DERE TEAM IS GENDER BALANCED, AND OURS AIN'T?
WELL, WE'LL JUST HAVE TO LEAN ON YOU, SUZU-HARA.
HOW DISAPPOINTING, NOT BEING ON SHINJI-KUN'S TEAM!
HEH, WELL...GO EASY ON ME.
...WHAT'S WRONG, AYANAMI?
ONCE WE WERE FRIENDS. PERHAPS MORE THAN FRIENDS.
NOW HE IS MY ENEMY, NOTHING BUT A TARGET FOR MY RIFLE AND ITS 6 MM PLASTIC PELLETS.

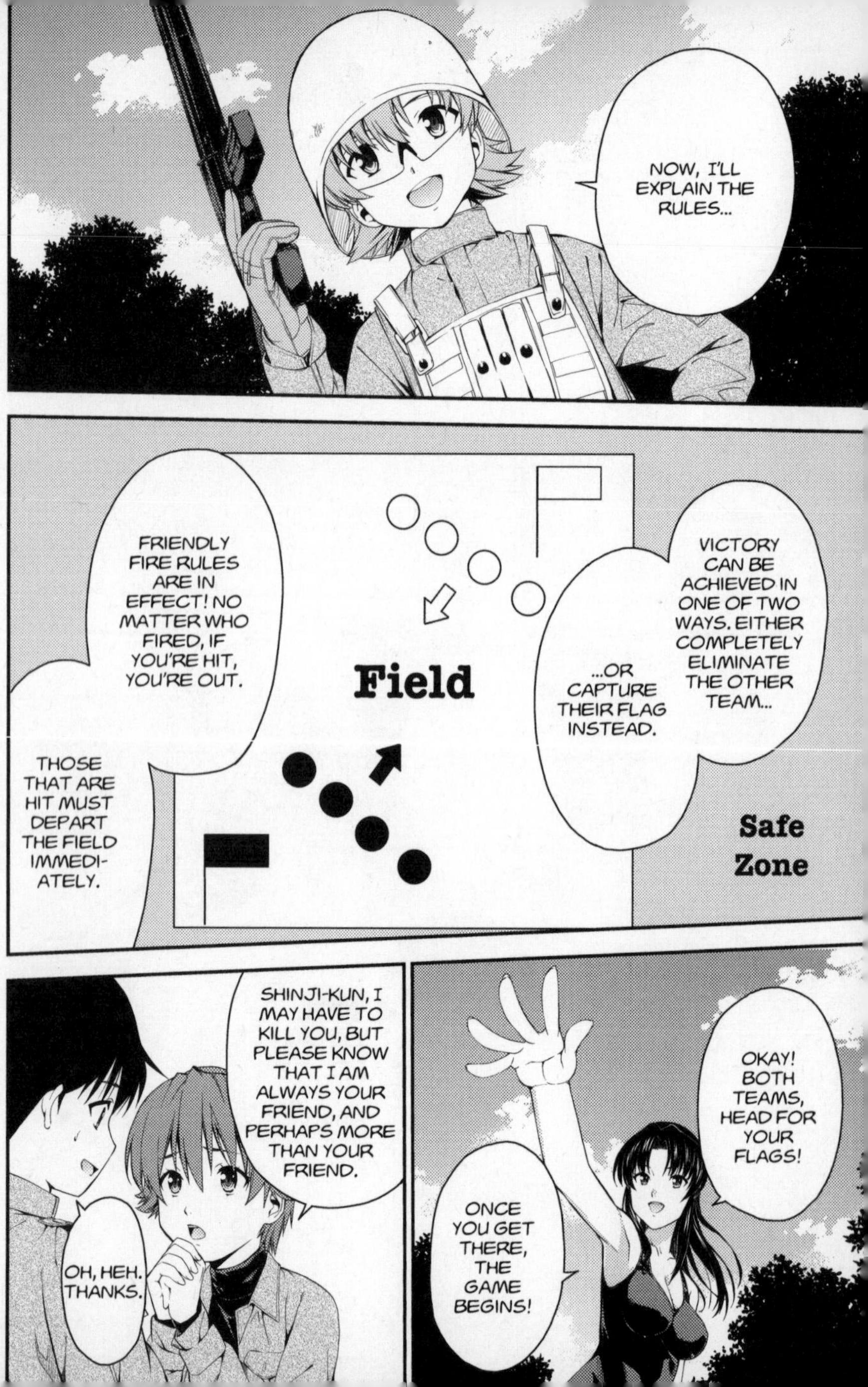
NOW, I'LL EXPLAIN THE RULES...
VICTORY CAN BE ACHIEVED IN ONE OF TWO WAYS. EITHER COMPLETELY ELIMINATE THE OTHER TEAM...
...OR CAPTURE THEIR FLAG INSTEAD.
Safe Zone
Field
FRIENDLY FIRE RULES ARE IN EFFECT! NO MATTER WHO FIRED, IF YOU'RE HIT, YOU'RE OUT.
THOSE THAT ARE HIT MUST DEPART THE FIELD IMMEDI-ATELY.
OKAY! BOTH TEAMS, HEAD FOR YOUR FLAGS!
ONCE YOU GET THERE, THE GAME BEGINS!
SHINJI-KUN, I MAY HAVE TO KILL YOU, BUT PLEASE KNOW THAT I AM ALWAYS YOUR FRIEND, AND PERHAPS MORE THAN YOUR FRIEND.
OH, HEH. THANKS.

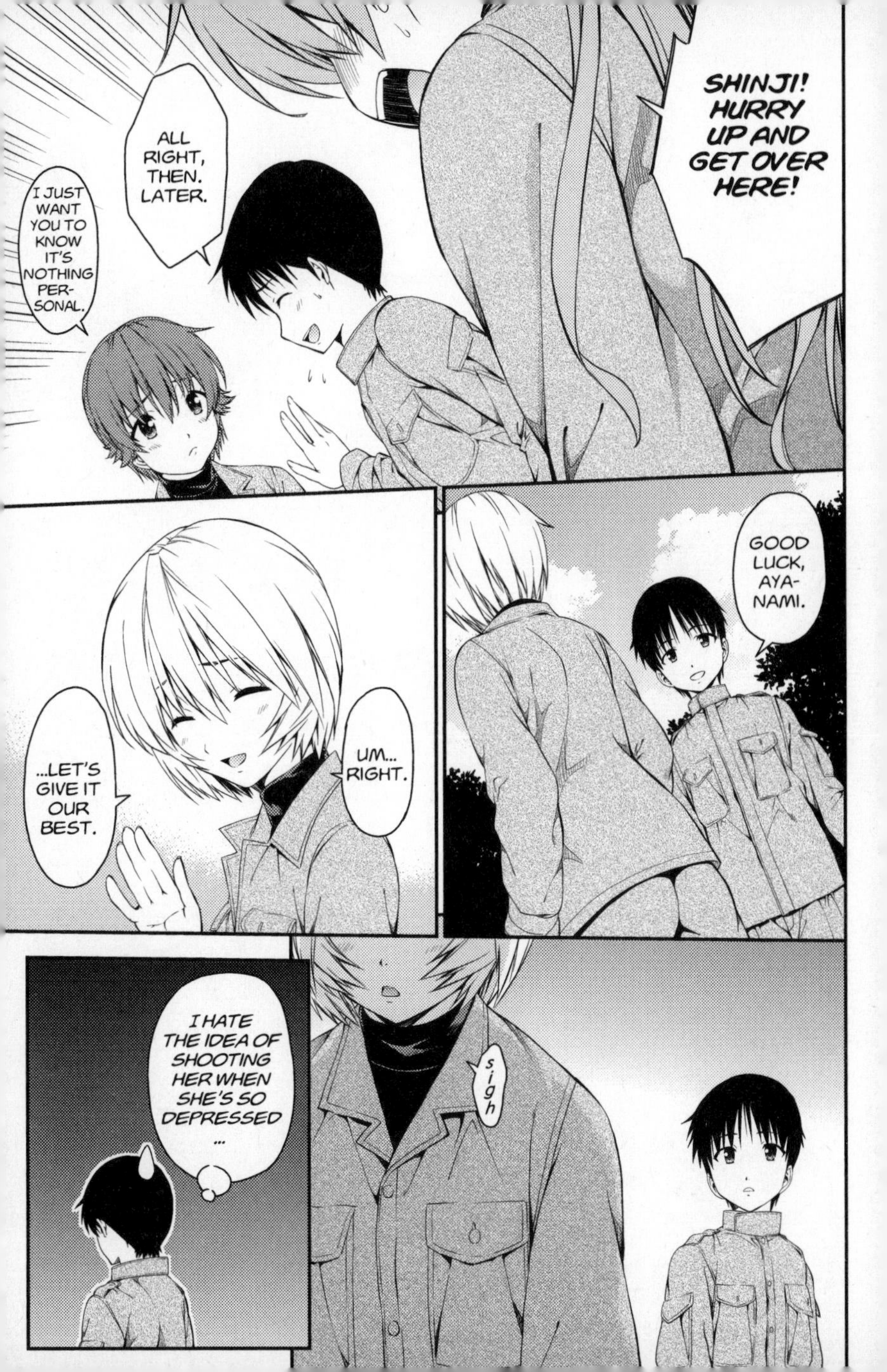
SHINJI! HURRY UP AND GET OVER HERE!
ALL RIGHT, THEN. LATER.
I JUST WANT YOU TO KNOW IT'S NOTHING PER-SONAL.
GOOD LUCK, AYA-NAMI.
UM... RIGHT.
...LET'S GIVE IT OUR BEST.
sigh
I HATE THE IDEA OF SHOOTING HER WHEN SHE'S SO DEPRESSED...

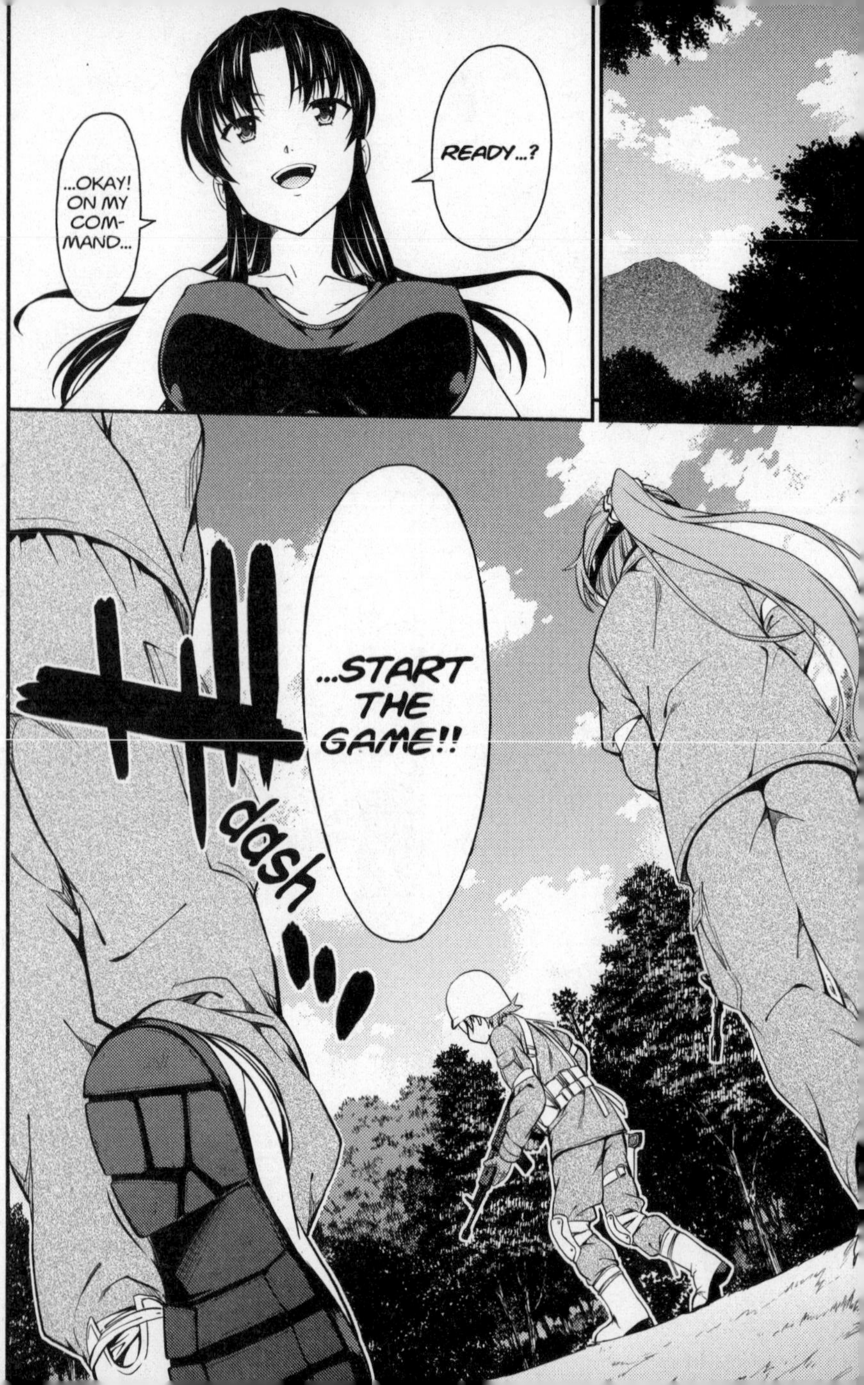
READY...?
...OKAY! ON MY COM-MAND...
...START THE GAME!!
dash...

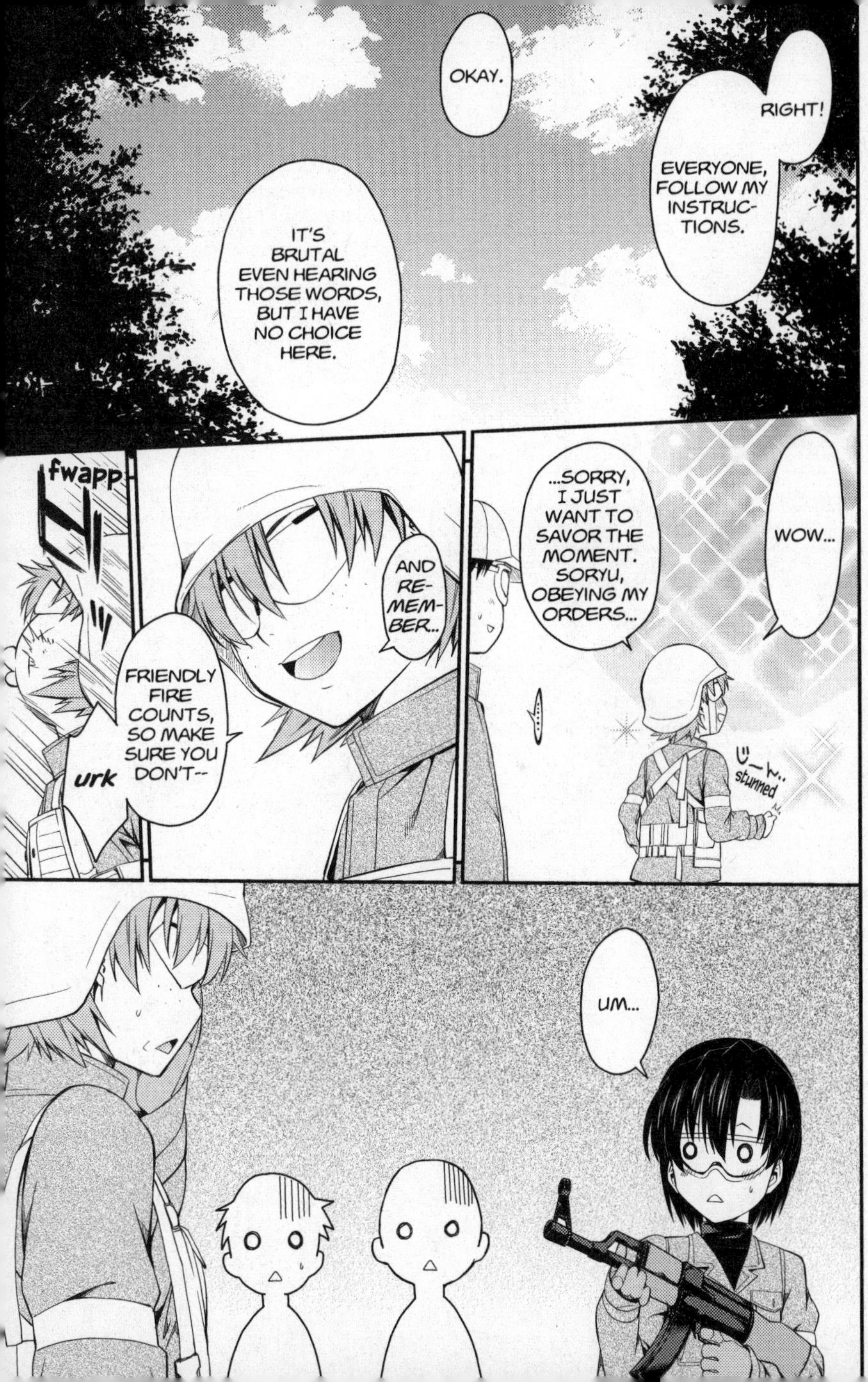
RIGHT!
EVERYONE, FOLLOW MY INSTRUCTIONS.
OKAY.
IT'S BRUTAL EVEN HEARING THOSE WORDS, BUT I HAVE NO CHOICE HERE.
WOW...
...SORRY, I JUST WANT TO SAVOR THE MOMENT. SORYU, OBEYING MY ORDERS...
じーん..
stunned
AND RE-MEM-BER...
FRIENDLY FIRE COUNTS, SO MAKE SURE YOU DON'T--
fwapp
urk
UM...

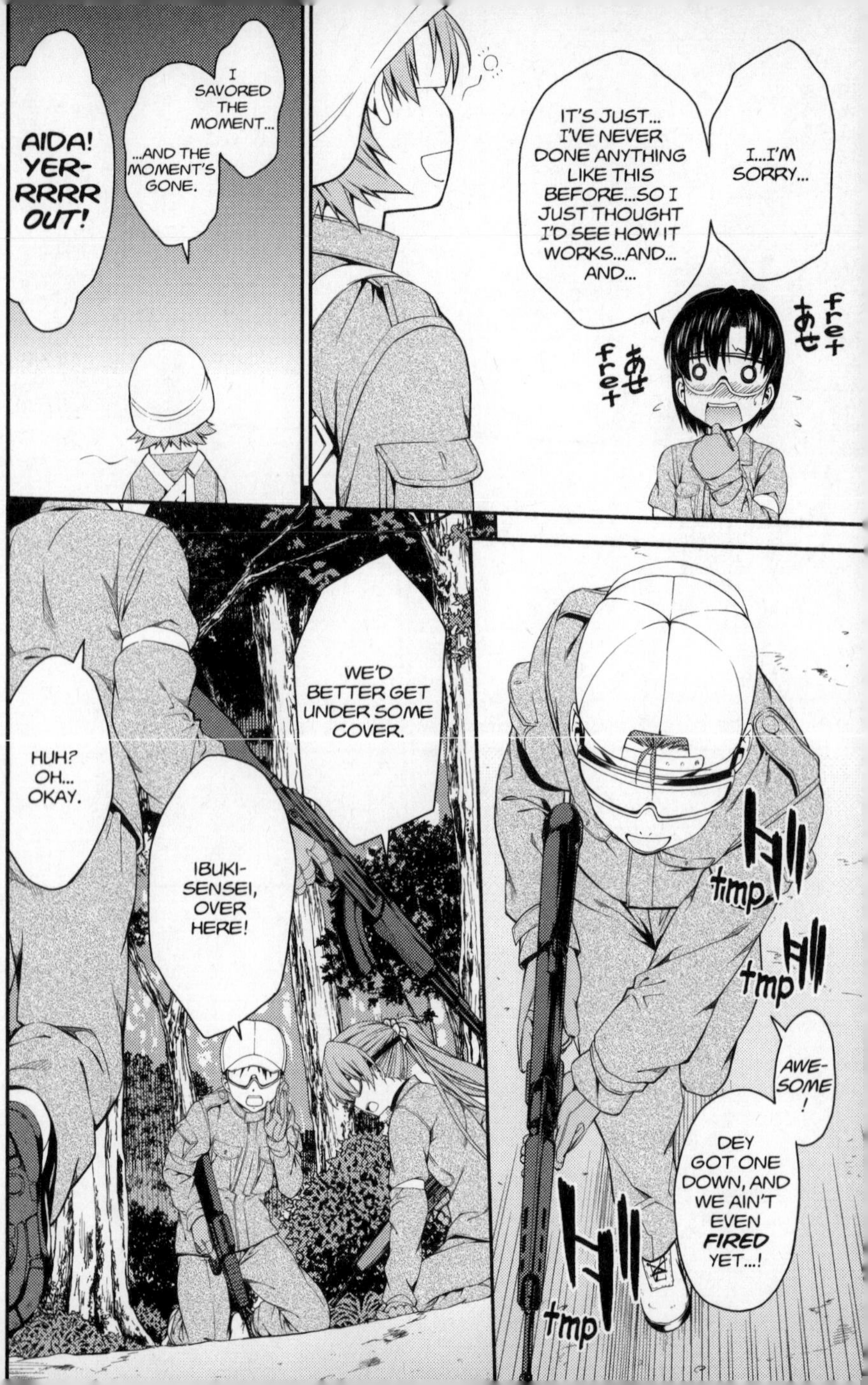

I...I'M SORRY...
IT'S JUST... I'VE NEVER DONE ANYTHING LIKE THIS BEFORE...SO I JUST THOUGHT I'D SEE HOW IT WORKS...AND... AND...
fret あせ
fret あせ
I SAVORED THE MOMENT...
...AND THE MOMENT'S GONE.
AIDA! YERRRRR OUT!
tmp
tmp
tmp
AWESOME!
DEY GOT ONE DOWN, AND WE AIN'T EVEN FIRED YET...!
WE'D BETTER GET UNDER SOME COVER.
IBUKI-SENSEI, OVER HERE!
HUH? OH... OKAY.

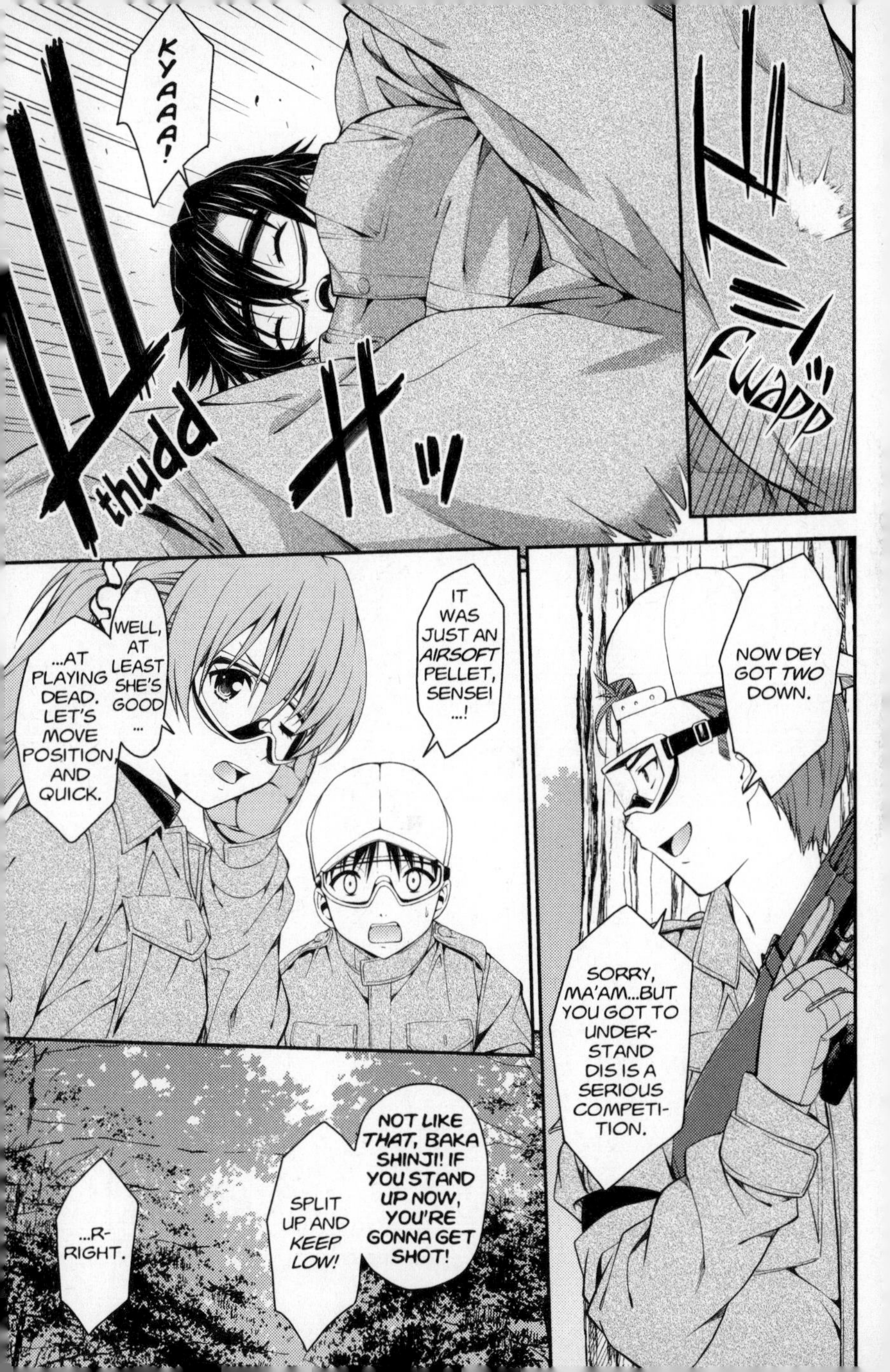
FWAPP
KYAAA!
thudd
NOW DEY GOT *TWO* DOWN.
SORRY, MA'AM...BUT YOU GOT TO UNDER-STAND DIS IS A SERIOUS COMPETI-TION.
IT WAS JUST AN *AIRSOFT* PELLET, SENSEI ...!
WELL, AT LEAST SHE'S GOOD ...
...AT PLAYING DEAD. LET'S MOVE POSITION, AND QUICK.
NOT LIKE *THAT*, BAKA SHINJI! IF YOU STAND UP NOW, YOU'RE GONNA GET SHOT!
SPLIT UP AND KEEP *LOW!*
...R-RIGHT.

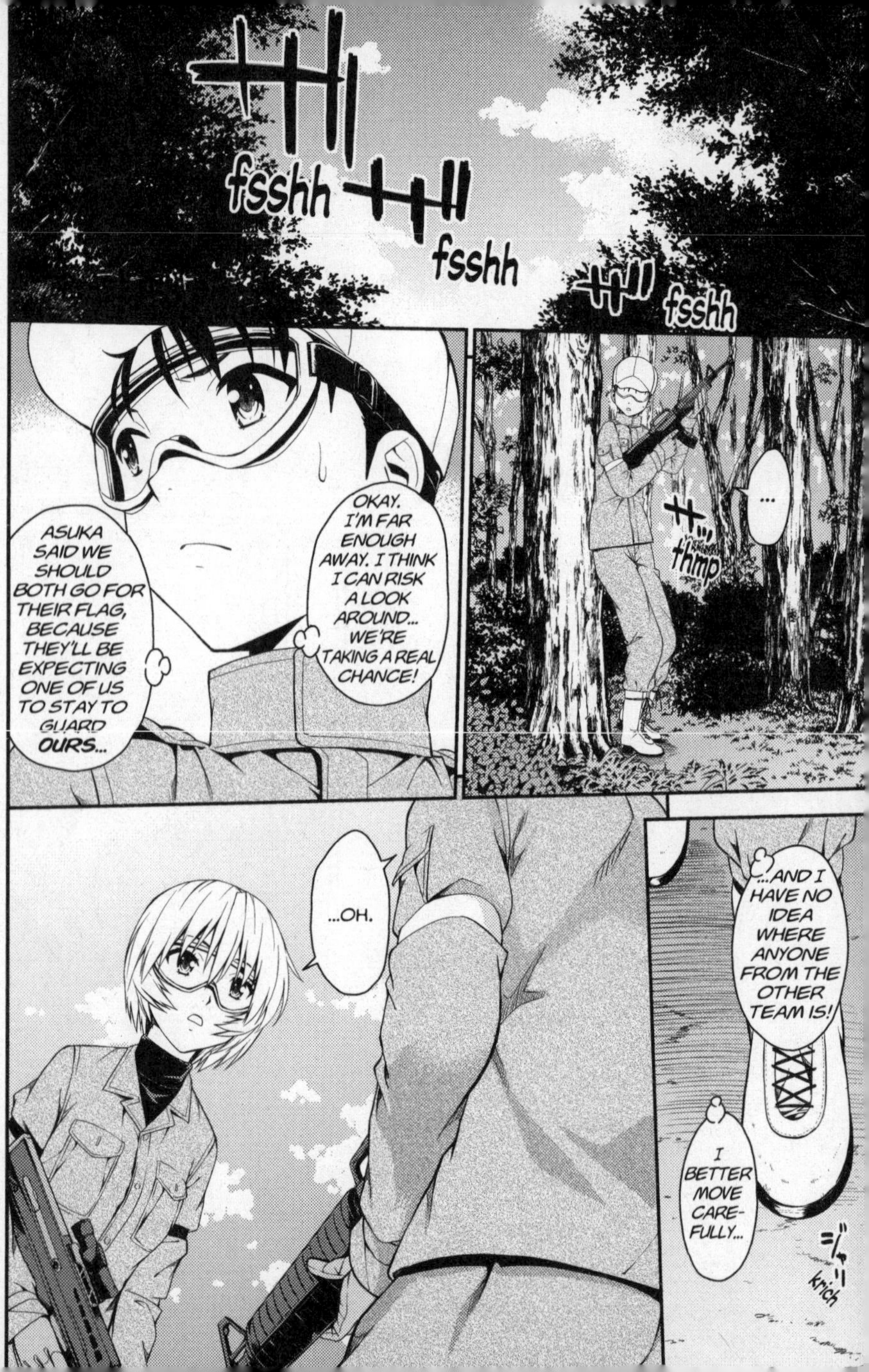
fsshh
fsshh
fsshh
...
thimp
OKAY. I'M FAR ENOUGH AWAY. I THINK I CAN RISK A LOOK AROUND... WE'RE TAKING A REAL CHANCE!
ASUKA SAID WE SHOULD BOTH GO FOR THEIR FLAG, BECAUSE THEY'LL BE EXPECTING ONE OF US TO STAY TO GUARD OURS...
...AND I HAVE NO IDEA WHERE ANYONE FROM THE OTHER TEAM IS!
I BETTER MOVE CARE-FULLY...
krich
...OH.

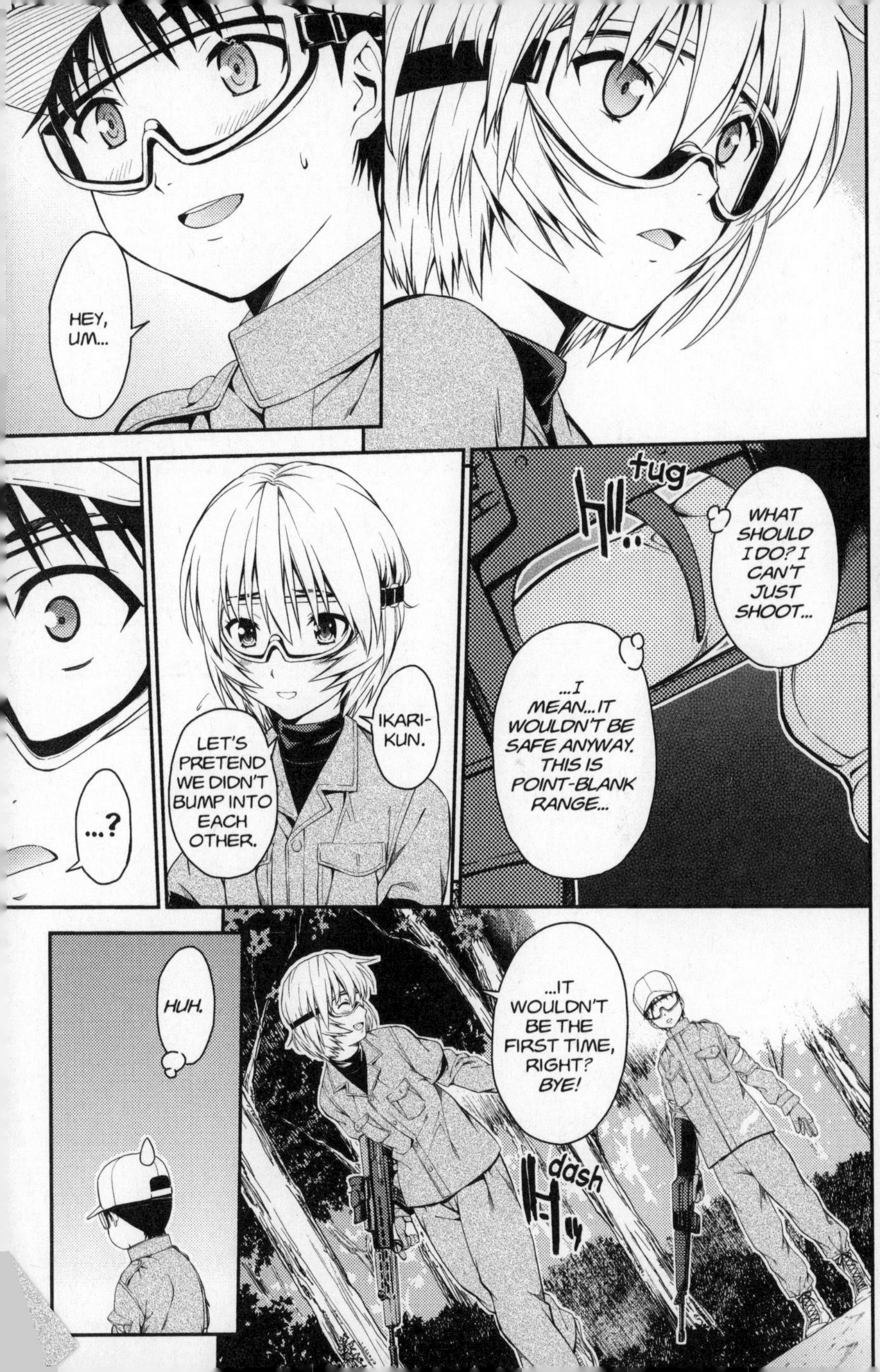
HEY, UM...
tug
WHAT SHOULD I DO? I CAN'T JUST SHOOT...
...I MEAN...IT WOULDN'T BE SAFE ANYWAY. THIS IS POINT-BLANK RANGE...
IKARI-KUN.
LET'S PRETEND WE DIDN'T BUMP INTO EACH OTHER.
...?
...IT WOULDN'T BE THE FIRST TIME, RIGHT? BYE!
dash
HUH.

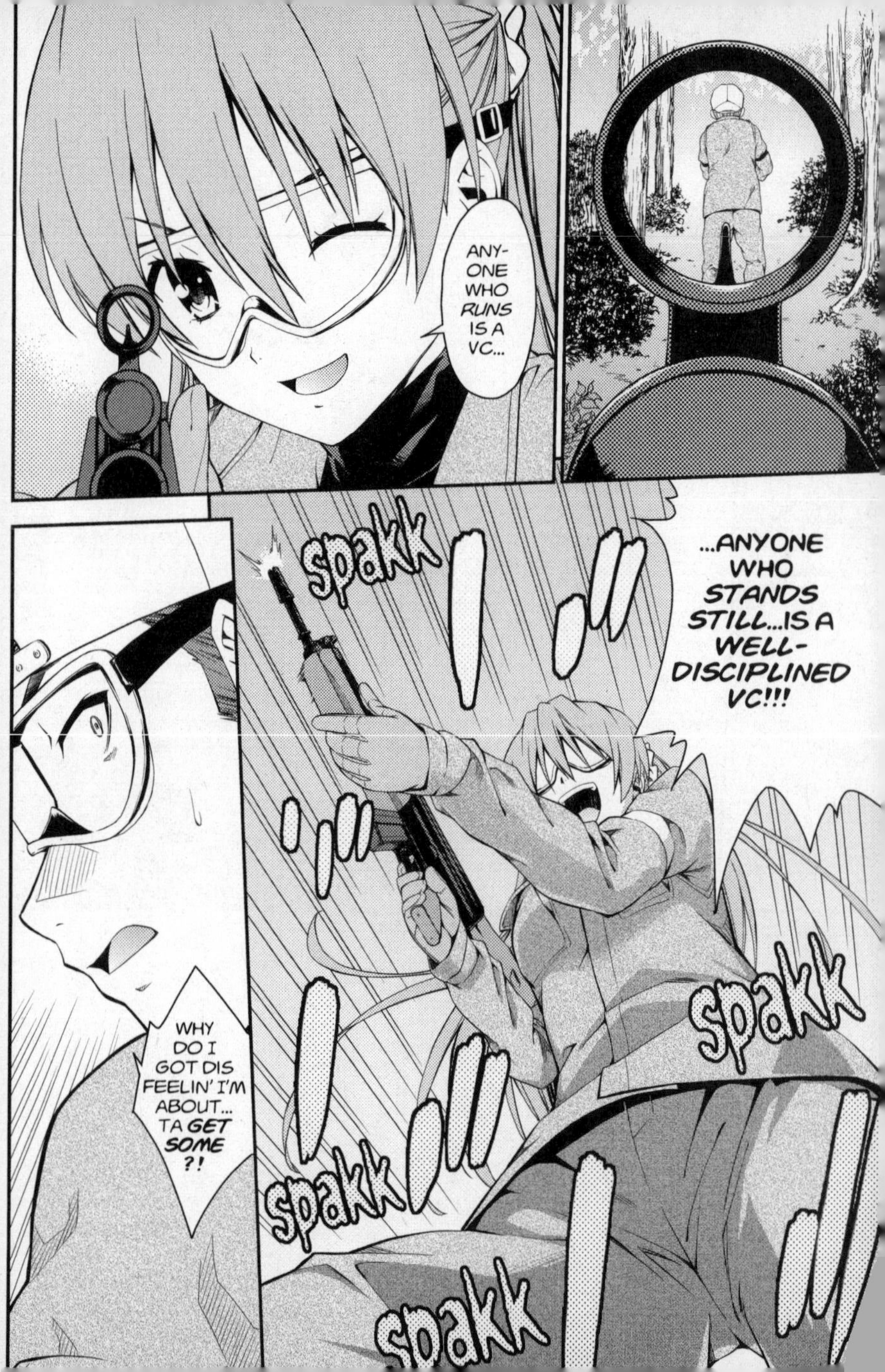
ANY-ONE WHO RUNS IS A VC...
...ANYONE WHO STANDS STILL...IS A WELL-DISCIPLINED VC!!!
spakk
spakk
spakk
spakk
WHY DO I GOT DIS FEELIN' I'M ABOUT... TA GET SOME ?!

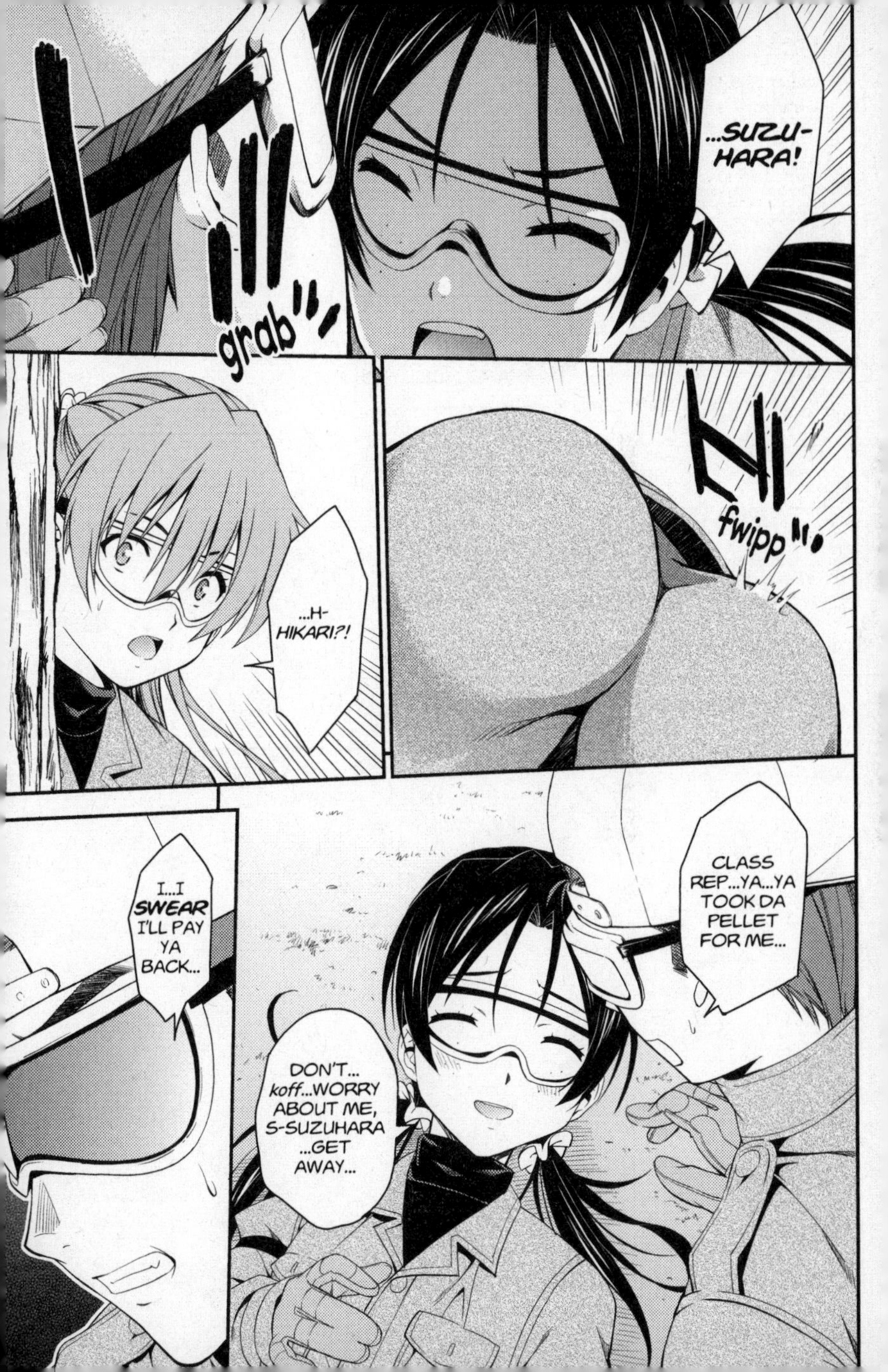
...SUZU-HARA!
grab
fwipp
...H-HIKARI?!
CLASS REP...YA...YA TOOK DA PELLET FOR ME...
DON'T... *koff*...WORRY ABOUT ME, S-SUZUHARA ...GET AWAY...
I...I **SWEAR** I'LL PAY YA BACK...

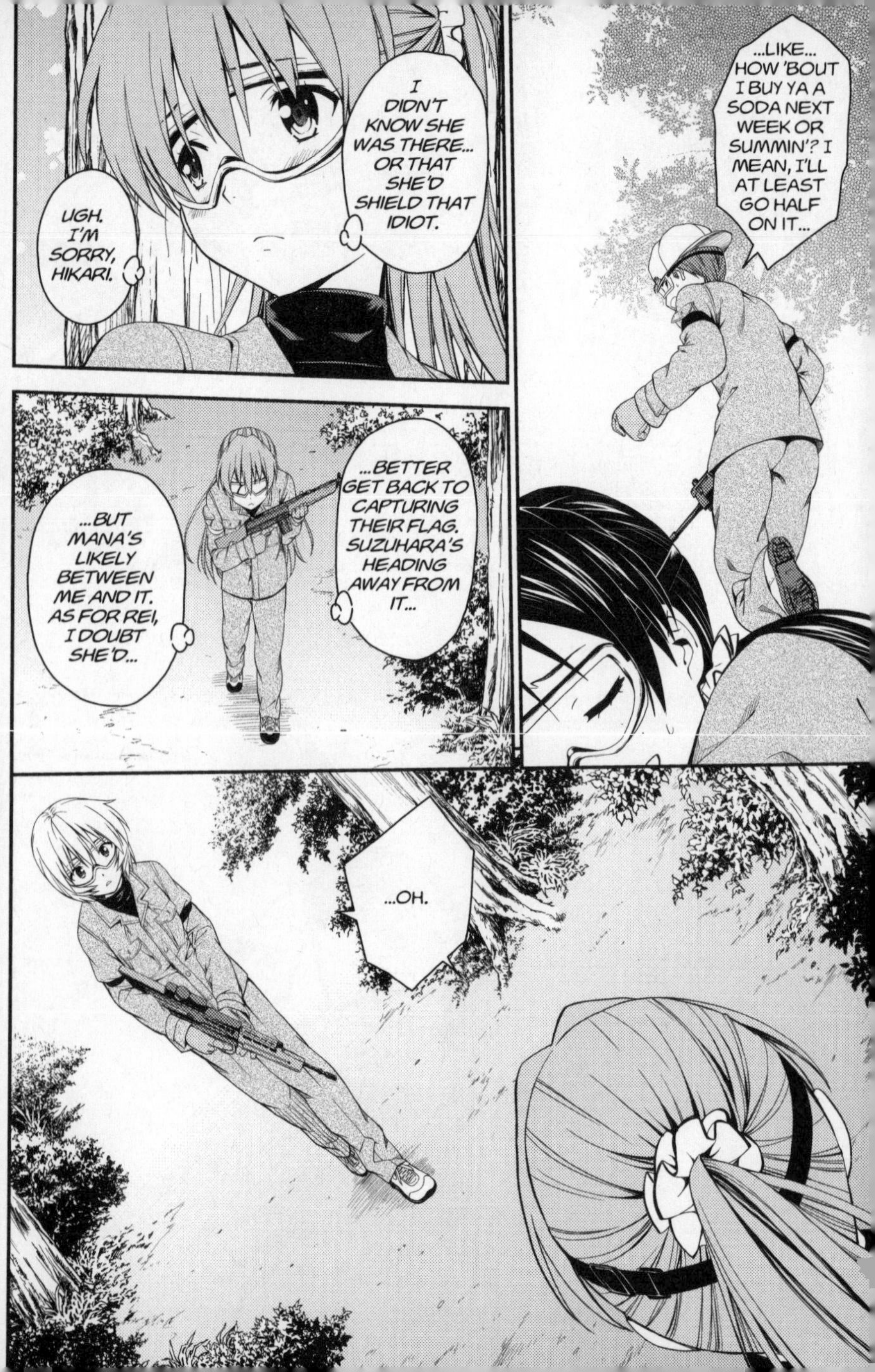
...LIKE... HOW 'BOUT I BUY YA A SODA NEXT WEEK OR SUMMIN'? I MEAN, I'LL AT LEAST GO HALF ON IT...
I DIDN'T KNOW SHE WAS THERE... OR THAT SHE'D SHIELD THAT IDIOT.
UGH. I'M SORRY, HIKARI.
...BETTER GET BACK TO CAPTURING THEIR FLAG. SUZUHARA'S HEADING AWAY FROM IT...
...BUT MANA'S LIKELY BETWEEN ME AND IT. AS FOR REI, I DOUBT SHE'D...
...OH.

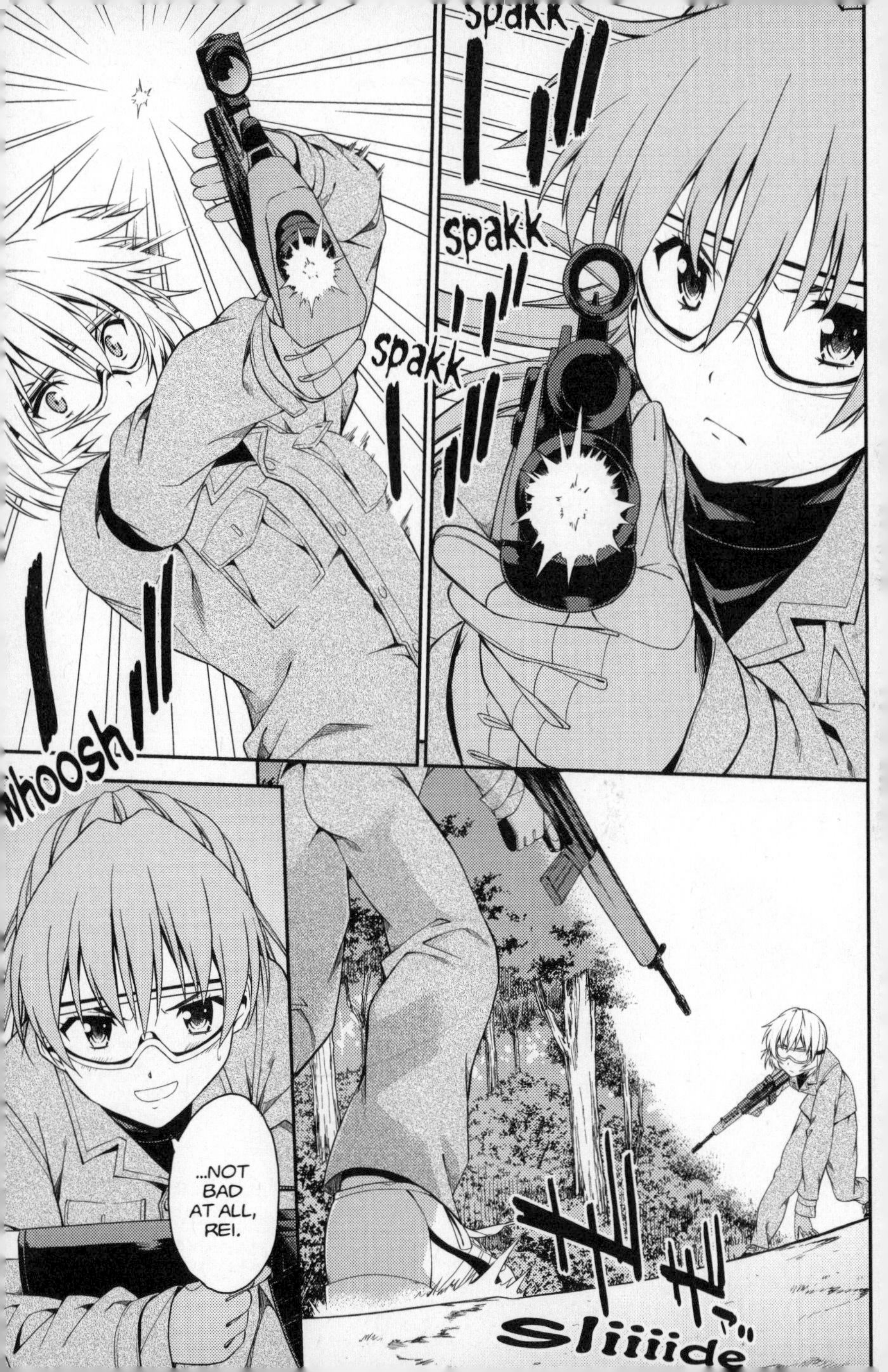
spakk
spakk
spakk
whoosh
Sliiiide
...NOT BAD AT ALL, REI.

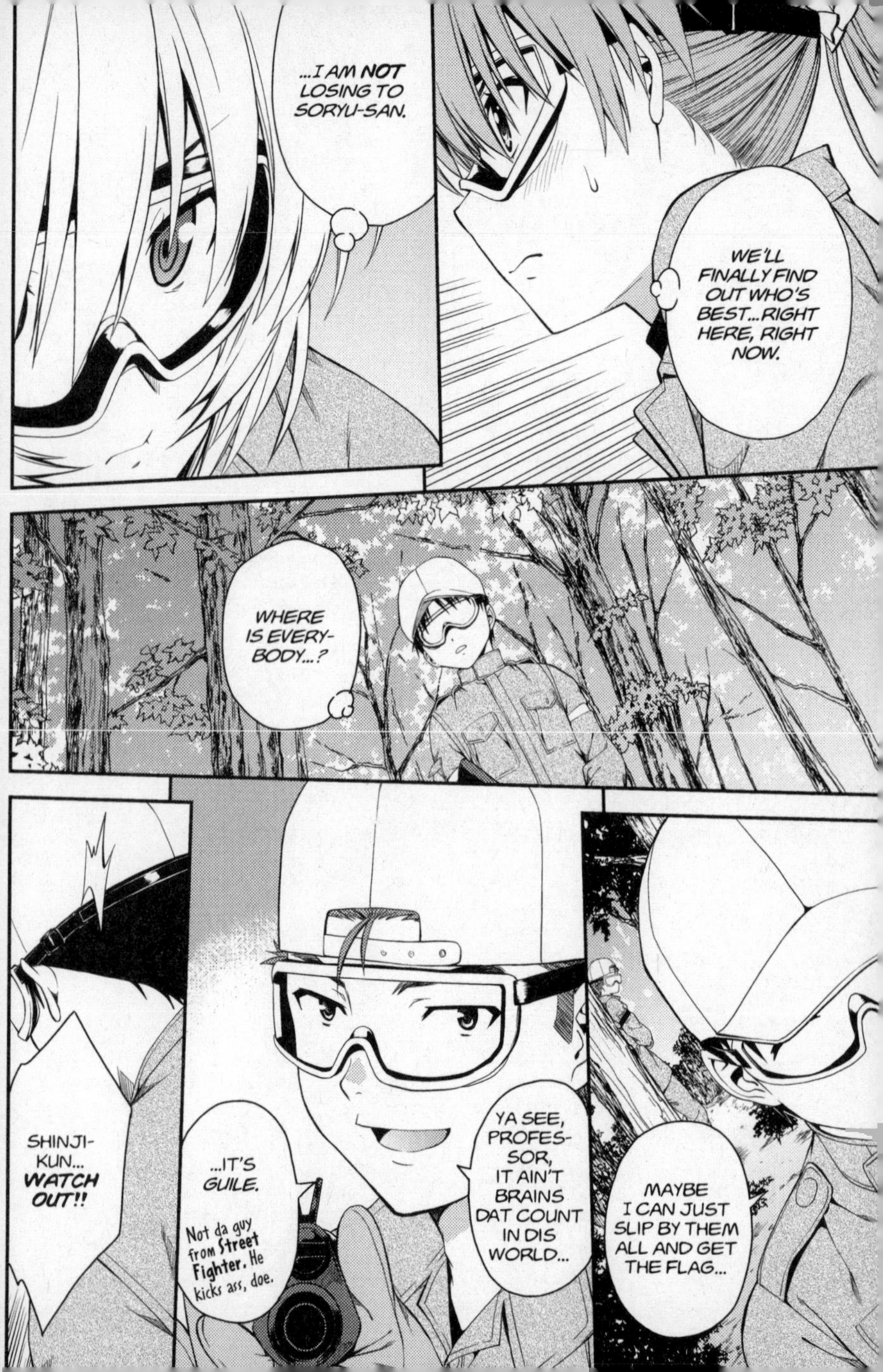
WE'LL FINALLY FIND OUT WHO'S BEST...RIGHT HERE, RIGHT NOW.
...I AM NOT LOSING TO SORYU-SAN.
WHERE IS EVERY-BODY...?
MAYBE I CAN JUST SLIP BY THEM ALL AND GET THE FLAG...
YA SEE, PROFES-SOR, IT AIN'T BRAINS DAT COUNT IN DIS WORLD...
...IT'S GUILE.
Not da guy from Street Fighter. He kicks ass, doe.
SHINJI-KUN... WATCH OUT!!

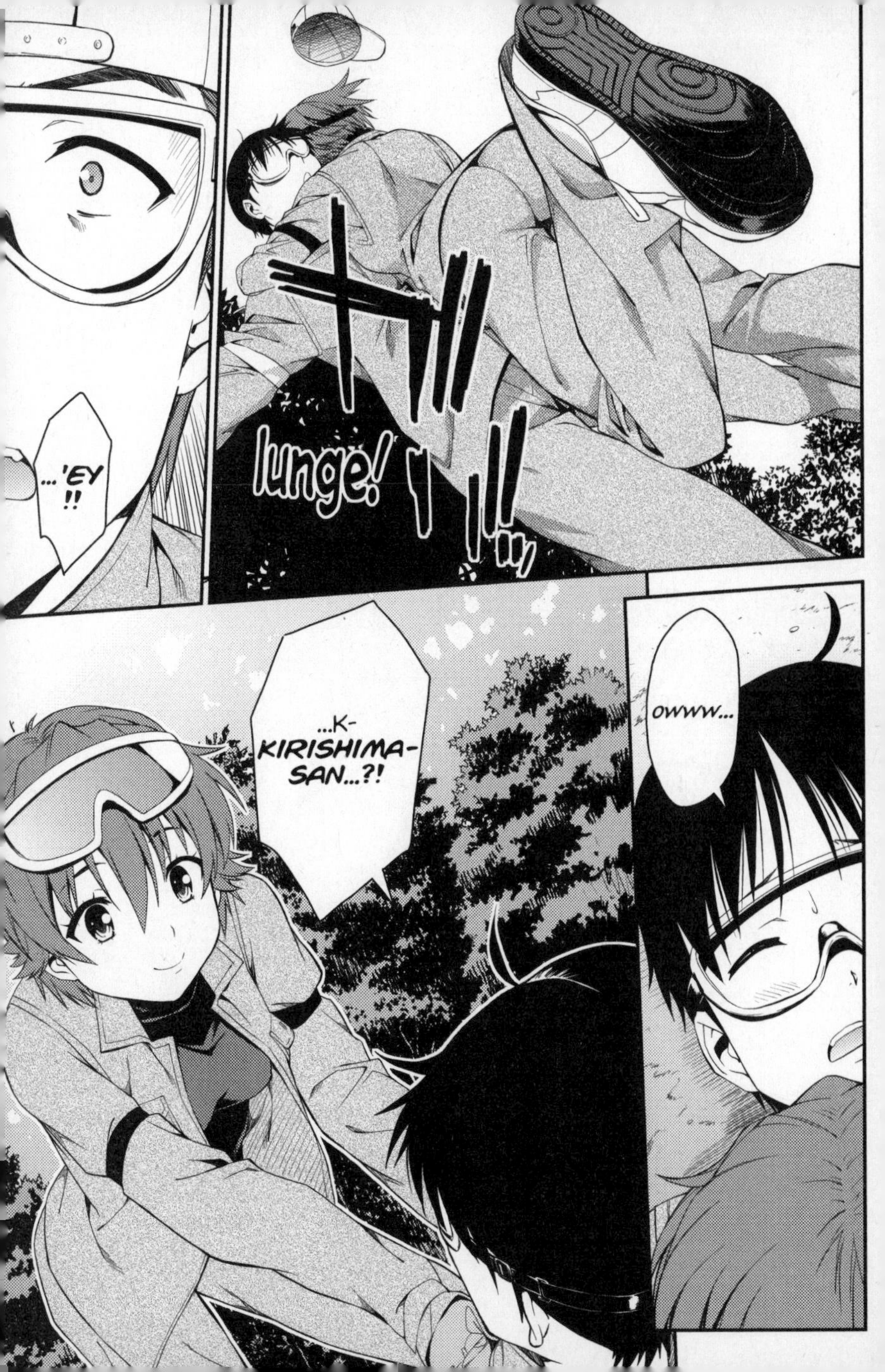
lunge!
...'EY !!
owww...
...K-KIRISHIMA-SAN...?!

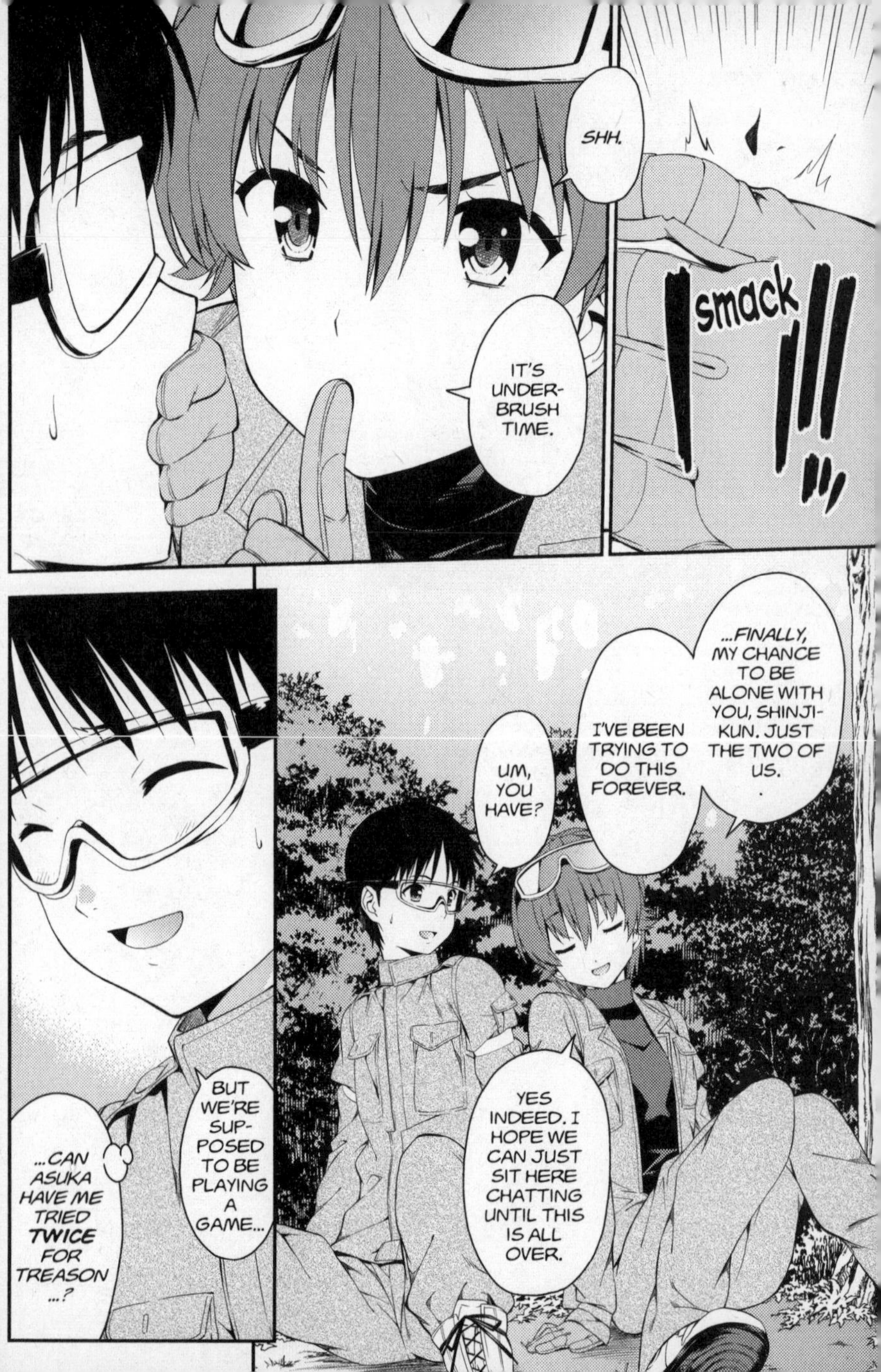
smack
SHH.
IT'S UNDER-BRUSH TIME.
...FINALLY, MY CHANCE TO BE ALONE WITH YOU, SHINJI-KUN. JUST THE TWO OF US.
I'VE BEEN TRYING TO DO THIS FOREVER.
UM, YOU HAVE?
YES INDEED. I HOPE WE CAN JUST SIT HERE CHATTING UNTIL THIS IS ALL OVER.
BUT WE'RE SUP-POSED TO BE PLAYING A GAME...
...CAN ASUKA HAVE ME TRIED **TWICE** FOR TREASON ...?

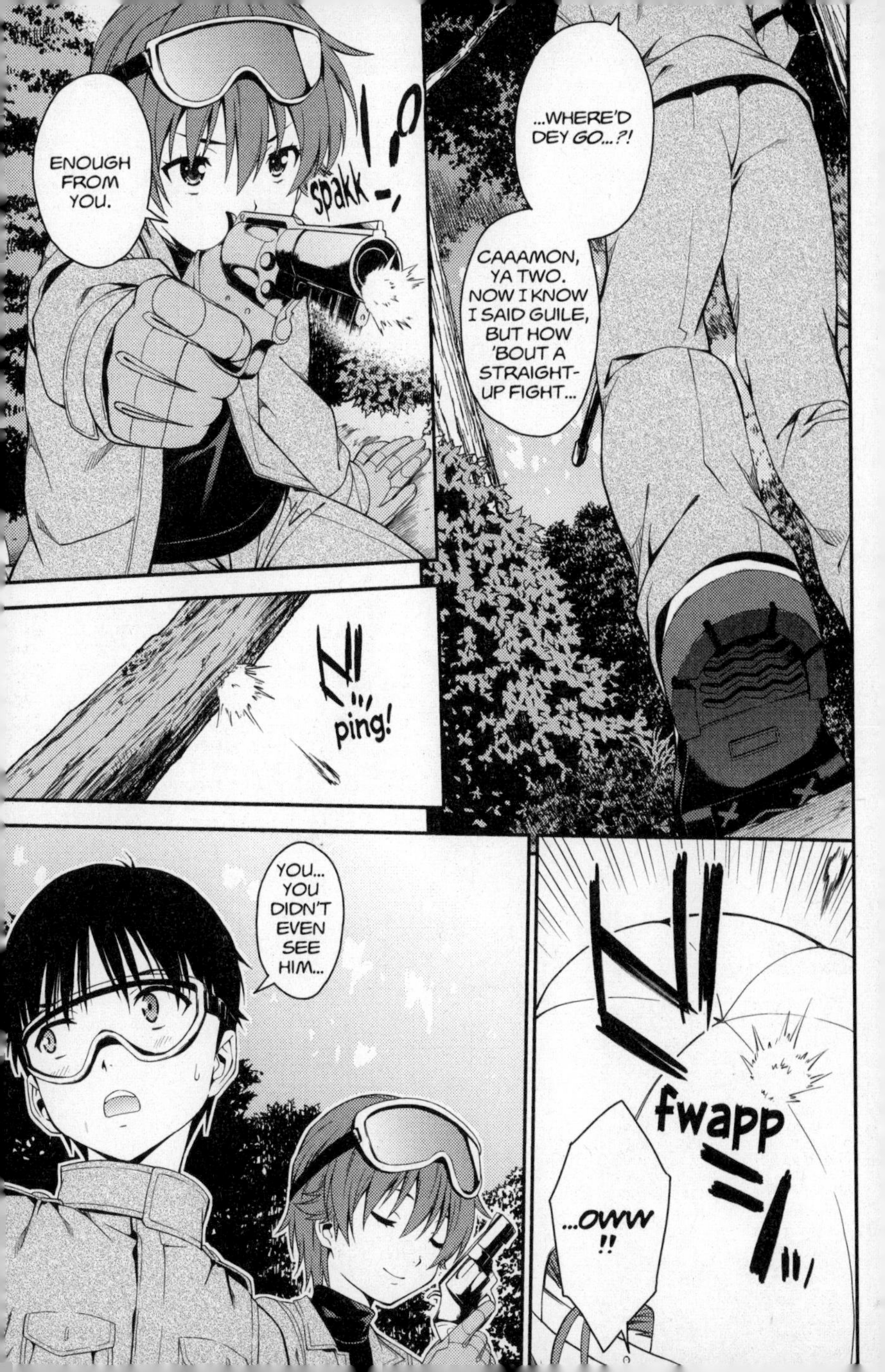
...WHERE'D DEY GO...?!
CAAAMON, YA TWO. NOW I KNOW I SAID GUILE, BUT HOW 'BOUT A STRAIGHT-UP FIGHT...
ENOUGH FROM YOU.
spakk
ping!
fwapp
...OWW !!
YOU... YOU DIDN'T EVEN SEE HIM...

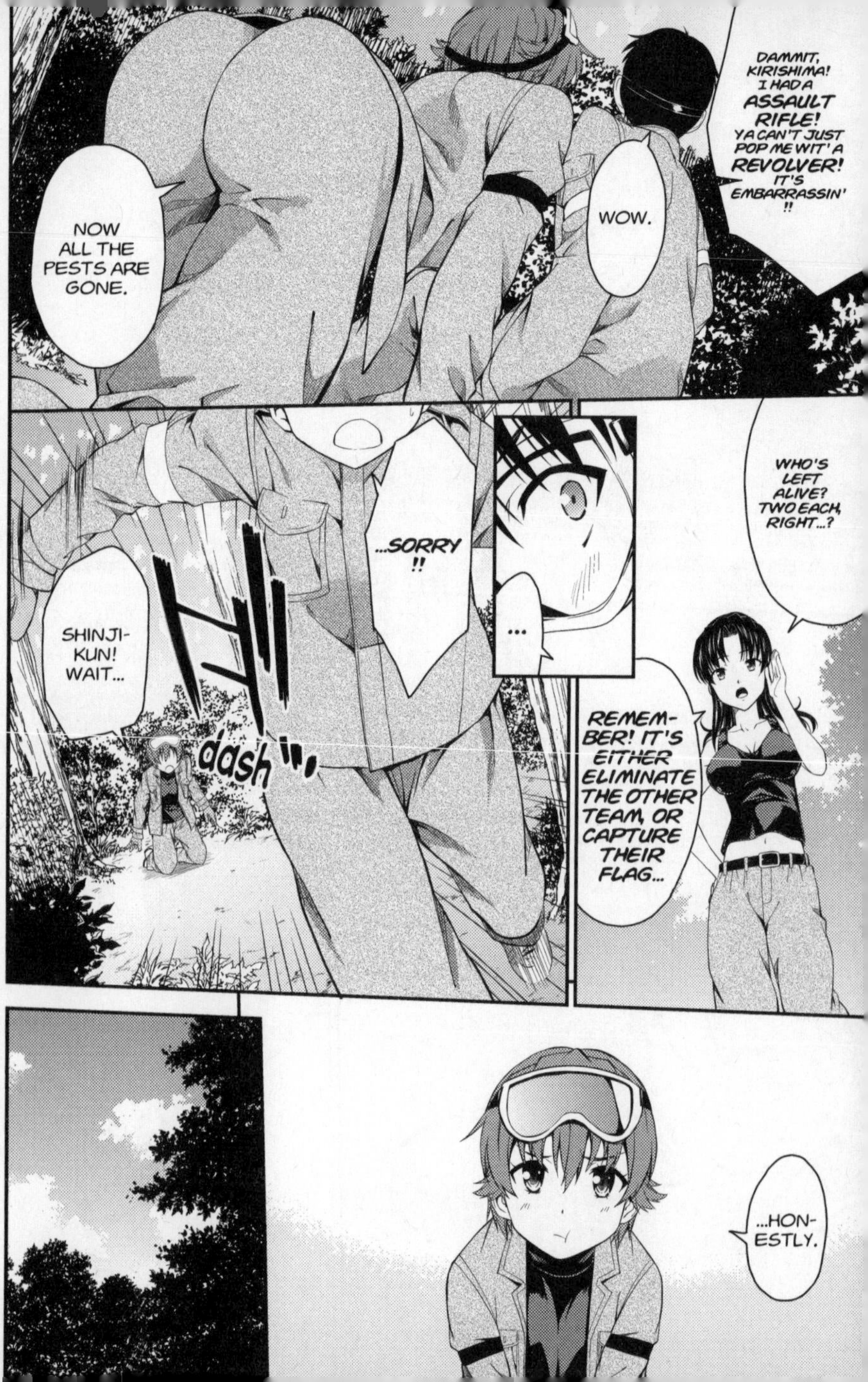
DAMMIT, KIRISHIMA! I HAD A ASSAULT RIFLE! YA CAN'T JUST POP ME WIT' A REVOLVER! IT'S EMBARRASSIN'!!
WOW.
NOW ALL THE PESTS ARE GONE.
WHO'S LEFT ALIVE? TWO EACH, RIGHT...?
REMEM-BER! IT'S EITHER ELIMINATE THE OTHER TEAM, OR CAPTURE THEIR FLAG...
...
...SORRY!!
SHINJI-KUN! WAIT...
dash
...HON-ESTLY.

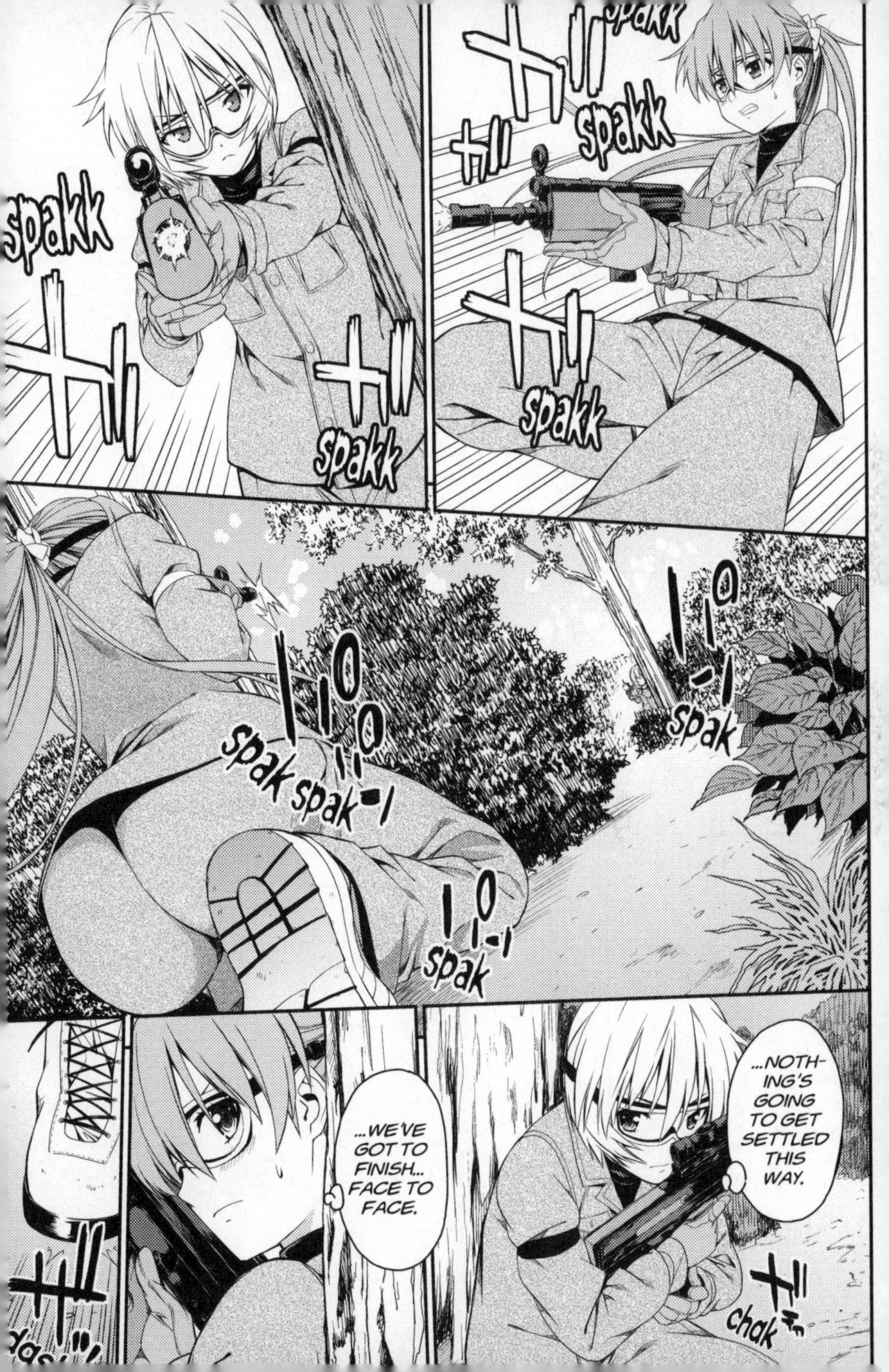

spakk
spakk
spakk
spakk
spakk
spak
spak spak
spak
...NOTHING'S GOING TO GET SETTLED THIS WAY.
chak
...WE'VE GOT TO FINISH... FACE TO FACE.

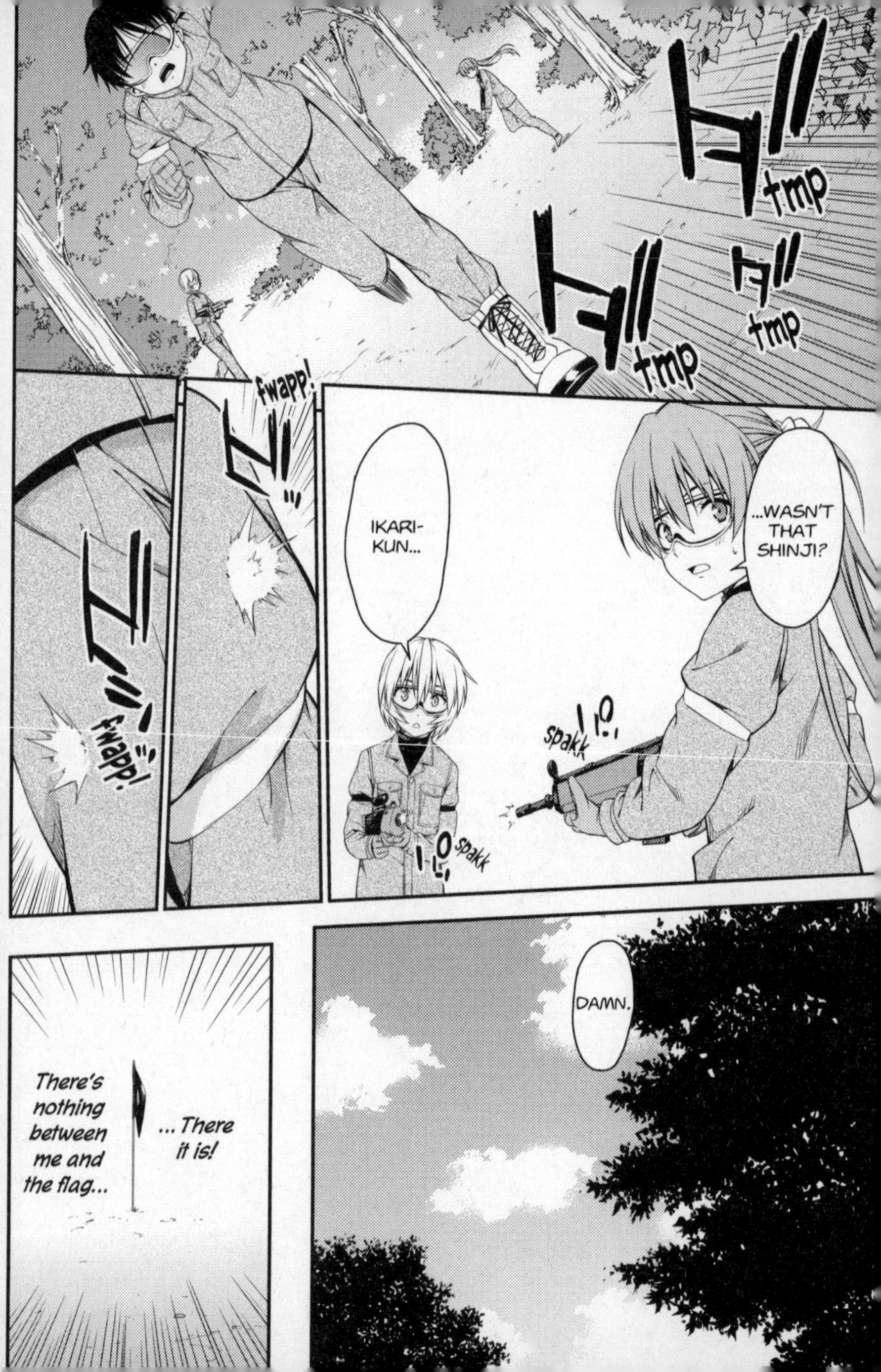
tmp
tmp
tmp
...WASN'T THAT SHINJI?
IKARI-KUN...
spakk
spakk
fwapp!
fwapp!
DAMN.
There's nothing between me and the flag...
...There it is!

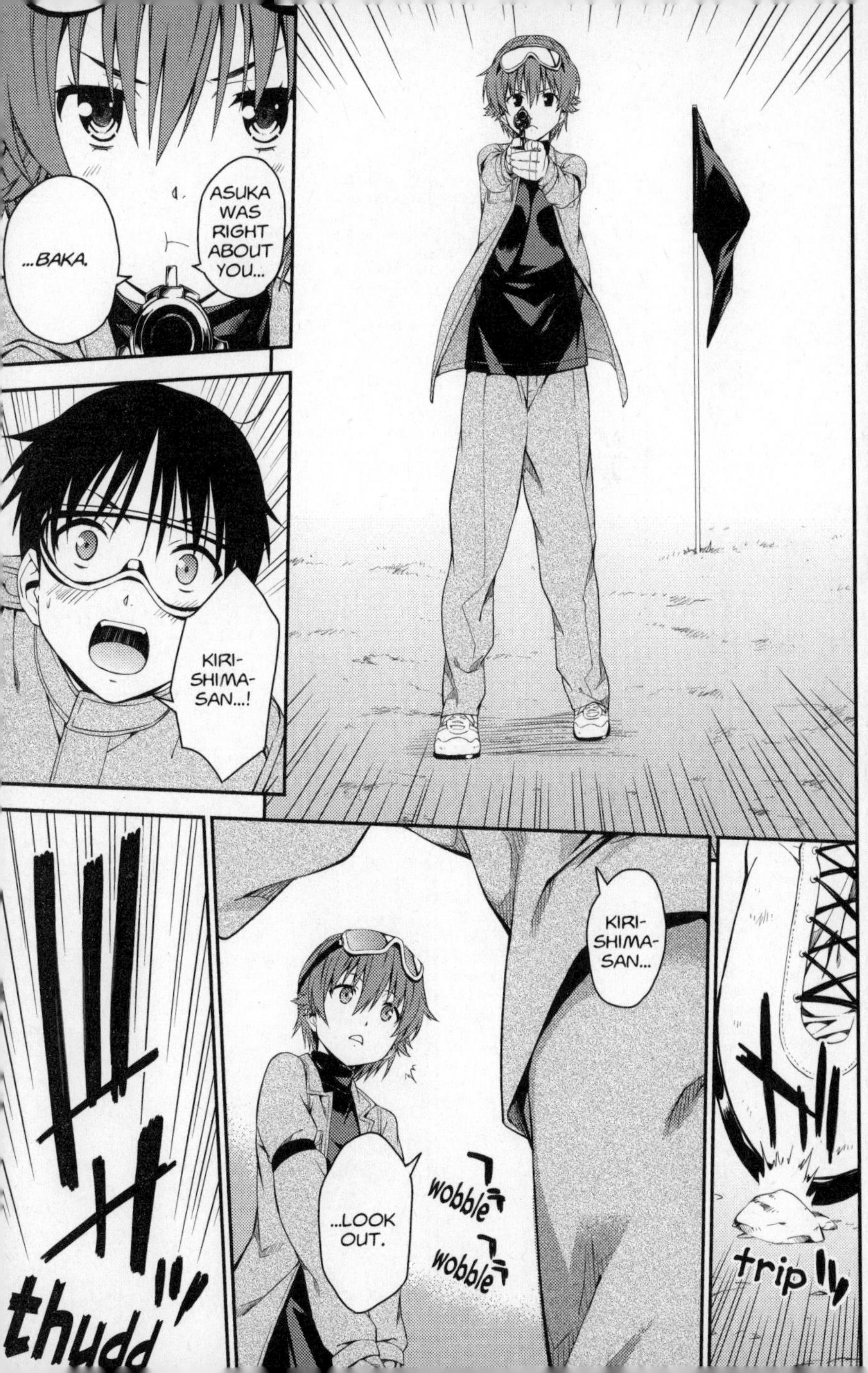
ASUKA WAS RIGHT ABOUT YOU...
...BAKA.
KIRI-SHIMA-SAN...!
trip
KIRI-SHIMA-SAN...
wobble
wobble
...LOOK OUT.
thudd

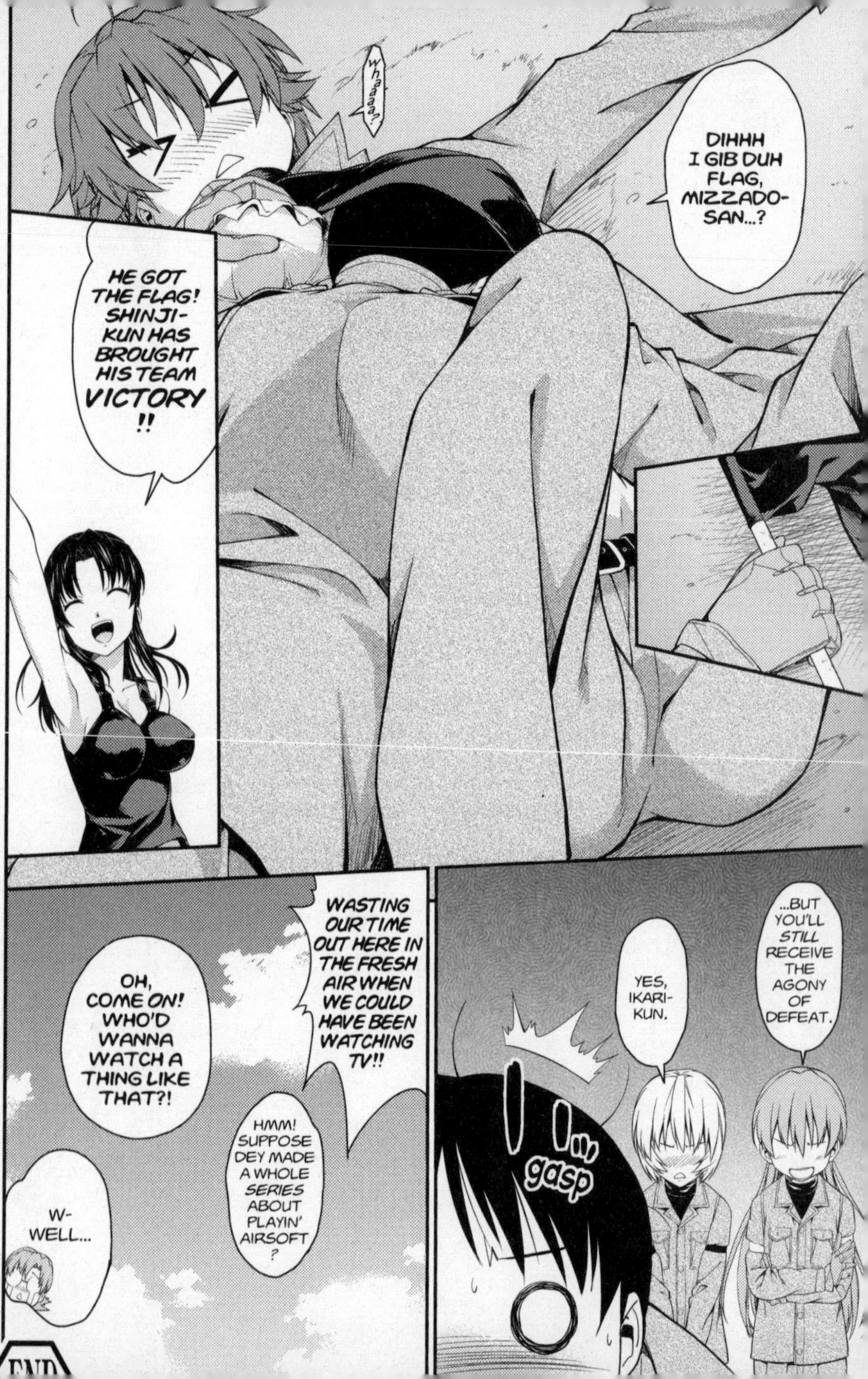
DIHHH I GIB DUH FLAG, MIZZADO-SAN...?
Whaaaa?!
HE GOT THE FLAG! SHINJI-KUN HAS BROUGHT HIS TEAM VICTORY !!
...BUT YOU'LL STILL RECEIVE THE AGONY OF DEFEAT.
YES, IKARI-KUN.
gasp
WASTING OUR TIME OUT HERE IN THE FRESH AIR WHEN WE COULD HAVE BEEN WATCHING TV!!
OH, COME ON! WHO'D WANNA WATCH A THING LIKE THAT?!
HMM! SUPPOSE DEY MADE A WHOLE SERIES ABOUT PLAYIN' AIRSOFT ?
W-WELL...
END

the shinji ikari raising project

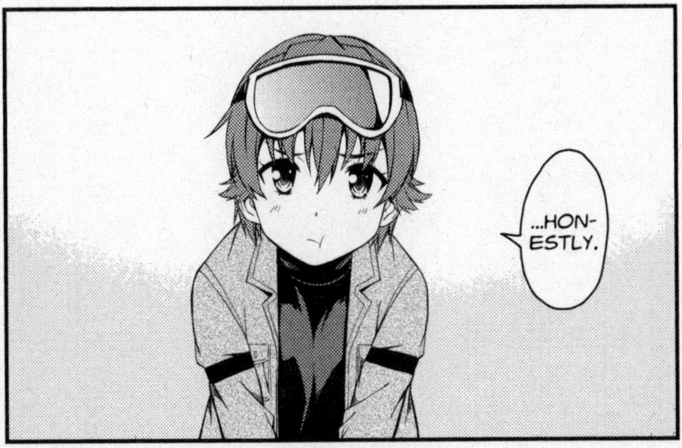
...HON-
ESTLY.

NEON GENESIS EVANGELION
THE SHINJI IKARI RAISING PROJECT

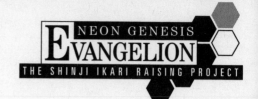

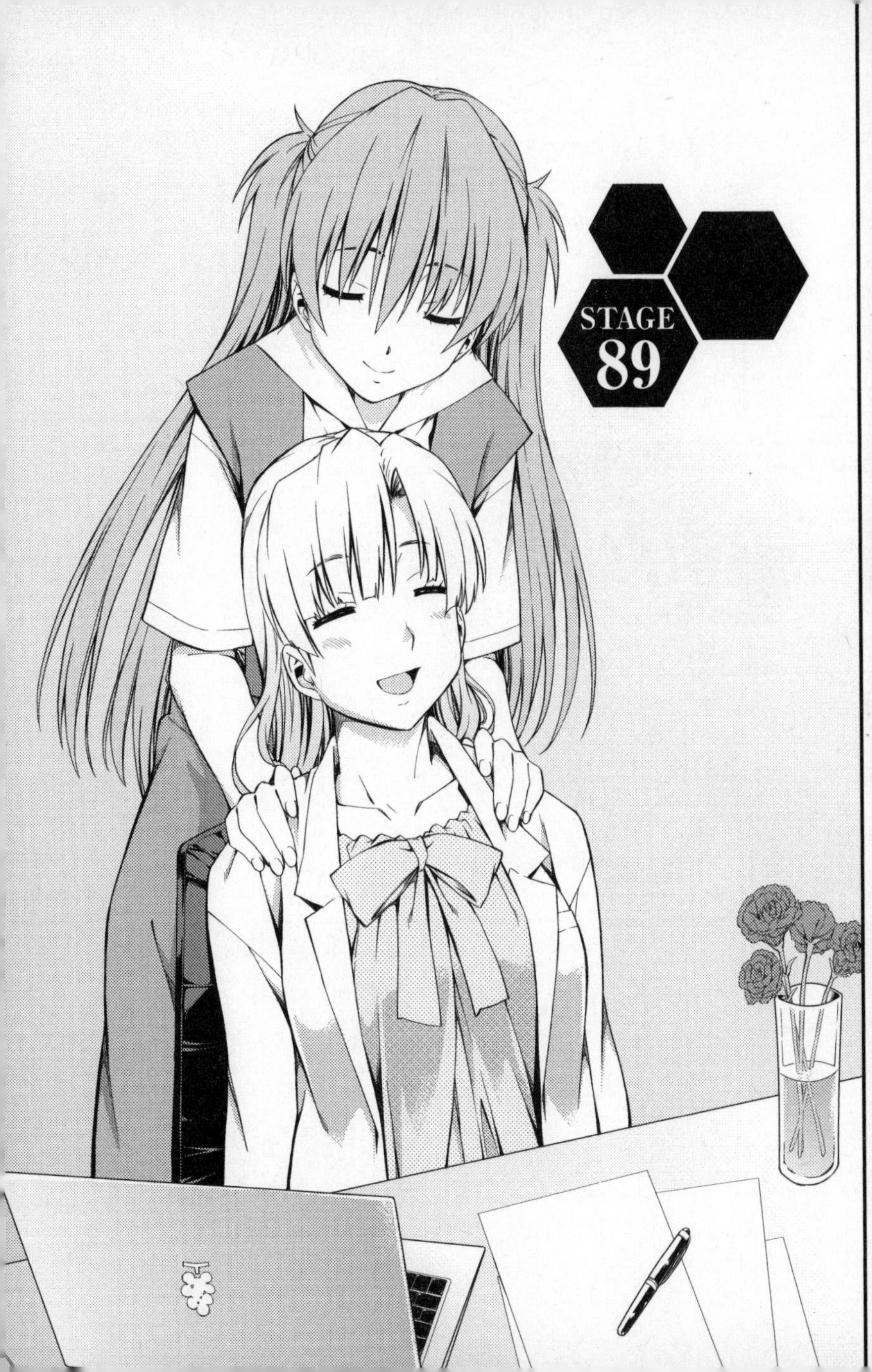
STAGE
89

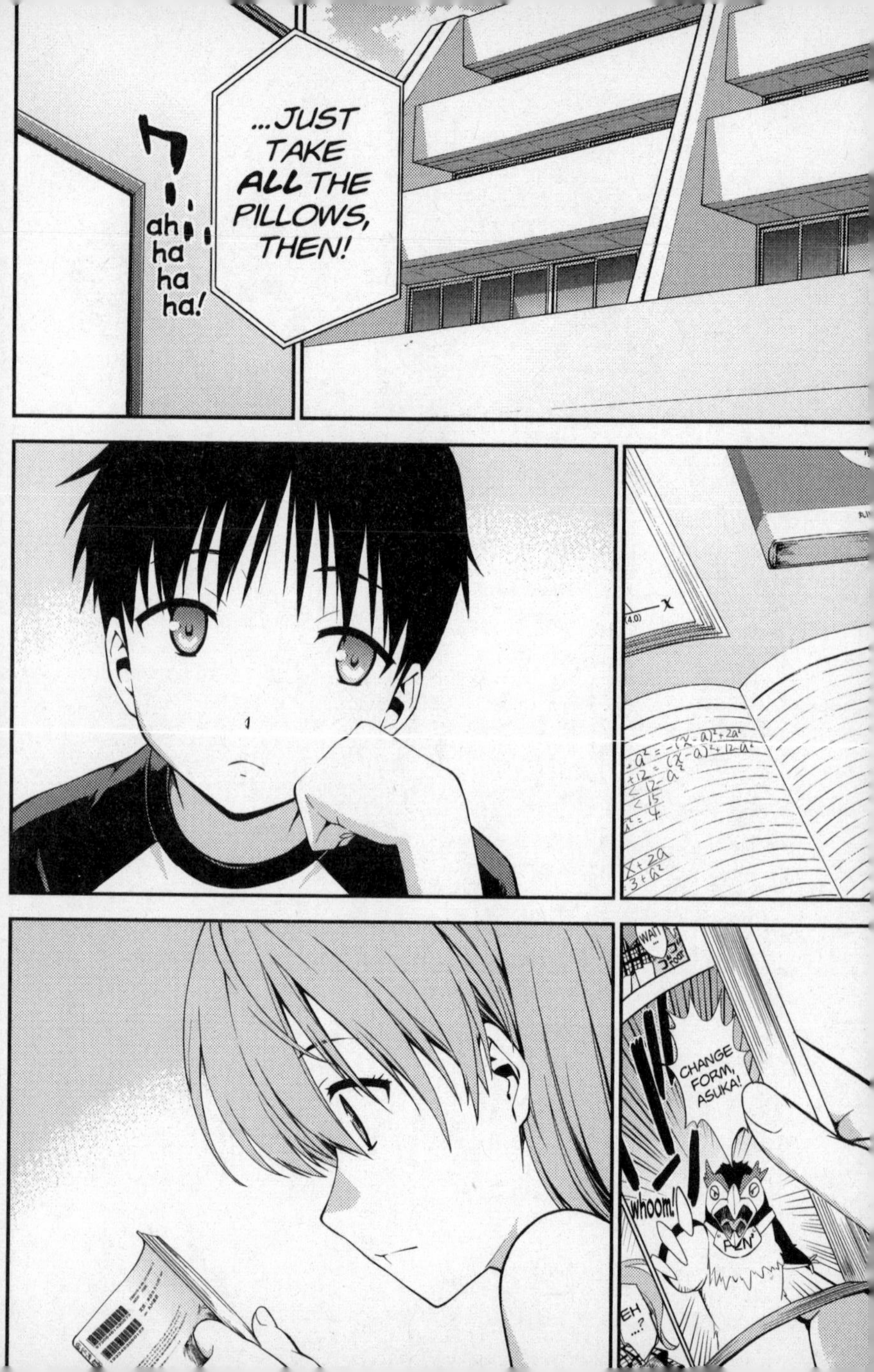
...JUST TAKE ALL THE PILLOWS, THEN!
ah ha ha ha!
WAIT ...
CHANGE FORM, ASUKA!
whoom!
PEN²
EH ...?

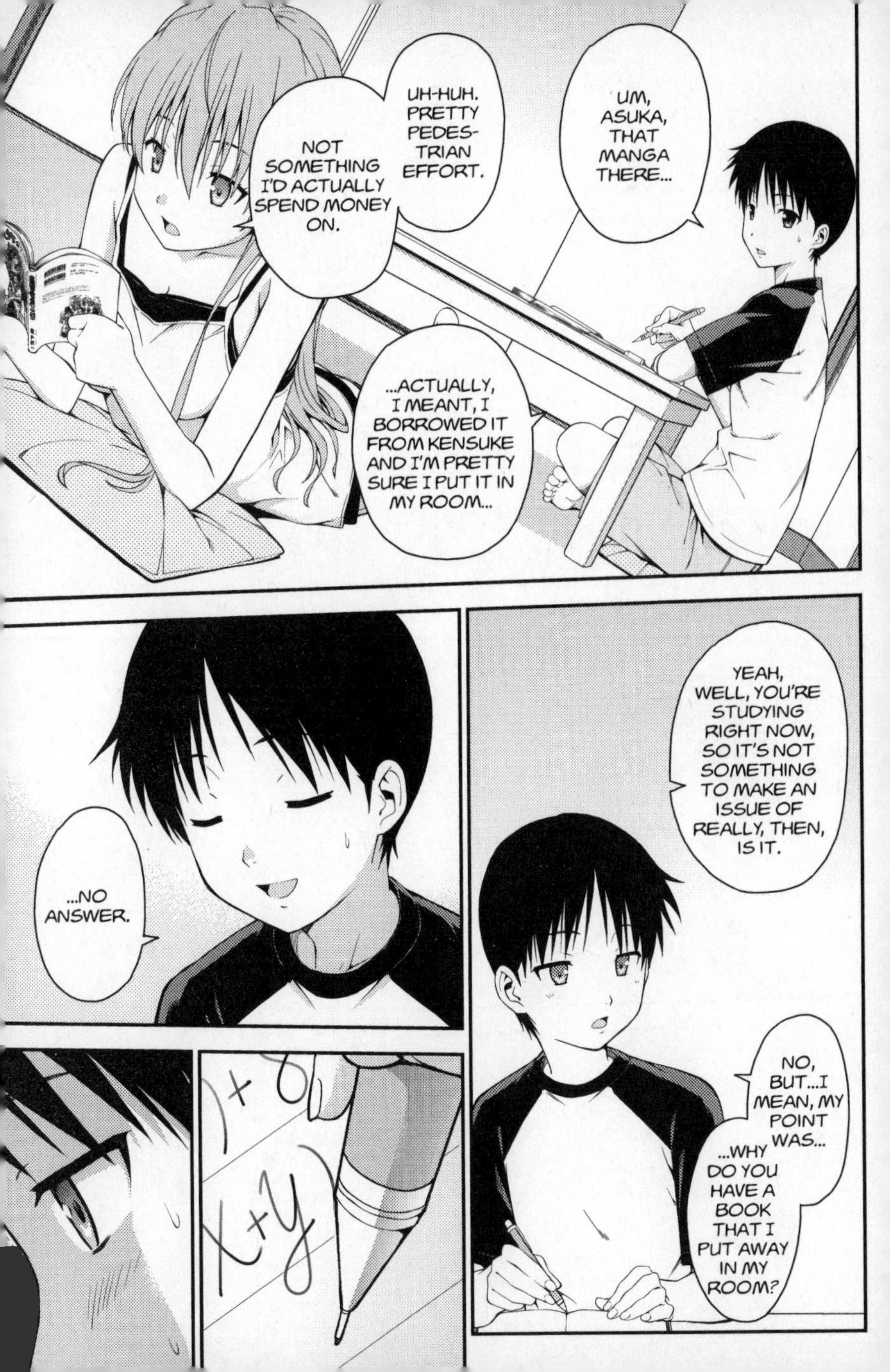
UM, ASUKA, THAT MANGA THERE...
UH-HUH. PRETTY PEDES-TRIAN EFFORT.
NOT SOMETHING I'D ACTUALLY SPEND MONEY ON.
...ACTUALLY, I MEANT, I BORROWED IT FROM KENSUKE AND I'M PRETTY SURE I PUT IT IN MY ROOM...
YEAH, WELL, YOU'RE STUDYING RIGHT NOW, SO IT'S NOT SOMETHING TO MAKE AN ISSUE OF REALLY, THEN, IS IT.
NO, BUT...I MEAN, MY POINT WAS...
...WHY DO YOU HAVE A BOOK THAT I PUT AWAY IN MY ROOM?
...NO ANSWER.
X+Y

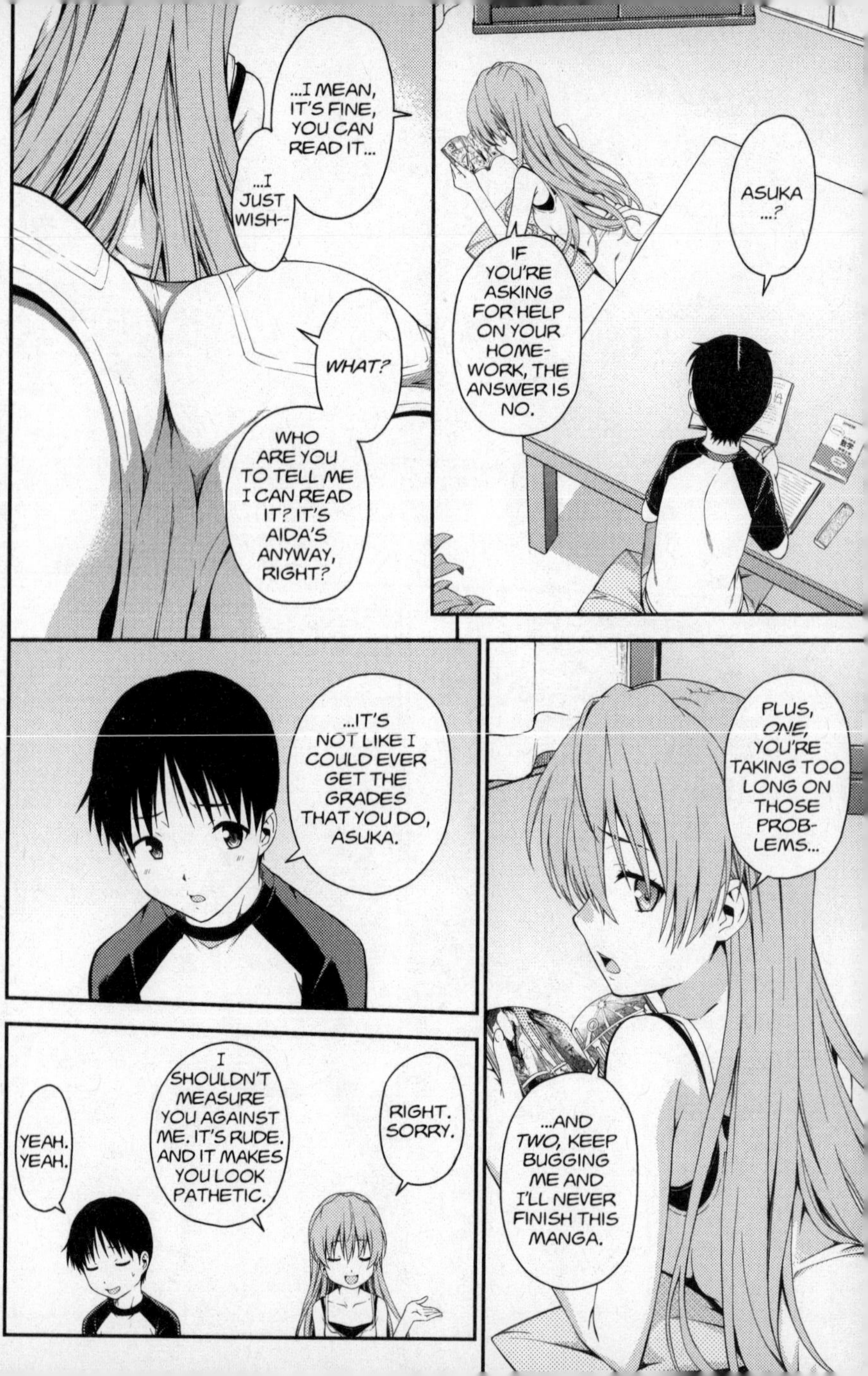
ASUKA ...?
IF YOU'RE ASKING FOR HELP ON YOUR HOME-WORK, THE ANSWER IS NO.
...I MEAN, IT'S FINE, YOU CAN READ IT...
...I JUST WISH--
WHAT?
WHO ARE YOU TO TELL ME I CAN READ IT? IT'S AIDA'S ANYWAY, RIGHT?
PLUS, *ONE*, YOU'RE TAKING TOO LONG ON THOSE PROB-LEMS...
...AND *TWO*, KEEP BUGGING ME AND I'LL NEVER FINISH THIS MANGA.
...IT'S NOT LIKE I COULD EVER GET THE GRADES THAT YOU DO, ASUKA.
RIGHT. SORRY.
I SHOULDN'T MEASURE YOU AGAINST ME. IT'S RUDE. AND IT MAKES YOU LOOK PATHETIC.
YEAH. YEAH.

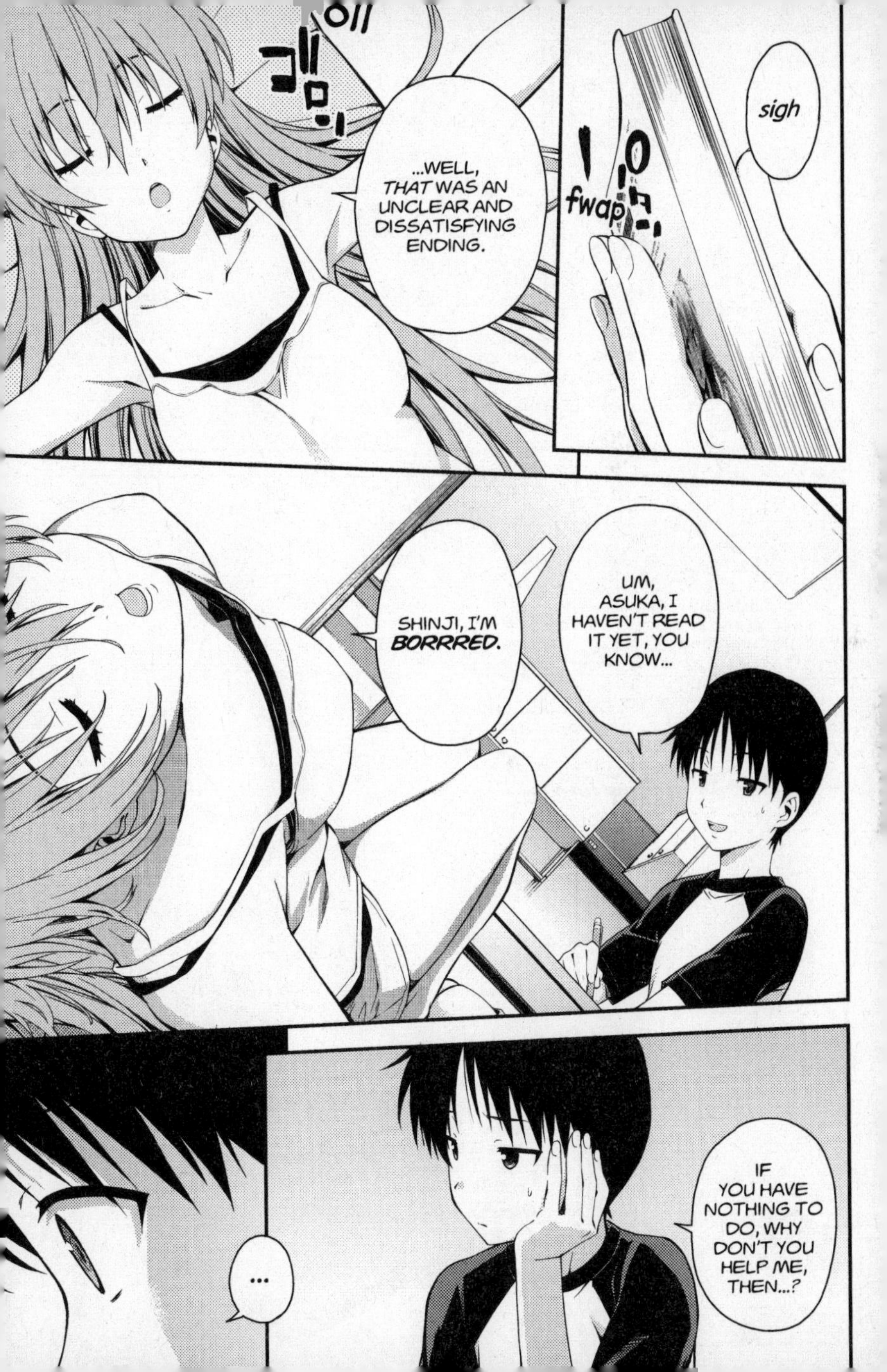
sigh
fwap
...WELL, THAT WAS AN UNCLEAR AND DISSATISFYING ENDING.
UM, ASUKA, I HAVEN'T READ IT YET, YOU KNOW...
SHINJI, I'M BORRRED.
IF YOU HAVE NOTHING TO DO, WHY DON'T YOU HELP ME, THEN...?
...

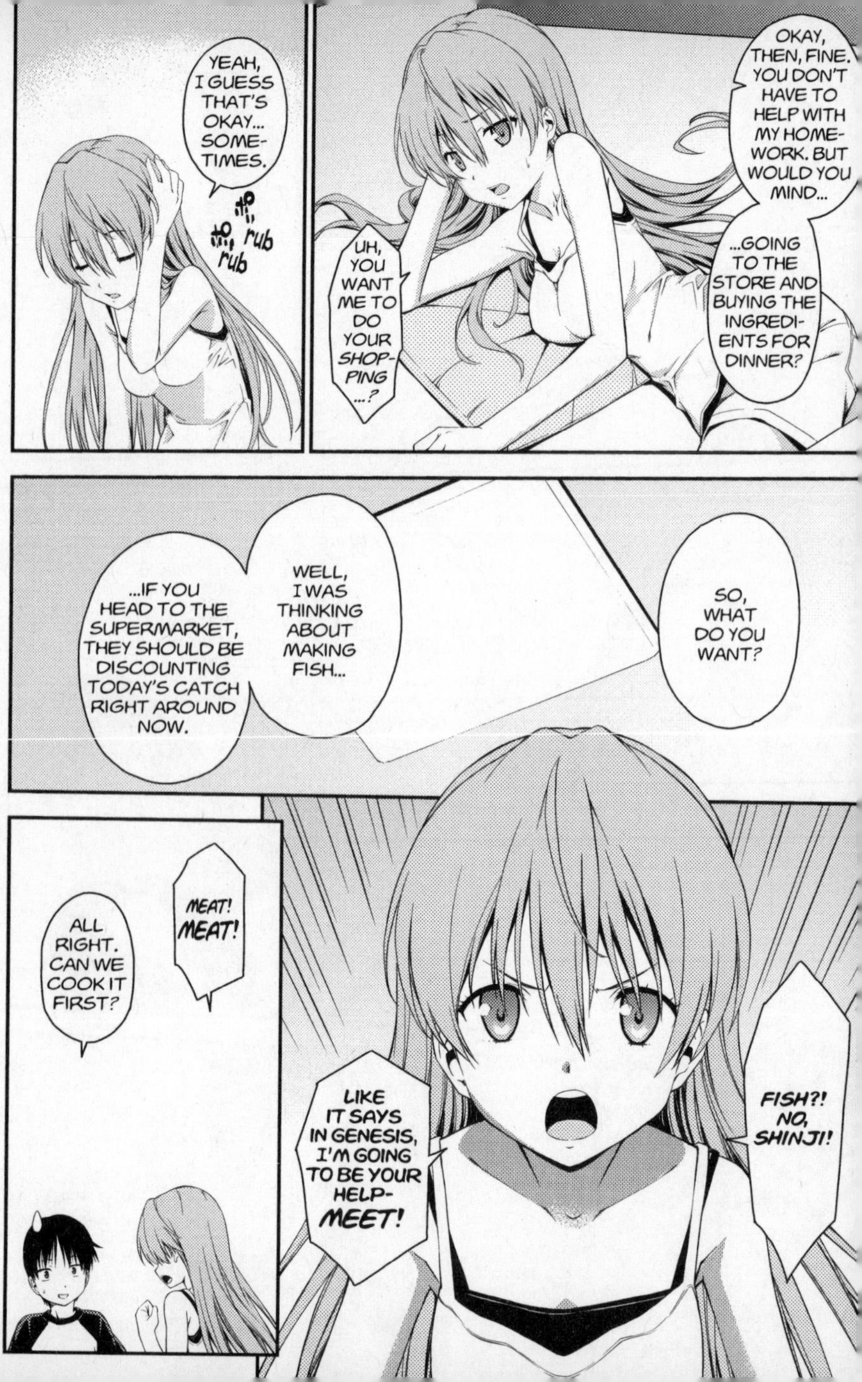
OKAY, THEN, FINE. YOU DON'T HAVE TO HELP WITH MY HOMEWORK. BUT WOULD YOU MIND...
...GOING TO THE STORE AND BUYING THE INGREDIENTS FOR DINNER?
UH, YOU WANT ME TO DO YOUR SHOPPING ...?
YEAH, I GUESS THAT'S OKAY... SOMETIMES.
rub
rub
SO, WHAT DO YOU WANT?
WELL, I WAS THINKING ABOUT MAKING FISH...
...IF YOU HEAD TO THE SUPERMARKET, THEY SHOULD BE DISCOUNTING TODAY'S CATCH RIGHT AROUND NOW.
FISH?! NO, SHINJI!
LIKE IT SAYS IN GENESIS, I'M GOING TO BE YOUR HELP-MEET!
MEAT! MEAT!
ALL RIGHT. CAN WE COOK IT FIRST?

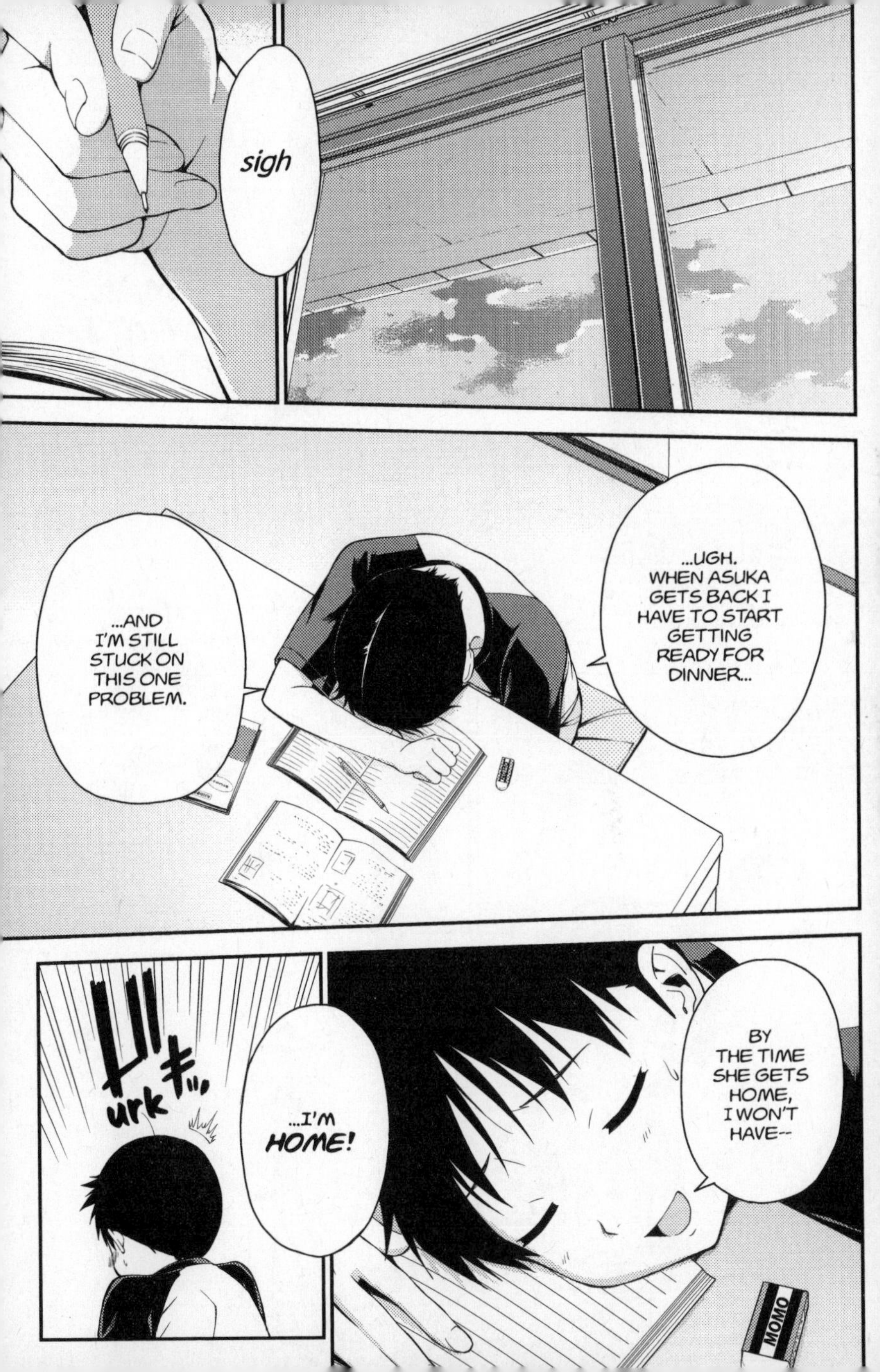
sigh
...UGH. WHEN ASUKA GETS BACK I HAVE TO START GETTING READY FOR DINNER...
...AND I'M STILL STUCK ON THIS ONE PROBLEM.
BY THE TIME SHE GETS HOME, I WON'T HAVE--
...I'M HOME!
urk
MOMO

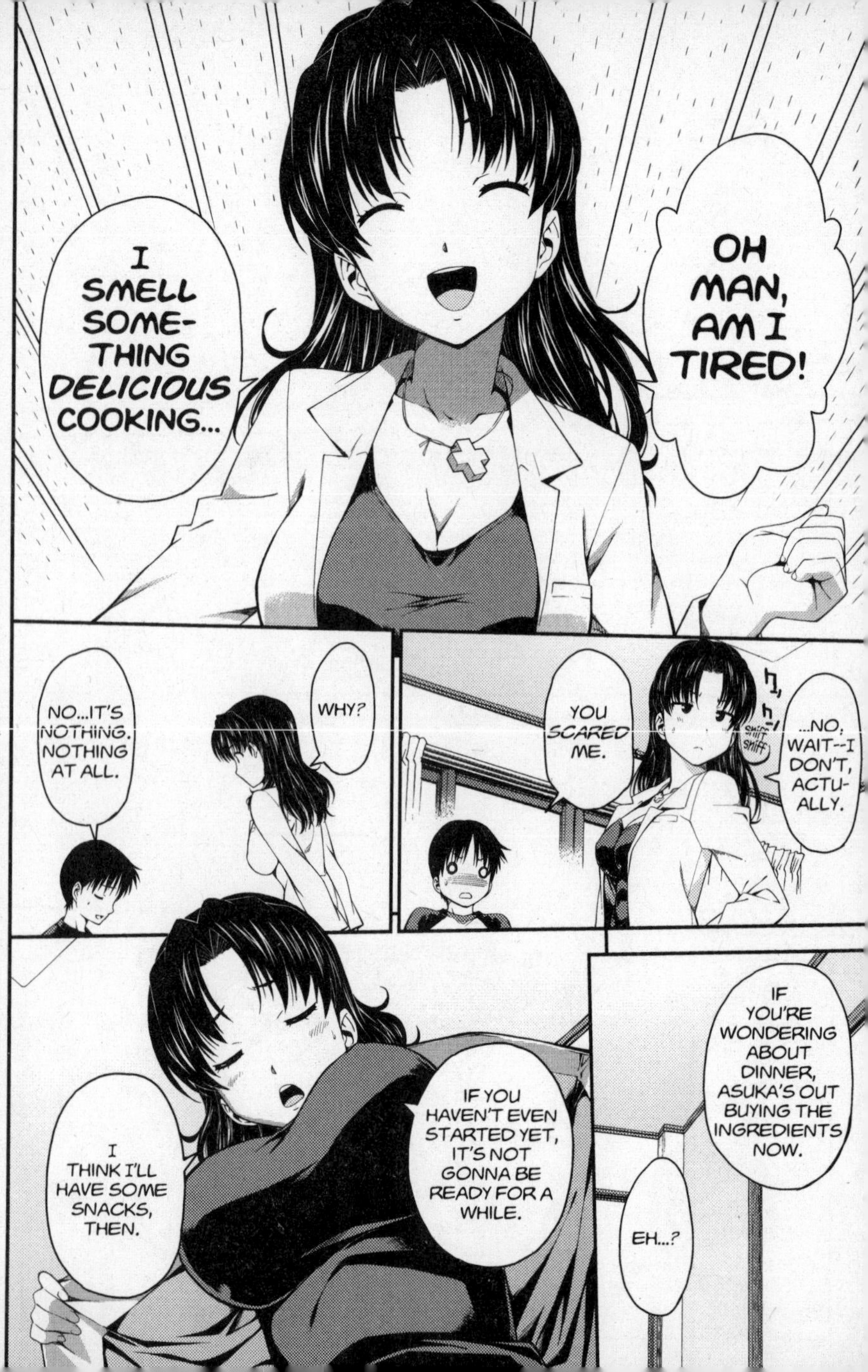
OH MAN, AM I TIRED!
I SMELL SOME-THING DELICIOUS COOKING...
SNIFF SNIFF
...NO, WAIT--I DON'T, ACTU-ALLY.
YOU SCARED ME.
WHY?
NO...IT'S NOTHING. NOTHING AT ALL.
IF YOU'RE WONDERING ABOUT DINNER, ASUKA'S OUT BUYING THE INGREDIENTS NOW.
EH...?
IF YOU HAVEN'T EVEN STARTED YET, IT'S NOT GONNA BE READY FOR A WHILE.
I THINK I'LL HAVE SOME SNACKS, THEN.

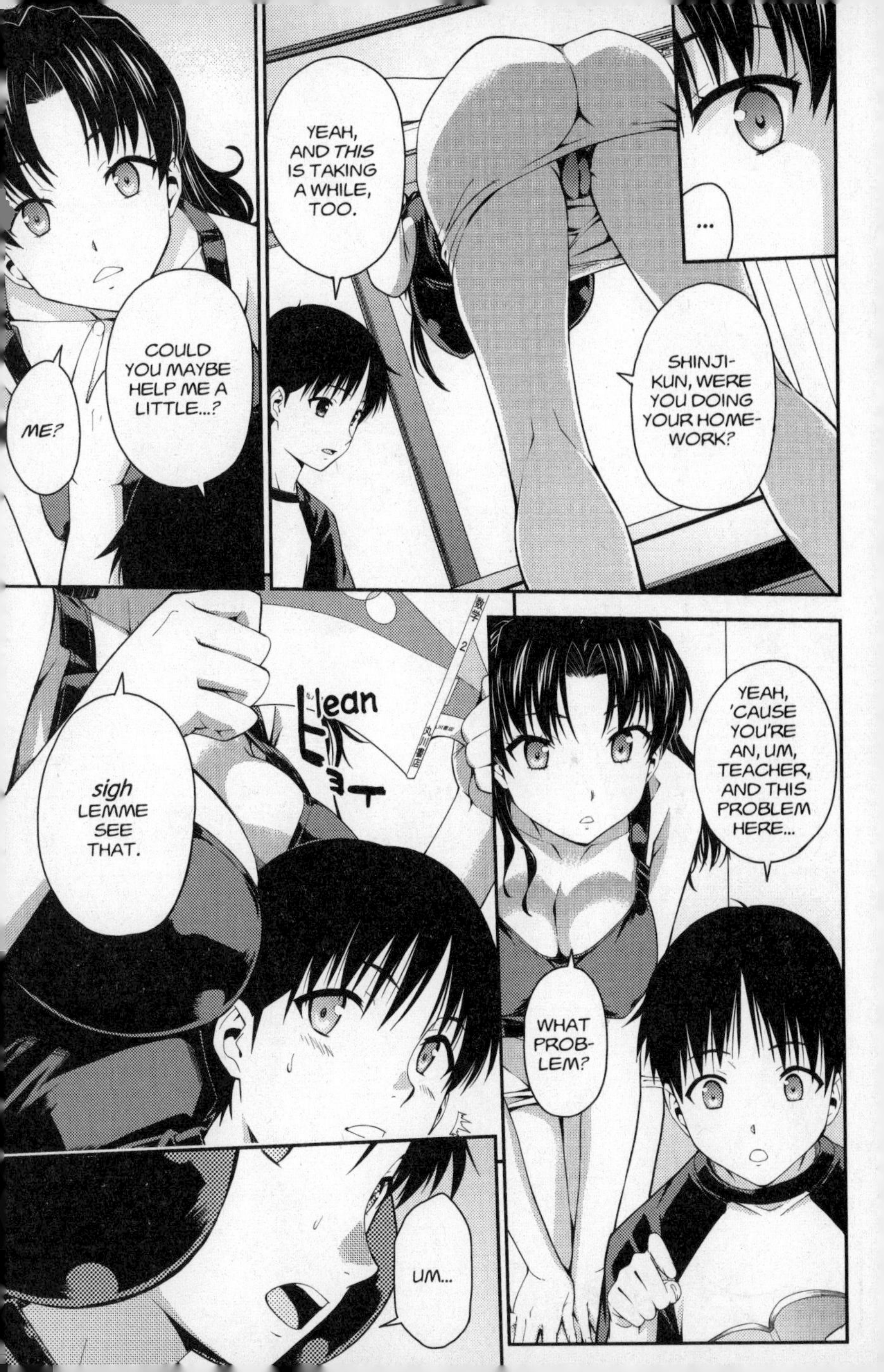
...
SHINJI-KUN, WERE YOU DOING YOUR HOMEWORK?
YEAH, AND THIS IS TAKING A WHILE, TOO.
COULD YOU MAYBE HELP ME A LITTLE...?
ME?
YEAH, 'CAUSE YOU'RE AN, UM, TEACHER, AND THIS PROBLEM HERE...
WHAT PROBLEM?
lean
sigh LEMME SEE THAT.
UM...

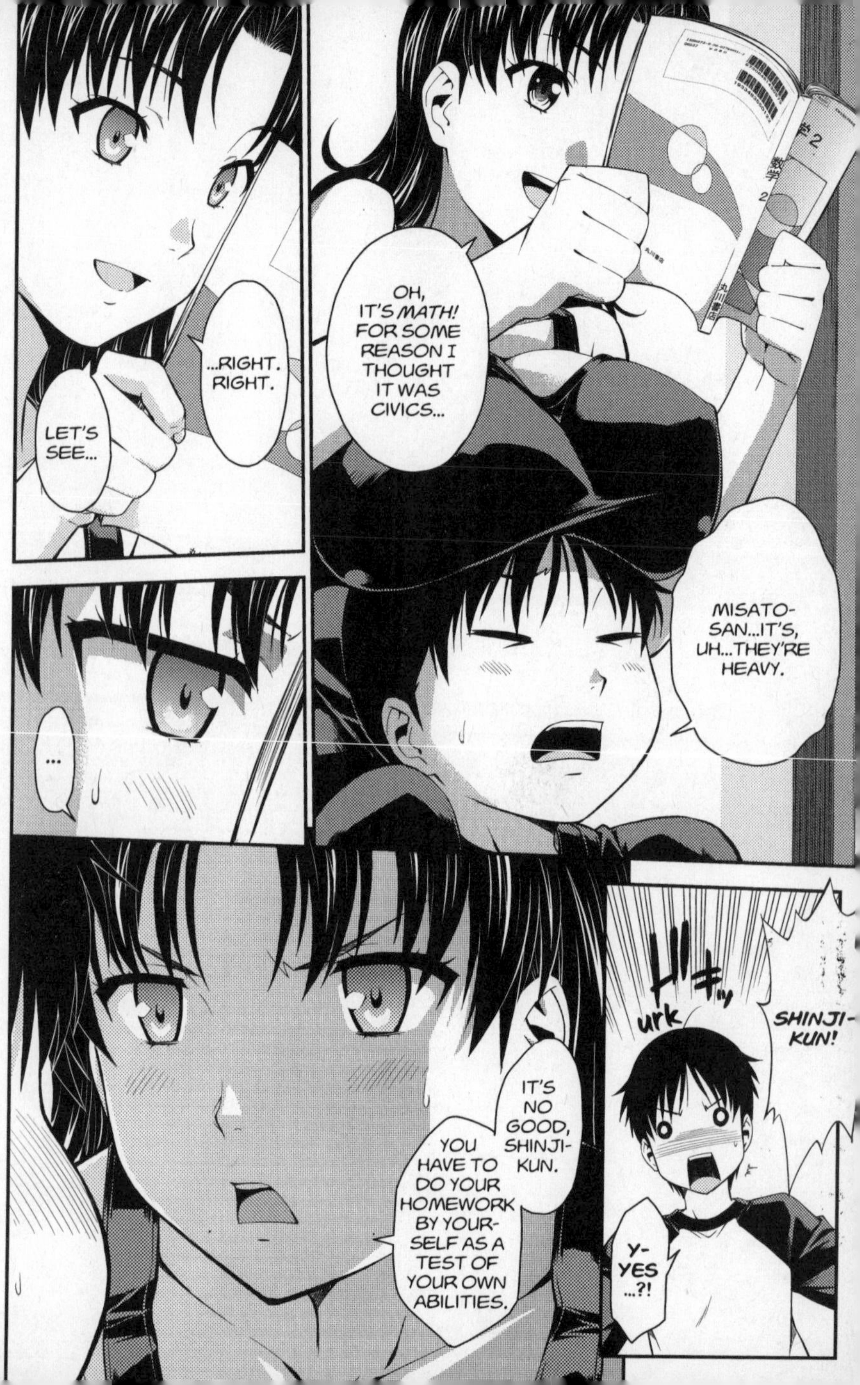
OH, IT'S *MATH!* FOR SOME REASON I THOUGHT IT WAS CIVICS...
MISATO-SAN...IT'S, UH...THEY'RE HEAVY.
...RIGHT. RIGHT.
LET'S SEE...
...
SHINJI-KUN!
ドキッ
urk
Y-YES ...?!
IT'S NO GOOD, SHINJI-KUN.
YOU HAVE TO DO YOUR HOMEWORK BY YOUR-SELF AS A TEST OF YOUR OWN ABILITIES.

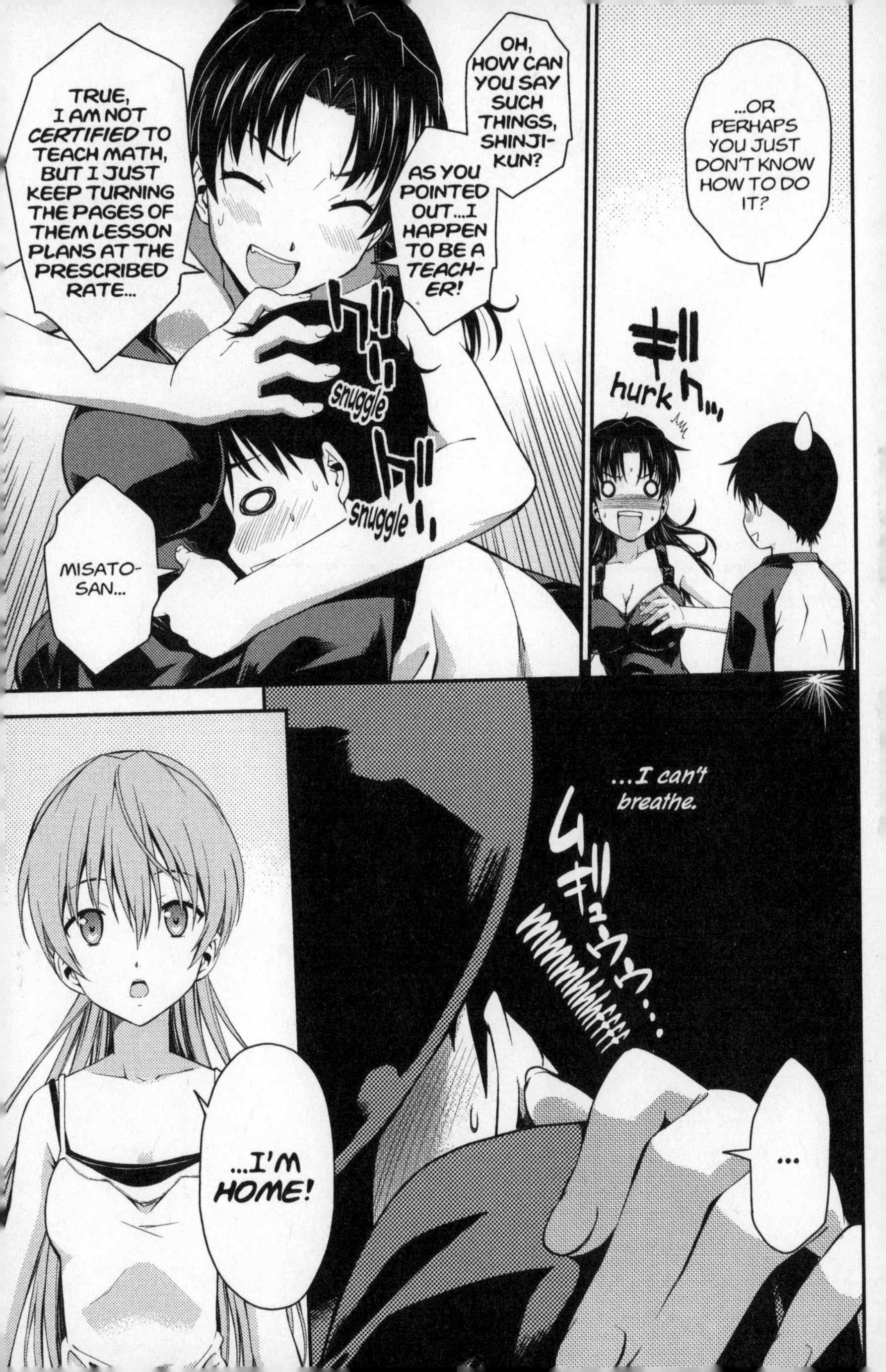
...OR PERHAPS YOU JUST DON'T KNOW HOW TO DO IT?
hurk
OH, HOW CAN YOU SAY SUCH THINGS, SHINJI-KUN?
AS YOU POINTED OUT...I HAPPEN TO BE A TEACHER!
TRUE, I AM NOT CERTIFIED TO TEACH MATH, BUT I JUST KEEP TURNING THE PAGES OF THEM LESSON PLANS AT THE PRESCRIBED RATE...
snuggle
snuggle
MISATO-SAN...
...I can't breathe.
...
...I'M HOME!

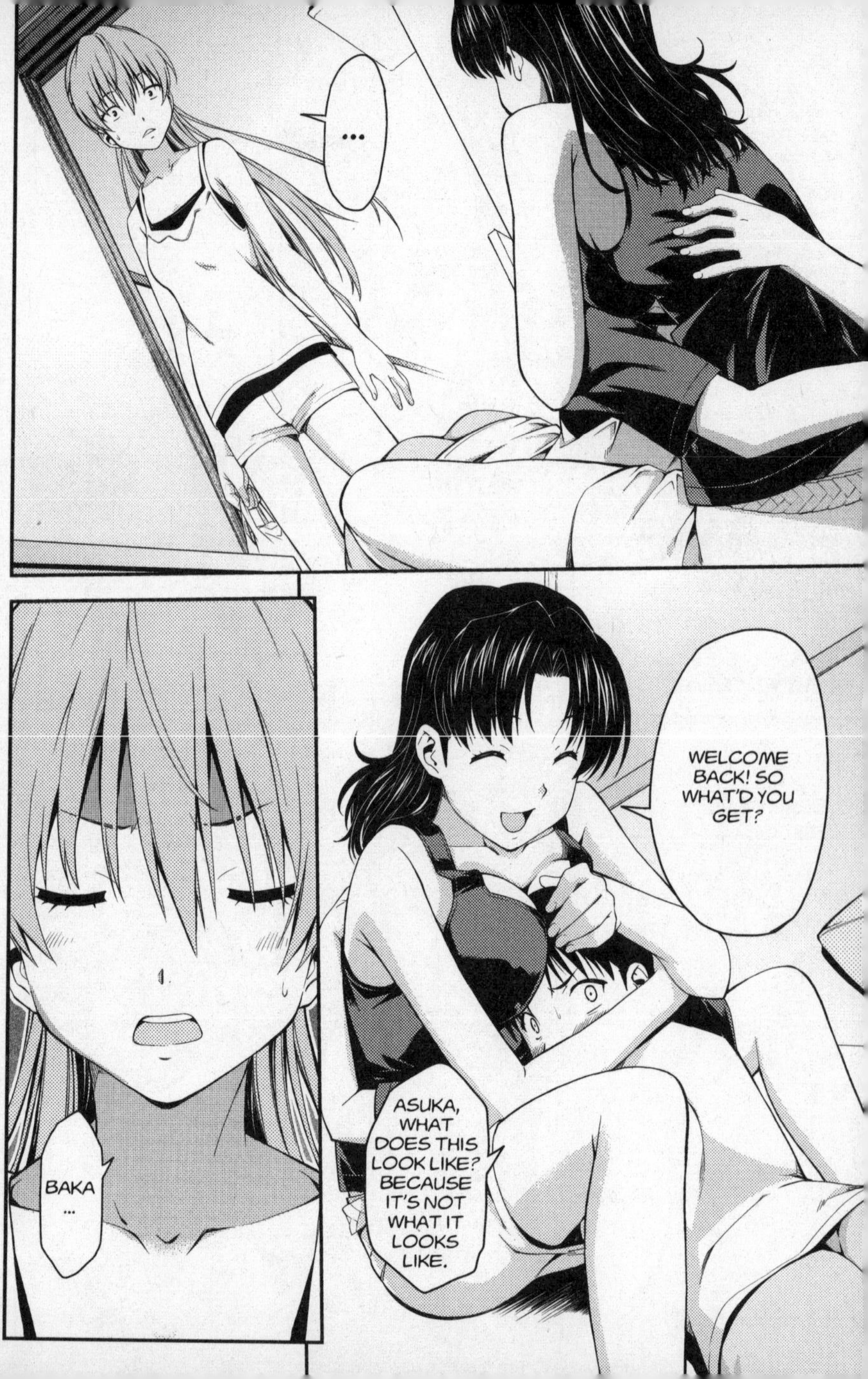
...
WELCOME BACK! SO WHAT'D YOU GET?
ASUKA, WHAT DOES THIS LOOK LIKE? BECAUSE IT'S NOT WHAT IT LOOKS LIKE.
BAKA ...

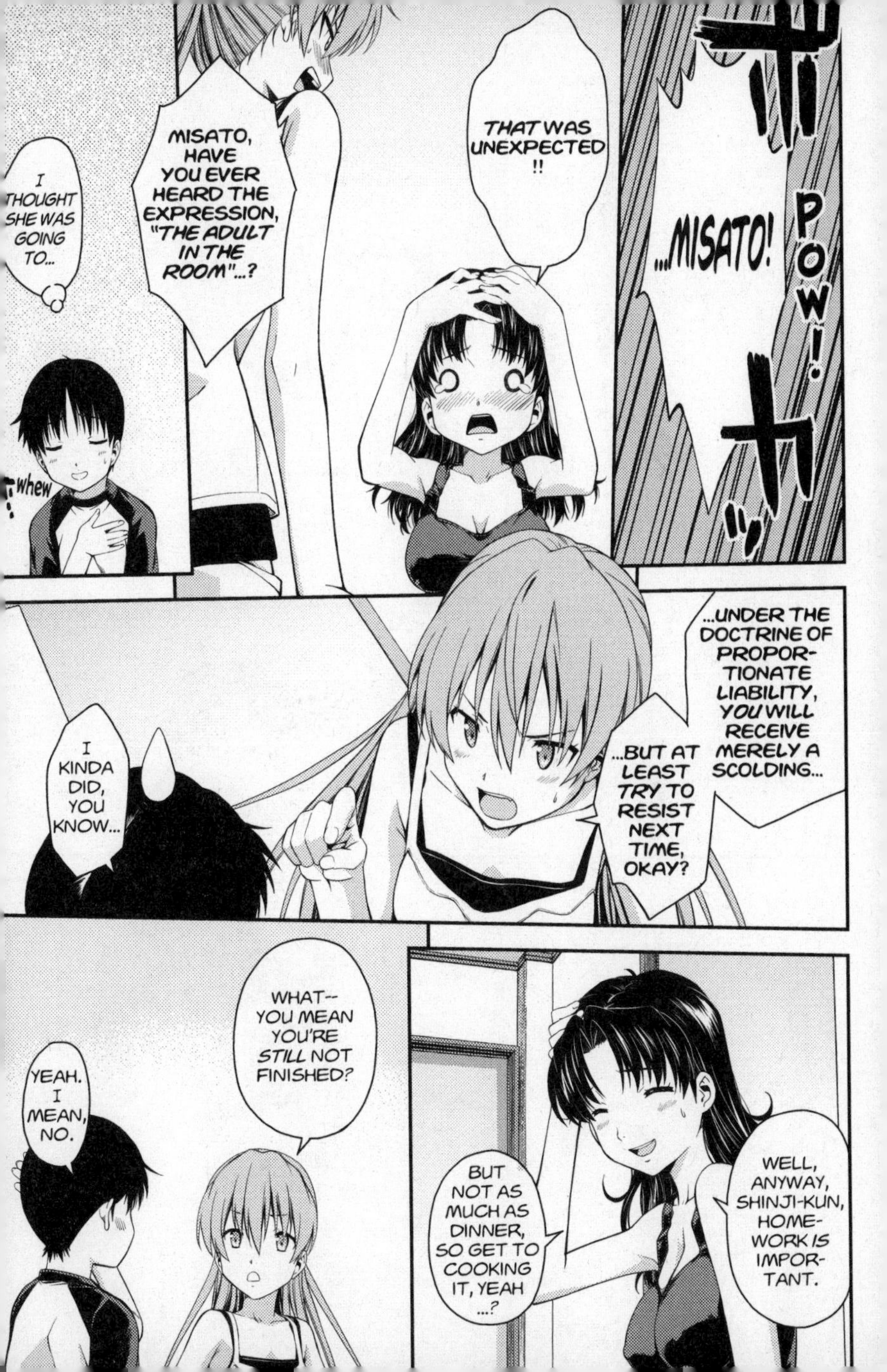
...MISATO!
POW!
THAT WAS UNEXPECTED !!
MISATO, HAVE YOU EVER HEARD THE EXPRESSION, "THE ADULT IN THE ROOM"...?
I THOUGHT SHE WAS GOING TO...
whew
...UNDER THE DOCTRINE OF PROPORTIONATE LIABILITY, YOU WILL RECEIVE MERELY A SCOLDING...
...BUT AT LEAST TRY TO RESIST NEXT TIME, OKAY?
I KINDA DID, YOU KNOW...
WELL, ANYWAY, SHINJI-KUN, HOMEWORK IS IMPORTANT.
BUT NOT AS MUCH AS DINNER, SO GET TO COOKING IT, YEAH ...?
WHAT-- YOU MEAN YOU'RE STILL NOT FINISHED?
YEAH. I MEAN, NO.

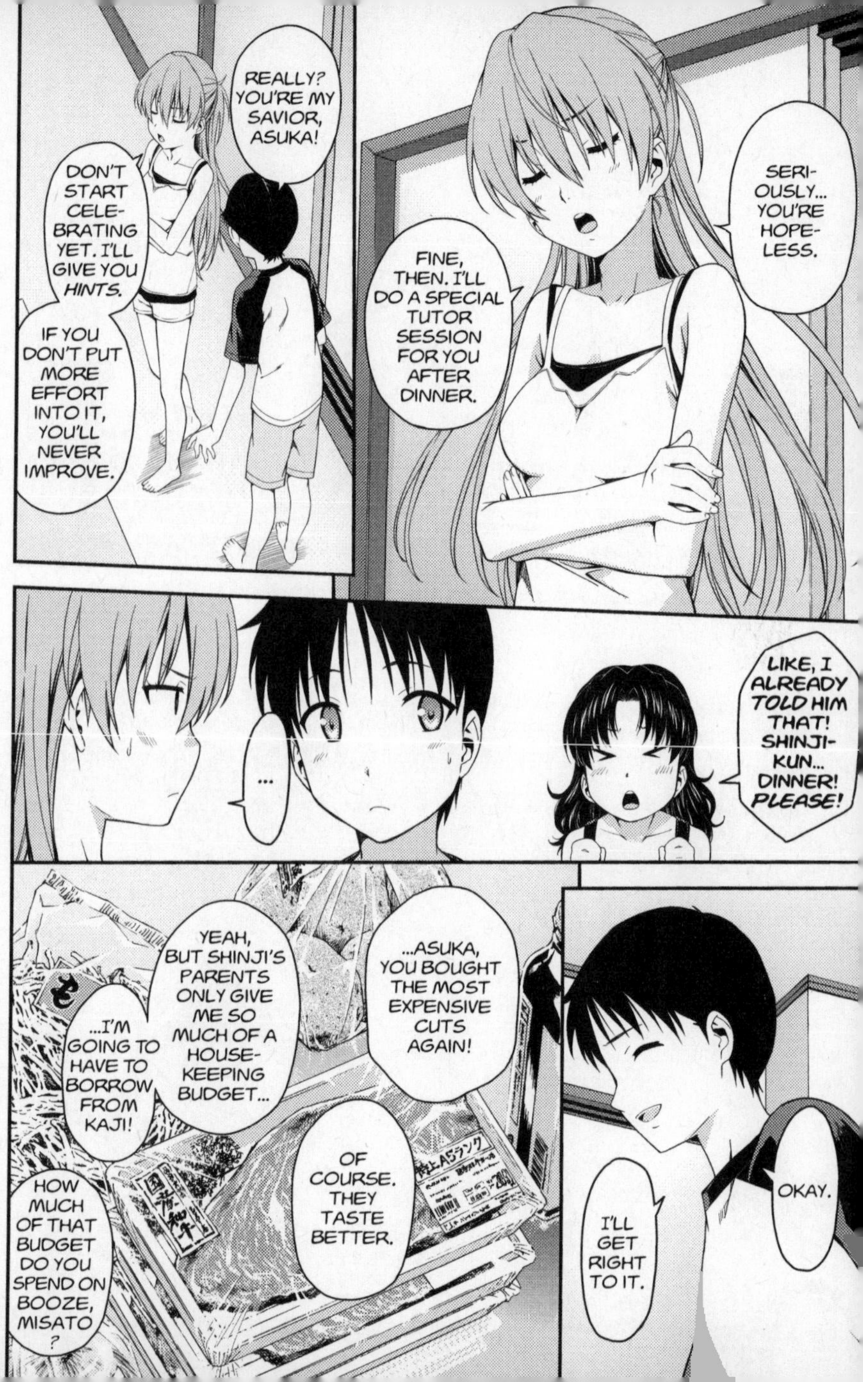
SERIOUSLY... YOU'RE HOPELESS.
FINE, THEN. I'LL DO A SPECIAL TUTOR SESSION FOR YOU AFTER DINNER.
REALLY? YOU'RE MY SAVIOR, ASUKA!
DON'T START CELEBRATING YET. I'LL GIVE YOU *HINTS*.
IF YOU DON'T PUT MORE EFFORT INTO IT, YOU'LL NEVER IMPROVE.
LIKE, I ALREADY *TOLD* HIM THAT! SHINJI-KUN... DINNER! *PLEASE!*
...
OKAY.
I'LL GET RIGHT TO IT.
...ASUKA, YOU BOUGHT THE MOST EXPENSIVE CUTS AGAIN!
OF COURSE. THEY TASTE BETTER.
YEAH, BUT SHINJI'S PARENTS ONLY GIVE ME SO MUCH OF A HOUSEKEEPING BUDGET...
...I'M GOING TO HAVE TO BORROW FROM KAJI!
HOW MUCH OF THAT BUDGET DO YOU SPEND ON BOOZE, MISATO?

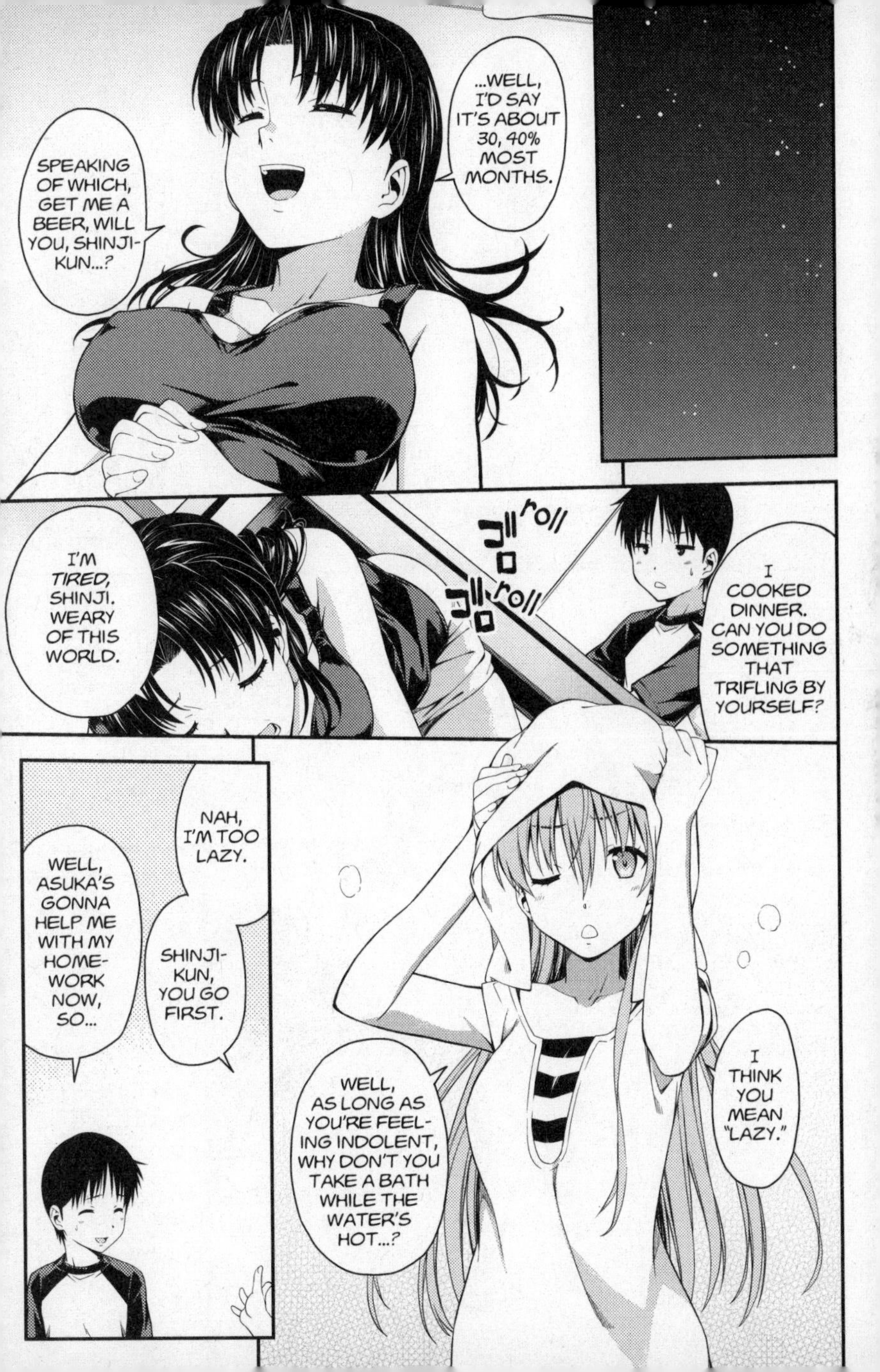
...WELL, I'D SAY IT'S ABOUT 30, 40% MOST MONTHS.
SPEAKING OF WHICH, GET ME A BEER, WILL YOU, SHINJI-KUN...?
I COOKED DINNER. CAN YOU DO SOMETHING THAT TRIFLING BY YOURSELF?
ゴロ roll
ゴロ roll
I'M TIRED, SHINJI. WEARY OF THIS WORLD.
I THINK YOU MEAN "LAZY."
WELL, AS LONG AS YOU'RE FEELING INDOLENT, WHY DON'T YOU TAKE A BATH WHILE THE WATER'S HOT...?
NAH, I'M TOO LAZY.
SHINJI-KUN, YOU GO FIRST.
WELL, ASUKA'S GONNA HELP ME WITH MY HOME-WORK NOW, SO...

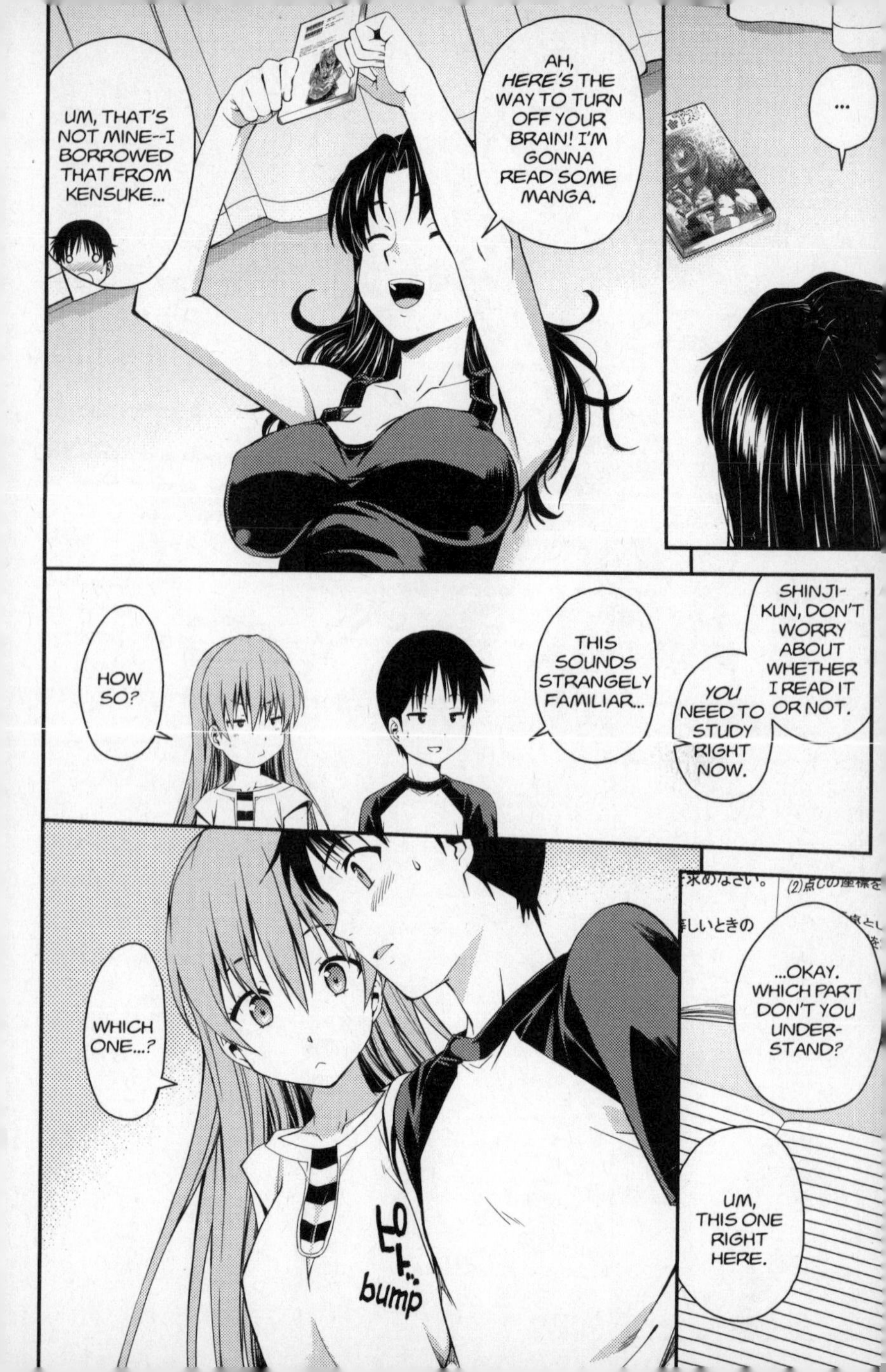
...
AH, HERE'S THE WAY TO TURN OFF YOUR BRAIN! I'M GONNA READ SOME MANGA.
UM, THAT'S NOT MINE--I BORROWED THAT FROM KENSUKE...
SHINJI-KUN, DON'T WORRY ABOUT WHETHER I READ IT OR NOT.
YOU NEED TO STUDY RIGHT NOW.
THIS SOUNDS STRANGELY FAMILIAR...
HOW SO?
...OKAY. WHICH PART DON'T YOU UNDERSTAND?
UM, THIS ONE RIGHT HERE.
WHICH ONE...?
bump

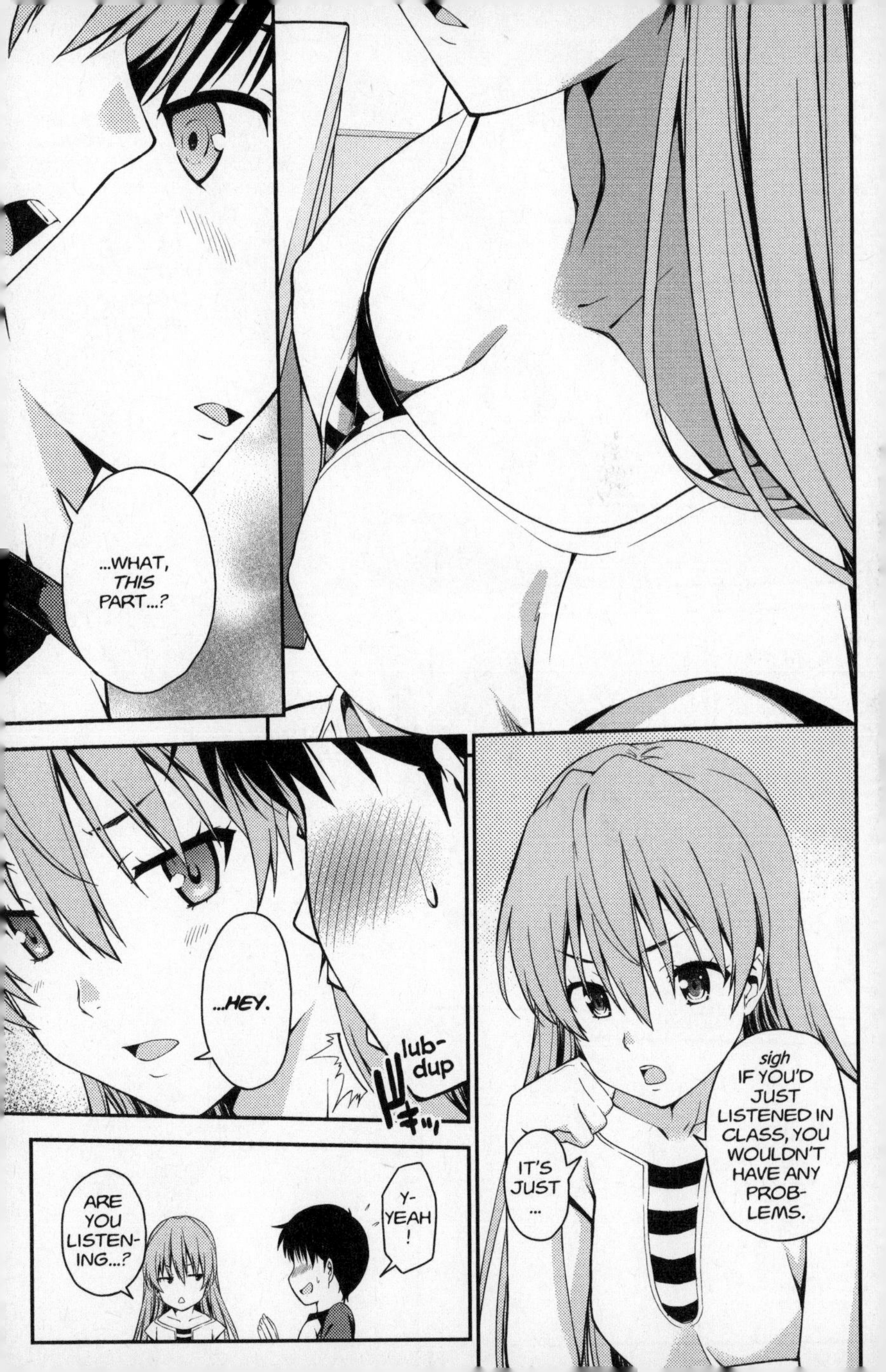
...WHAT, THIS PART...?
sigh IF YOU'D JUST LISTENED IN CLASS, YOU WOULDN'T HAVE ANY PROB-LEMS.
IT'S JUST ...
...HEY.
lub-dup
Y-YEAH!
ARE YOU LISTEN-ING...?

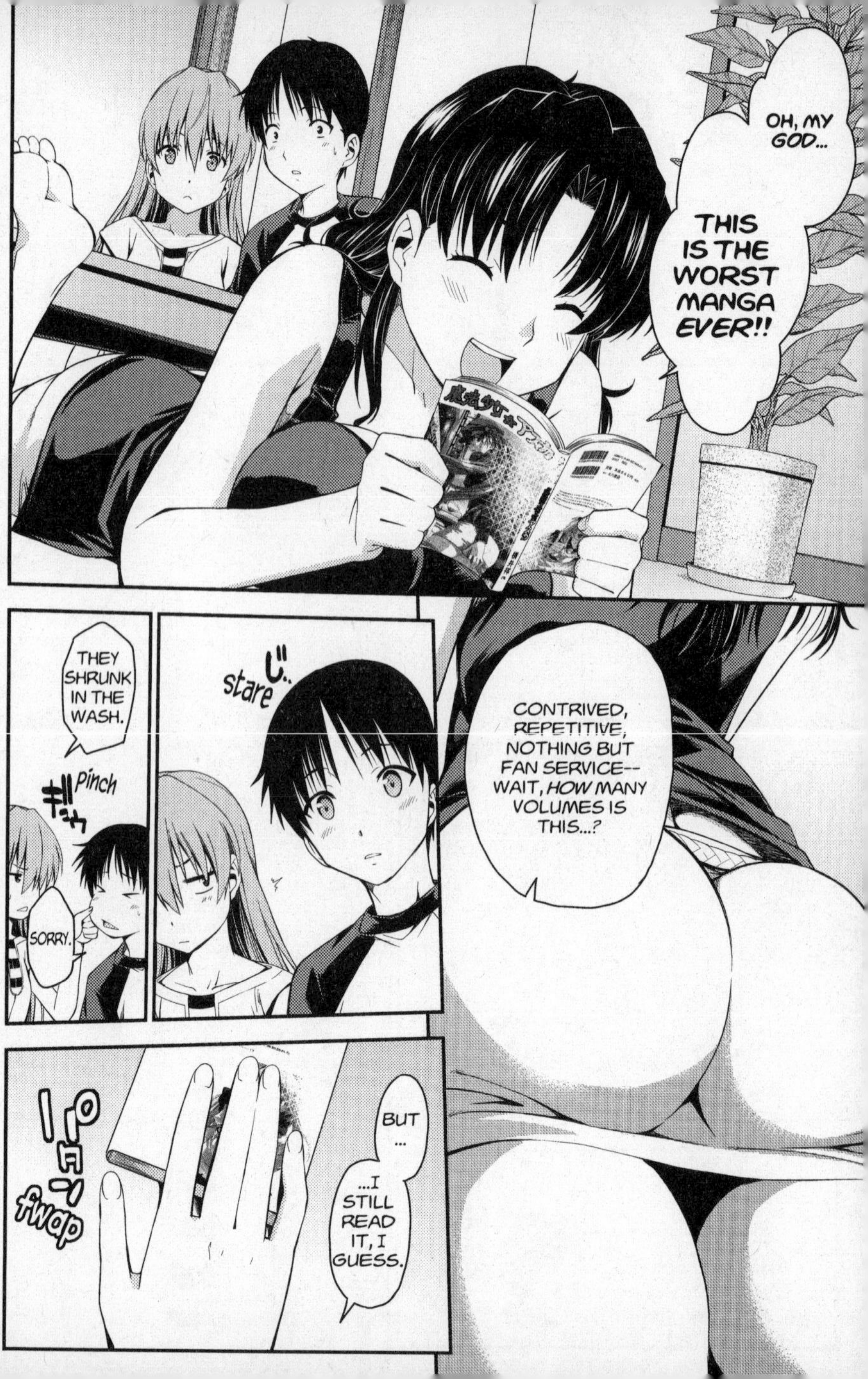
OH, MY GOD...
THIS IS THE WORST MANGA EVER!!
CONTRIVED, REPETITIVE, NOTHING BUT FAN SERVICE-- WAIT, HOW MANY VOLUMES IS THIS...?
stare
THEY SHRUNK IN THE WASH.
pinch
SORRY.
fwap
BUT ...
...I STILL READ IT, I GUESS.

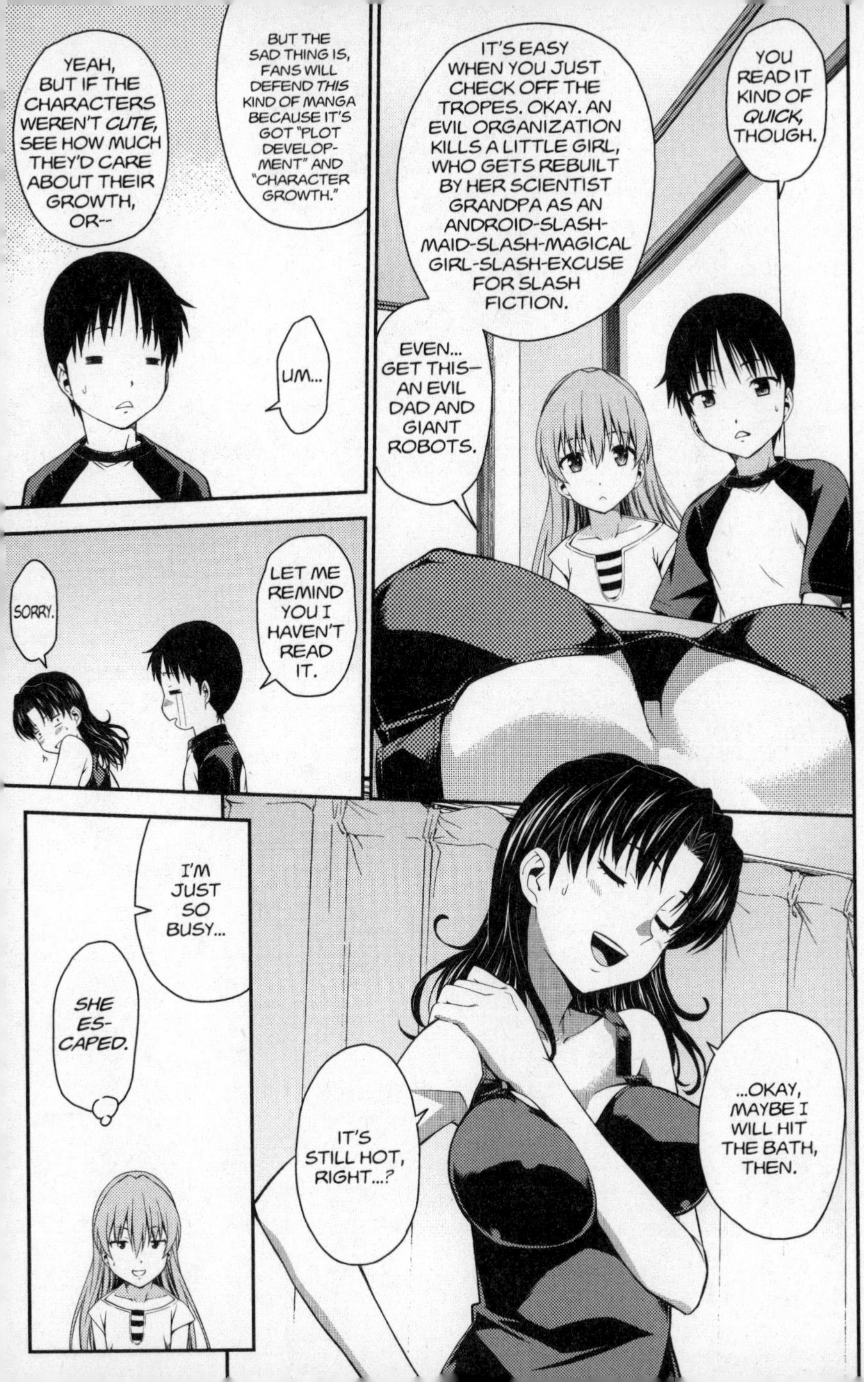

YOU READ IT KIND OF *QUICK*, THOUGH.
IT'S EASY WHEN YOU JUST CHECK OFF THE TROPES. OKAY. AN EVIL ORGANIZATION KILLS A LITTLE GIRL, WHO GETS REBUILT BY HER SCIENTIST GRANDPA AS AN ANDROID-SLASH-MAID-SLASH-MAGICAL GIRL-SLASH-EXCUSE FOR SLASH FICTION.
EVEN... GET THIS— AN EVIL DAD AND GIANT ROBOTS.
BUT THE SAD THING IS, FANS WILL DEFEND *THIS* KIND OF MANGA BECAUSE IT'S GOT "PLOT DEVELOP-MENT" AND "CHARACTER GROWTH."
YEAH, BUT IF THE CHARACTERS WEREN'T *CUTE*, SEE HOW MUCH THEY'D CARE ABOUT THEIR GROWTH, OR--
UM...
LET ME REMIND YOU I HAVEN'T READ IT.
SORRY.
...OKAY, MAYBE I WILL HIT THE BATH, THEN.
IT'S STILL HOT, RIGHT...?
I'M JUST SO BUSY...
SHE ES-CAPED.

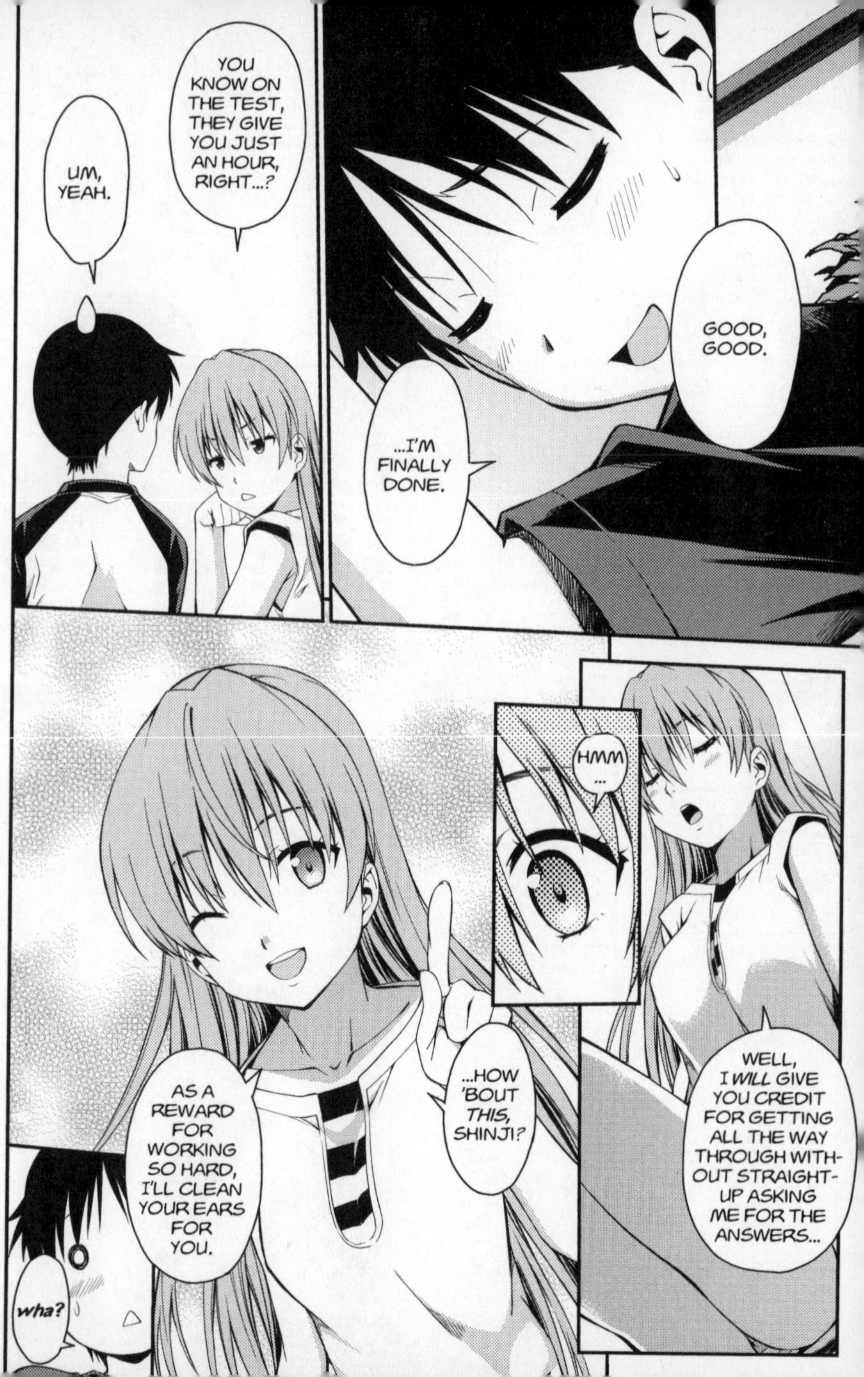
GOOD, GOOD.
...I'M FINALLY DONE.
YOU KNOW ON THE TEST, THEY GIVE YOU JUST AN HOUR, RIGHT...?
UM, YEAH.
HMM...
WELL, I *WILL* GIVE YOU CREDIT FOR GETTING ALL THE WAY THROUGH WITH-OUT STRAIGHT-UP ASKING ME FOR THE ANSWERS...
...HOW 'BOUT *THIS*, SHINJI?
AS A REWARD FOR WORKING SO HARD, I'LL CLEAN YOUR EARS FOR YOU.
wha?

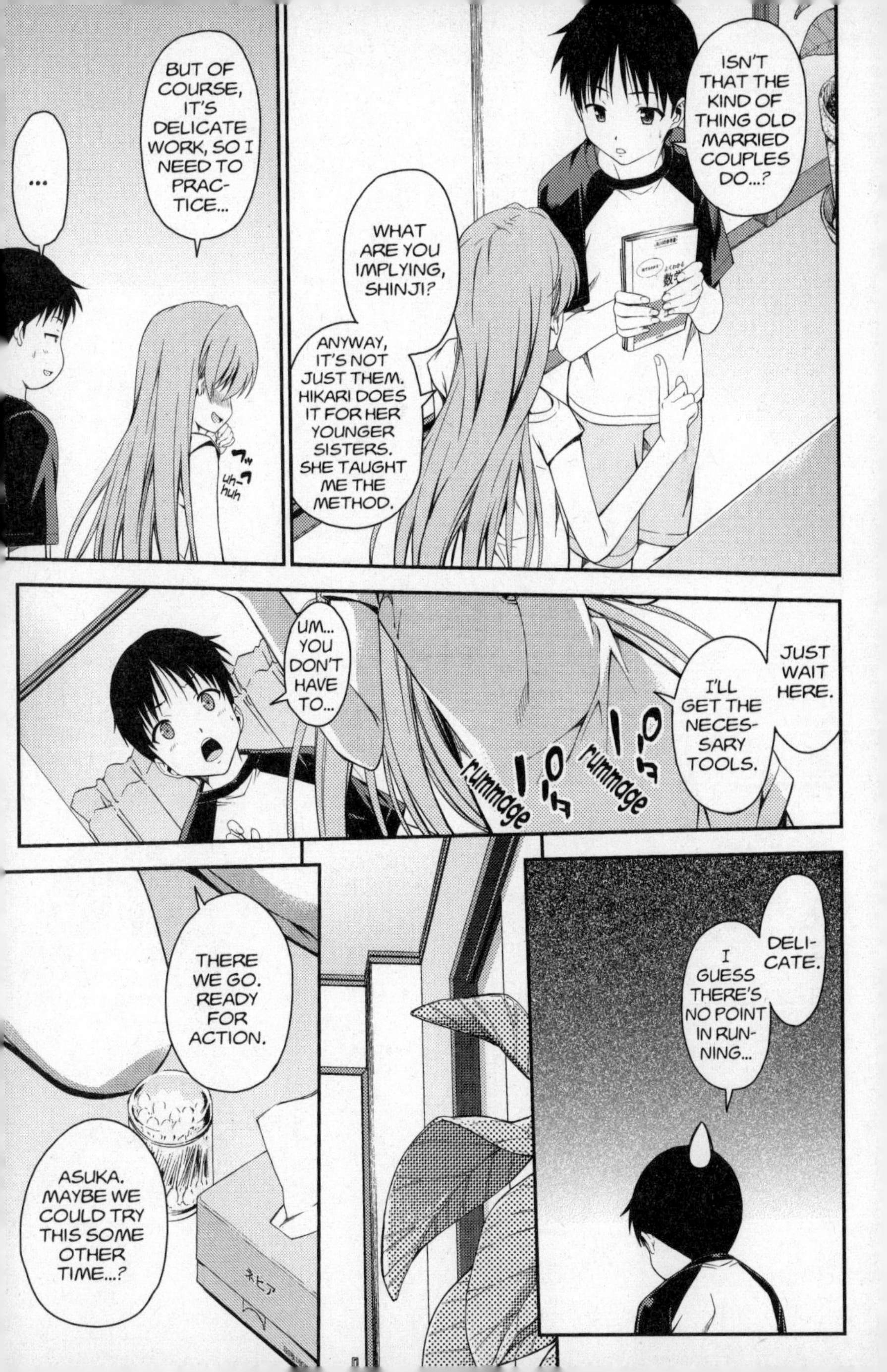
ISN'T THAT THE KIND OF THING OLD MARRIED COUPLES DO...?
WHAT ARE YOU IMPLYING, SHINJI?
ANYWAY, IT'S NOT JUST THEM. HIKARI DOES IT FOR HER YOUNGER SISTERS. SHE TAUGHT ME THE METHOD.
BUT OF COURSE, IT'S DELICATE WORK, SO I NEED TO PRACTICE...
...
uh-huh
JUST WAIT HERE.
I'LL GET THE NECESSARY TOOLS.
rummage
rummage
UM... YOU DON'T HAVE TO...
DELICATE.
I GUESS THERE'S NO POINT IN RUNNING...
THERE WE GO. READY FOR ACTION.
ASUKA. MAYBE WE COULD TRY THIS SOME OTHER TIME...?

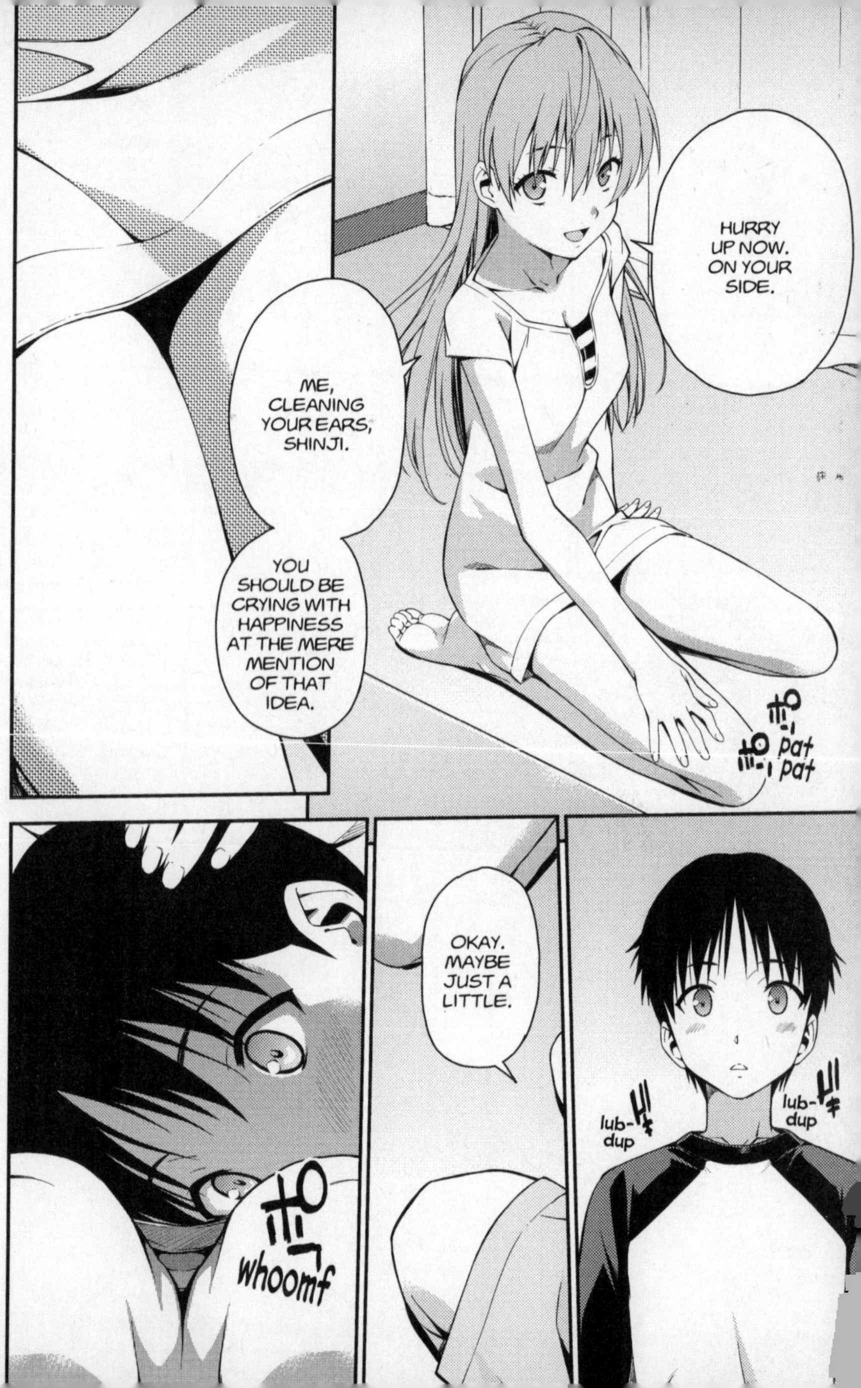
HURRY UP NOW. ON YOUR SIDE.
ME, CLEANING YOUR EARS, SHINJI.
YOU SHOULD BE CRYING WITH HAPPINESS AT THE MERE MENTION OF THAT IDEA.
pat pat
lub-dup
lub-dup
OKAY. MAYBE JUST A LITTLE.
whoomf

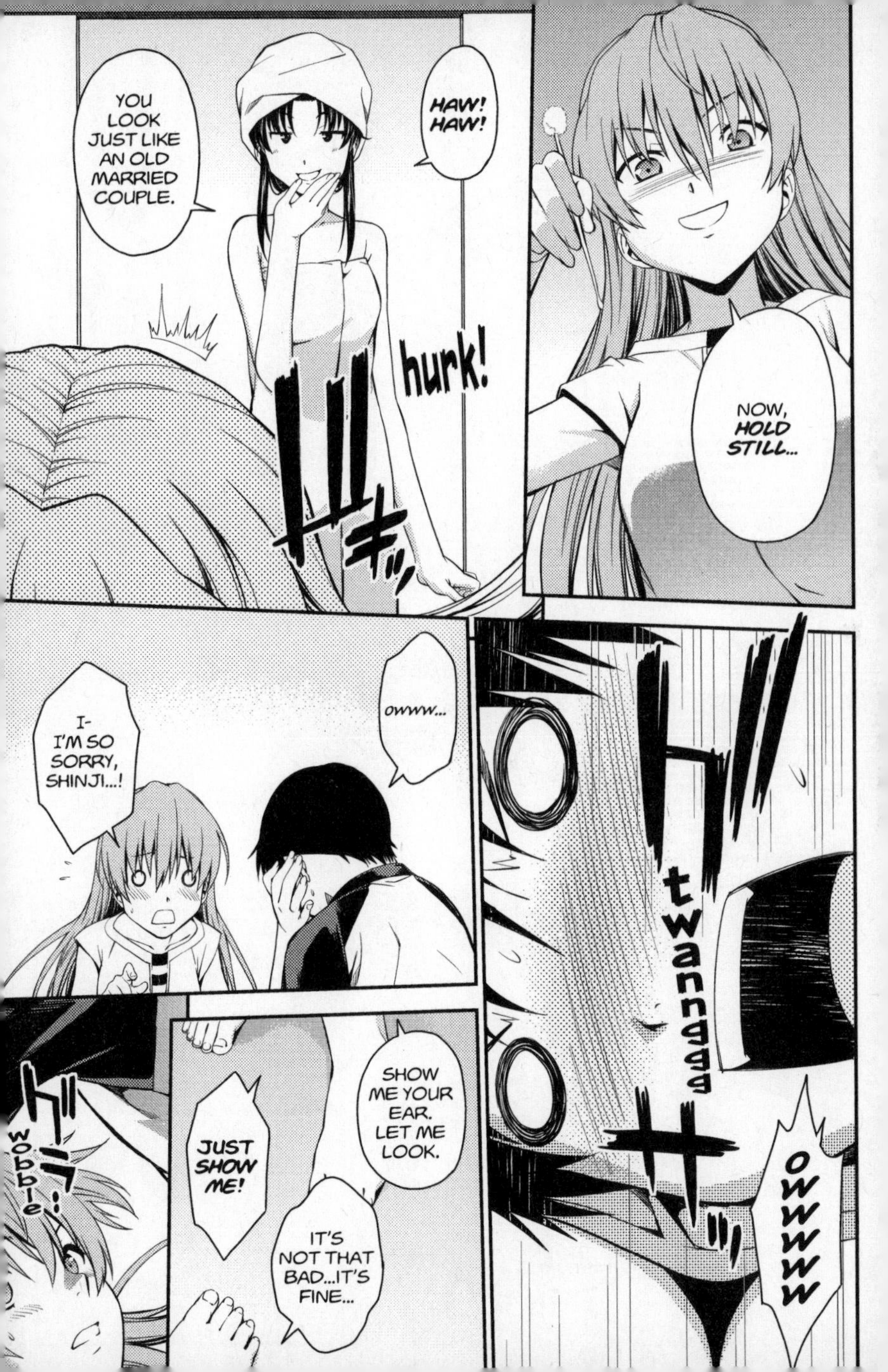
NOW, HOLD STILL...
HAW! HAW!
YOU LOOK JUST LIKE AN OLD MARRIED COUPLE.
hurk!
twannggg
OWWWWW
owww...
I- I'M SO SORRY, SHINJI...!
SHOW ME YOUR EAR. LET ME LOOK.
JUST SHOW ME!
IT'S NOT THAT BAD...IT'S FINE...
wobble

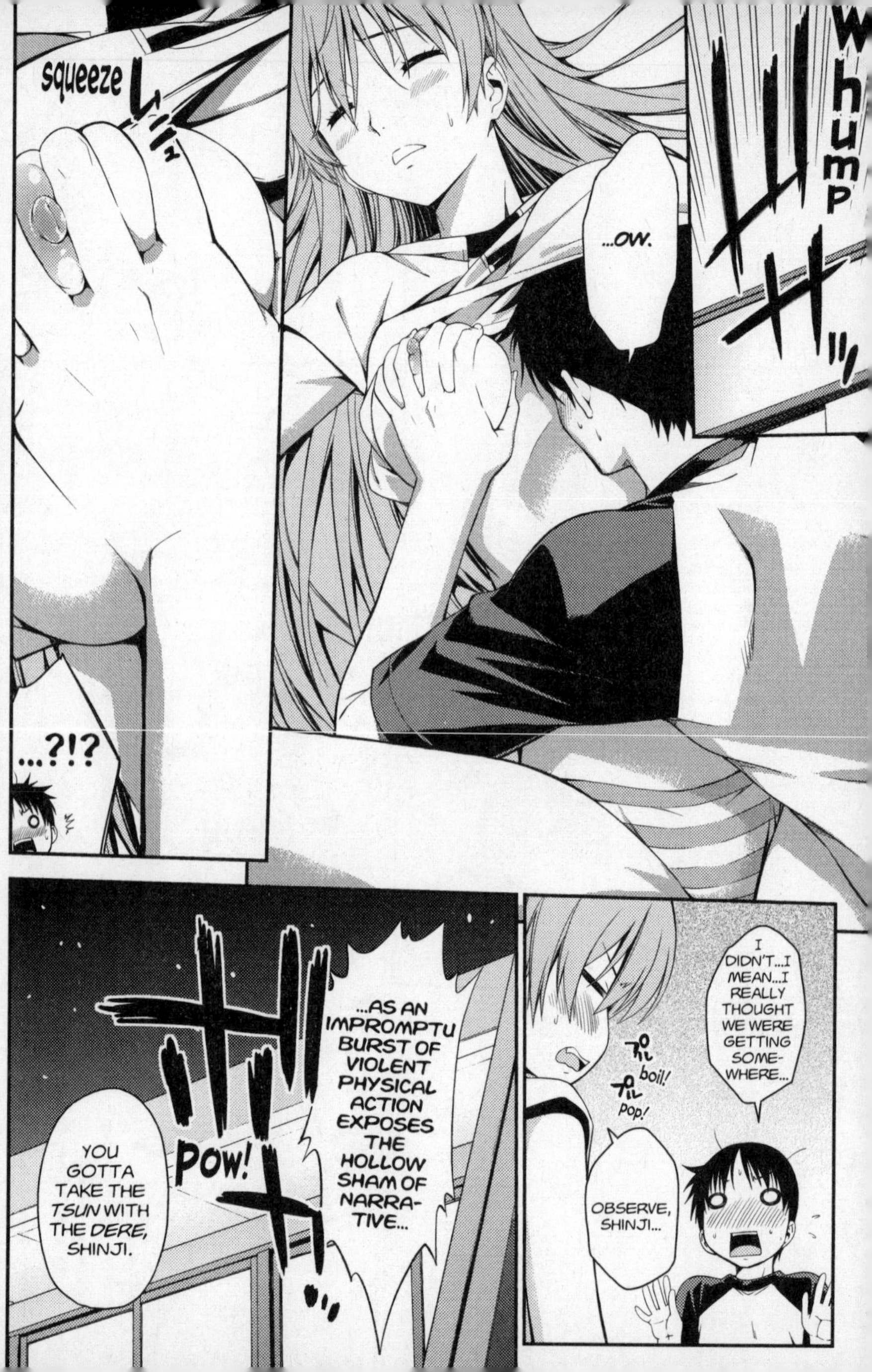

WHUMP
...OW.
squeeze
...?!?
I DIDN'T...I MEAN...I REALLY THOUGHT WE WERE GETTING SOME-WHERE...
boil!
pop!
OBSERVE, SHINJI...
...AS AN IMPROMPTU BURST OF VIOLENT PHYSICAL ACTION EXPOSES THE HOLLOW SHAM OF NARRA-TIVE...
POW!
YOU GOTTA TAKE THE *TSUN* WITH THE *DERE*, SHINJI.

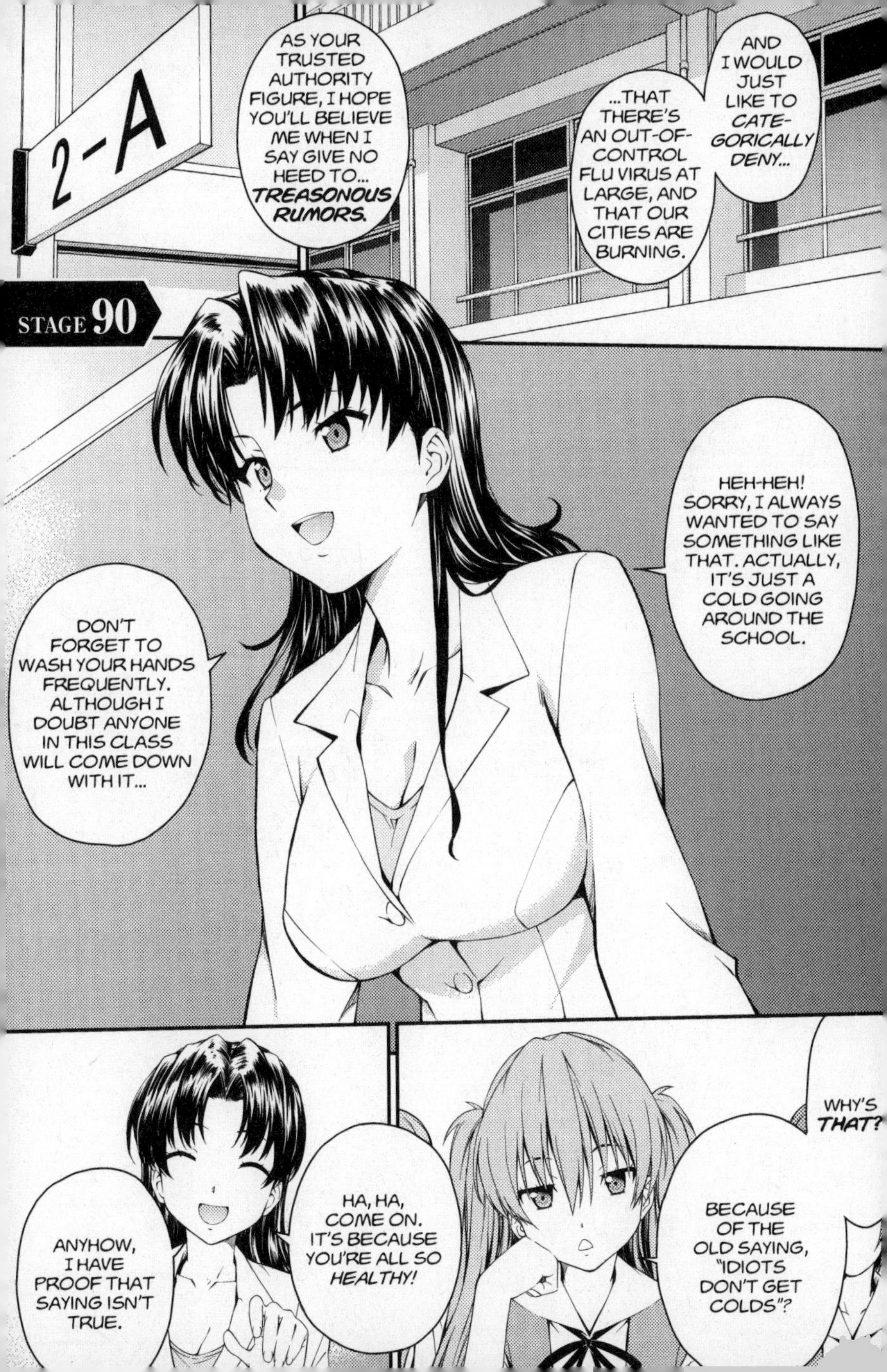
2-A
STAGE 90
AND I WOULD JUST LIKE TO *CATEGORICALLY DENY*...
...THAT THERE'S AN OUT-OF-CONTROL FLU VIRUS AT LARGE, AND THAT OUR CITIES ARE BURNING.
AS YOUR TRUSTED AUTHORITY FIGURE, I HOPE YOU'LL BELIEVE ME WHEN I SAY GIVE NO HEED TO... ***TREASONOUS RUMORS.***
HEH-HEH! SORRY, I ALWAYS WANTED TO SAY SOMETHING LIKE THAT. ACTUALLY, IT'S JUST A COLD GOING AROUND THE SCHOOL.
DON'T FORGET TO WASH YOUR HANDS FREQUENTLY. ALTHOUGH I DOUBT ANYONE IN THIS CLASS WILL COME DOWN WITH IT...
WHY'S ***THAT?***
BECAUSE OF THE OLD SAYING, "IDIOTS DON'T GET COLDS"?
HA, HA, COME ON. IT'S BECAUSE YOU'RE ALL SO *HEALTHY!*
ANYHOW, I HAVE PROOF THAT SAYING ISN'T TRUE.

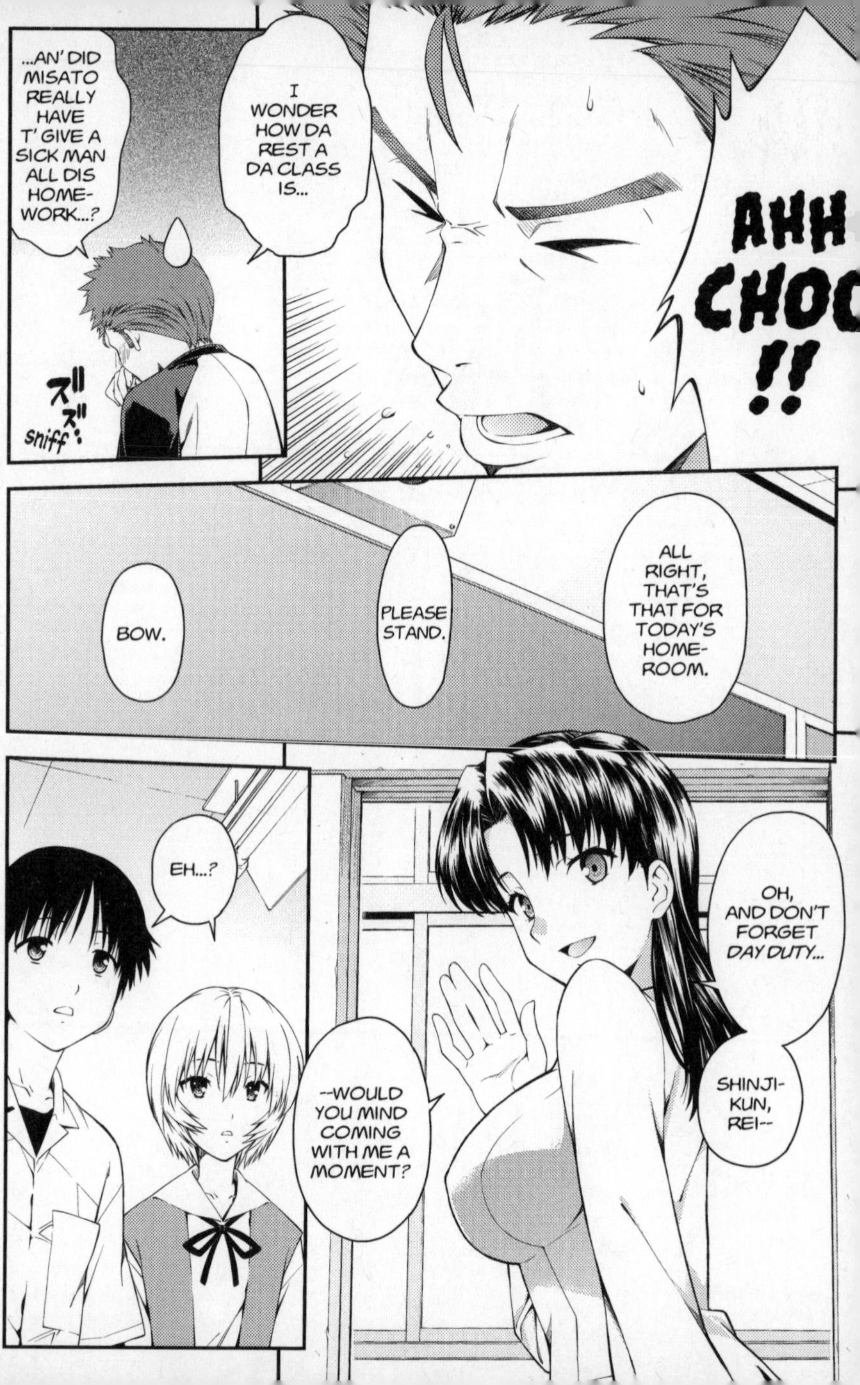
I WONDER HOW DA REST A DA CLASS IS...
AHH CHOO!!
...AN' DID MISATO REALLY HAVE T' GIVE A SICK MAN ALL DIS HOMEWORK...?
ズズ
sniff
ALL RIGHT, THAT'S THAT FOR TODAY'S HOMEROOM.
PLEASE STAND.
BOW.
OH, AND DON'T FORGET DAY DUTY...
SHINJI-KUN, REI--
--WOULD YOU MIND COMING WITH ME A MOMENT?
EH...?

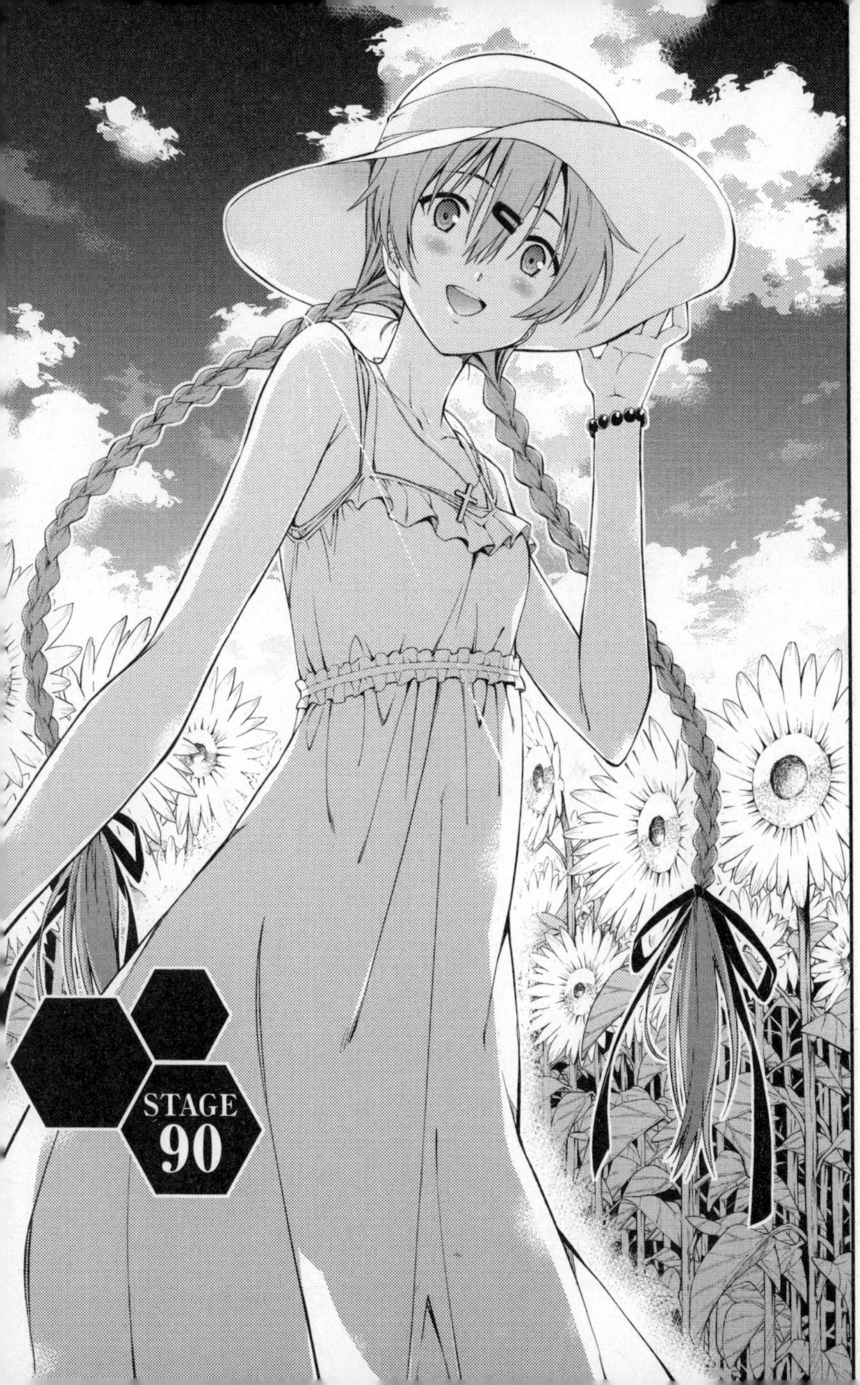
STAGE
90

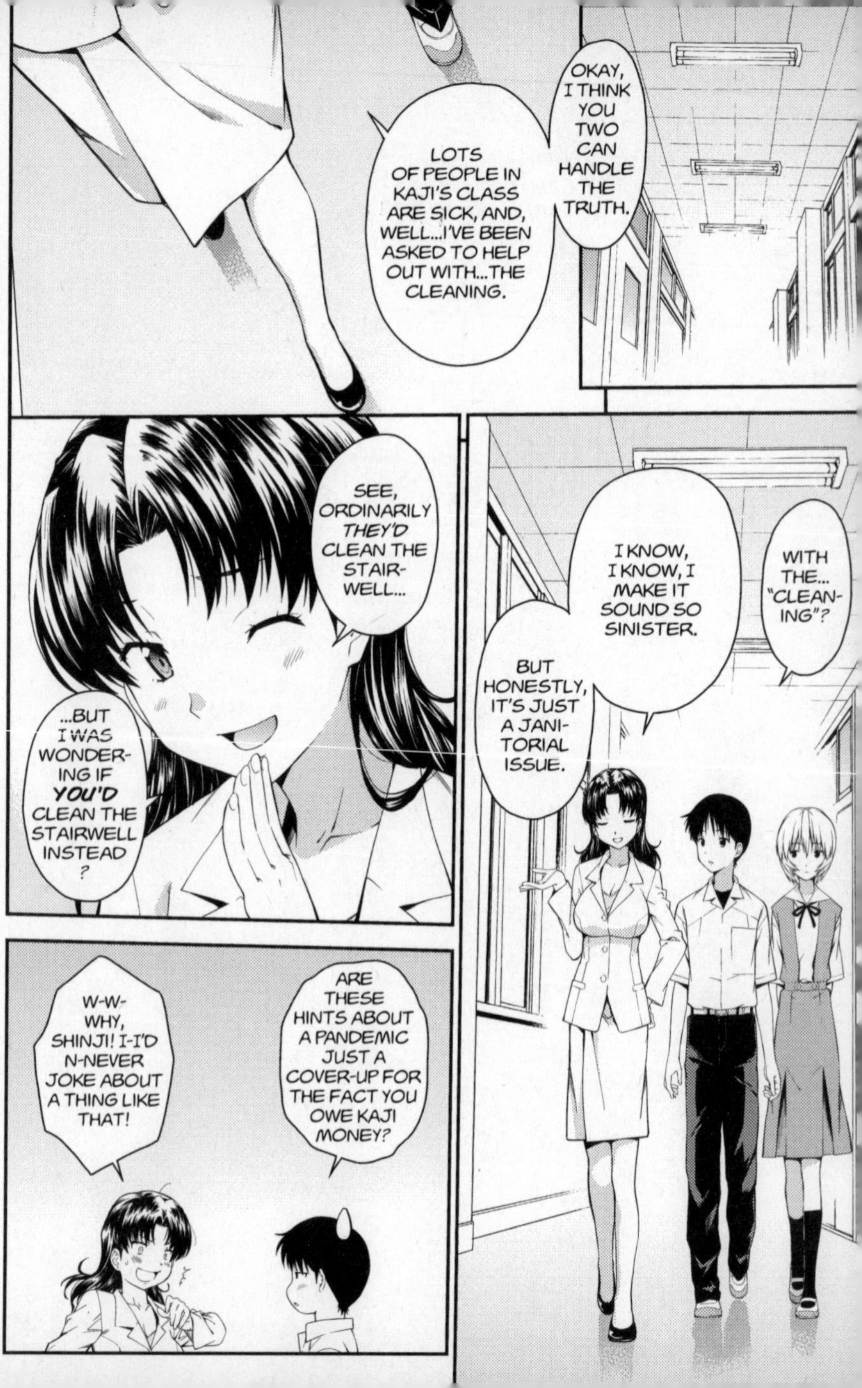
OKAY, I THINK YOU TWO CAN HANDLE THE TRUTH.
LOTS OF PEOPLE IN KAJI'S CLASS ARE SICK, AND, WELL...I'VE BEEN ASKED TO HELP OUT WITH...THE CLEANING.
WITH THE... "CLEANING"?
I KNOW, I KNOW, I MAKE IT SOUND SO SINISTER.
BUT HONESTLY, IT'S JUST A JANITORIAL ISSUE.
SEE, ORDINARILY *THEY'D* CLEAN THE STAIRWELL...
...BUT I WAS WONDERING IF ***YOU'D*** CLEAN THE STAIRWELL INSTEAD?
ARE THESE HINTS ABOUT A PANDEMIC JUST A COVER-UP FOR THE FACT YOU OWE KAJI MONEY?
W-W-WHY, SHINJI! I-I'D N-NEVER JOKE ABOUT A THING LIKE THAT!

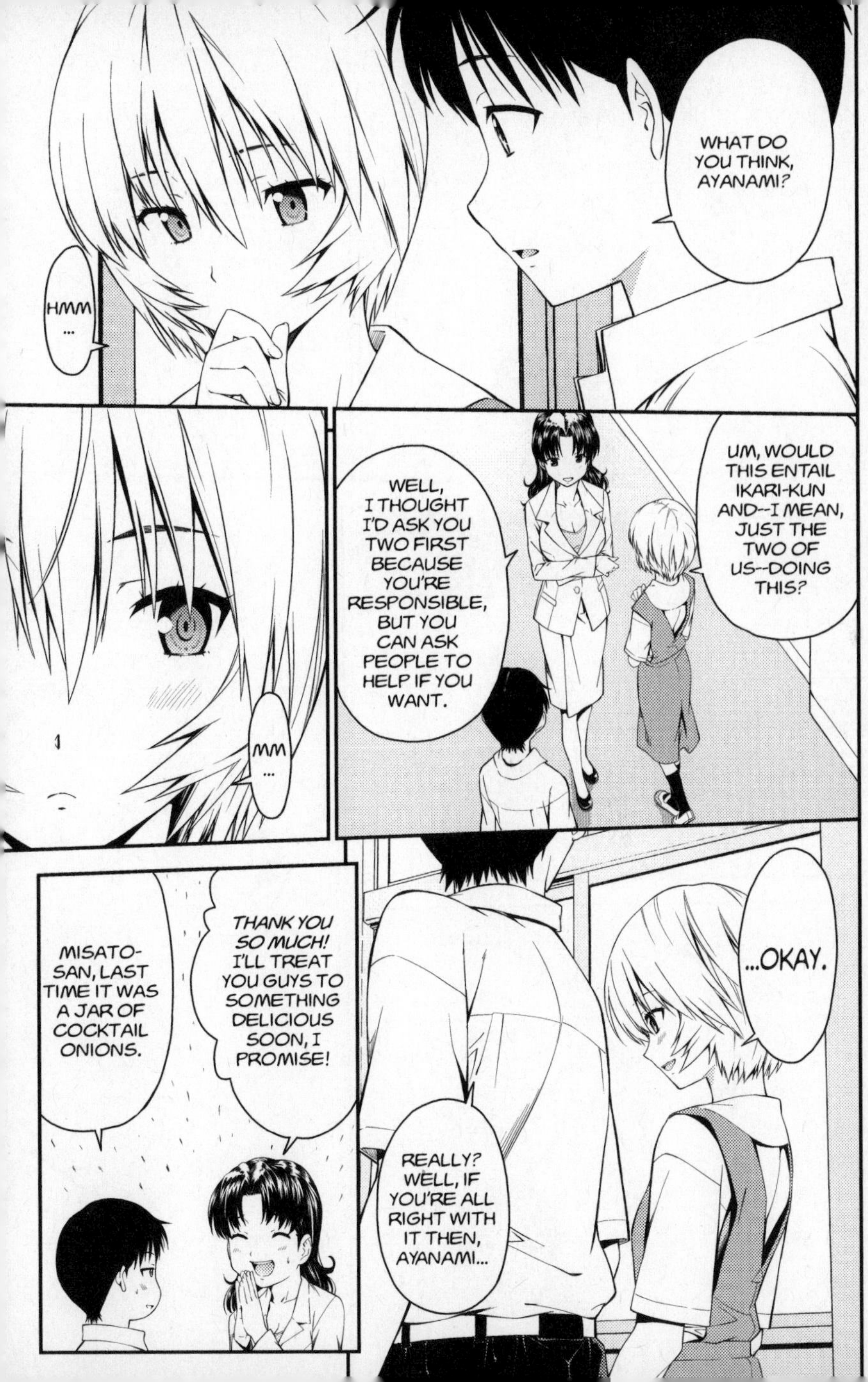
WHAT DO YOU THINK, AYANAMI?
HMM ...
UM, WOULD THIS ENTAIL IKARI-KUN AND--I MEAN, JUST THE TWO OF US--DOING THIS?
WELL, I THOUGHT I'D ASK YOU TWO FIRST BECAUSE YOU'RE RESPONSIBLE, BUT YOU CAN ASK PEOPLE TO HELP IF YOU WANT.
MM ...
...OKAY.
REALLY? WELL, IF YOU'RE ALL RIGHT WITH IT THEN, AYANAMI...
THANK YOU SO MUCH! I'LL TREAT YOU GUYS TO SOMETHING DELICIOUS SOON, I PROMISE!
MISATO-SAN, LAST TIME IT WAS A JAR OF COCKTAIL ONIONS.

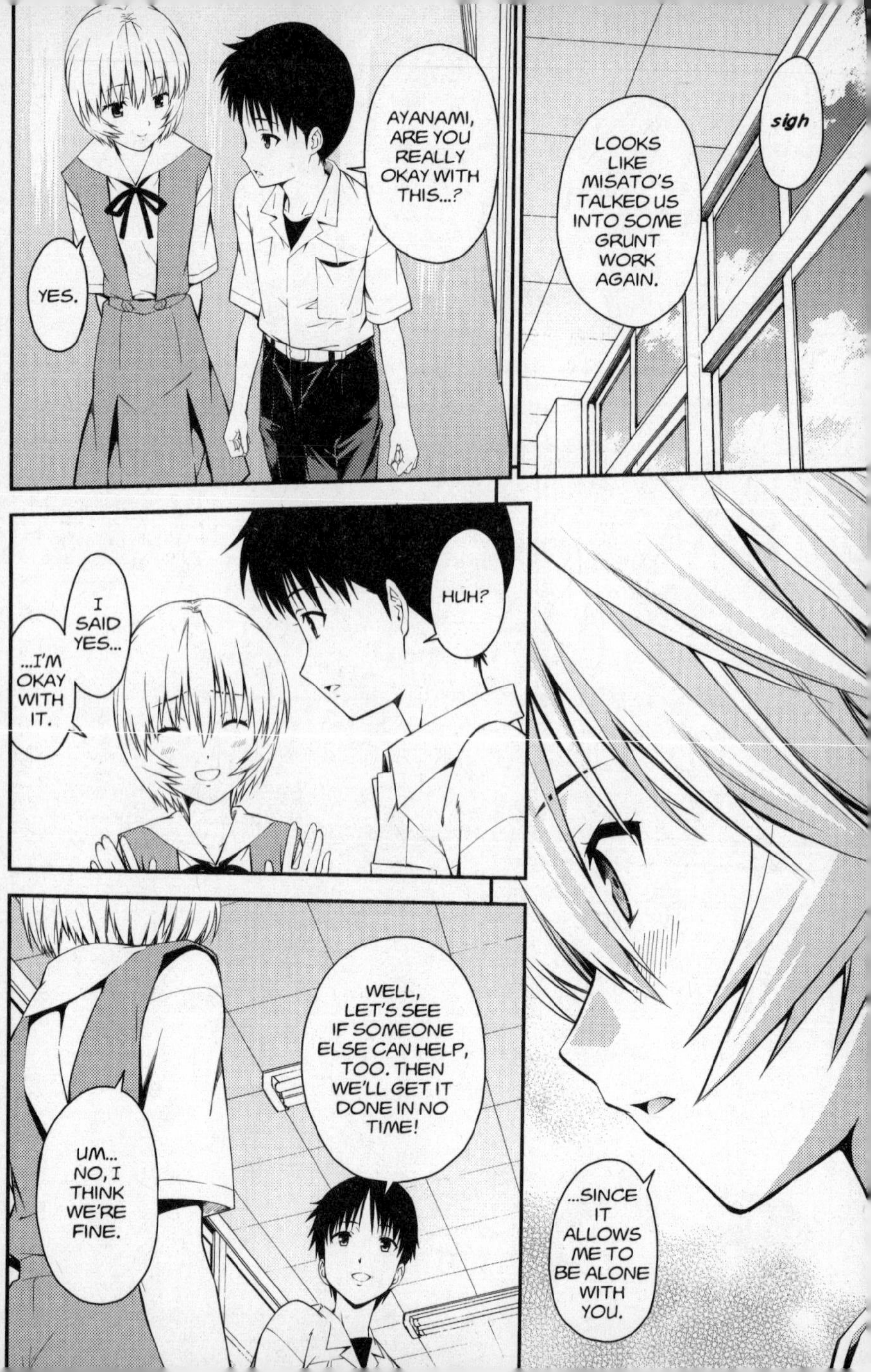
sigh
LOOKS LIKE MISATO'S TALKED US INTO SOME GRUNT WORK AGAIN.
AYANAMI, ARE YOU REALLY OKAY WITH THIS...?
YES.
...SINCE IT ALLOWS ME TO BE ALONE WITH YOU.
HUH?
I SAID YES...
...I'M OKAY WITH IT.
WELL, LET'S SEE IF SOMEONE ELSE CAN HELP, TOO. THEN WE'LL GET IT DONE IN NO TIME!
UM... NO, I THINK WE'RE FINE.

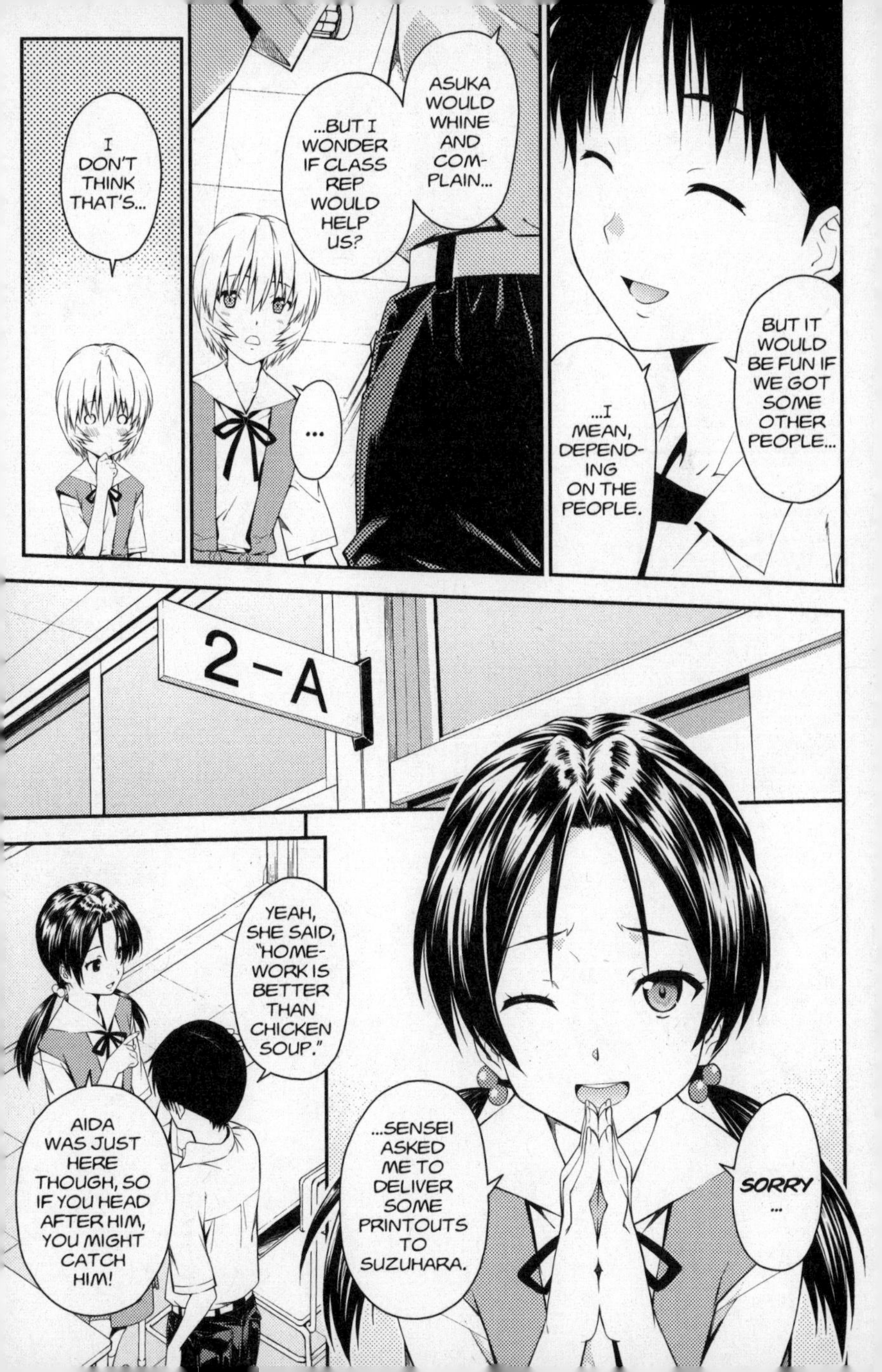

BUT IT WOULD BE FUN IF WE GOT SOME OTHER PEOPLE...
...I MEAN, DEPENDING ON THE PEOPLE.
ASUKA WOULD WHINE AND COM-PLAIN...
...BUT I WONDER IF CLASS REP WOULD HELP US?
...
I DON'T THINK THAT'S...
2-A
SORRY...
...SENSEI ASKED ME TO DELIVER SOME PRINTOUTS TO SUZUHARA.
YEAH, SHE SAID, "HOME-WORK IS BETTER THAN CHICKEN SOUP."
AIDA WAS JUST HERE THOUGH, SO IF YOU HEAD AFTER HIM, YOU MIGHT CATCH HIM!

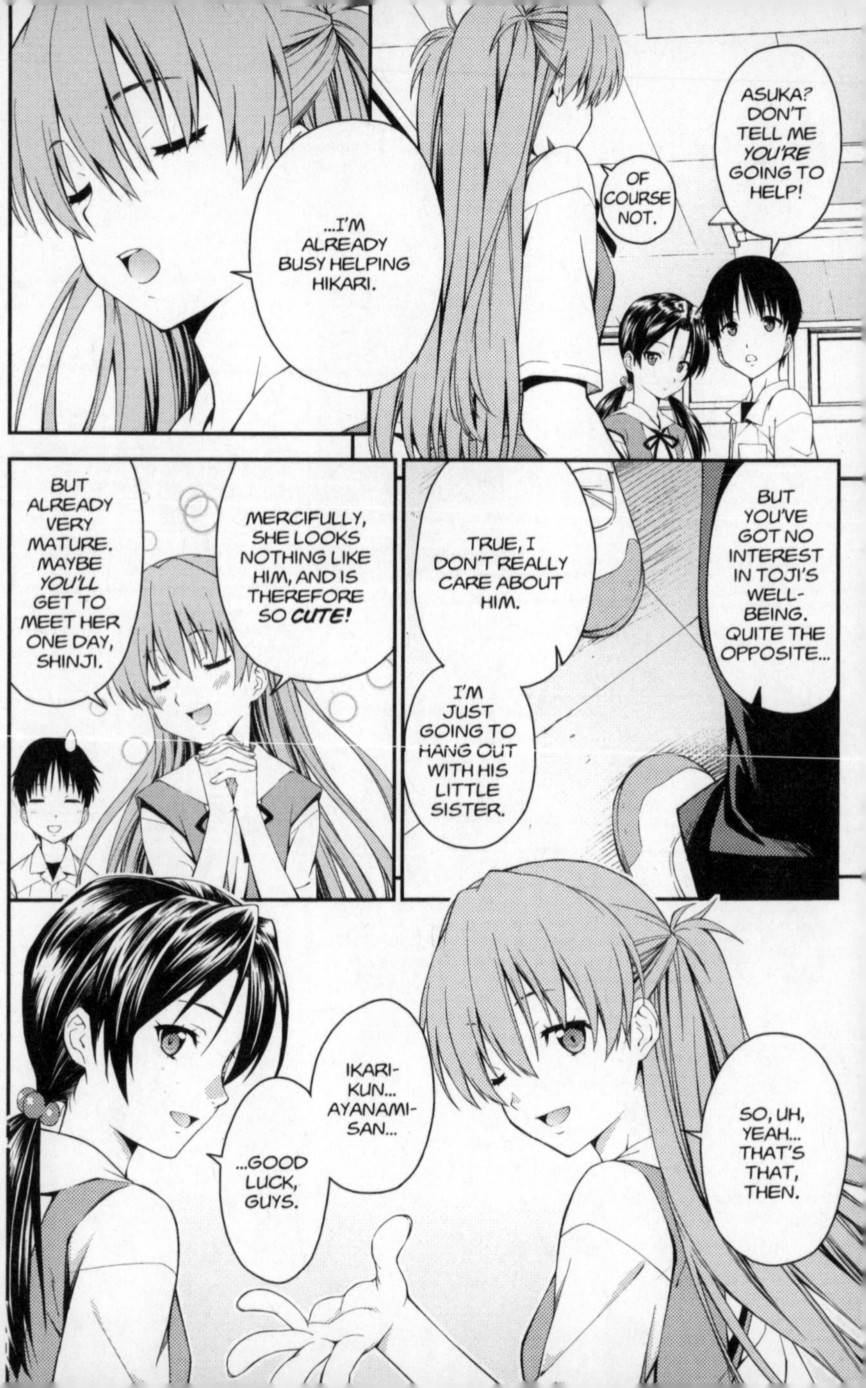
ASUKA? DON'T TELL ME *YOU'RE* GOING TO HELP!
OF COURSE NOT.
...I'M ALREADY BUSY HELPING HIKARI.
BUT YOU'VE GOT NO INTEREST IN TOJI'S WELL-BEING. QUITE THE OPPOSITE...
TRUE, I DON'T REALLY CARE ABOUT HIM.
I'M JUST GOING TO HANG OUT WITH HIS LITTLE SISTER.
MERCIFULLY, SHE LOOKS NOTHING LIKE HIM, AND IS THEREFORE SO ***CUTE!***
BUT ALREADY VERY MATURE. MAYBE *YOU'LL* GET TO MEET HER ONE DAY, SHINJI.
SO, UH, YEAH... THAT'S THAT, THEN.
IKARI-KUN... AYANAMI-SAN...
...GOOD LUCK, GUYS.

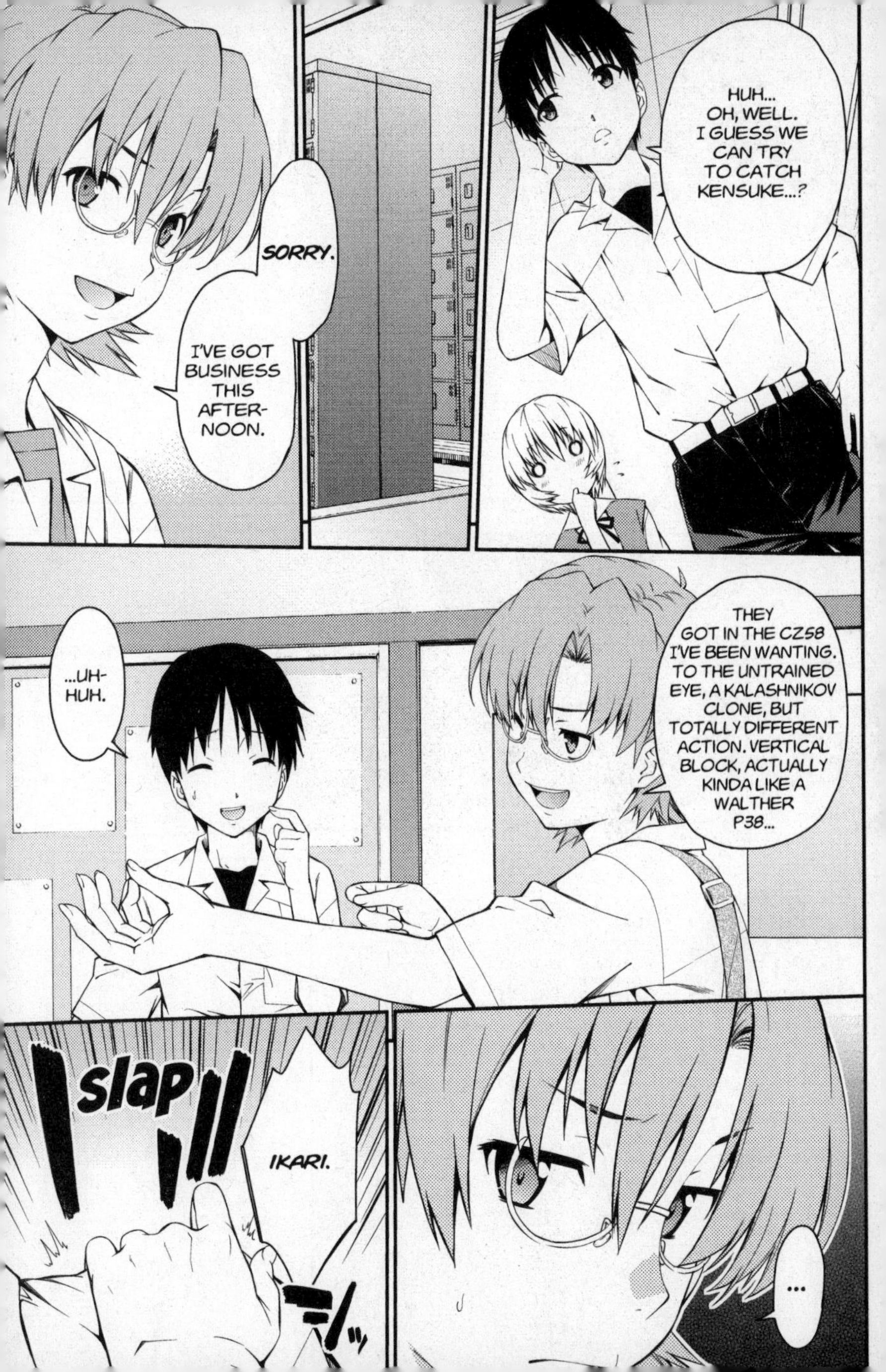
HUH...
OH, WELL.
I GUESS WE CAN TRY TO CATCH KENSUKE...?
SORRY.
I'VE GOT BUSINESS THIS AFTER-NOON.
THEY GOT IN THE CZ58 I'VE BEEN WANTING. TO THE UNTRAINED EYE, A KALASHNIKOV CLONE, BUT TOTALLY DIFFERENT ACTION. VERTICAL BLOCK, ACTUALLY KINDA LIKE A WALTHER P38...
...UH-HUH.
...
slap
IKARI.

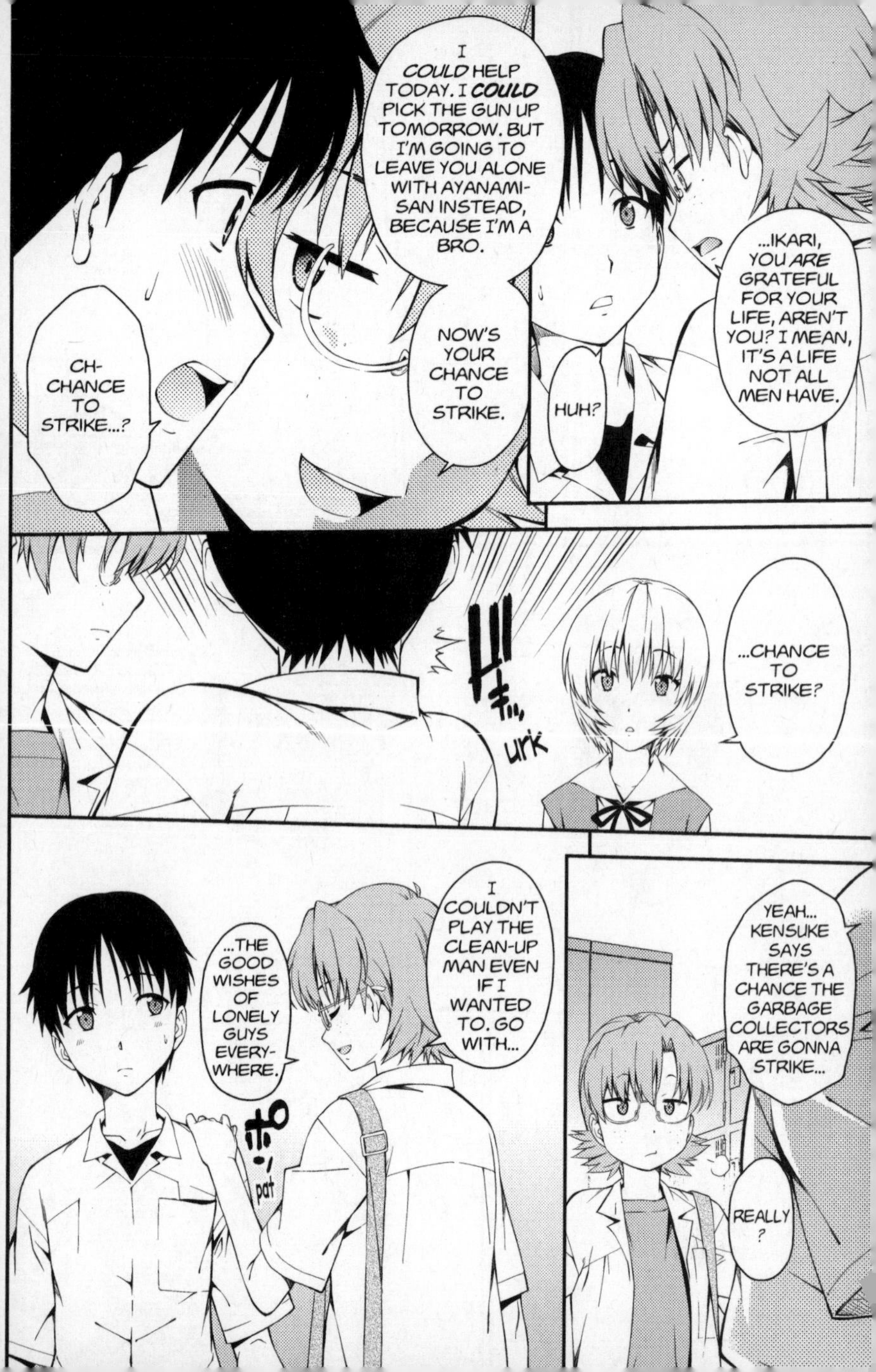
...IKARI, YOU *ARE* GRATEFUL FOR YOUR LIFE, AREN'T YOU? I MEAN, IT'S A LIFE NOT ALL MEN HAVE.
HUH?
I *COULD* HELP TODAY. I ***COULD*** PICK THE GUN UP TOMORROW. BUT I'M GOING TO LEAVE YOU ALONE WITH AYANAMI-SAN INSTEAD, BECAUSE I'M A BRO.
NOW'S YOUR CHANCE TO STRIKE.
CH-CHANCE TO STRIKE...?
...CHANCE TO STRIKE?
urk
YEAH... KENSUKE SAYS THERE'S A CHANCE THE GARBAGE COLLECTORS ARE GONNA STRIKE...
REALLY?
I COULDN'T PLAY THE CLEAN-UP MAN EVEN IF I WANTED TO. GO WITH...
...THE GOOD WISHES OF LONELY GUYS EVERY-WHERE.
pat

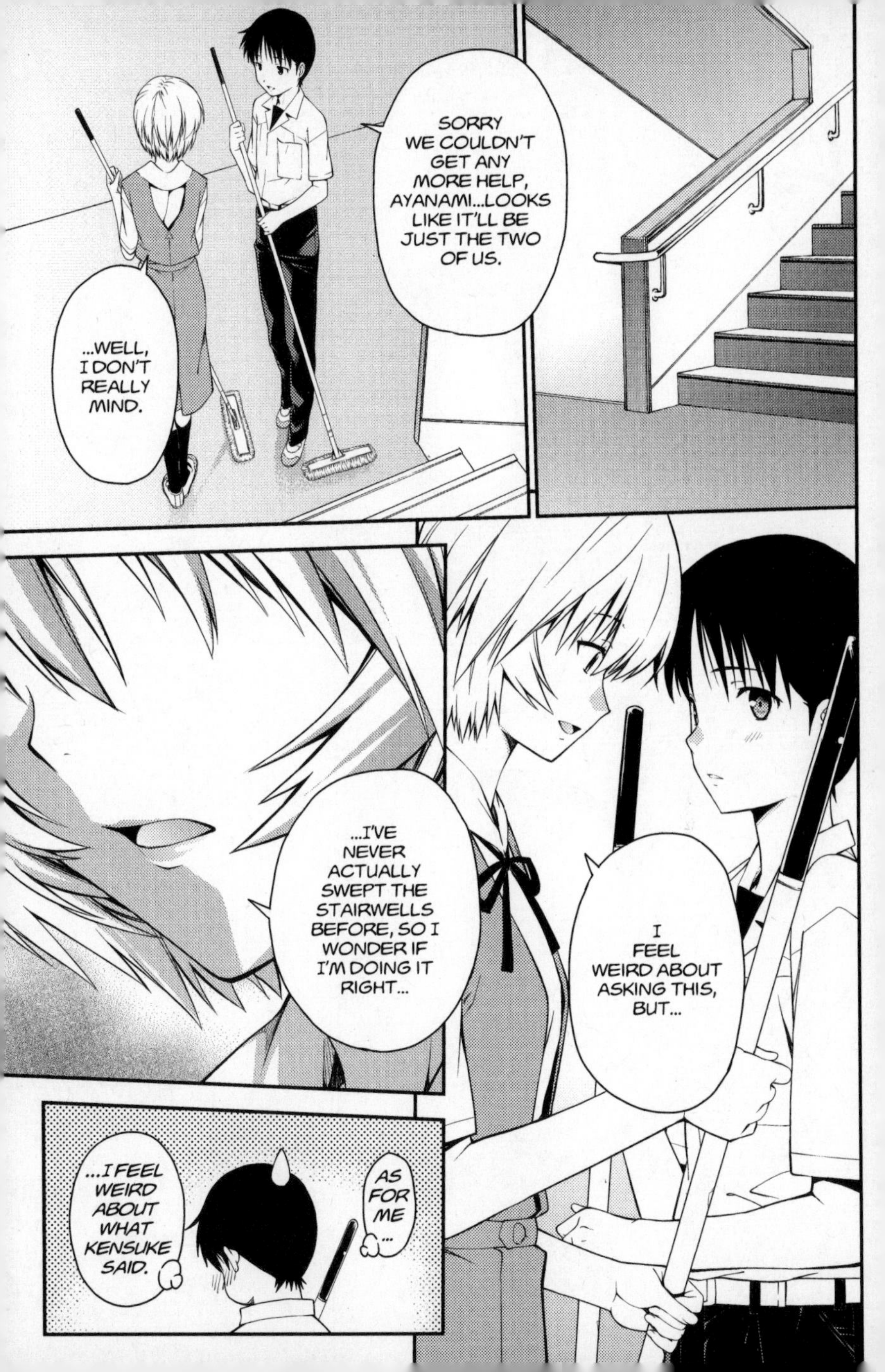
SORRY WE COULDN'T GET ANY MORE HELP, AYANAMI...LOOKS LIKE IT'LL BE JUST THE TWO OF US.
...WELL, I DON'T REALLY MIND.
I FEEL WEIRD ABOUT ASKING THIS, BUT...
...I'VE NEVER ACTUALLY SWEPT THE STAIRWELLS BEFORE, SO I WONDER IF I'M DOING IT RIGHT...
AS FOR ME...
...I FEEL WEIRD ABOUT WHAT KENSUKE SAID.

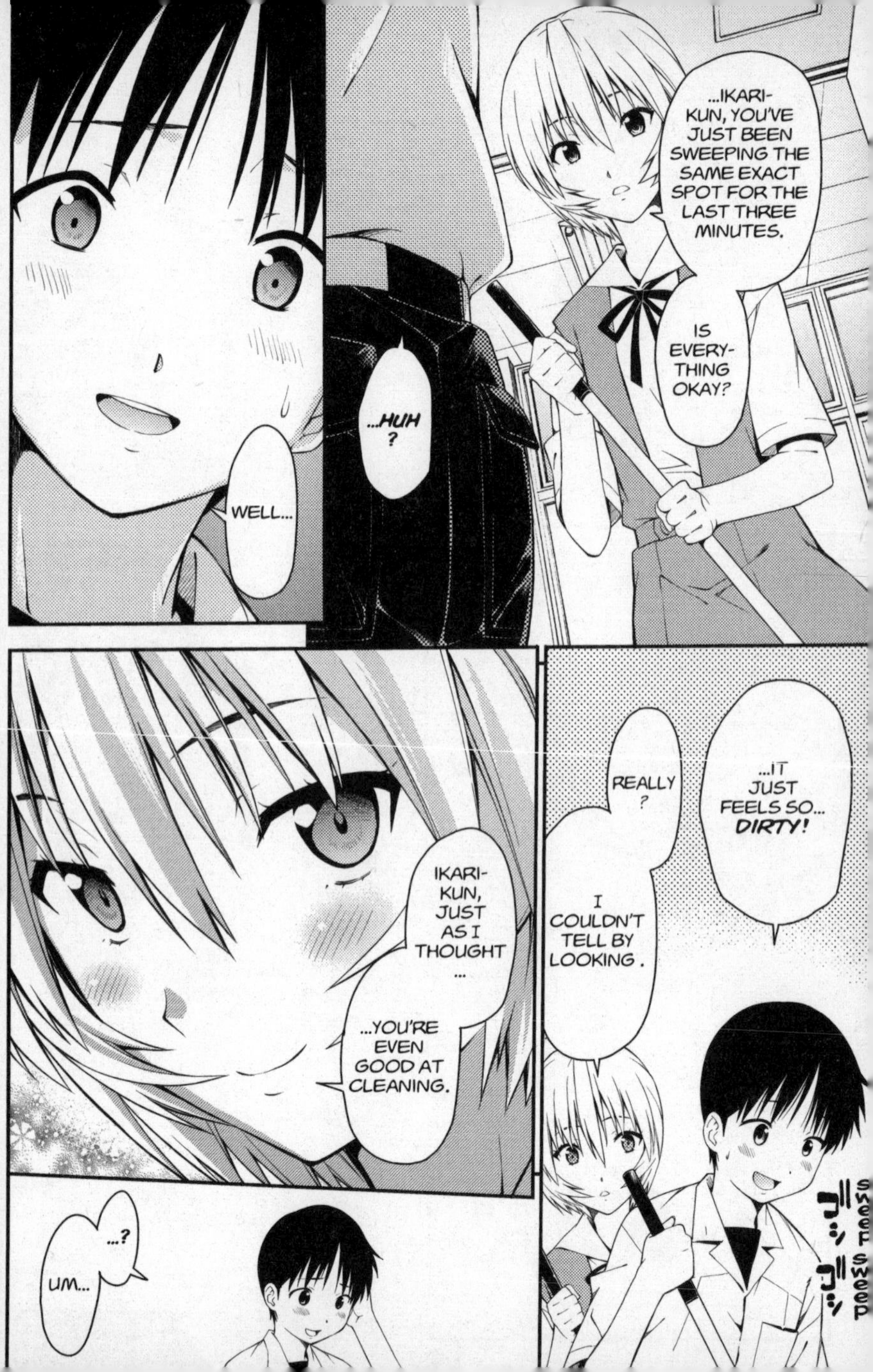
...IKARI-KUN, YOU'VE JUST BEEN SWEEPING THE SAME EXACT SPOT FOR THE LAST THREE MINUTES.
IS EVERYTHING OKAY?
...HUH?
WELL...
...IT JUST FEELS SO... DIRTY!
REALLY?
I COULDN'T TELL BY LOOKING.
SWEEP SWEEP
IKARI-KUN, JUST AS I THOUGHT...
...YOU'RE EVEN GOOD AT CLEANING.
...?
UM...

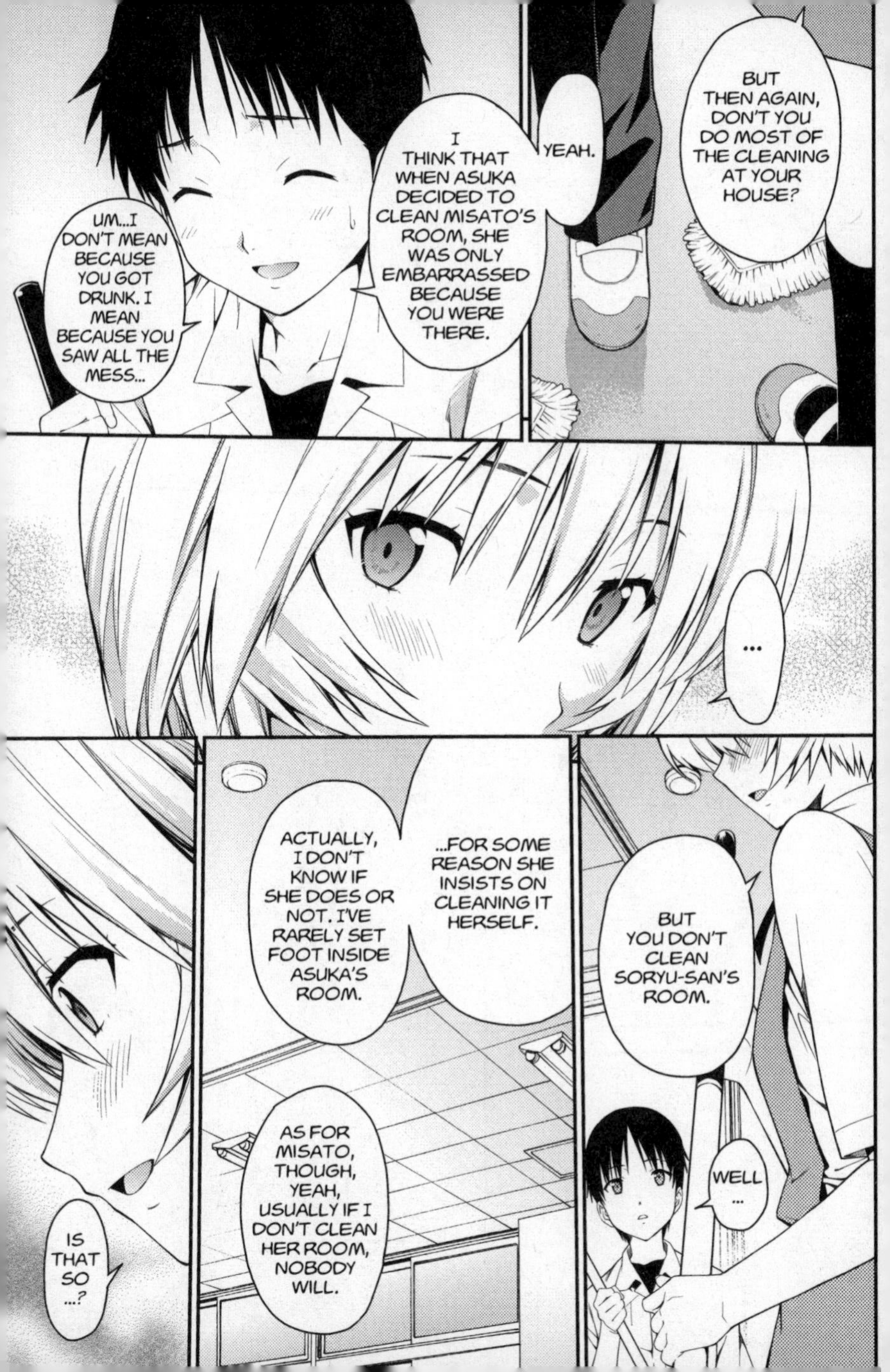
BUT THEN AGAIN, DON'T YOU DO MOST OF THE CLEANING AT YOUR HOUSE?
YEAH.
I THINK THAT WHEN ASUKA DECIDED TO CLEAN MISATO'S ROOM, SHE WAS ONLY EMBARRASSED BECAUSE YOU WERE THERE.
UM...I DON'T MEAN BECAUSE YOU GOT DRUNK. I MEAN BECAUSE YOU SAW ALL THE MESS...
...
BUT YOU DON'T CLEAN SORYU-SAN'S ROOM.
WELL ...
ACTUALLY, I DON'T KNOW IF SHE DOES OR NOT. I'VE RARELY SET FOOT INSIDE ASUKA'S ROOM.
...FOR SOME REASON SHE INSISTS ON CLEANING IT HERSELF.
AS FOR MISATO, THOUGH, YEAH, USUALLY IF I DON'T CLEAN HER ROOM, NOBODY WILL.
IS THAT SO ...?

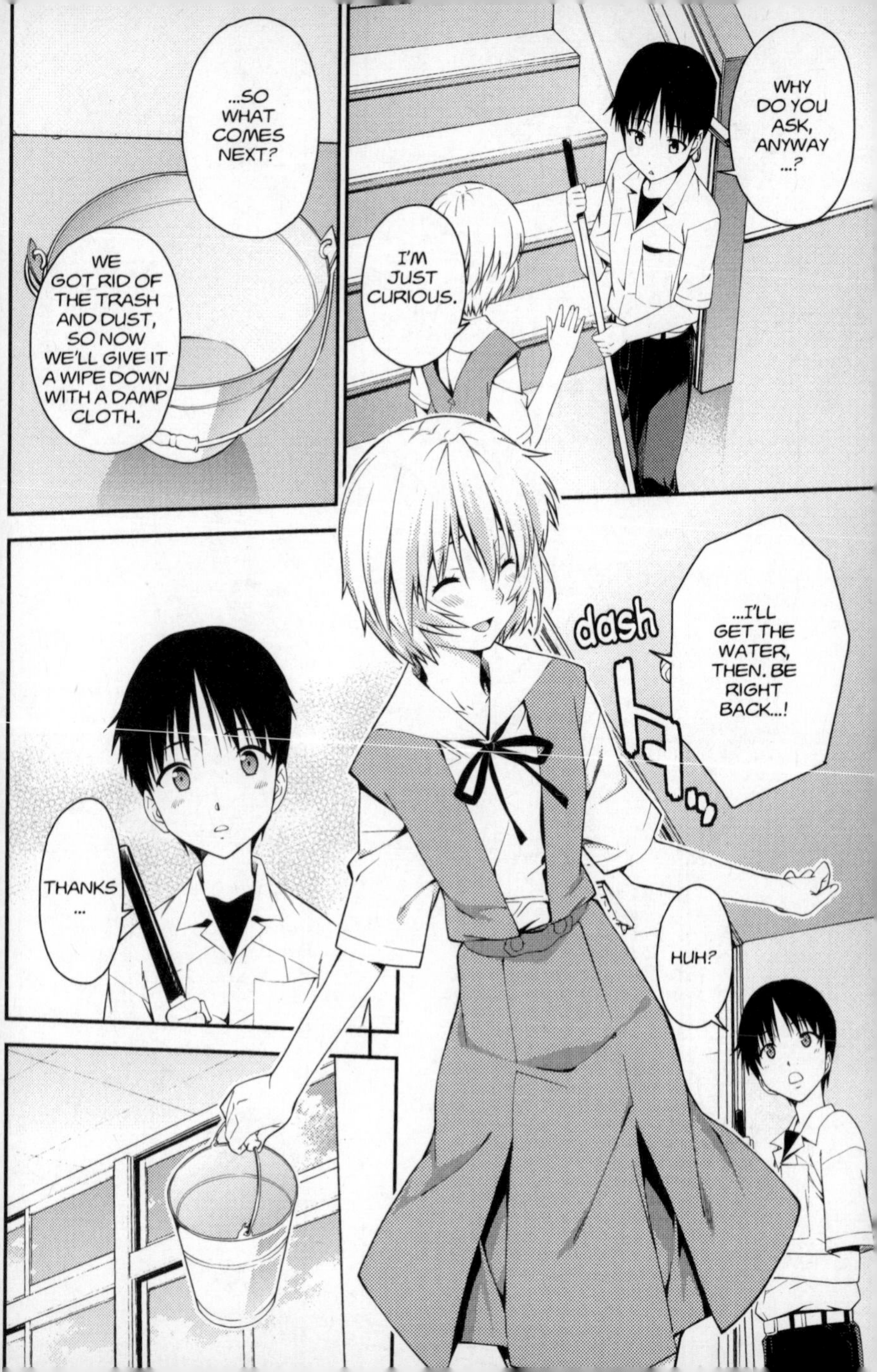
WHY DO YOU ASK, ANYWAY ...?
I'M JUST CURIOUS.
...SO WHAT COMES NEXT?
WE GOT RID OF THE TRASH AND DUST, SO NOW WE'LL GIVE IT A WIPE DOWN WITH A DAMP CLOTH.
...I'LL GET THE WATER, THEN. BE RIGHT BACK...!
dash
HUH?
THANKS ...

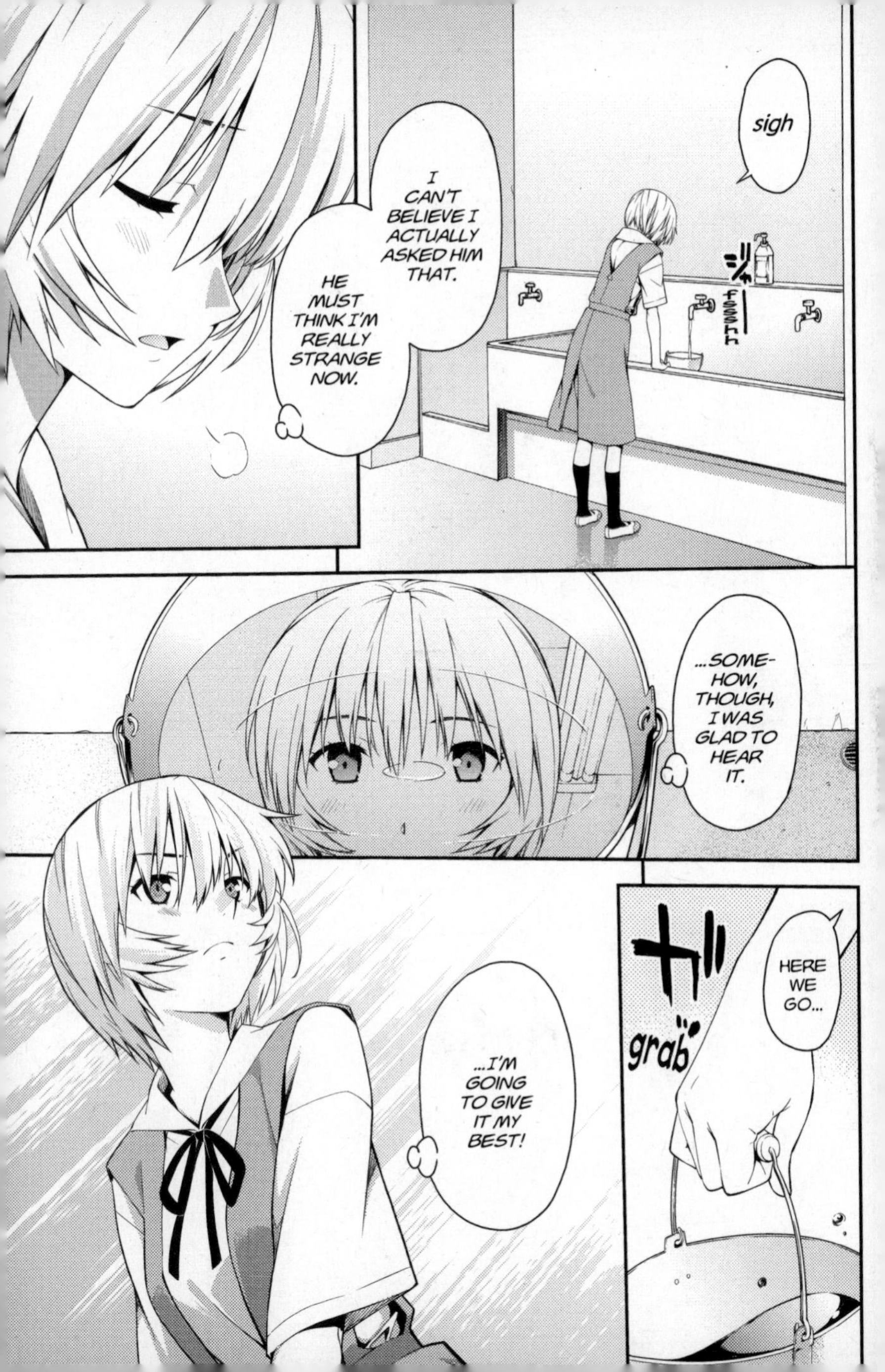
sigh
fsssh
I CAN'T BELIEVE I ACTUALLY ASKED HIM THAT.
HE MUST THINK I'M REALLY STRANGE NOW.
...SOMEHOW, THOUGH, I WAS GLAD TO HEAR IT.
HERE WE GO...
grab
...I'M GOING TO GIVE IT MY BEST!

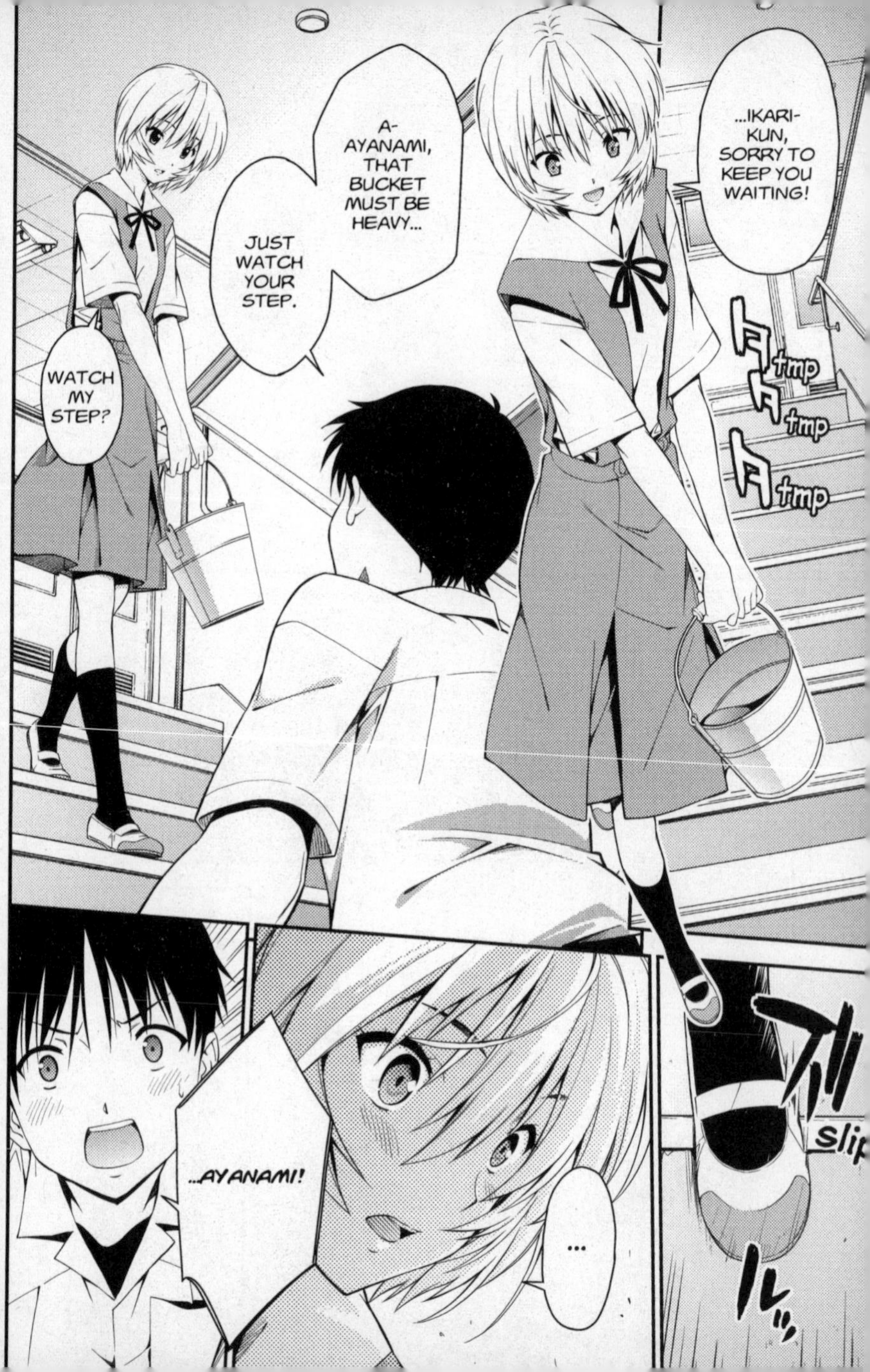
...IKARI-KUN, SORRY TO KEEP YOU WAITING!
tmp
tmp
tmp
A- AYANAMI, THAT BUCKET MUST BE HEAVY...
JUST WATCH YOUR STEP.
WATCH MY STEP?
Sli
...
...AYANAMI!

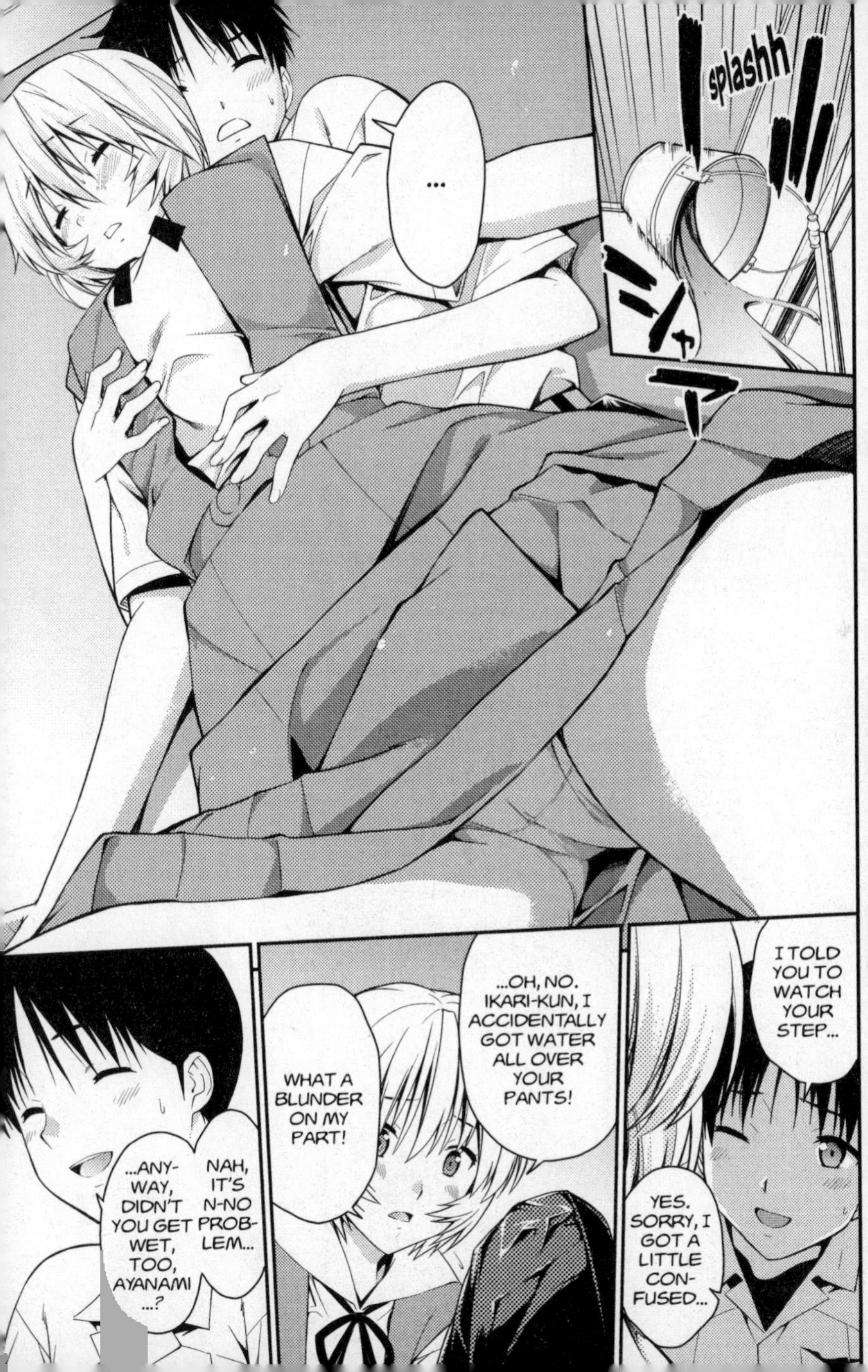
splashh
...
I TOLD YOU TO WATCH YOUR STEP...
YES. SORRY, I GOT A LITTLE CON-FUSED...
...OH, NO. IKARI-KUN, I ACCIDENTALLY GOT WATER ALL OVER YOUR PANTS!
WHAT A BLUNDER ON MY PART!
NAH, IT'S N-NO PROB-LEM...
...ANY-WAY, DIDN'T YOU GET WET, TOO, AYANAMI ...?

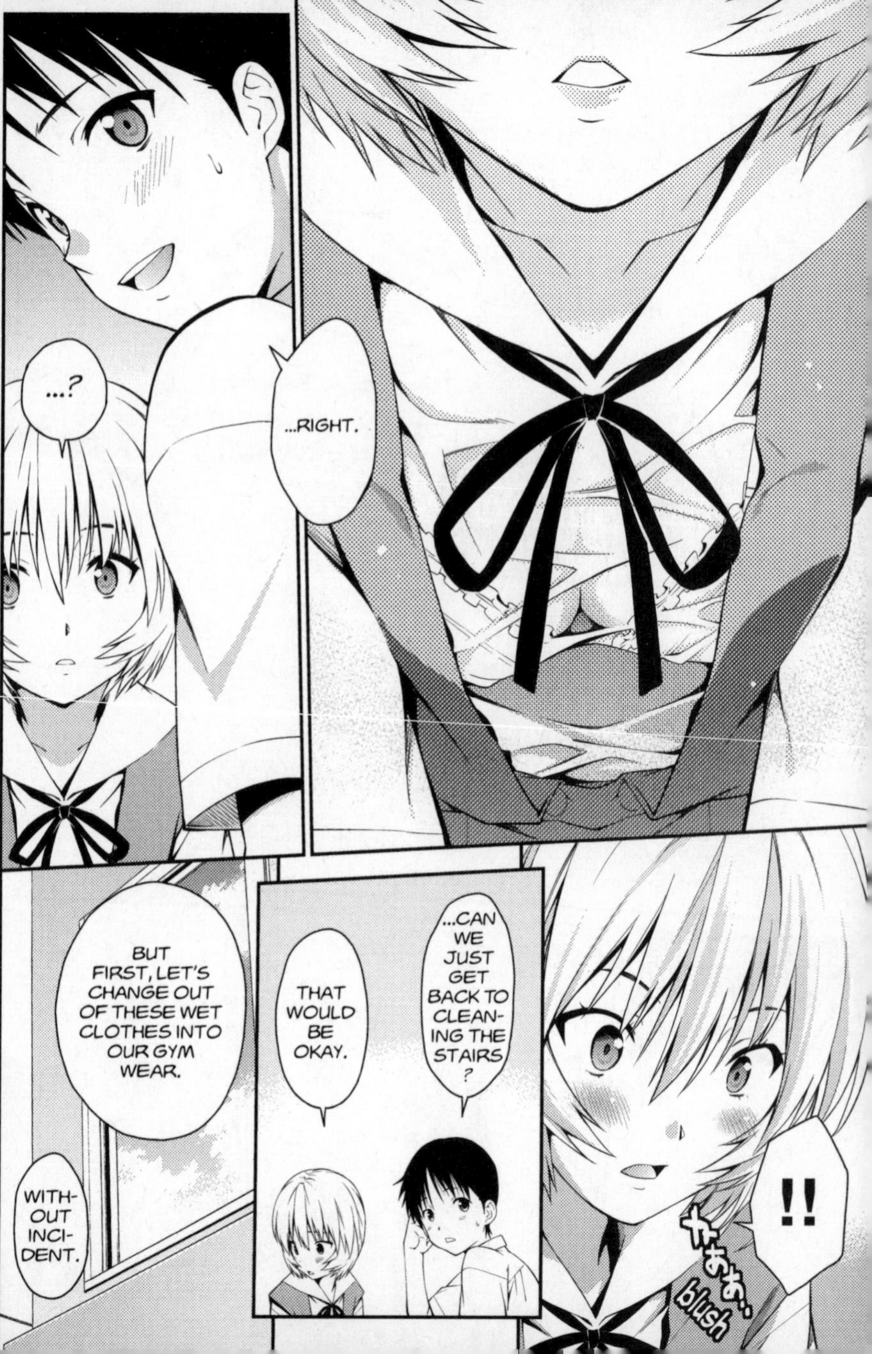
...RIGHT.
...?
!!
かぁぁ…
blush
...CAN WE JUST GET BACK TO CLEANING THE STAIRS?
THAT WOULD BE OKAY.
BUT FIRST, LET'S CHANGE OUT OF THESE WET CLOTHES INTO OUR GYM WEAR.
WITHOUT INCIDENT.

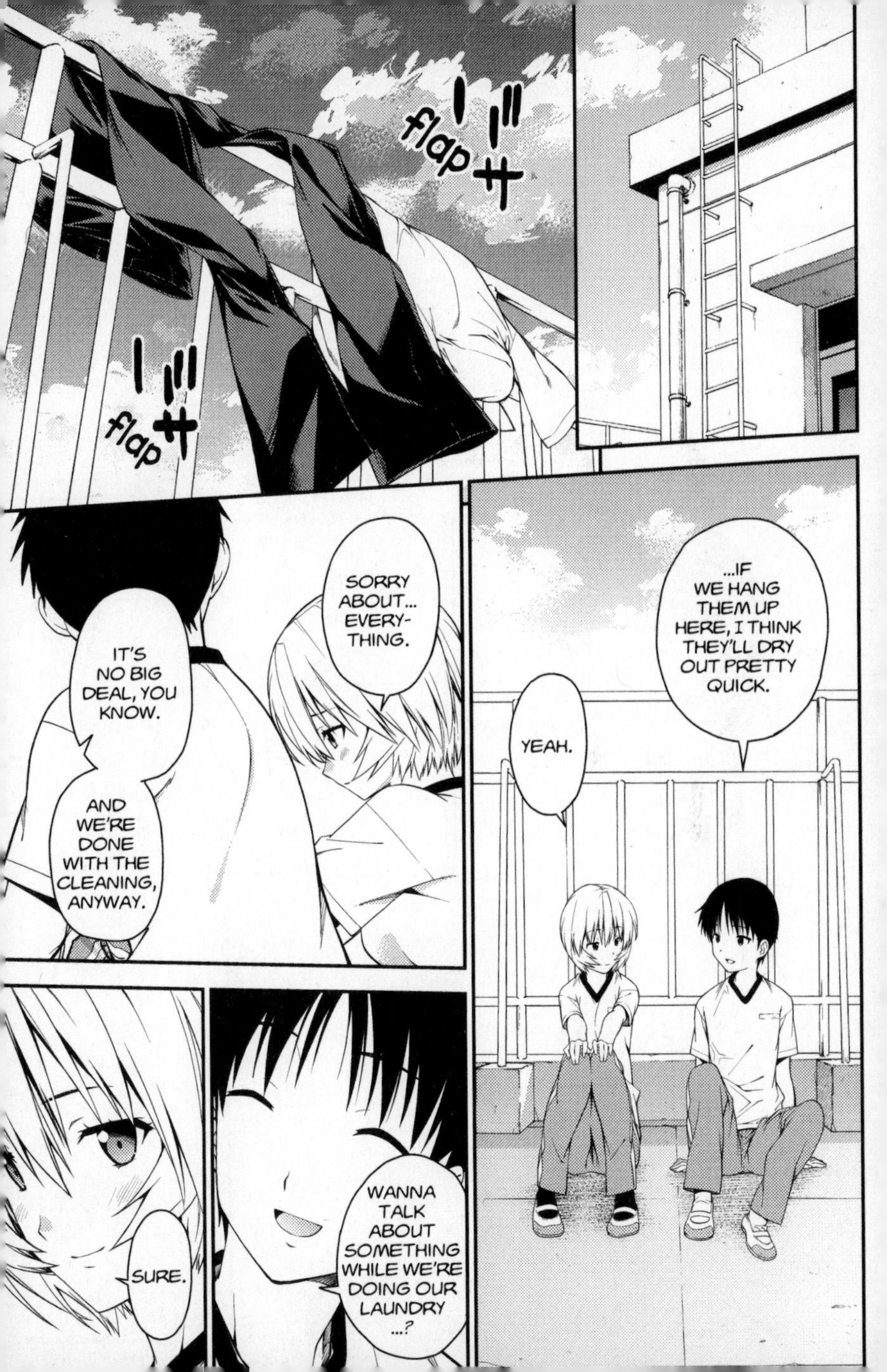
flap
flap
...IF WE HANG THEM UP HERE, I THINK THEY'LL DRY OUT PRETTY QUICK.
YEAH.
SORRY ABOUT... EVERY-THING.
IT'S NO BIG DEAL, YOU KNOW.
AND WE'RE DONE WITH THE CLEANING, ANYWAY.
WANNA TALK ABOUT SOMETHING WHILE WE'RE DOING OUR LAUNDRY ...?
SURE.

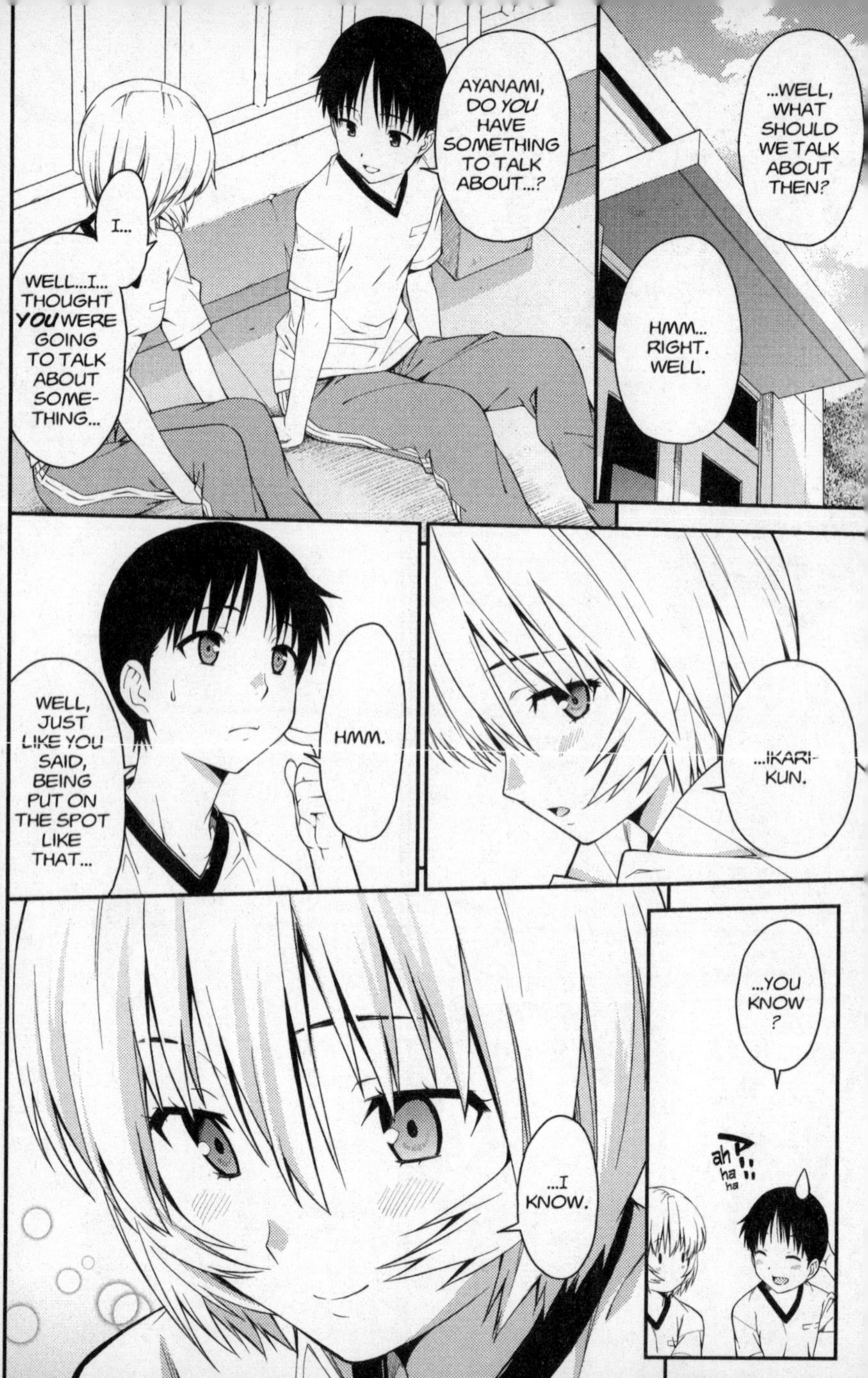
...WELL, WHAT SHOULD WE TALK ABOUT THEN?
HMM... RIGHT. WELL.
AYANAMI, DO YOU HAVE SOMETHING TO TALK ABOUT...?
I...
WELL...I... THOUGHT YOU WERE GOING TO TALK ABOUT SOME-THING...
...IKARI-KUN.
HMM.
WELL, JUST LIKE YOU SAID, BEING PUT ON THE SPOT LIKE THAT...
...YOU KNOW?
ah ha ha
...I KNOW.

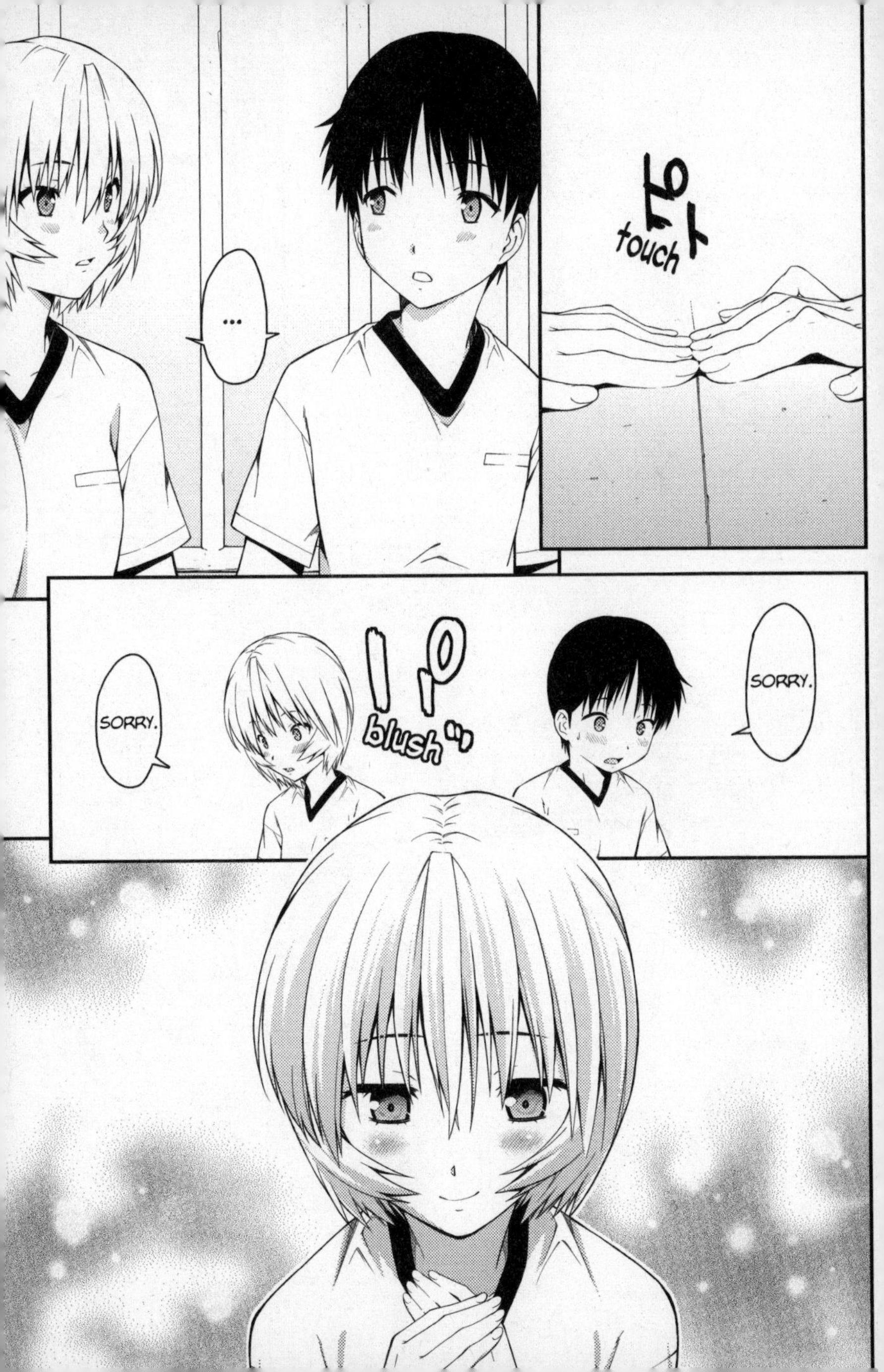
touch
...
SORRY.
blush
SORRY.

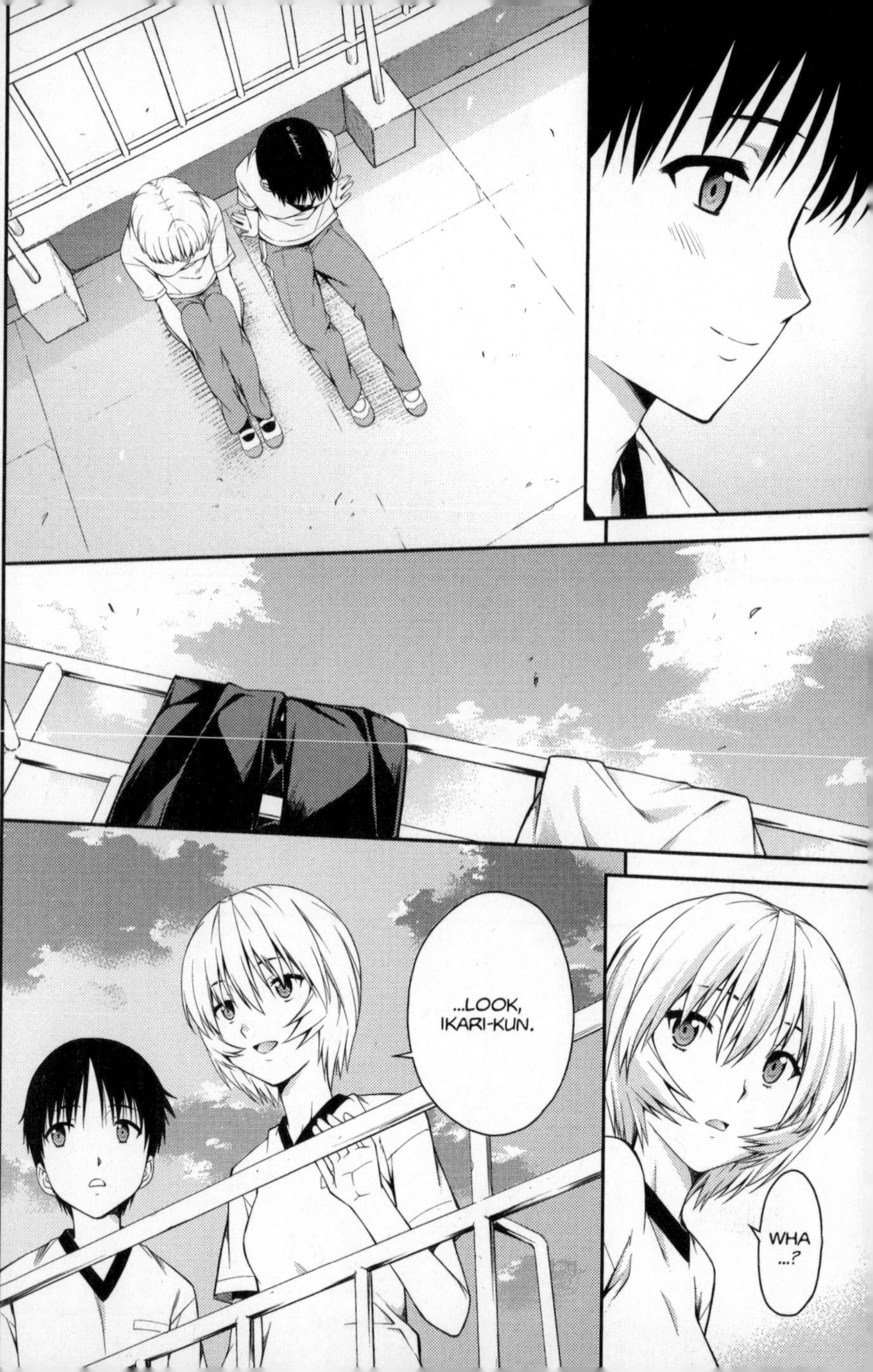
WHA ...?
...LOOK, IKARI-KUN.

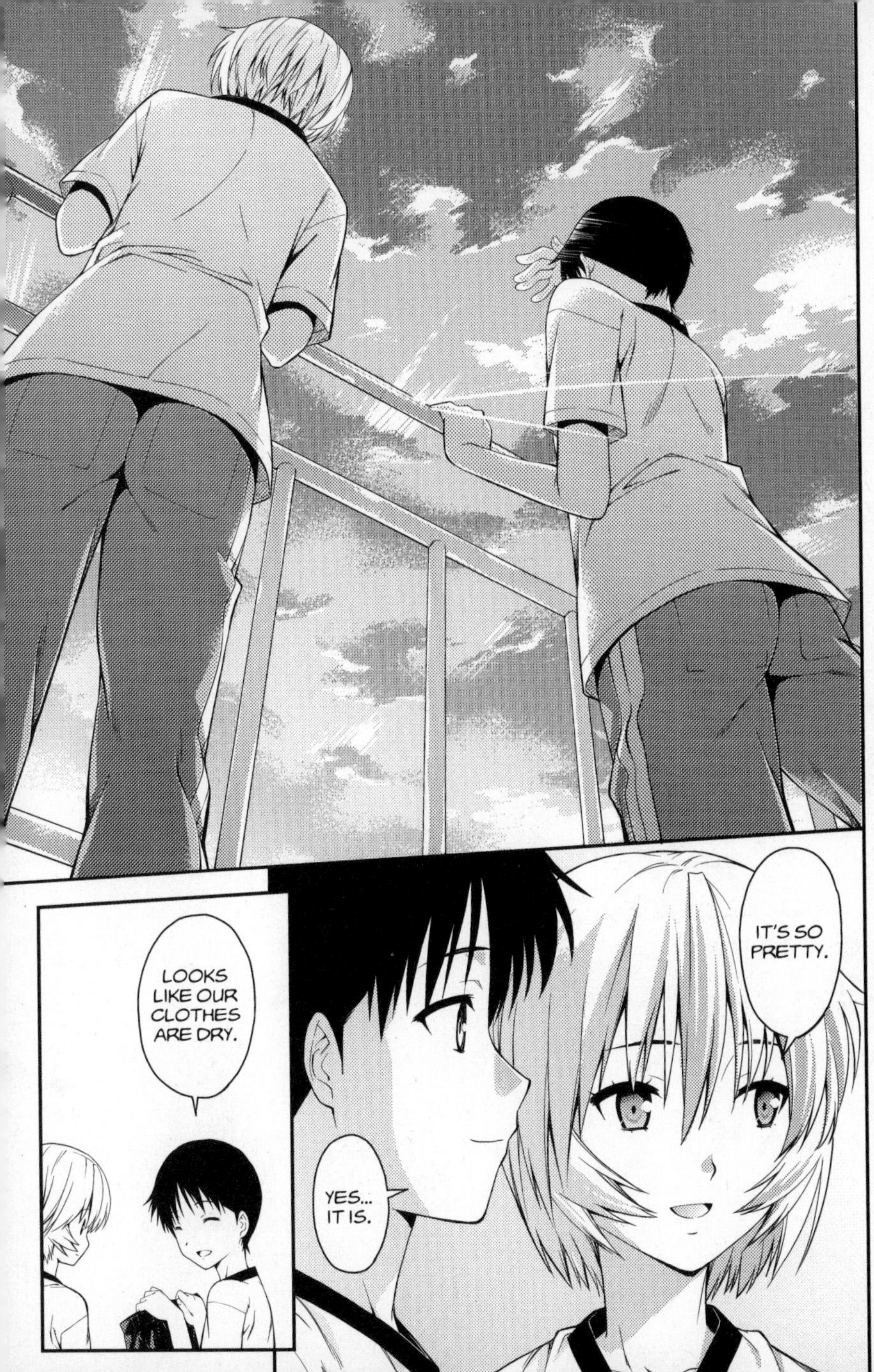
IT'S SO PRETTY.
YES... IT IS.
LOOKS LIKE OUR CLOTHES ARE DRY.

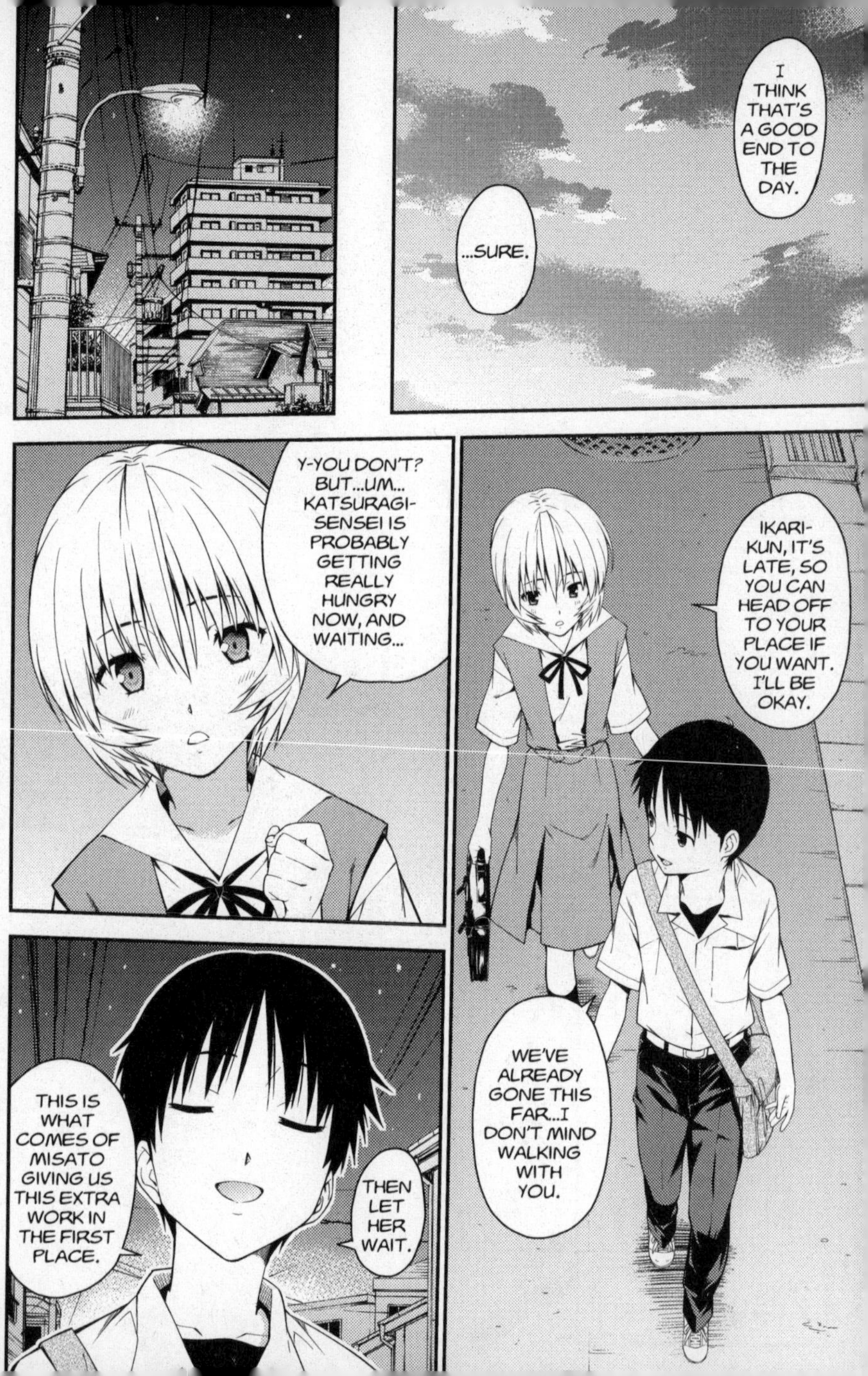
I THINK THAT'S A GOOD END TO THE DAY.
...SURE.
IKARI-KUN, IT'S LATE, SO YOU CAN HEAD OFF TO YOUR PLACE IF YOU WANT. I'LL BE OKAY.
WE'VE ALREADY GONE THIS FAR...I DON'T MIND WALKING WITH YOU.
Y-YOU DON'T? BUT...UM... KATSURAGI-SENSEI IS PROBABLY GETTING REALLY HUNGRY NOW, AND WAITING...
THEN LET HER WAIT.
THIS IS WHAT COMES OF MISATO GIVING US THIS EXTRA WORK IN THE FIRST PLACE.

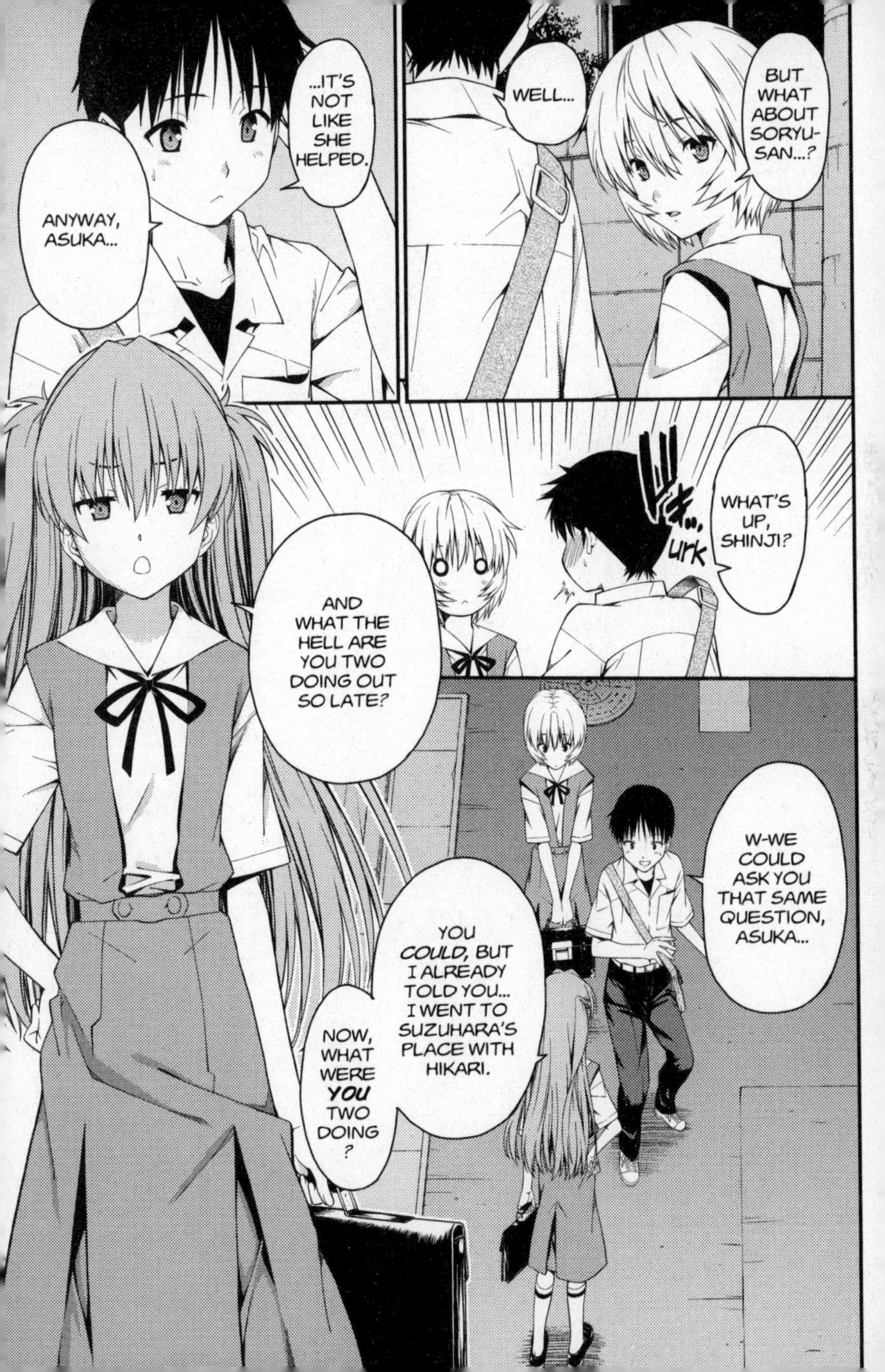

BUT WHAT ABOUT SORYU-SAN...?
WELL...
...IT'S NOT LIKE SHE HELPED.
ANYWAY, ASUKA...
URK
WHAT'S UP, SHINJI?
AND WHAT THE HELL ARE YOU TWO DOING OUT SO LATE?
W-WE COULD ASK YOU THAT SAME QUESTION, ASUKA...
YOU *COULD*, BUT I ALREADY TOLD YOU... I WENT TO SUZUHARA'S PLACE WITH HIKARI.
NOW, WHAT WERE ***YOU*** TWO DOING?

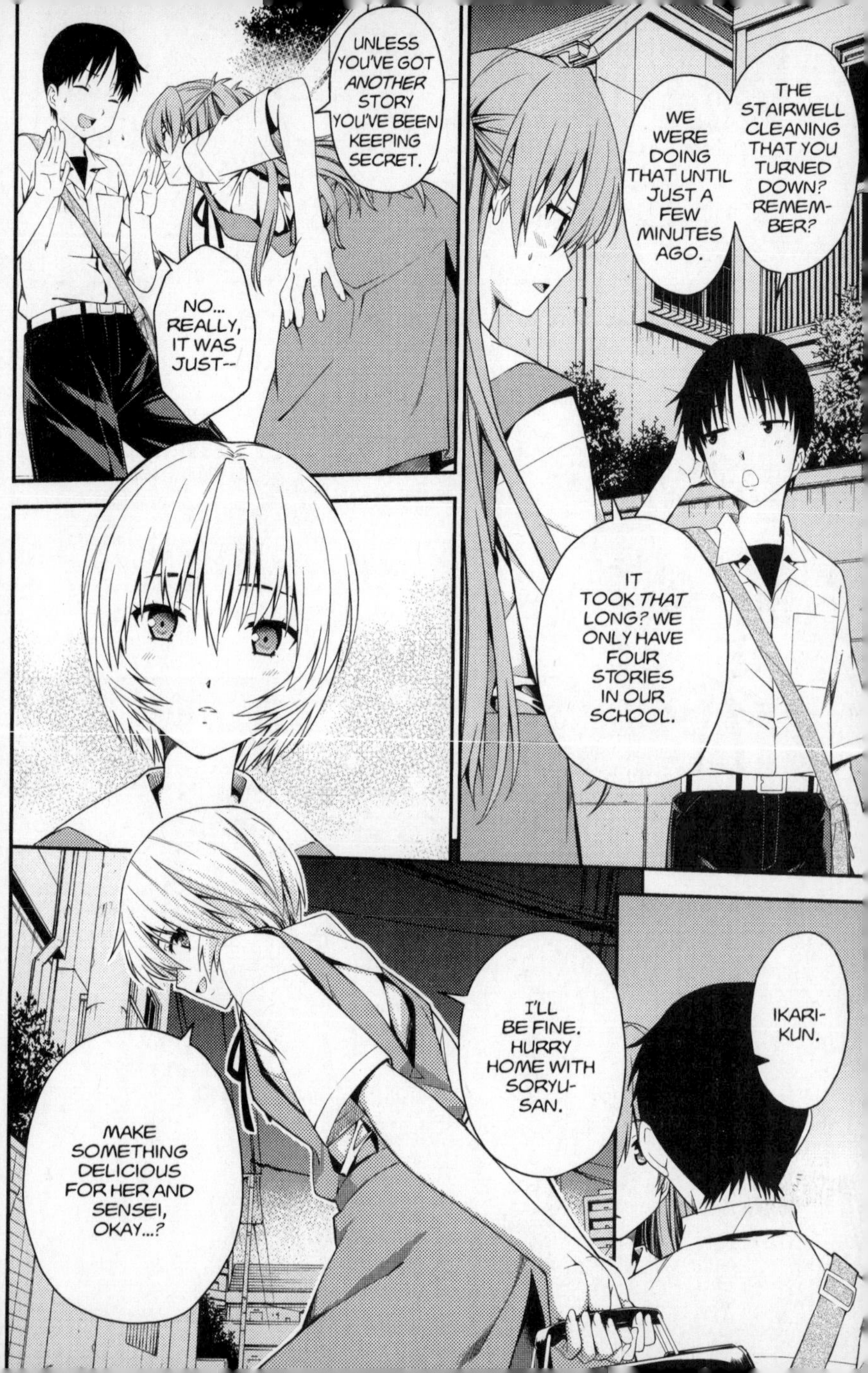
THE STAIRWELL CLEANING THAT YOU TURNED DOWN? REMEMBER?
WE WERE DOING THAT UNTIL JUST A FEW MINUTES AGO.
IT TOOK *THAT* LONG? WE ONLY HAVE FOUR STORIES IN OUR SCHOOL.
UNLESS YOU'VE GOT *ANOTHER* STORY YOU'VE BEEN KEEPING SECRET.
NO... REALLY, IT WAS JUST--
IKARI-KUN.
I'LL BE FINE. HURRY HOME WITH SORYU-SAN.
MAKE SOMETHING DELICIOUS FOR HER AND SENSEI, OKAY...?

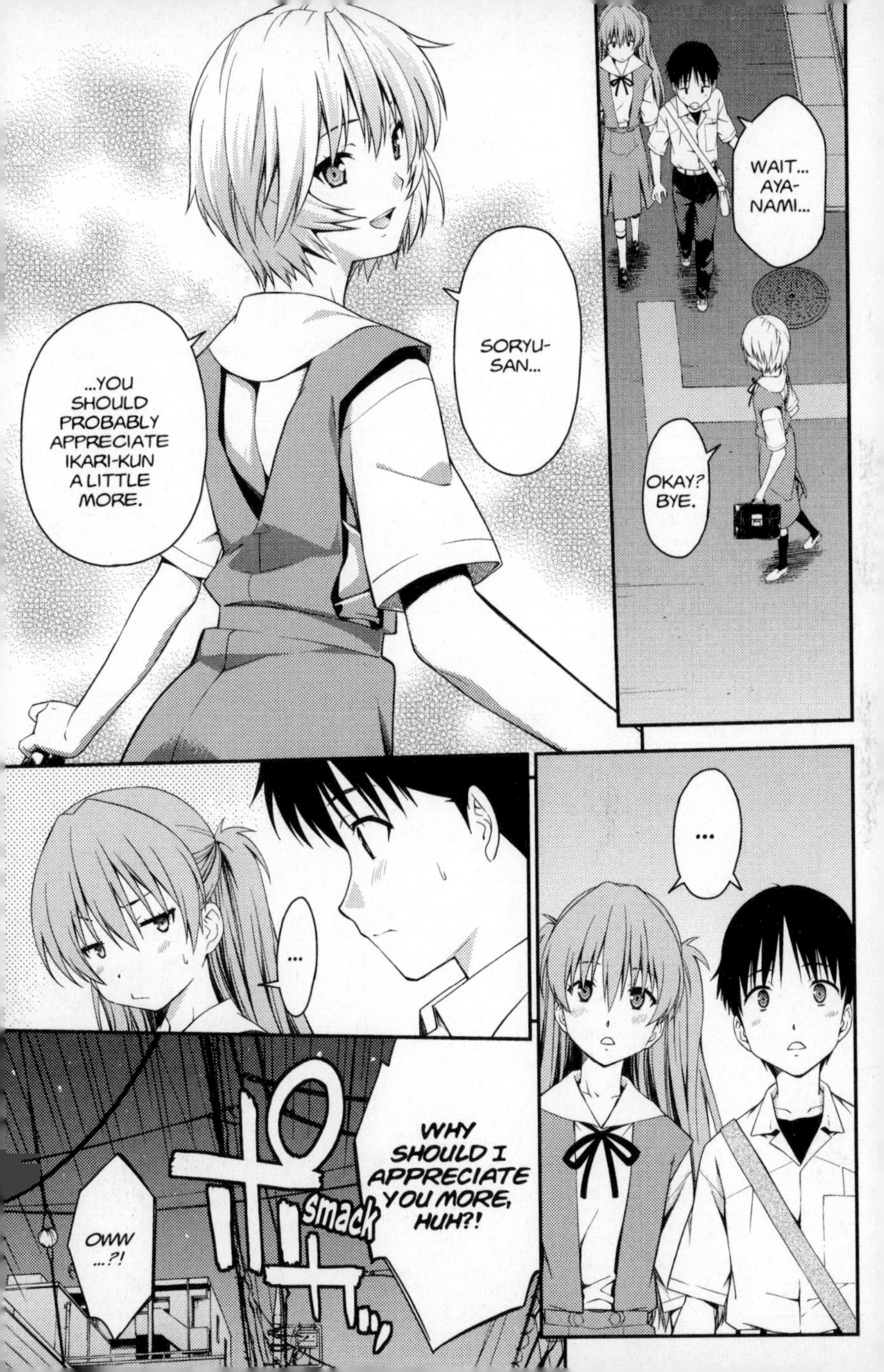
WAIT... AYA-NAMI...
OKAY? BYE.
SORYU-SAN...
...YOU SHOULD PROBABLY APPRECIATE IKARI-KUN A LITTLE MORE.
...
...
WHY SHOULD I APPRECIATE YOU MORE, HUH?!
smack
OWW ...?!

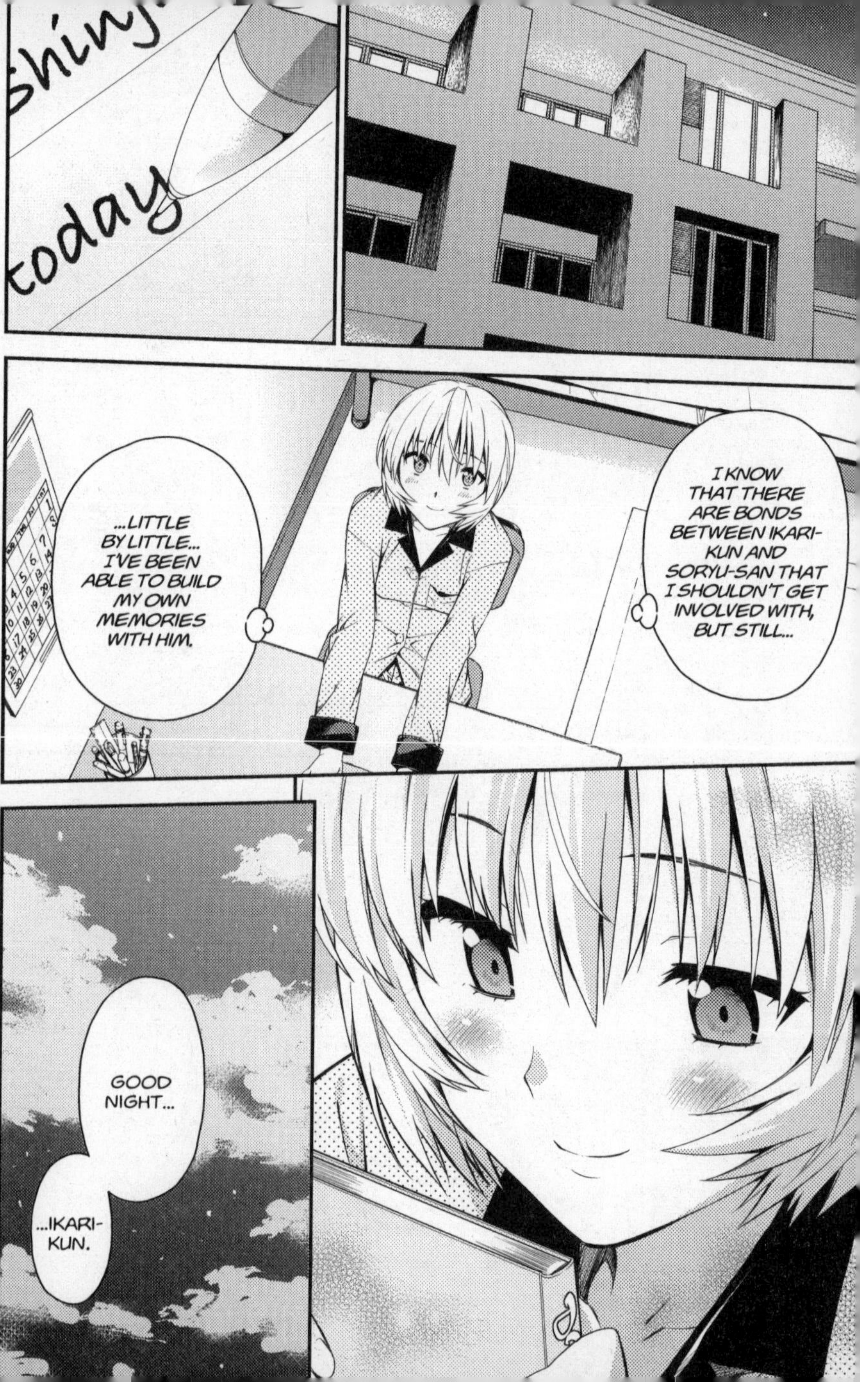
Shinj
today
I KNOW THAT THERE ARE BONDS BETWEEN IKARI-KUN AND SORYU-SAN THAT I SHOULDN'T GET INVOLVED WITH, BUT STILL...
...LITTLE BY LITTLE... I'VE BEEN ABLE TO BUILD MY OWN MEMORIES WITH HIM.
GOOD NIGHT...
...IKARI-KUN.

the shinji ikari raising project

NEON GENESIS EVANGELION
THE SHINJI IKARI RAISING PROJECT

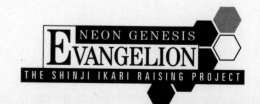

EXTRA STAGE 1

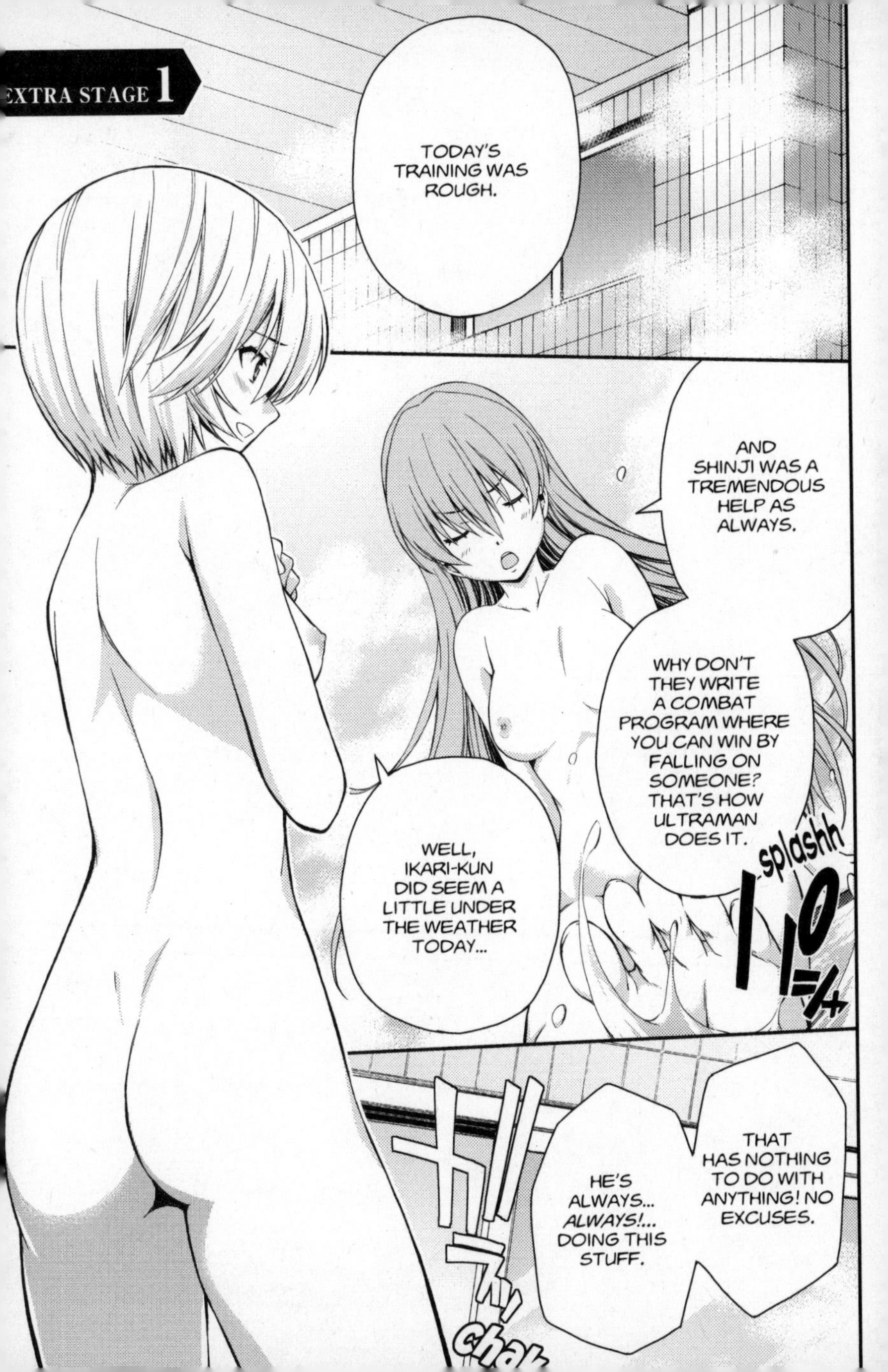
TODAY'S TRAINING WAS ROUGH.
AND SHINJI WAS A TREMENDOUS HELP AS ALWAYS.
WHY DON'T THEY WRITE A COMBAT PROGRAM WHERE YOU CAN WIN BY FALLING ON SOMEONE? THAT'S HOW ULTRAMAN DOES IT.
WELL, IKARI-KUN DID SEEM A LITTLE UNDER THE WEATHER TODAY...
splashh
THAT HAS NOTHING TO DO WITH ANYTHING! NO EXCUSES.
HE'S ALWAYS... ALWAYS!... DOING THIS STUFF.
chak

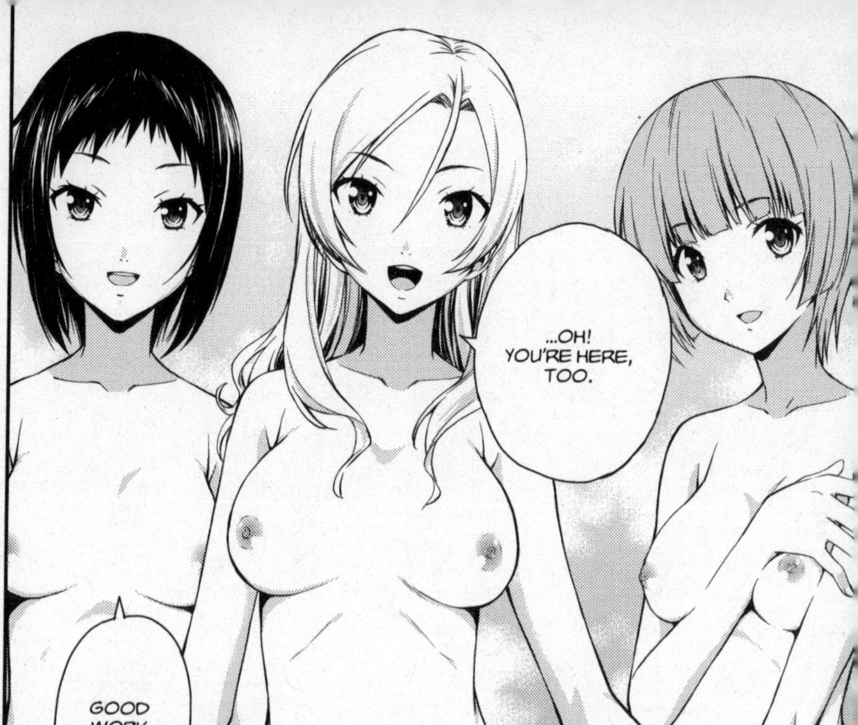
...OH! YOU'RE HERE, TOO.
GOOD WORK TODAY.
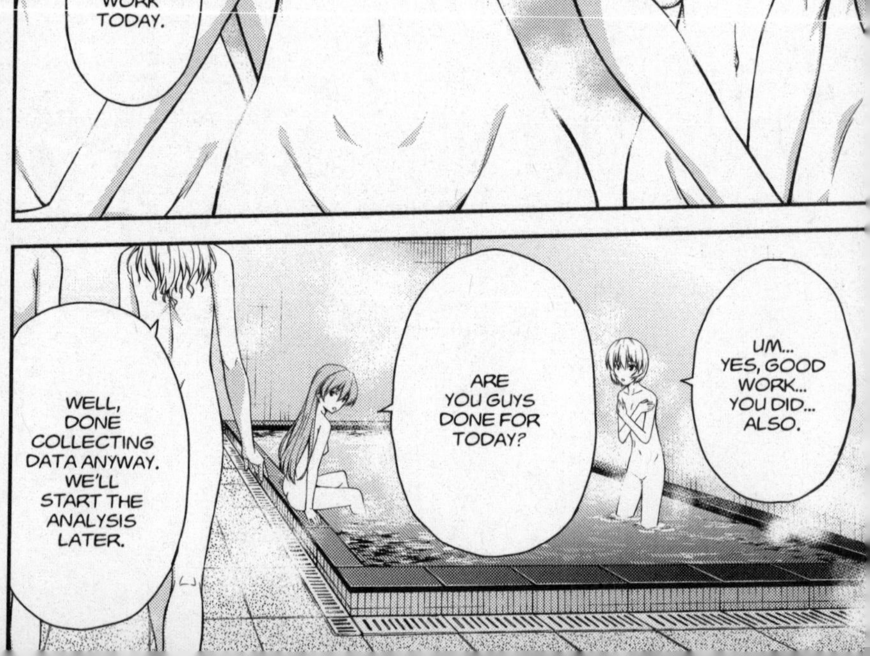
UM... YES, GOOD WORK... YOU DID... ALSO.
ARE YOU GUYS DONE FOR TODAY?
WELL, DONE COLLECTING DATA ANYWAY. WE'LL START THE ANALYSIS LATER.

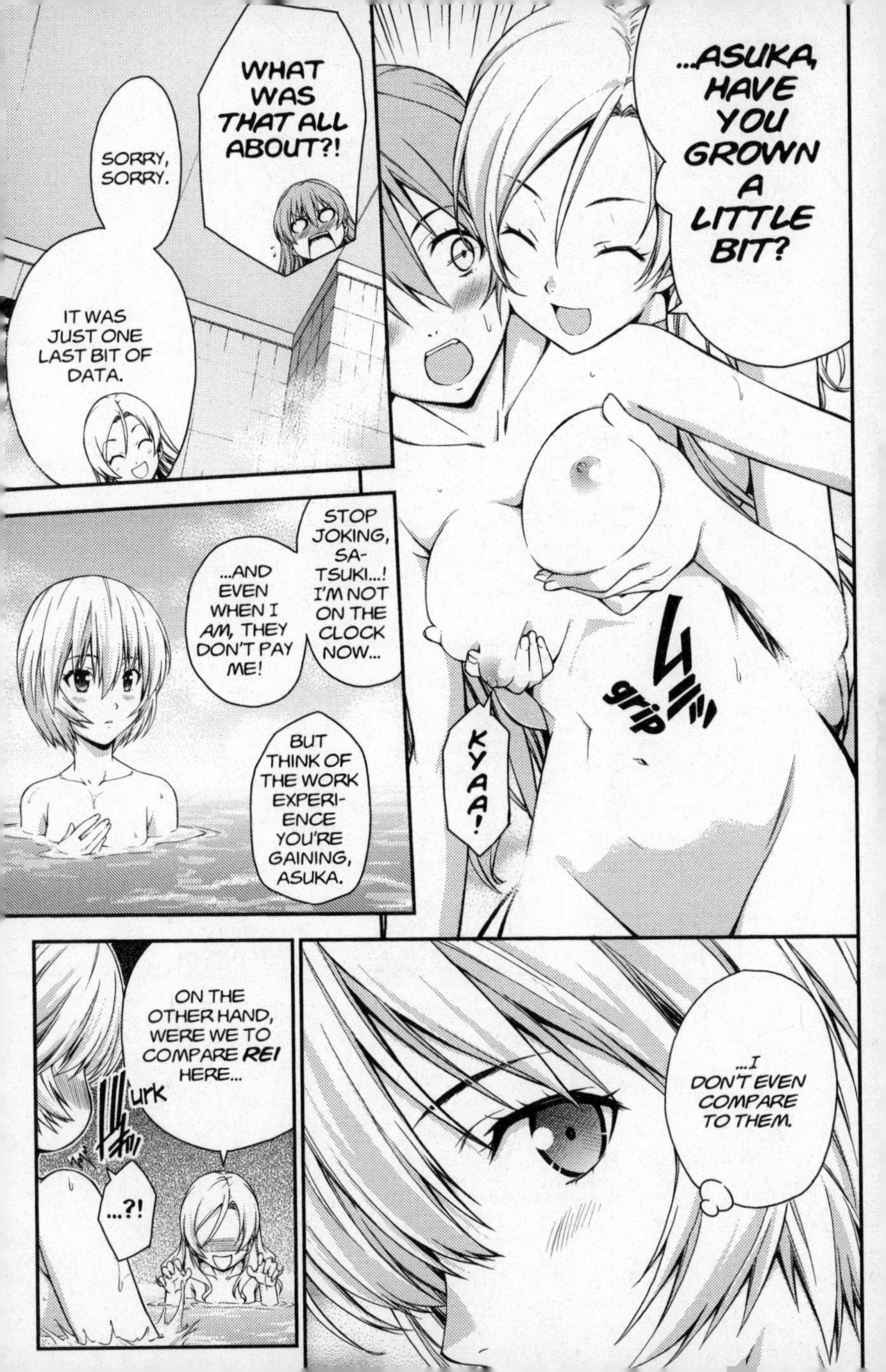
...ASUKA, HAVE YOU GROWN A LITTLE BIT?
grip
KYAA!
WHAT WAS THAT ALL ABOUT?!
SORRY, SORRY.
IT WAS JUST ONE LAST BIT OF DATA.
STOP JOKING, SA-TSUKI...! I'M NOT ON THE CLOCK NOW...
...AND EVEN WHEN I *AM*, THEY DON'T PAY ME!
BUT THINK OF THE WORK EXPERIENCE YOU'RE GAINING, ASUKA.
...I DON'T EVEN COMPARE TO THEM.
ON THE OTHER HAND, WERE WE TO COMPARE **REI** HERE...
urk
...?!

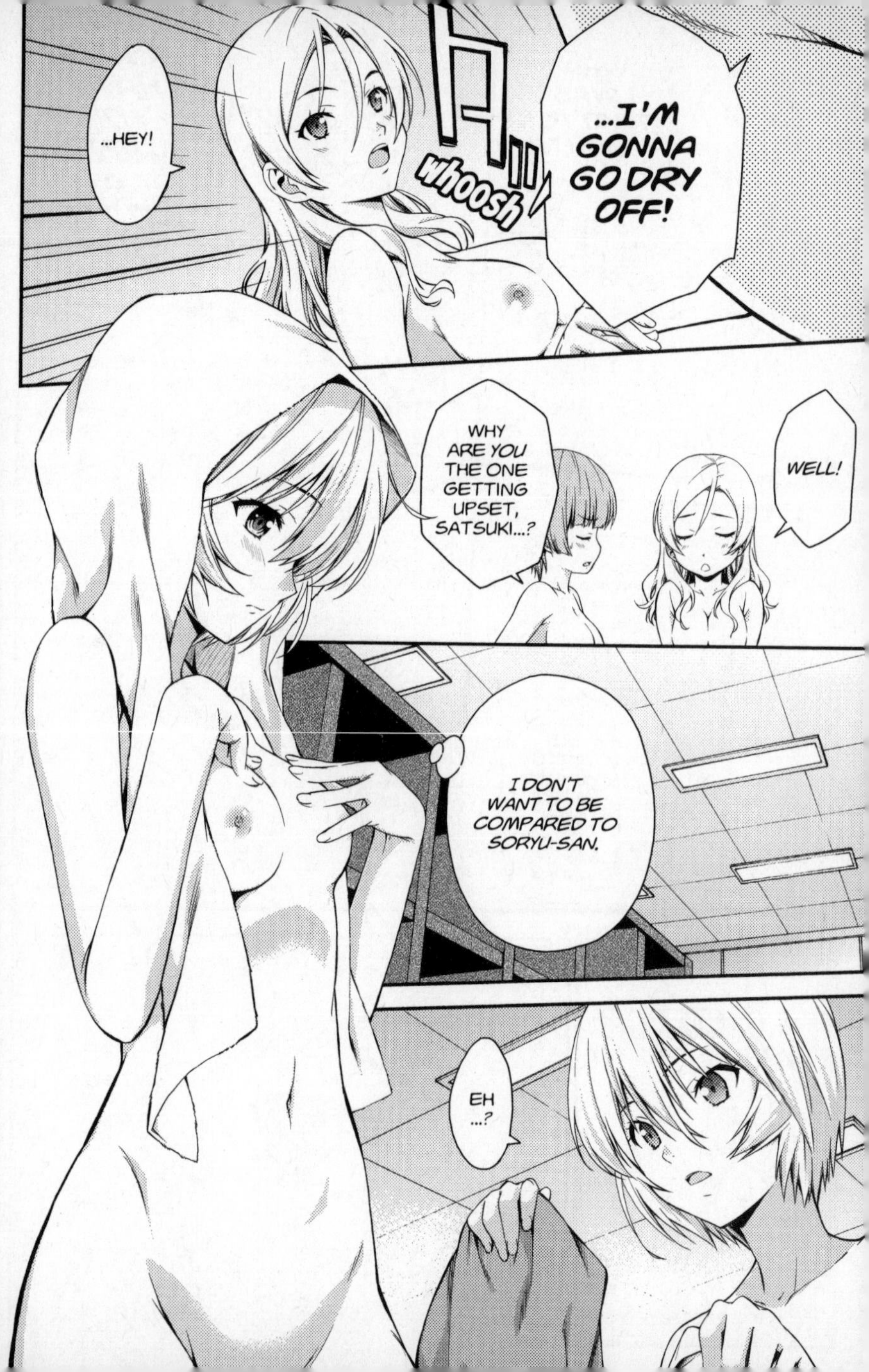
...I'M GONNA GO DRY OFF!
whoosh
...HEY!
WELL!
WHY ARE YOU THE ONE GETTING UPSET, SATSUKI...?
I DON'T WANT TO BE COMPARED TO SORYU-SAN.
EH ...?

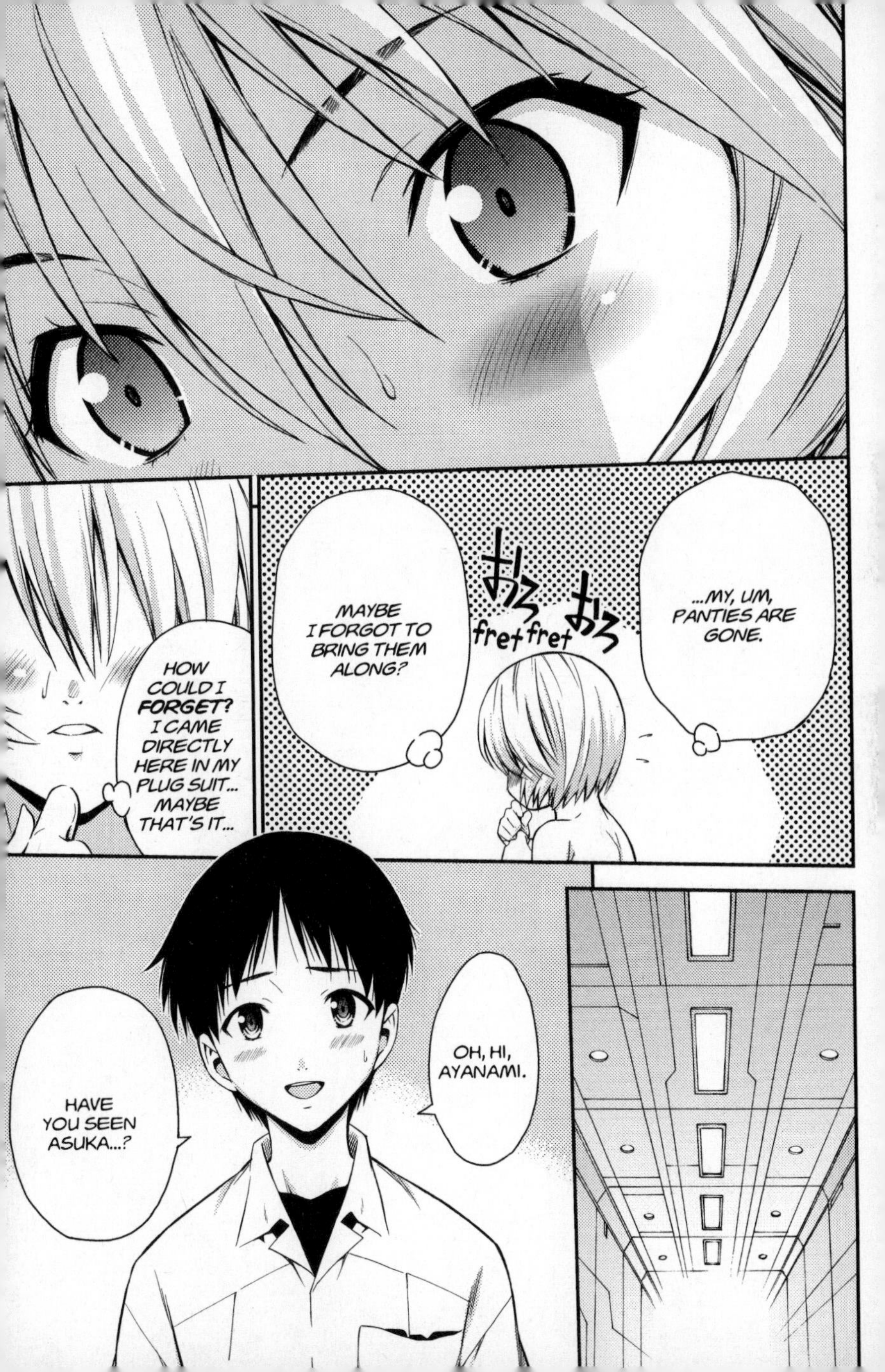
...MY, UM, PANTIES ARE GONE.
おろ おろ
fret fret
MAYBE I FORGOT TO BRING THEM ALONG?
HOW COULD I **FORGET?** I CAME DIRECTLY HERE IN MY PLUG SUIT... MAYBE THAT'S IT...
OH, HI, AYANAMI.
HAVE YOU SEEN ASUKA...?

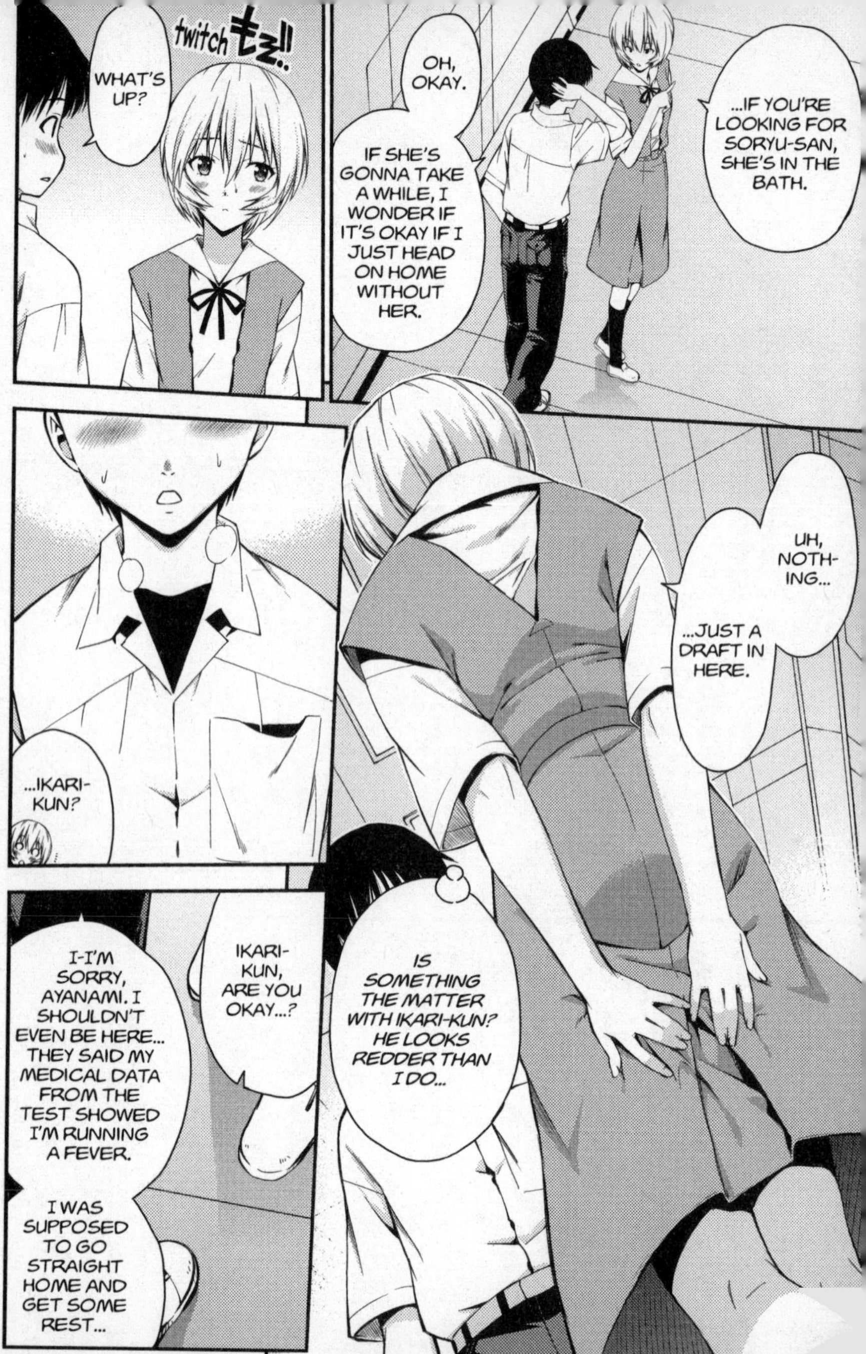
...IF YOU'RE LOOKING FOR SORYU-SAN, SHE'S IN THE BATH.
OH, OKAY.
IF SHE'S GONNA TAKE A WHILE, I WONDER IF IT'S OKAY IF I JUST HEAD ON HOME WITHOUT HER.
twitch もぞ!!
WHAT'S UP?
UH, NOTHING...
...JUST A DRAFT IN HERE.
IS SOMETHING THE MATTER WITH IKARI-KUN? HE LOOKS REDDER THAN I DO...
...IKARI-KUN?
IKARI-KUN, ARE YOU OKAY...?
I-I'M SORRY, AYANAMI. I SHOULDN'T EVEN BE HERE... THEY SAID MY MEDICAL DATA FROM THE TEST SHOWED I'M RUNNING A FEVER.
I WAS SUPPOSED TO GO STRAIGHT HOME AND GET SOME REST...

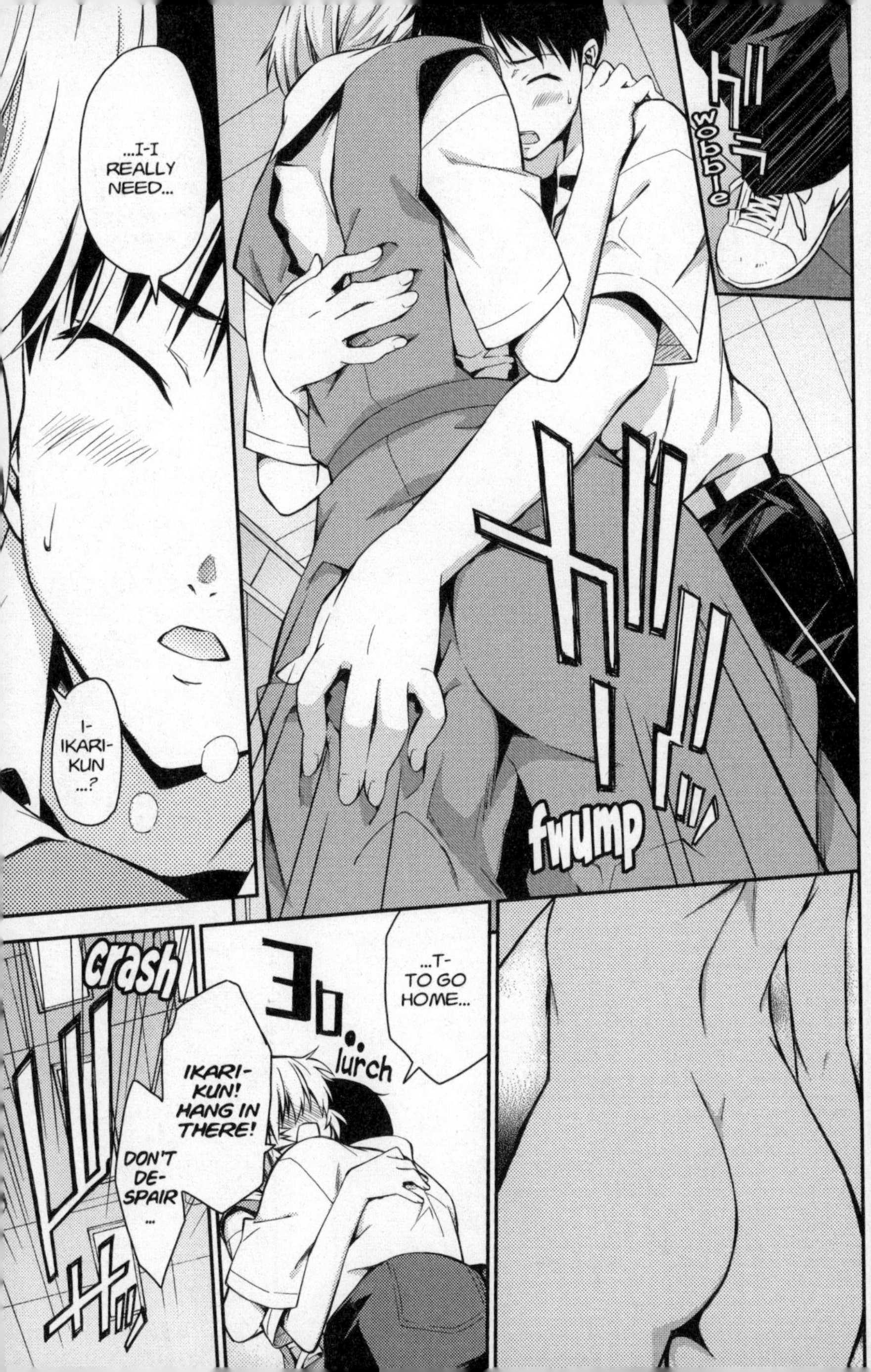
wobble
fwump
...I-I REALLY NEED...
I-IKARI-KUN ...?
...T- TO GO HOME...
lurch
IKARI-KUN! HANG IN THERE!
DON'T DE-SPAIR ...
crash

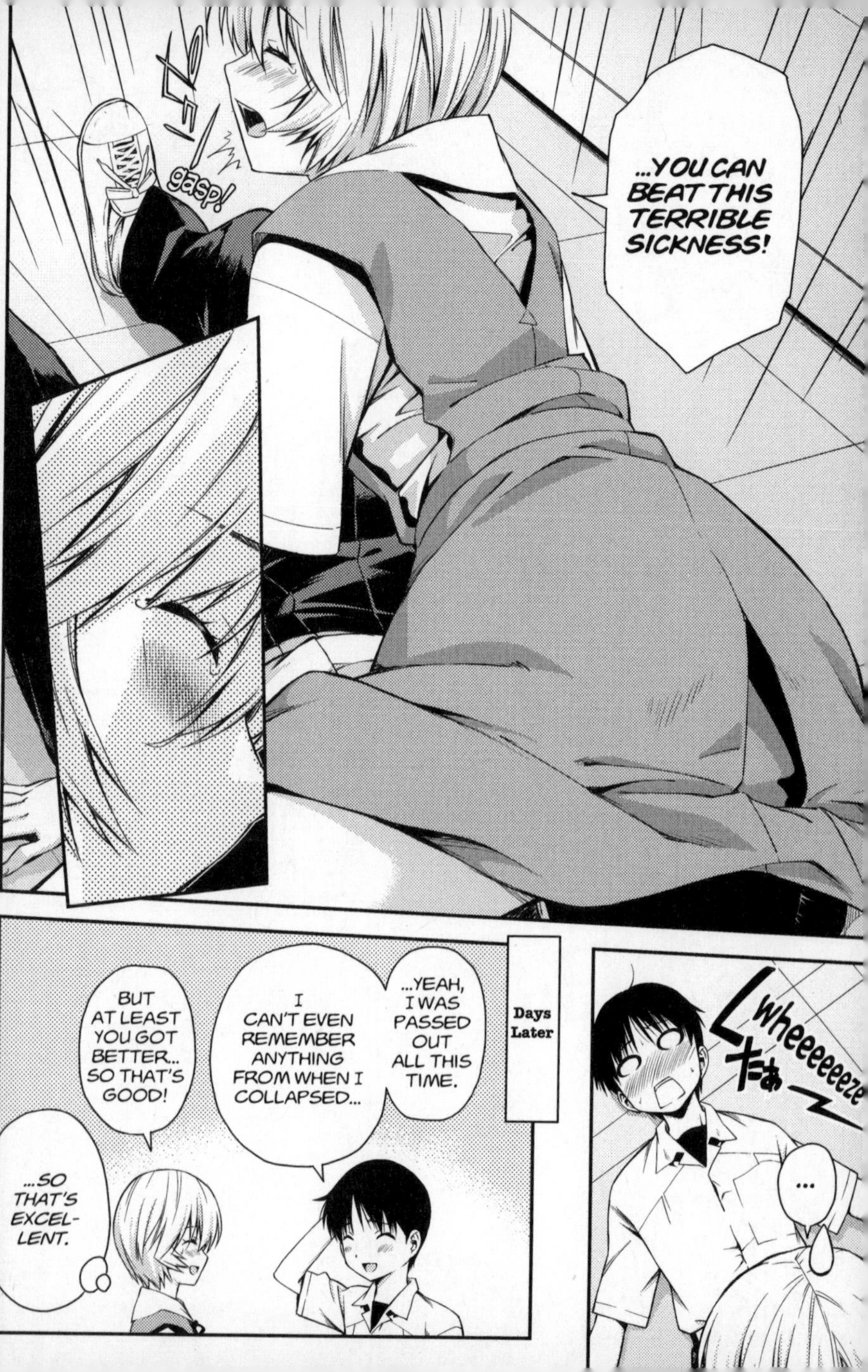
...YOU CAN BEAT THIS TERRIBLE SICKNESS!
gasp!
wheeeeeeze
...
Days Later
...YEAH, I WAS PASSED OUT ALL THIS TIME.
I CAN'T EVEN REMEMBER ANYTHING FROM WHEN I COLLAPSED...
BUT AT LEAST YOU GOT BETTER... SO THAT'S GOOD!
...SO THAT'S EXCEL-LENT.

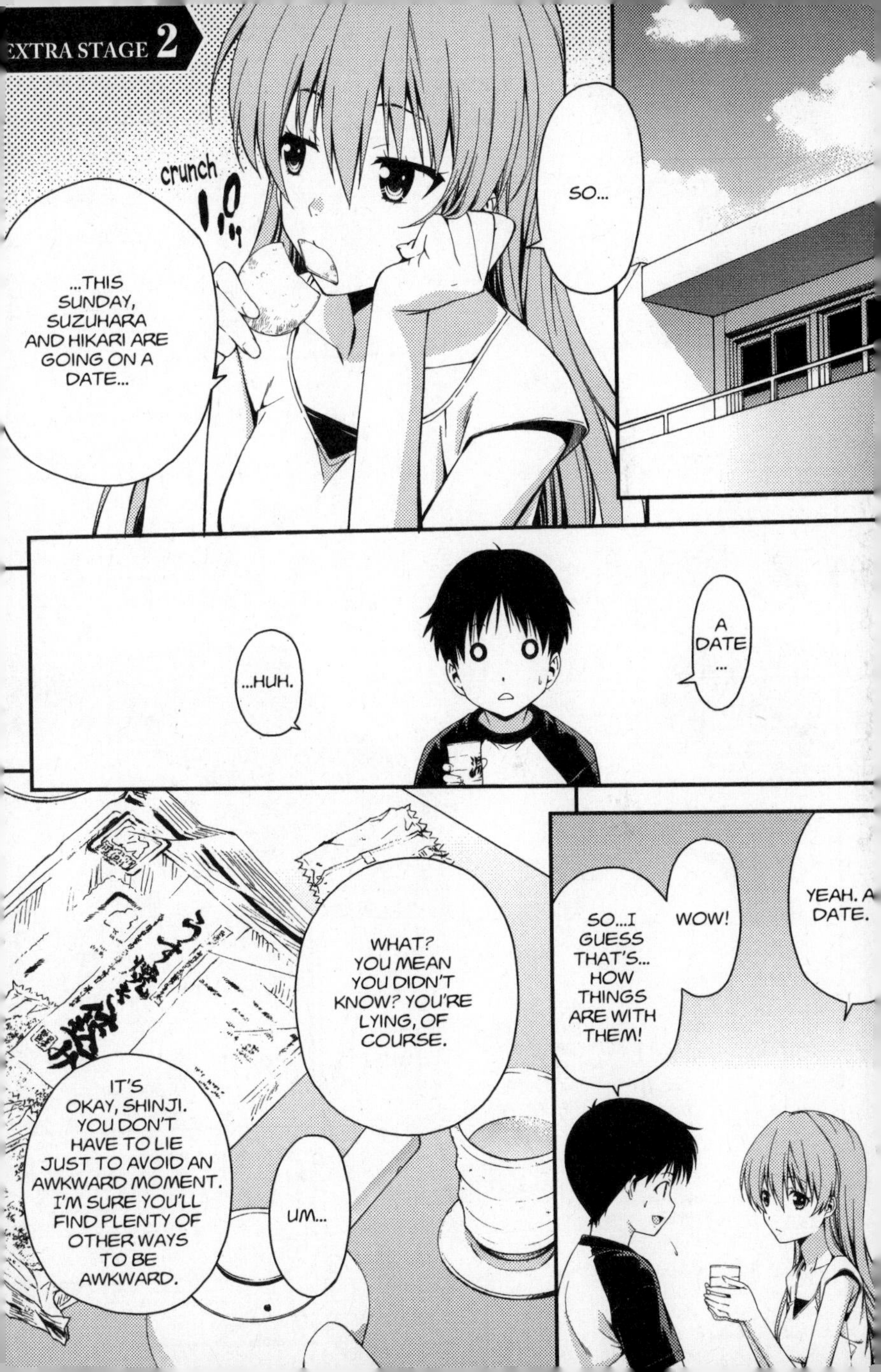
EXTRA STAGE 2
SO...
crunch
...THIS SUNDAY, SUZUHARA AND HIKARI ARE GOING ON A DATE...
A DATE ...
...HUH.
YEAH. A DATE.
WOW!
SO...I GUESS THAT'S... HOW THINGS ARE WITH THEM!
WHAT? YOU MEAN YOU DIDN'T KNOW? YOU'RE LYING, OF COURSE.
UM...
IT'S OKAY, SHINJI. YOU DON'T HAVE TO LIE JUST TO AVOID AN AWKWARD MOMENT. I'M SURE YOU'LL FIND PLENTY OF OTHER WAYS TO BE AWKWARD.

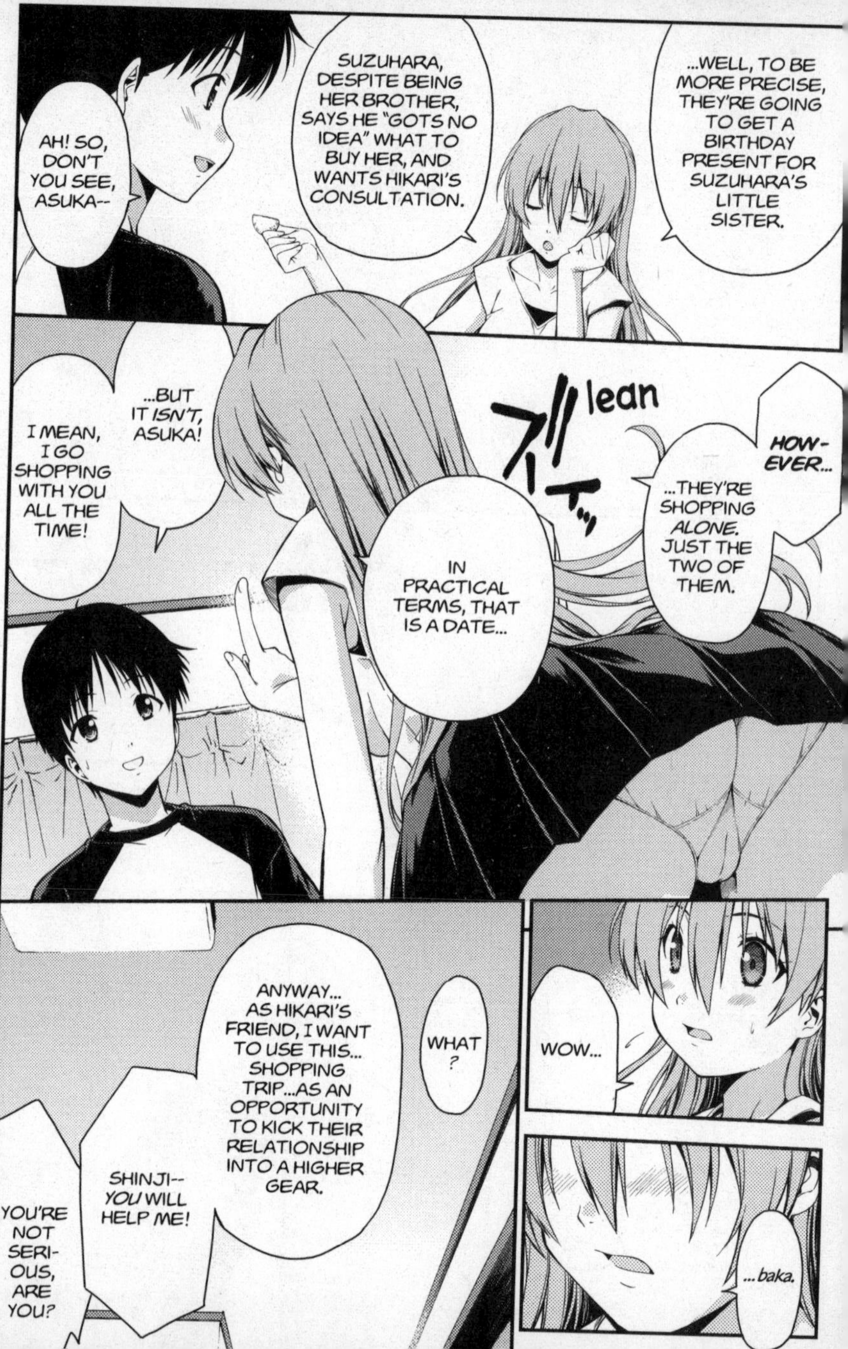
...WELL, TO BE MORE PRECISE, THEY'RE GOING TO GET A BIRTHDAY PRESENT FOR SUZUHARA'S LITTLE SISTER.
SUZUHARA, DESPITE BEING HER BROTHER, SAYS HE "GOTS NO IDEA" WHAT TO BUY HER, AND WANTS HIKARI'S CONSULTATION.
AH! SO, DON'T YOU SEE, ASUKA--
HOW-EVER...
...THEY'RE SHOPPING *ALONE*. JUST THE TWO OF THEM.
lean
IN PRACTICAL TERMS, THAT IS A DATE...
...BUT IT *ISN'T*, ASUKA!
I MEAN, I GO SHOPPING WITH YOU ALL THE TIME!
WOW...
...baka.
WHAT?
ANYWAY... AS HIKARI'S FRIEND, I WANT TO USE THIS... SHOPPING TRIP...AS AN OPPORTUNITY TO KICK THEIR RELATIONSHIP INTO A HIGHER GEAR.
SHINJI-- *YOU* WILL HELP ME!
YOU'RE NOT SERI-OUS, ARE YOU?

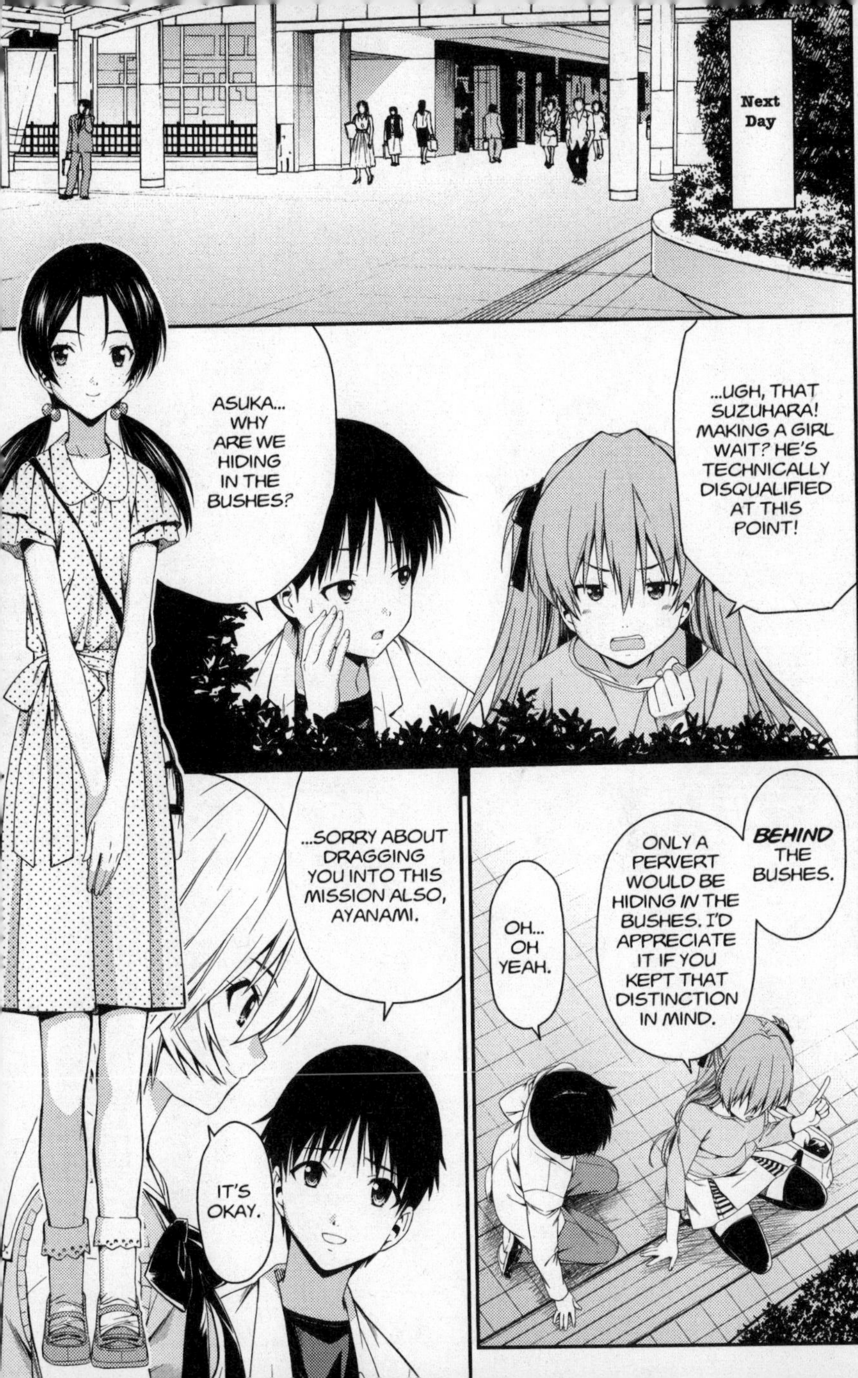
Next Day
...UGH, THAT SUZUHARA! MAKING A GIRL WAIT? HE'S TECHNICALLY DISQUALIFIED AT THIS POINT!
ASUKA... WHY ARE WE HIDING IN THE BUSHES?
BEHIND THE BUSHES.
ONLY A PERVERT WOULD BE HIDING *IN* THE BUSHES. I'D APPRECIATE IT IF YOU KEPT THAT DISTINCTION IN MIND.
OH... OH YEAH.
...SORRY ABOUT DRAGGING YOU INTO THIS MISSION ALSO, AYANAMI.
IT'S OKAY.

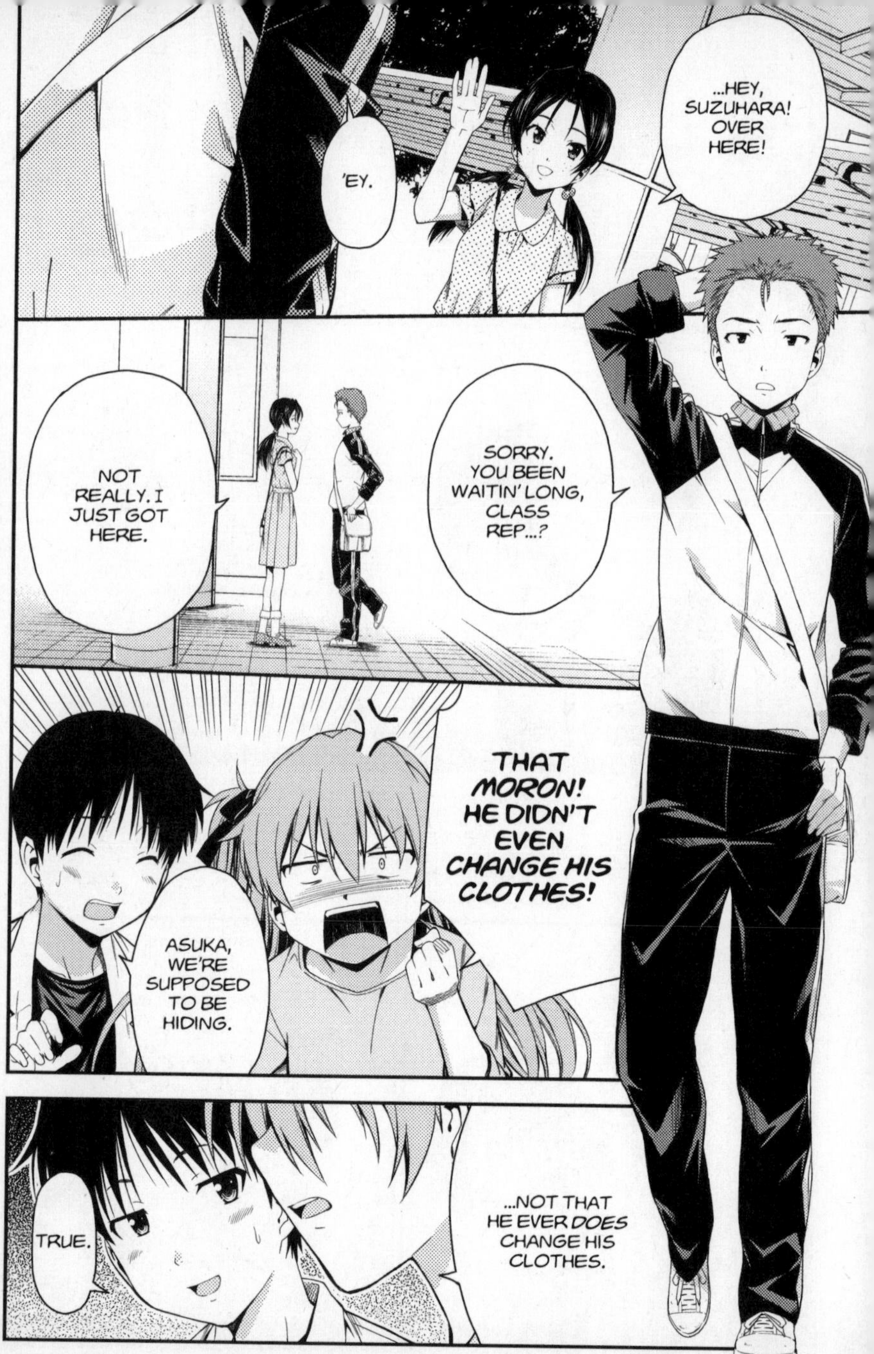
...HEY, SUZUHARA! OVER HERE!
'EY.
SORRY. YOU BEEN WAITIN' LONG, CLASS REP...?
NOT REALLY. I JUST GOT HERE.
THAT *MORON*! HE DIDN'T EVEN *CHANGE HIS CLOTHES*!
ASUKA, WE'RE SUPPOSED TO BE HIDING.
...NOT THAT HE EVER *DOES* CHANGE HIS CLOTHES.
TRUE.

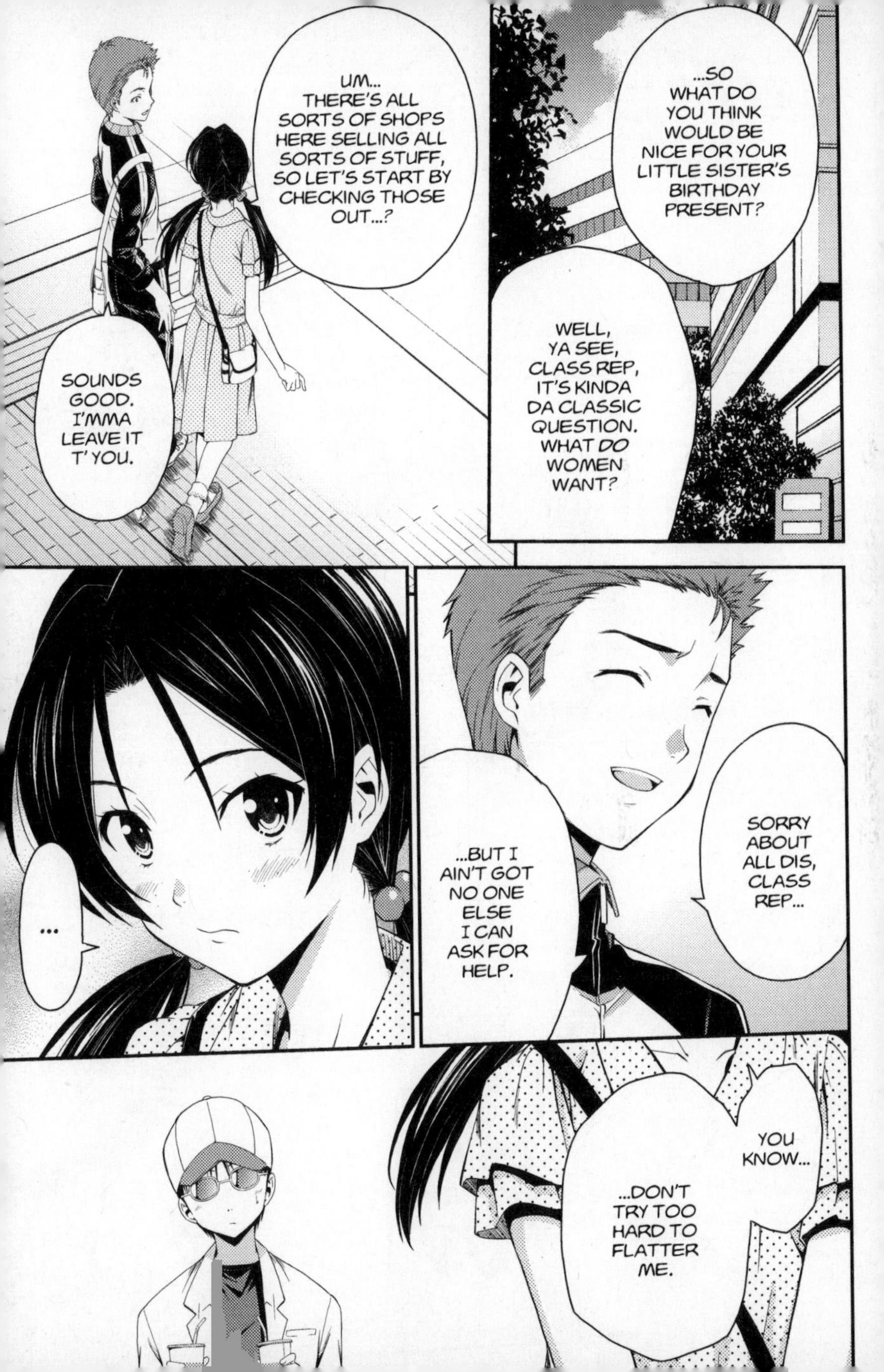
...SO WHAT DO YOU THINK WOULD BE NICE FOR YOUR LITTLE SISTER'S BIRTHDAY PRESENT?
WELL, YA SEE, CLASS REP, IT'S KINDA DA CLASSIC QUESTION. WHAT *DO* WOMEN WANT?
UM... THERE'S ALL SORTS OF SHOPS HERE SELLING ALL SORTS OF STUFF, SO LET'S START BY CHECKING THOSE OUT...?
SOUNDS GOOD. I'MMA LEAVE IT T' YOU.
SORRY ABOUT ALL DIS, CLASS REP...
...BUT I AIN'T GOT NO ONE ELSE I CAN ASK FOR HELP.
...
YOU KNOW...
...DON'T TRY TOO HARD TO FLATTER ME.

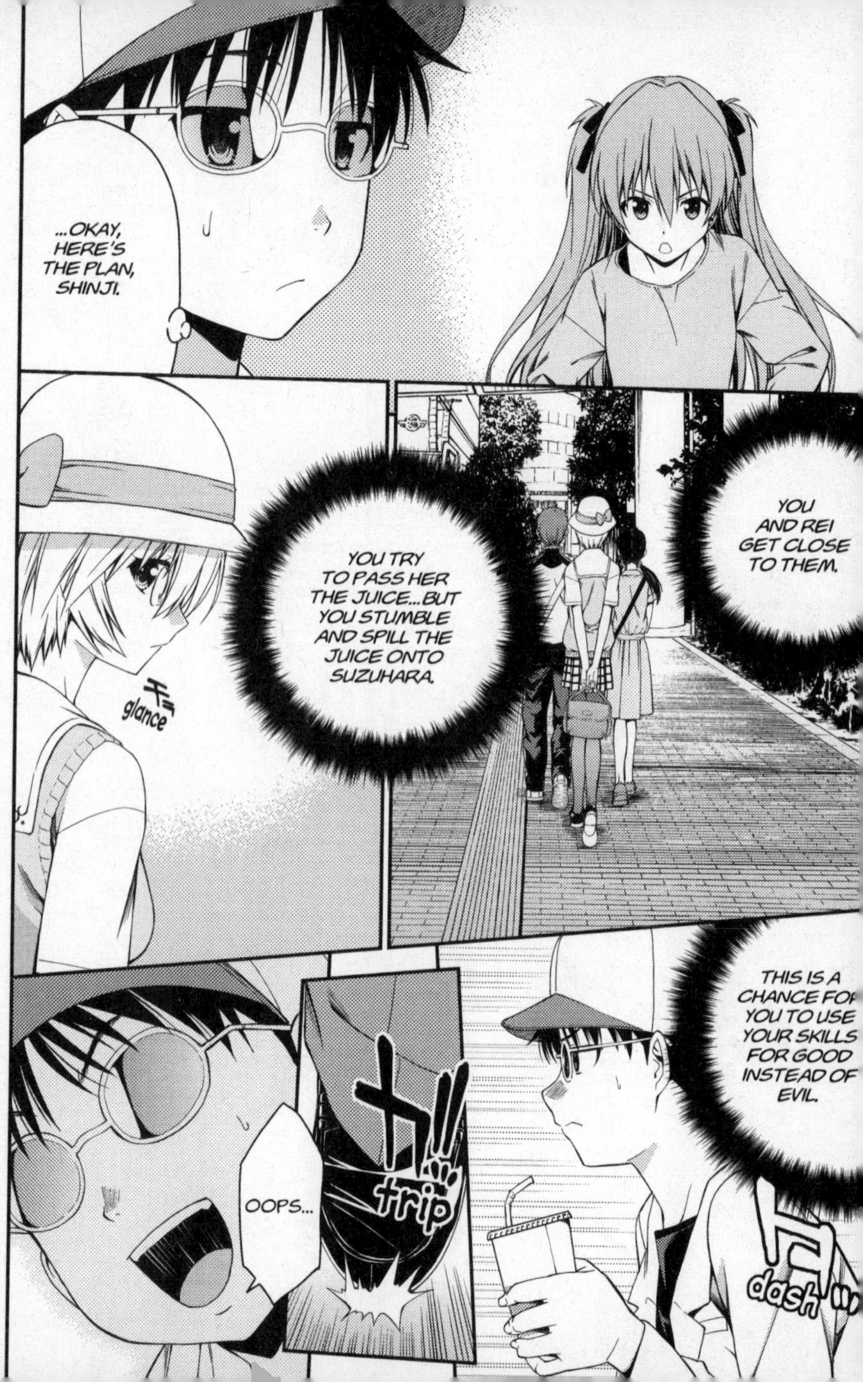
...OKAY, HERE'S THE PLAN, SHINJI.
YOU AND REI GET CLOSE TO THEM.
YOU TRY TO PASS HER THE JUICE...BUT YOU STUMBLE AND SPILL THE JUICE ONTO SUZUHARA.
glance
THIS IS A CHANCE FOR YOU TO USE YOUR SKILLS FOR GOOD INSTEAD OF EVIL.
dash
trip
OOPS...

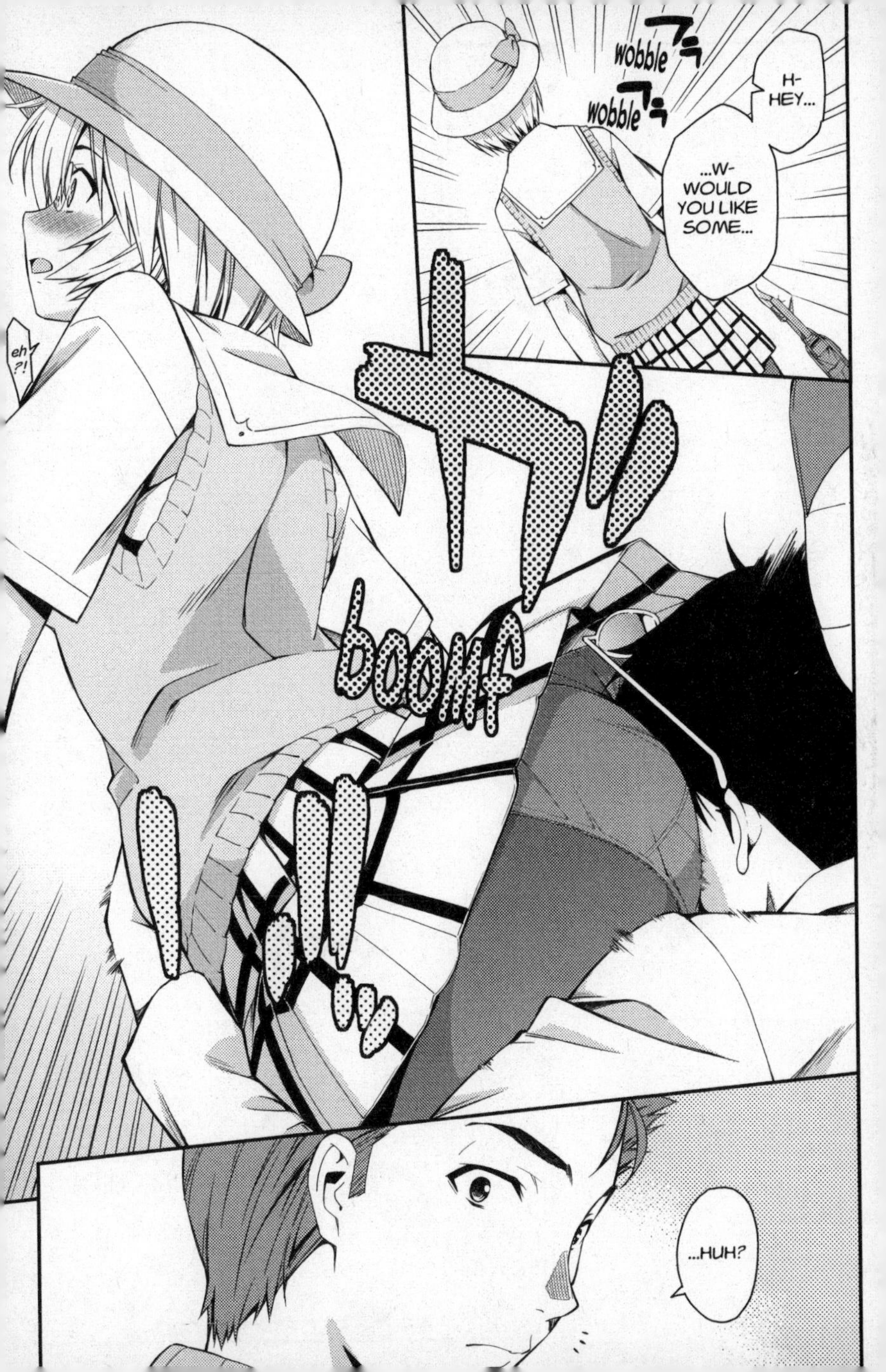
wobble
wobble
H-HEY...
...W-WOULD YOU LIKE SOME...
eh?!
boomf
...HUH?

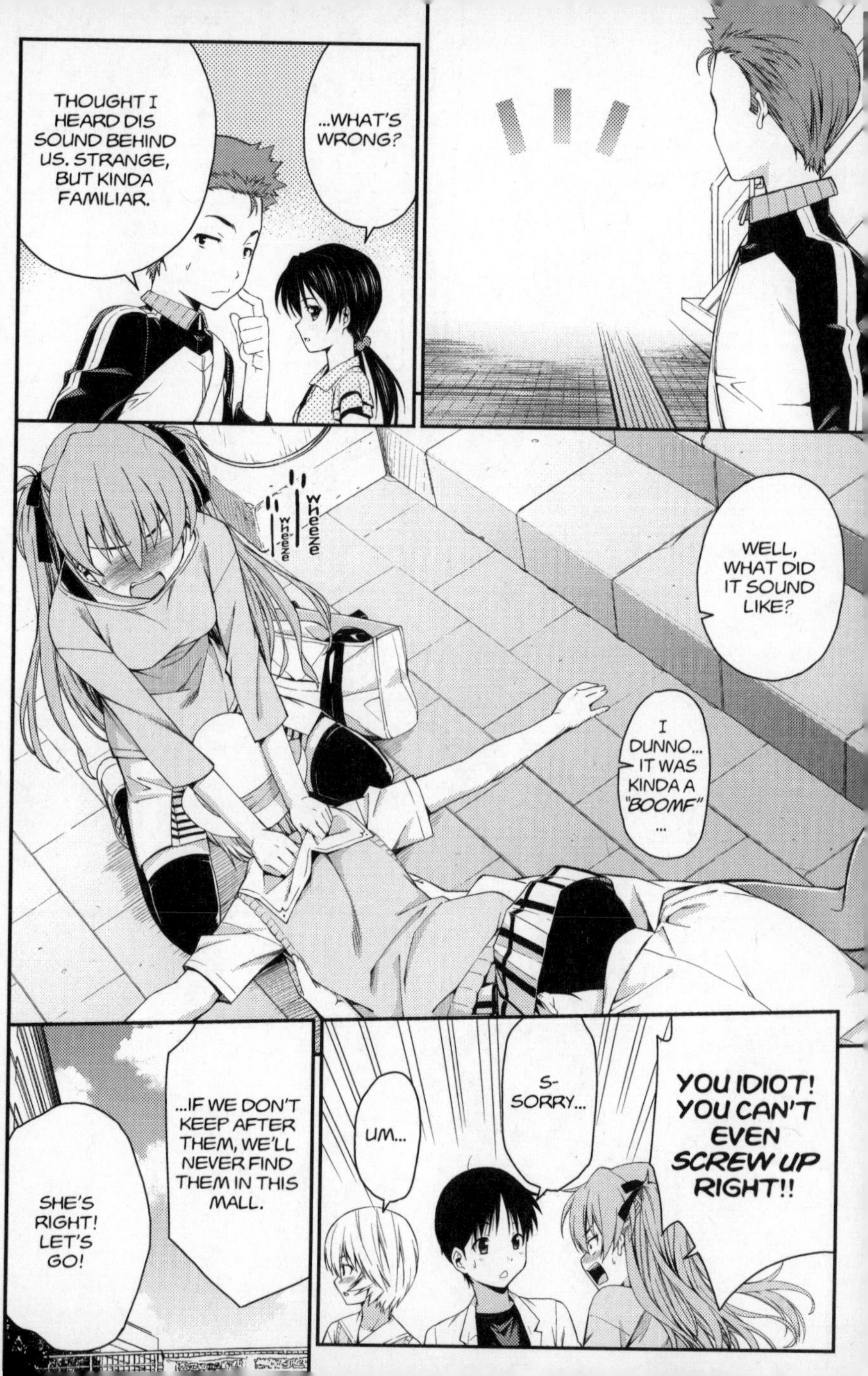
...WHAT'S WRONG?
THOUGHT I HEARD DIS SOUND BEHIND US. STRANGE, BUT KINDA FAMILIAR.
WELL, WHAT DID IT SOUND LIKE?
I DUNNO... IT WAS KINDA A "BOOMF"...
wheeze wheeze
YOU IDIOT! YOU CAN'T EVEN SCREW UP RIGHT!!
S-SORRY...
UM...
...IF WE DON'T KEEP AFTER THEM, WE'LL NEVER FIND THEM IN THIS MALL.
SHE'S RIGHT! LET'S GO!

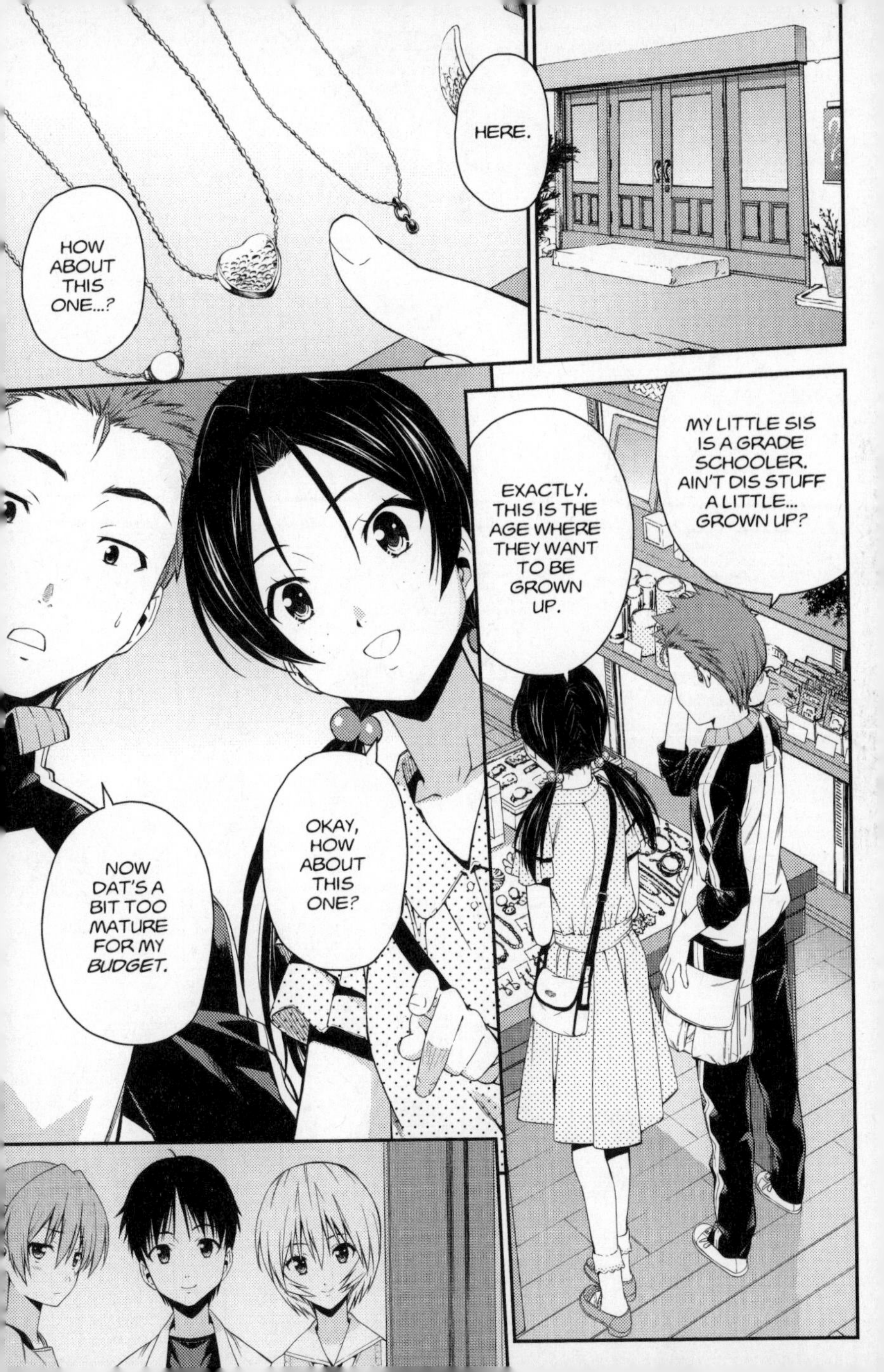
HERE.
HOW ABOUT THIS ONE...?
MY LITTLE SIS IS A GRADE SCHOOLER. AIN'T DIS STUFF A LITTLE... GROWN UP?
EXACTLY. THIS IS THE AGE WHERE THEY WANT TO BE GROWN UP.
OKAY, HOW ABOUT THIS ONE?
NOW DAT'S A BIT TOO MATURE FOR MY *BUDGET*.

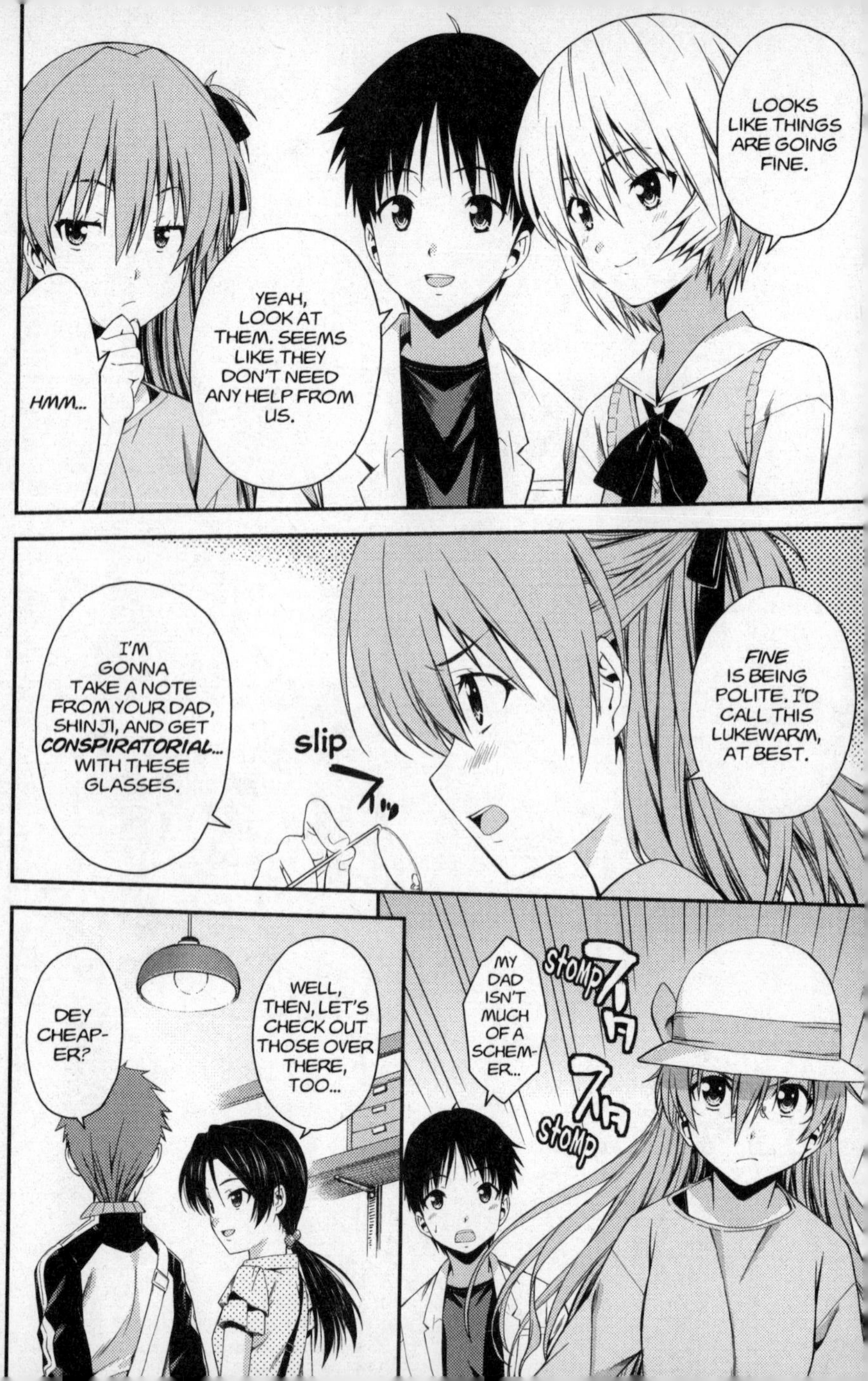
LOOKS LIKE THINGS ARE GOING FINE.
YEAH, LOOK AT THEM. SEEMS LIKE THEY DON'T NEED ANY HELP FROM US.
HMM...
FINE IS BEING POLITE. I'D CALL THIS LUKEWARM, AT BEST.
slip
I'M GONNA TAKE A NOTE FROM YOUR DAD, SHINJI, AND GET CONSPIRATORIAL... WITH THESE GLASSES.
stomp
stomp
MY DAD ISN'T MUCH OF A SCHEMER...
WELL, THEN, LET'S CHECK OUT THOSE OVER THERE, TOO...
DEY CHEAPER?

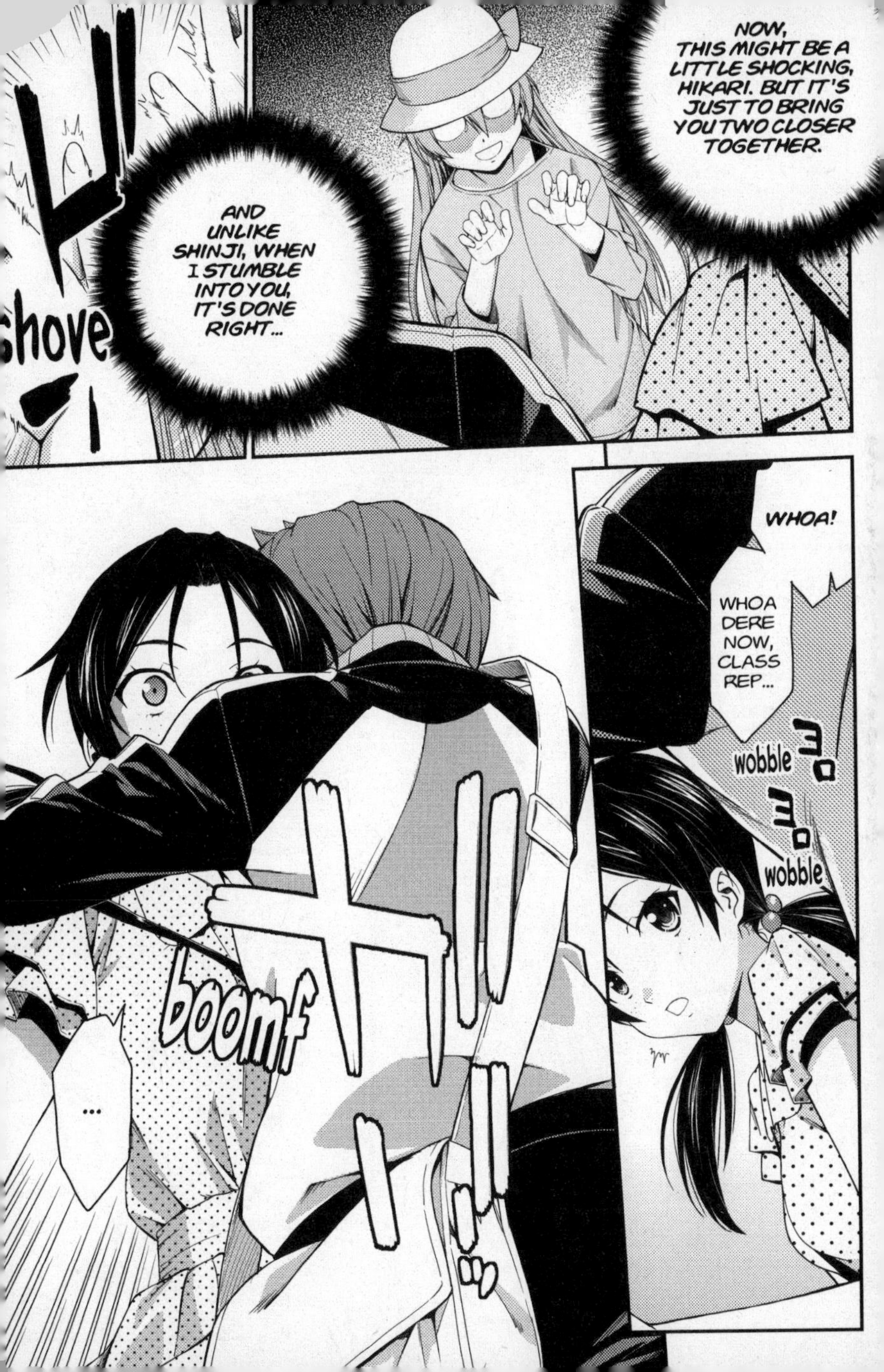
NOW, THIS MIGHT BE A LITTLE SHOCKING, HIKARI. BUT IT'S JUST TO BRING YOU TWO CLOSER TOGETHER.
AND UNLIKE SHINJI, WHEN I STUMBLE INTO YOU, IT'S DONE RIGHT...
shove
WHOA!
WHOA DERE NOW, CLASS REP...
wobble
wobble
boomf
...

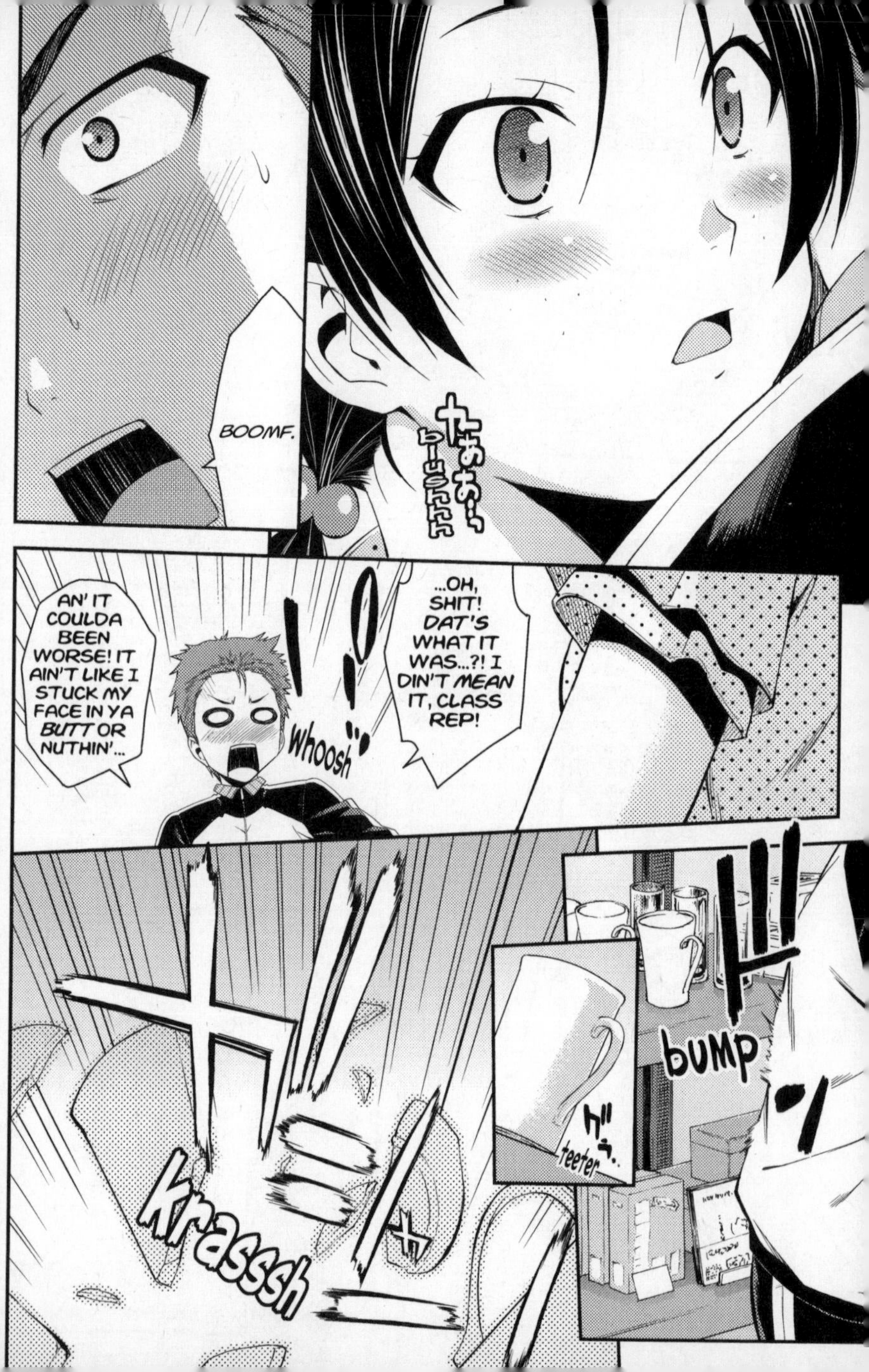
BOOMF.
...OH, SHIT! DAT'S WHAT IT WAS...?! I DIN'T MEAN IT, CLASS REP!
whoosh
AN' IT COULDA BEEN WORSE! IT AIN'T LIKE I STUCK MY FACE IN YA BUTT OR NUTHIN'...
bump
teeter
krasssh

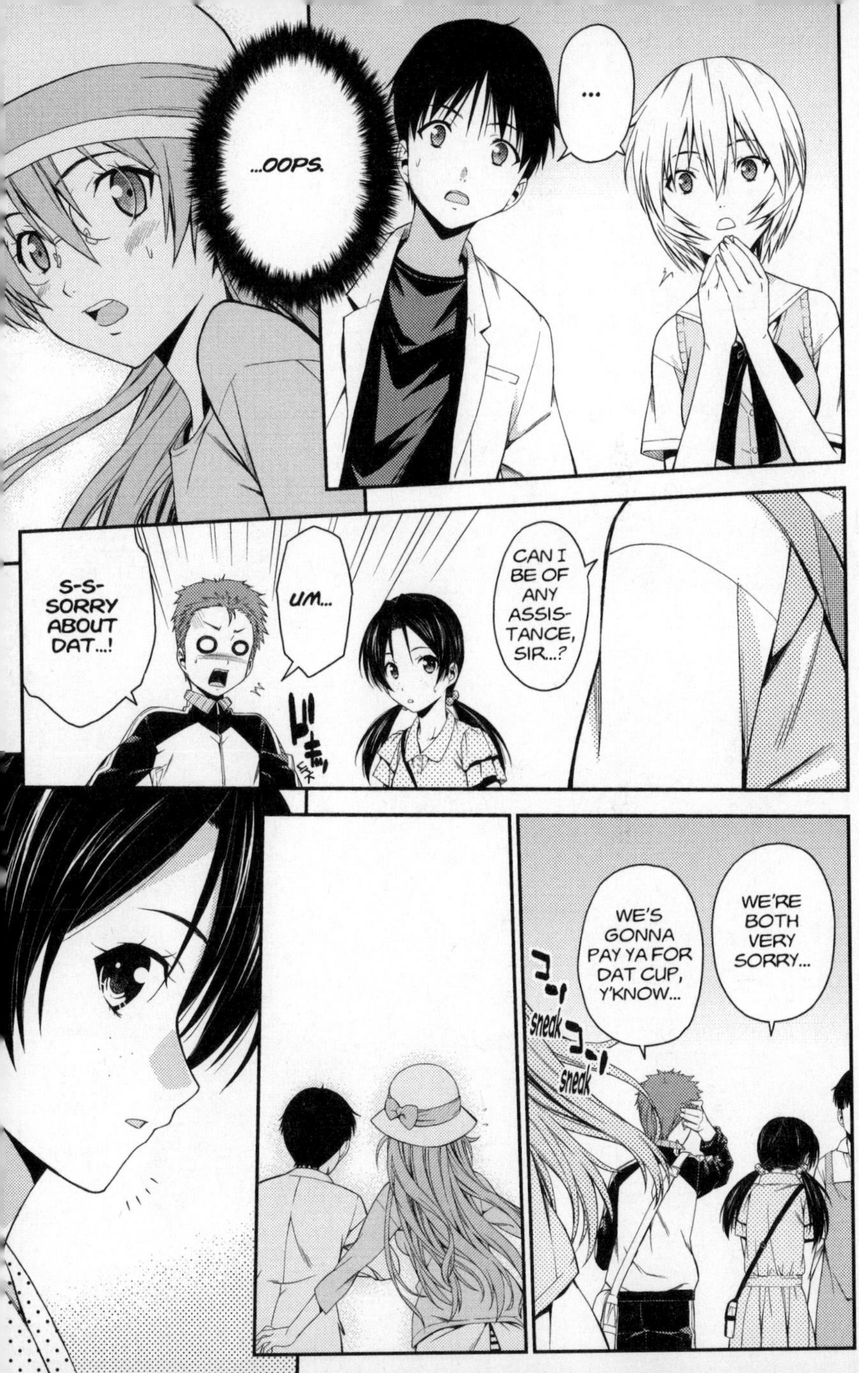
...
...OOPS.
CAN I BE OF ANY ASSIS-TANCE, SIR...?
UM...
S-S-SORRY ABOUT DAT...!
WE'RE BOTH VERY SORRY...
WE'S GONNA PAY YA FOR DAT CUP, Y'KNOW...
sneak
sneak

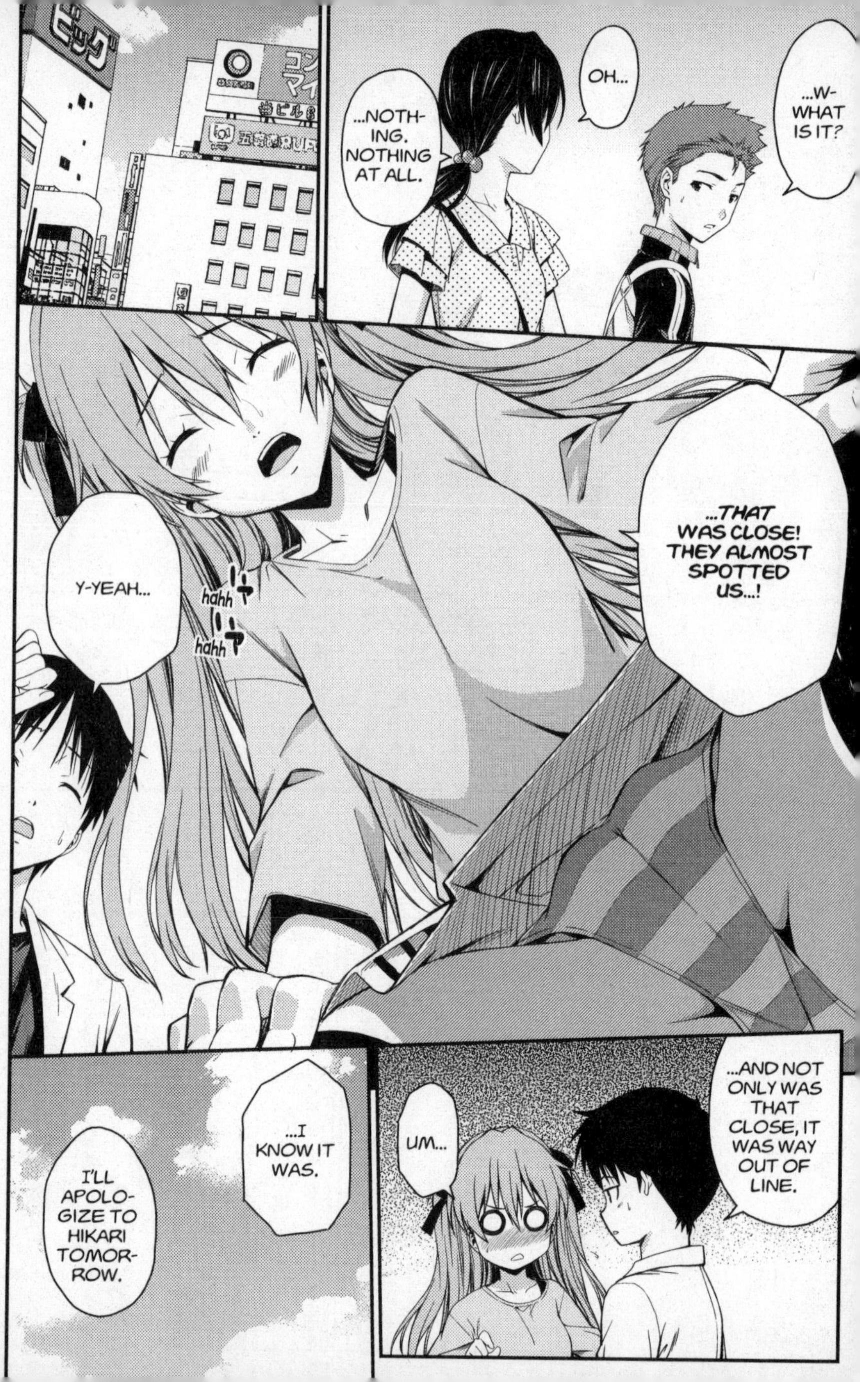
...W- WHAT IS IT?
OH...
...NOTH- ING. NOTHING AT ALL.
...THAT WAS CLOSE! THEY ALMOST SPOTTED US...!
hahh hahh
Y-YEAH...
...AND NOT ONLY WAS THAT CLOSE, IT WAS WAY OUT OF LINE.
UM...
...I KNOW IT WAS.
I'LL APOLO- GIZE TO HIKARI TOMOR- ROW.

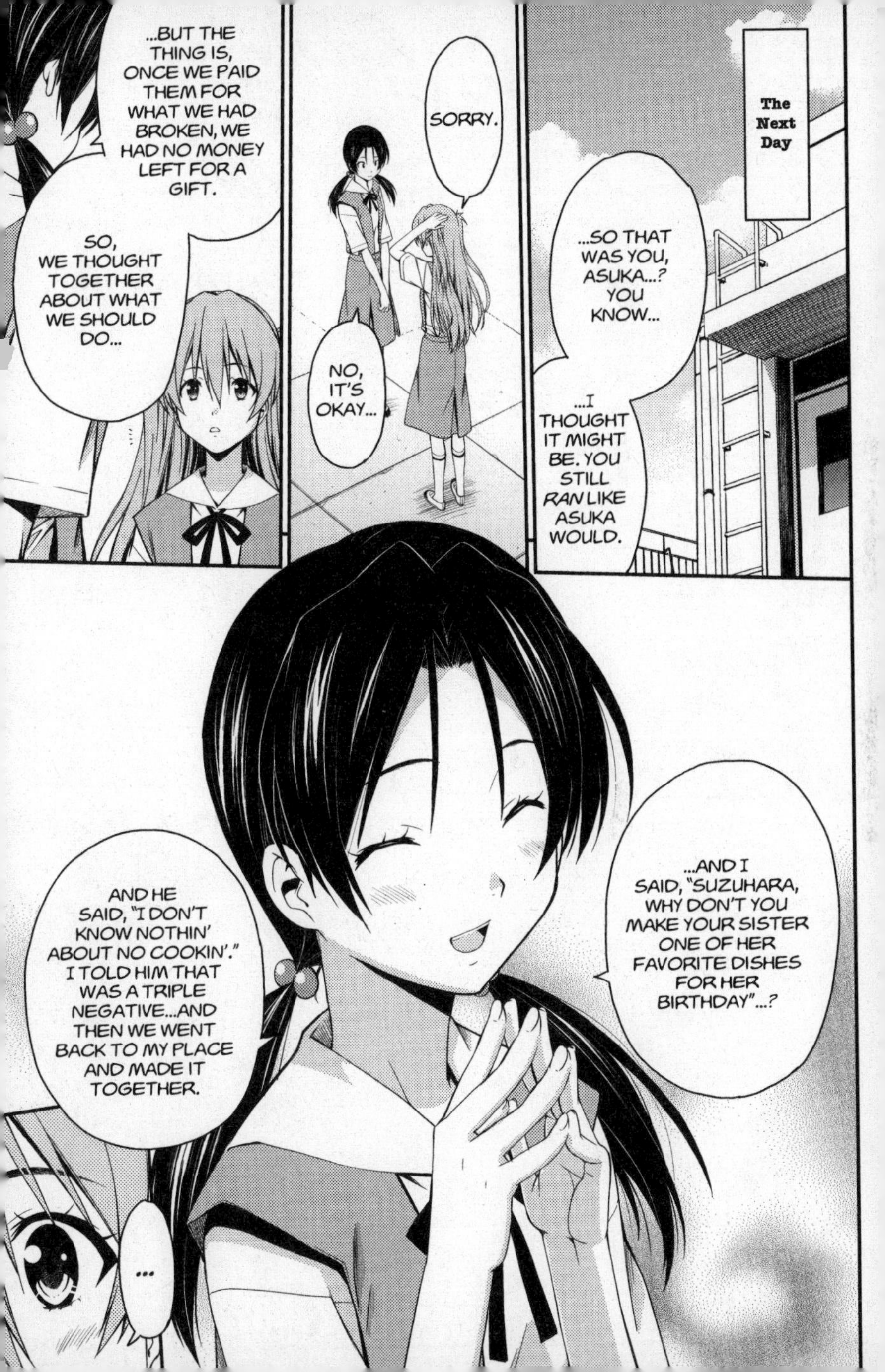
The Next Day
...SO THAT WAS YOU, ASUKA...? YOU KNOW...
...I THOUGHT IT MIGHT BE. YOU STILL *RAN* LIKE ASUKA WOULD.
SORRY.
NO, IT'S OKAY...
...BUT THE THING IS, ONCE WE PAID THEM FOR WHAT WE HAD BROKEN, WE HAD NO MONEY LEFT FOR A GIFT.
SO, WE THOUGHT TOGETHER ABOUT WHAT WE SHOULD DO...
...AND I SAID, "SUZUHARA, WHY DON'T YOU MAKE YOUR SISTER ONE OF HER FAVORITE DISHES FOR HER BIRTHDAY"...?
AND HE SAID, "I DON'T KNOW NOTHIN' ABOUT NO COOKIN'." I TOLD HIM THAT WAS A TRIPLE NEGATIVE...AND THEN WE WENT BACK TO MY PLACE AND MADE IT TOGETHER.
...

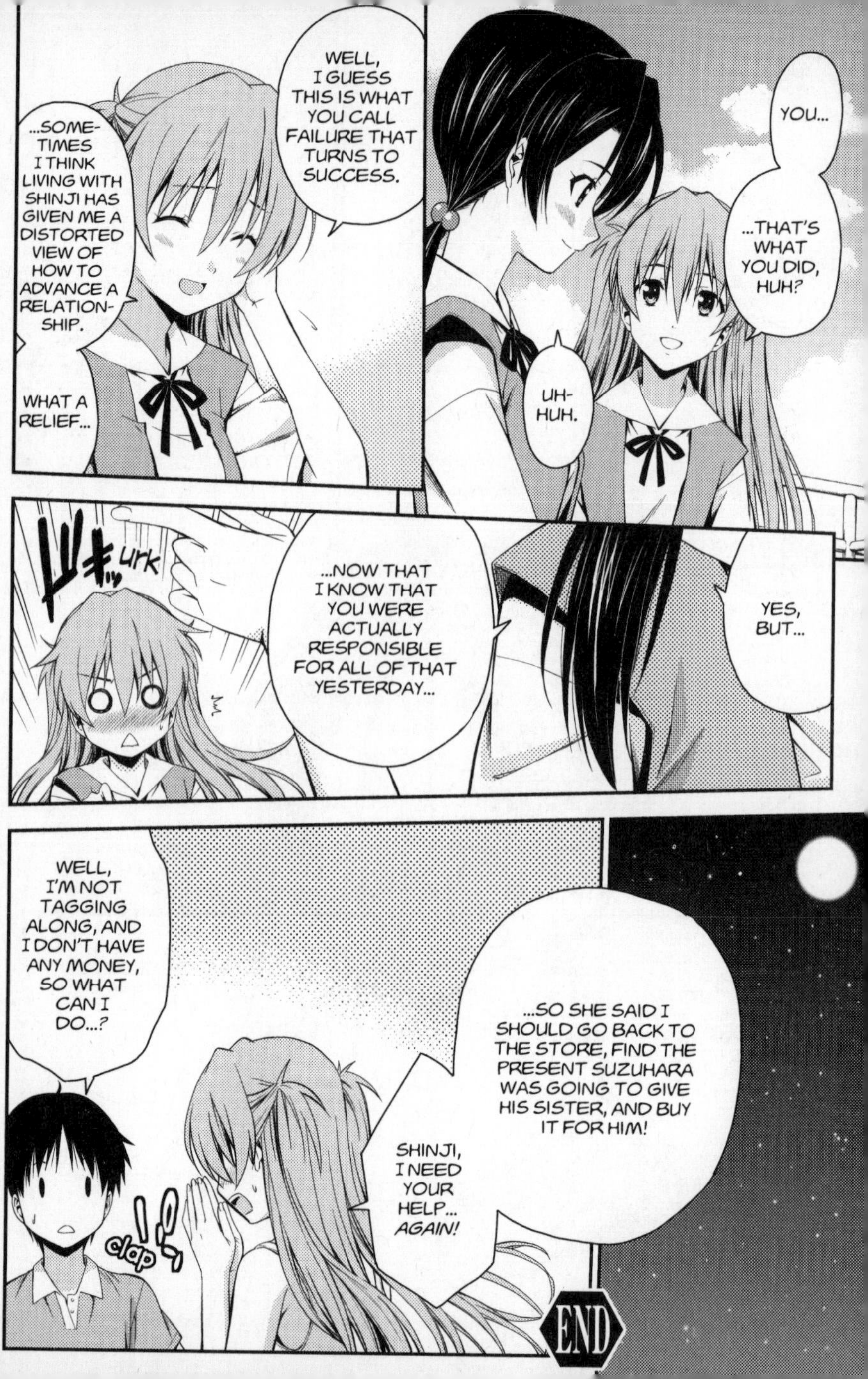
YOU...
...THAT'S WHAT YOU DID, HUH?
UH-HUH.
WELL, I GUESS THIS IS WHAT YOU CALL FAILURE THAT TURNS TO SUCCESS.
...SOME-TIMES I THINK LIVING WITH SHINJI HAS GIVEN ME A DISTORTED VIEW OF HOW TO ADVANCE A RELATION-SHIP.
WHAT A RELIEF...
YES, BUT...
...NOW THAT I KNOW THAT YOU WERE ACTUALLY RESPONSIBLE FOR ALL OF THAT YESTERDAY...
urk
...SO SHE SAID I SHOULD GO BACK TO THE STORE, FIND THE PRESENT SUZUHARA WAS GOING TO GIVE HIS SISTER, AND BUY IT FOR HIM!
WELL, I'M NOT TAGGING ALONG, AND I DON'T HAVE ANY MONEY, SO WHAT CAN I DO...?
SHINJI, I NEED YOUR HELP... *AGAIN!*
clap
END

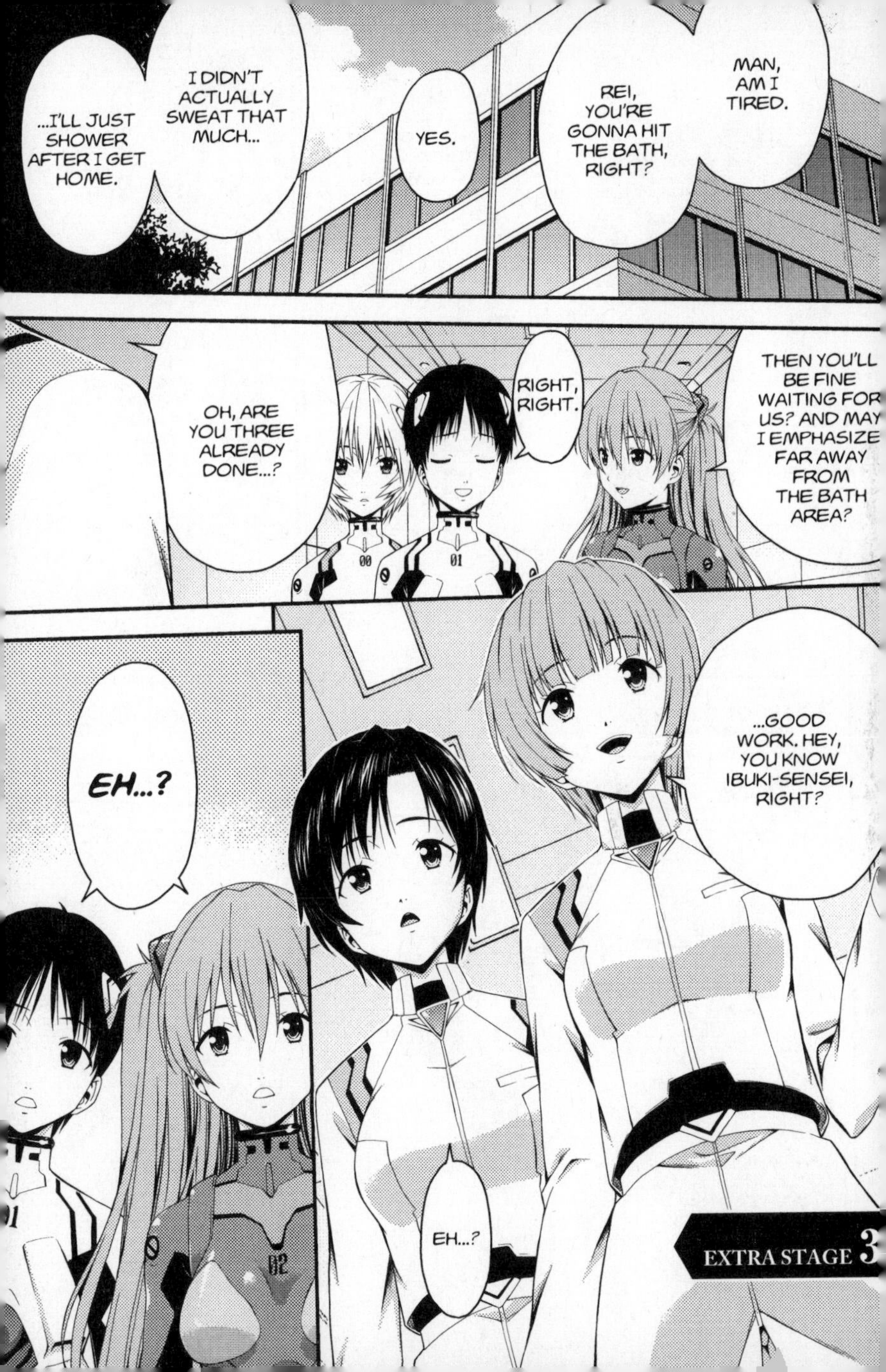
MAN, AM I TIRED.
REI, YOU'RE GONNA HIT THE BATH, RIGHT?
YES.
I DIDN'T ACTUALLY SWEAT THAT MUCH...
...I'LL JUST SHOWER AFTER I GET HOME.
THEN YOU'LL BE FINE WAITING FOR US? AND MAY I EMPHASIZE FAR AWAY FROM THE BATH AREA?
RIGHT, RIGHT.
OH, ARE YOU THREE ALREADY DONE...?
...GOOD WORK. HEY, YOU KNOW IBUKI-SENSEI, RIGHT?
EXTRA STAGE 3
EH...?
EH...?

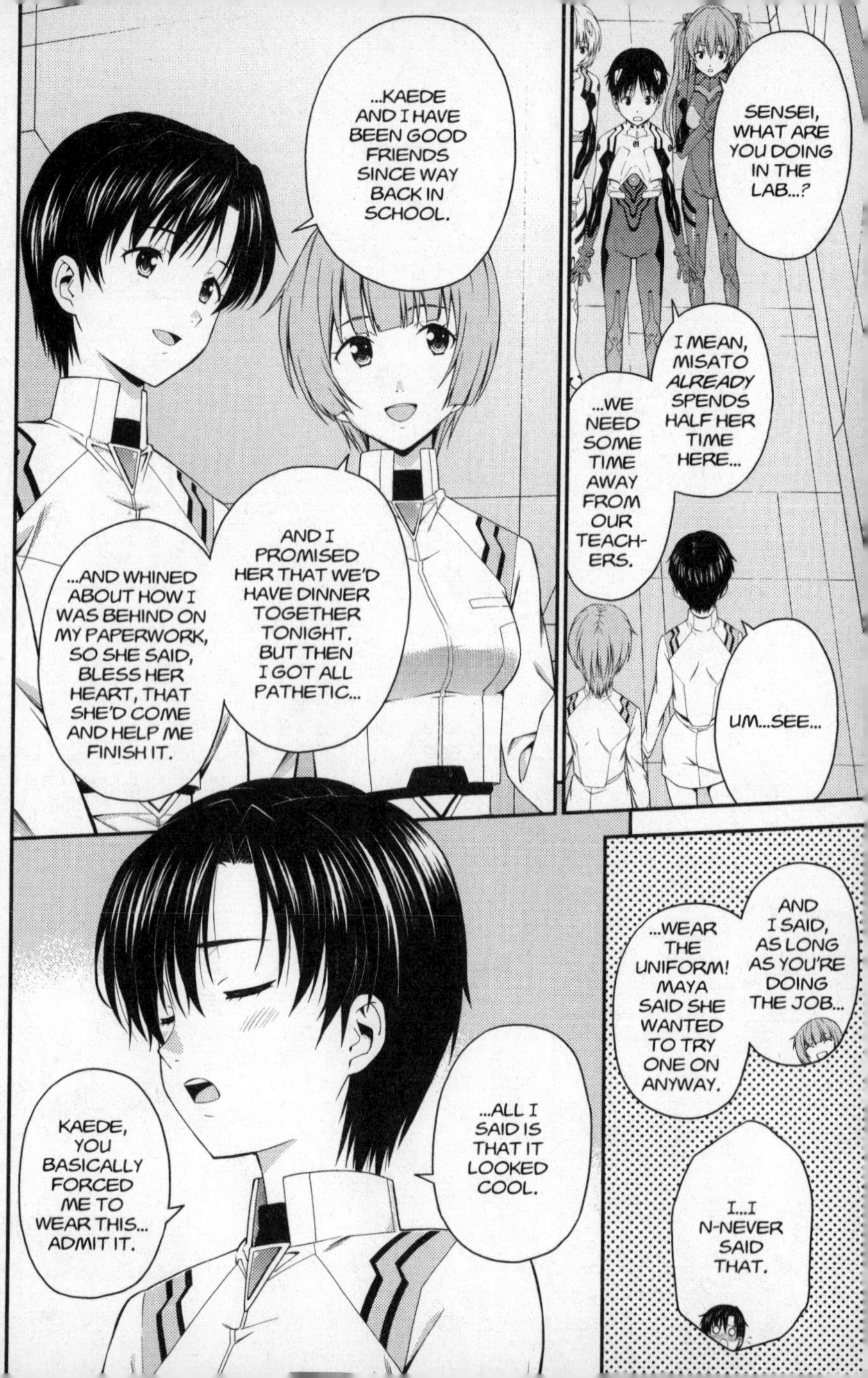
SENSEI, WHAT ARE YOU DOING IN THE LAB...?
I MEAN, MISATO ALREADY SPENDS HALF HER TIME HERE...
...WE NEED SOME TIME AWAY FROM OUR TEACH-ERS.
UM...SEE...
...KAEDE AND I HAVE BEEN GOOD FRIENDS SINCE WAY BACK IN SCHOOL.
AND I PROMISED HER THAT WE'D HAVE DINNER TOGETHER TONIGHT. BUT THEN I GOT ALL PATHETIC...
...AND WHINED ABOUT HOW I WAS BEHIND ON MY PAPERWORK, SO SHE SAID, BLESS HER HEART, THAT SHE'D COME AND HELP ME FINISH IT.
AND I SAID, AS LONG AS YOU'RE DOING THE JOB...
...WEAR THE UNIFORM! MAYA SAID SHE WANTED TO TRY ONE ON ANYWAY.
I...I N-NEVER SAID THAT.
...ALL I SAID IS THAT IT LOOKED COOL.
KAEDE, YOU BASICALLY FORCED ME TO WEAR THIS... ADMIT IT.

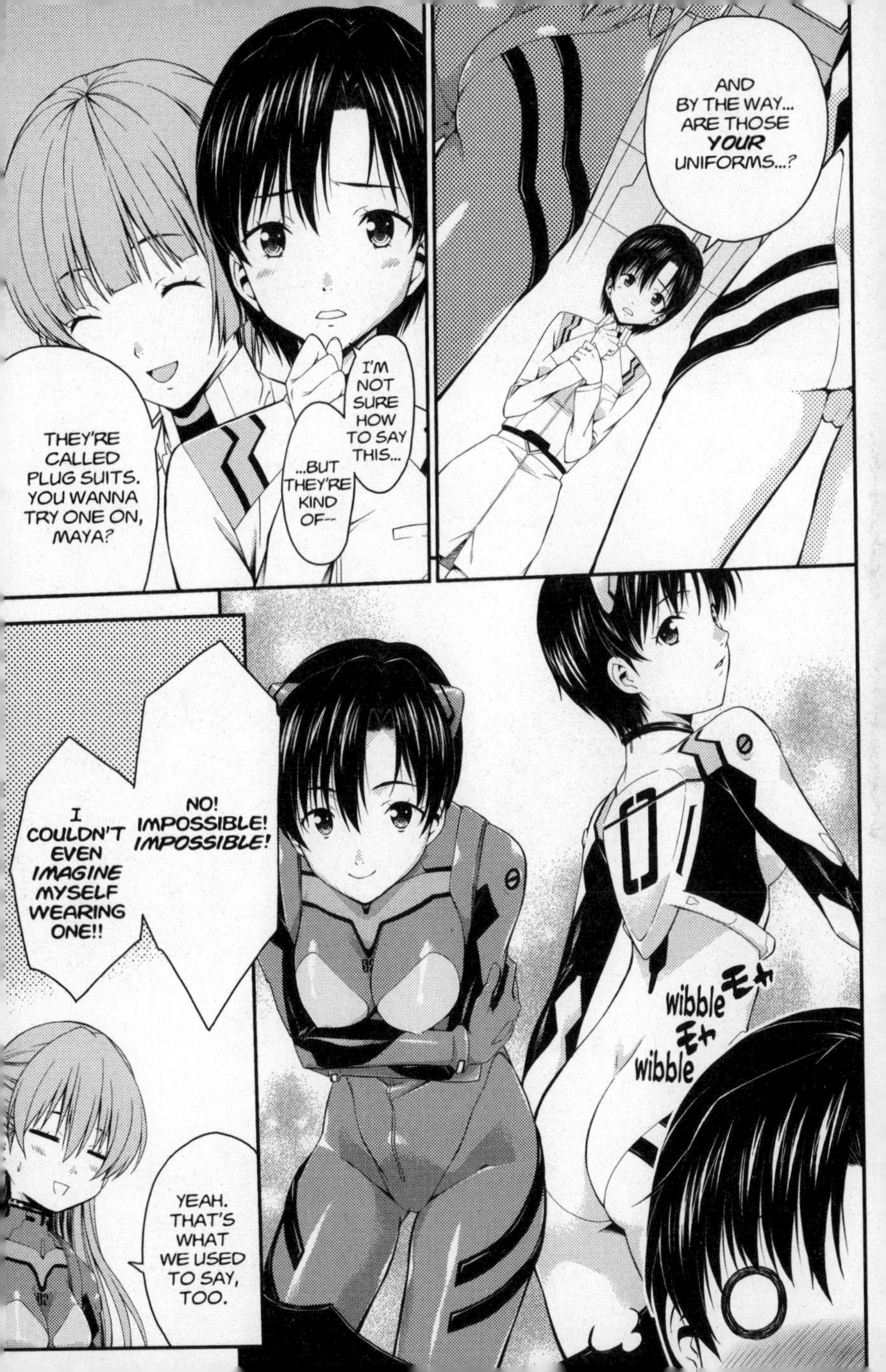
AND BY THE WAY... ARE THOSE YOUR UNIFORMS...?
I'M NOT SURE HOW TO SAY THIS...
...BUT THEY'RE KIND OF--
THEY'RE CALLED PLUG SUITS. YOU WANNA TRY ONE ON, MAYA?
wibble モャ
モャ wibble
NO! IMPOSSIBLE! IMPOSSIBLE!
I COULDN'T EVEN IMAGINE MYSELF WEARING ONE!!
YEAH. THAT'S WHAT WE USED TO SAY, TOO.

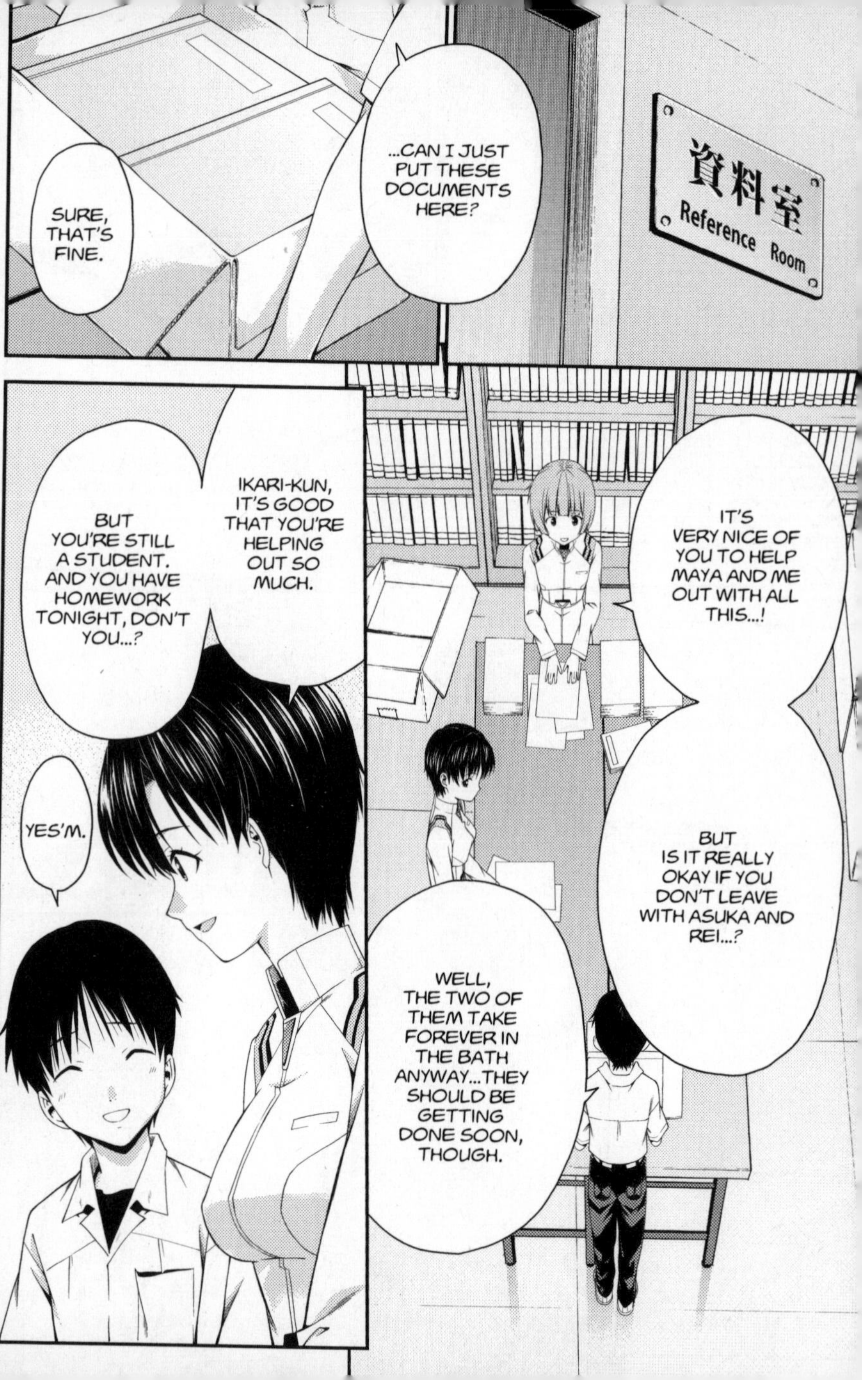
資料室
Reference Room
...CAN I JUST PUT THESE DOCUMENTS HERE?
SURE, THAT'S FINE.
IT'S VERY NICE OF YOU TO HELP MAYA AND ME OUT WITH ALL THIS...!
BUT IS IT REALLY OKAY IF YOU DON'T LEAVE WITH ASUKA AND REI...?
WELL, THE TWO OF THEM TAKE FOREVER IN THE BATH ANYWAY...THEY SHOULD BE GETTING DONE SOON, THOUGH.
IKARI-KUN, IT'S GOOD THAT YOU'RE HELPING OUT SO MUCH.
BUT YOU'RE STILL A STUDENT. AND YOU HAVE HOMEWORK TONIGHT, DON'T YOU...?
YES'M.

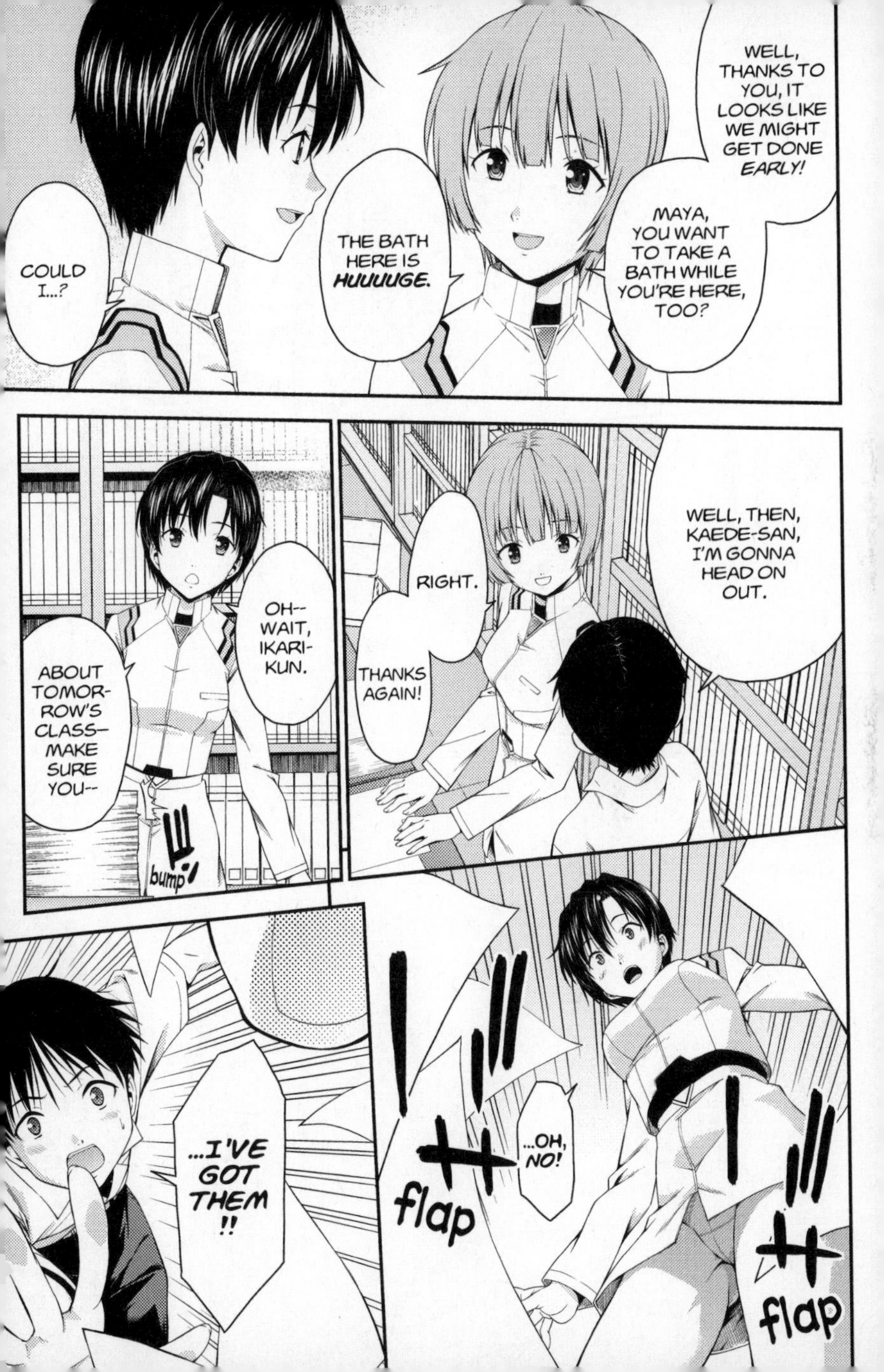
WELL, THANKS TO YOU, IT LOOKS LIKE WE MIGHT GET DONE *EARLY!*
MAYA, YOU WANT TO TAKE A BATH WHILE YOU'RE HERE, TOO?
THE BATH HERE IS **HUUUUGE.**
COULD I...?
WELL, THEN, KAEDE-SAN, I'M GONNA HEAD ON OUT.
RIGHT.
THANKS AGAIN!
OH-- WAIT, IKARI-KUN.
ABOUT TOMOR-ROW'S CLASS— MAKE SURE YOU--
bump
flap
...OH, NO!
flap
...I'VE GOT THEM !!

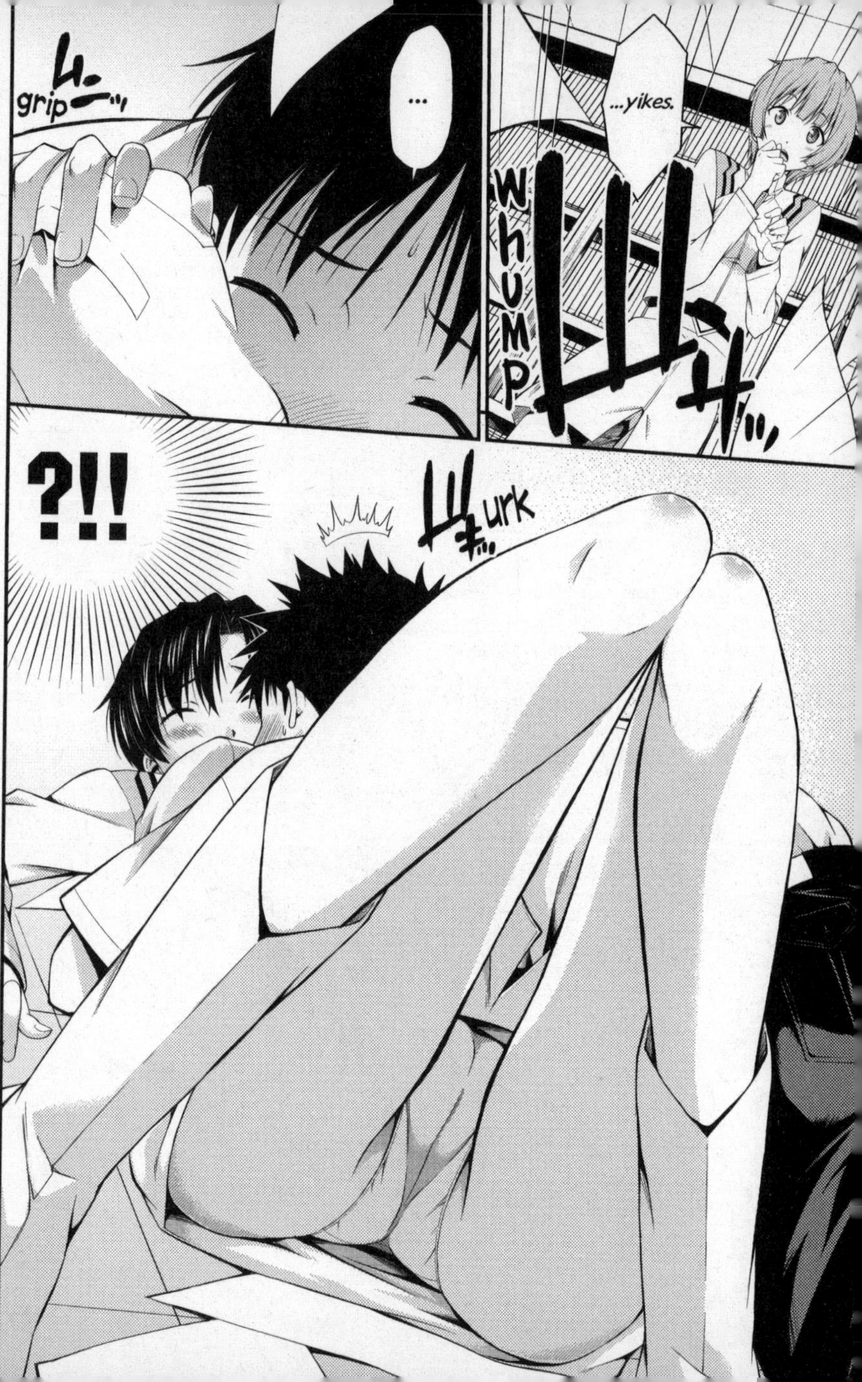
...yikes.
WHUMP
...
grip
?!!
urk

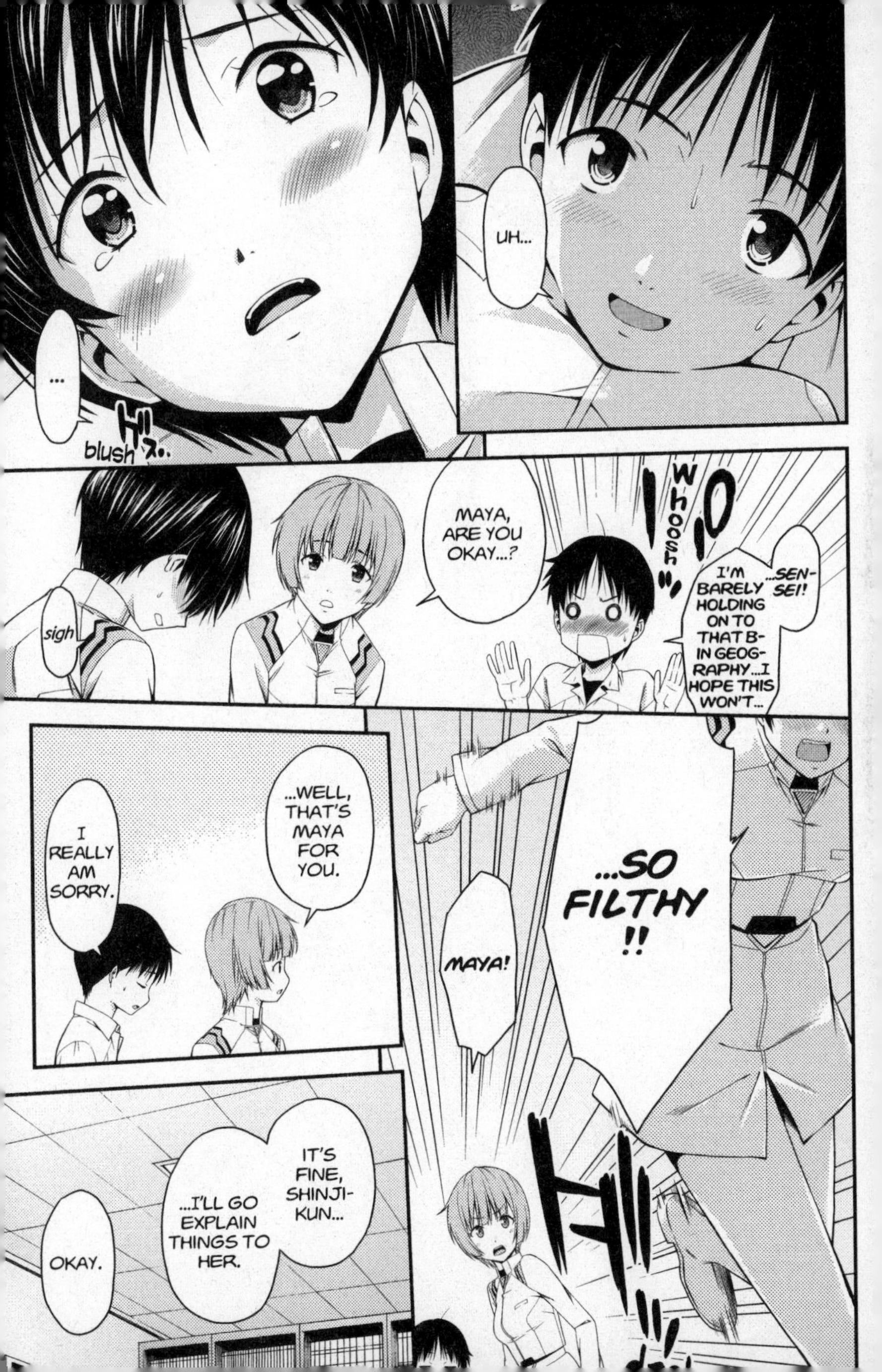
UH...
...
blush
...SEN-SEI!
I'M BARELY HOLDING ON TO THAT B- IN GEOGRAPHY...I HOPE THIS WON'T...
Whoosh
MAYA, ARE YOU OKAY...?
sigh
...SO FILTHY!!
MAYA!
...WELL, THAT'S MAYA FOR YOU.
I REALLY AM SORRY.
IT'S FINE, SHINJI-KUN...
...I'LL GO EXPLAIN THINGS TO HER.
OKAY.

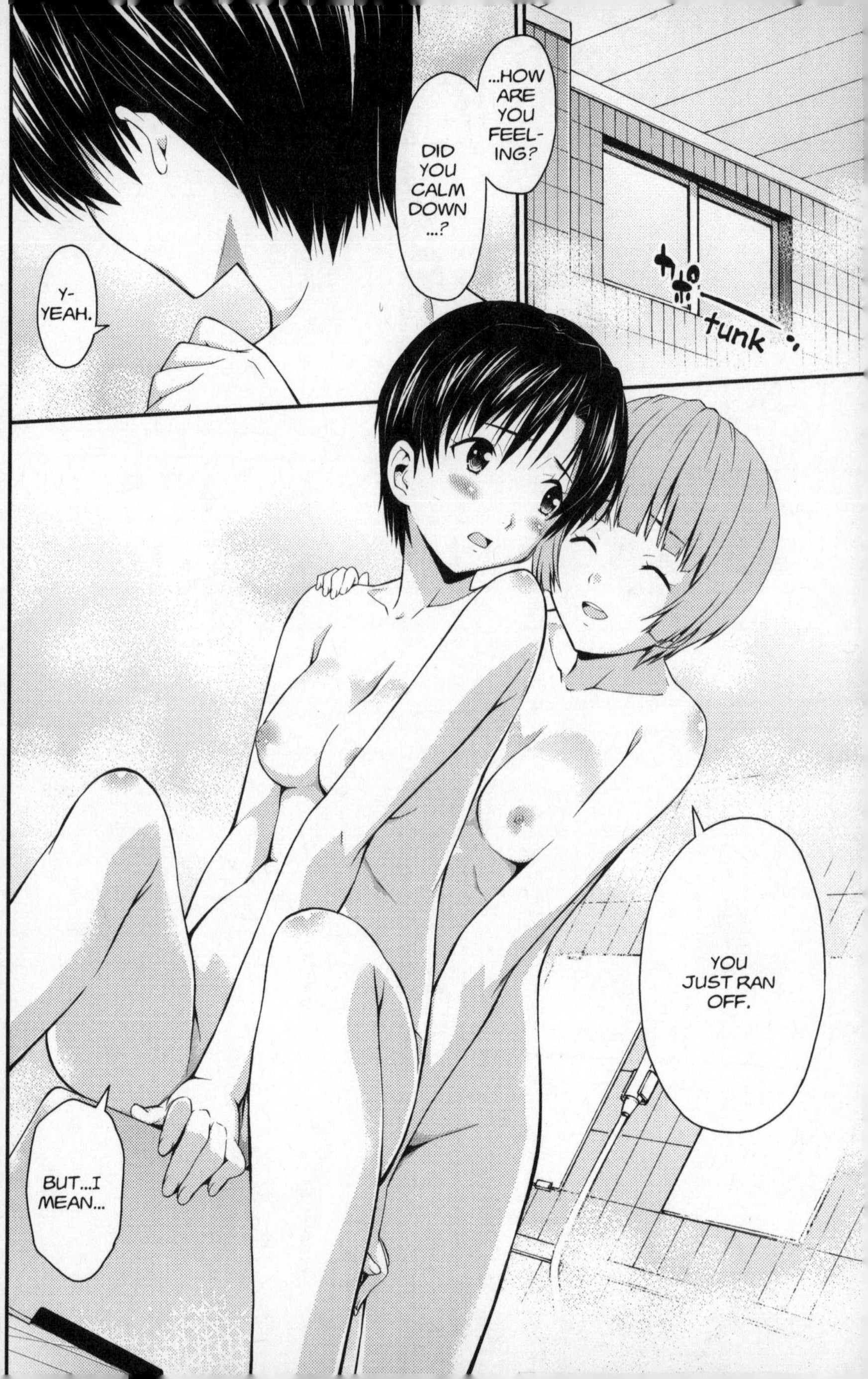
...HOW ARE YOU FEEL-ING?
DID YOU CALM DOWN ...?
tunk
Y-YEAH.
YOU JUST RAN OFF.
BUT...I MEAN...

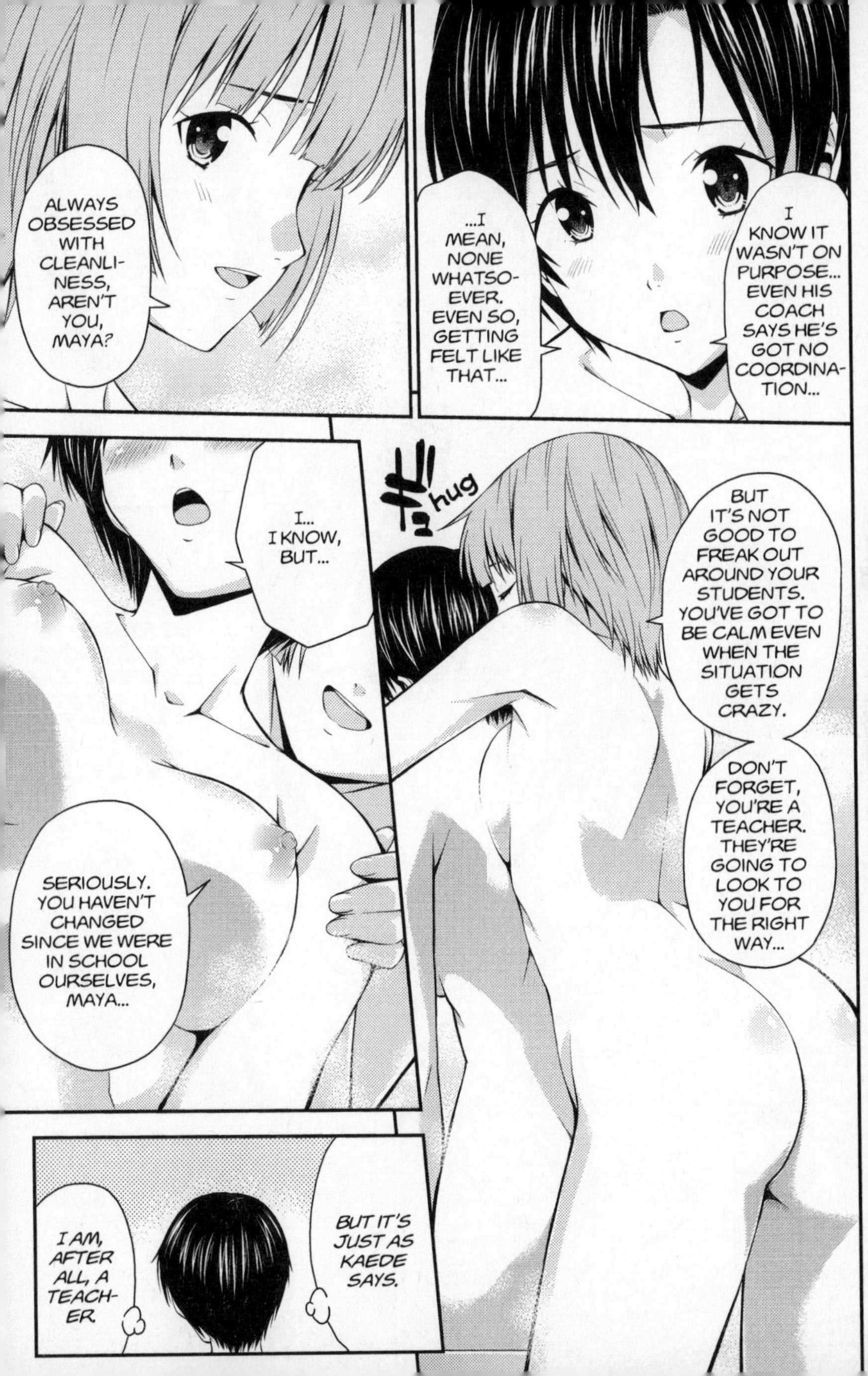
I KNOW IT WASN'T ON PURPOSE... EVEN HIS COACH SAYS HE'S GOT NO COORDINATION...
...I MEAN, NONE WHATSOEVER. EVEN SO, GETTING FELT LIKE THAT...
ALWAYS OBSESSED WITH CLEANLINESS, AREN'T YOU, MAYA?
hug
BUT IT'S NOT GOOD TO FREAK OUT AROUND YOUR STUDENTS. YOU'VE GOT TO BE CALM EVEN WHEN THE SITUATION GETS CRAZY.
DON'T FORGET, YOU'RE A TEACHER. THEY'RE GOING TO LOOK TO YOU FOR THE RIGHT WAY...
I... I KNOW, BUT...
SERIOUSLY. YOU HAVEN'T CHANGED SINCE WE WERE IN SCHOOL OURSELVES, MAYA...
BUT IT'S JUST AS KAEDE SAYS.
I AM, AFTER ALL, A TEACHER.

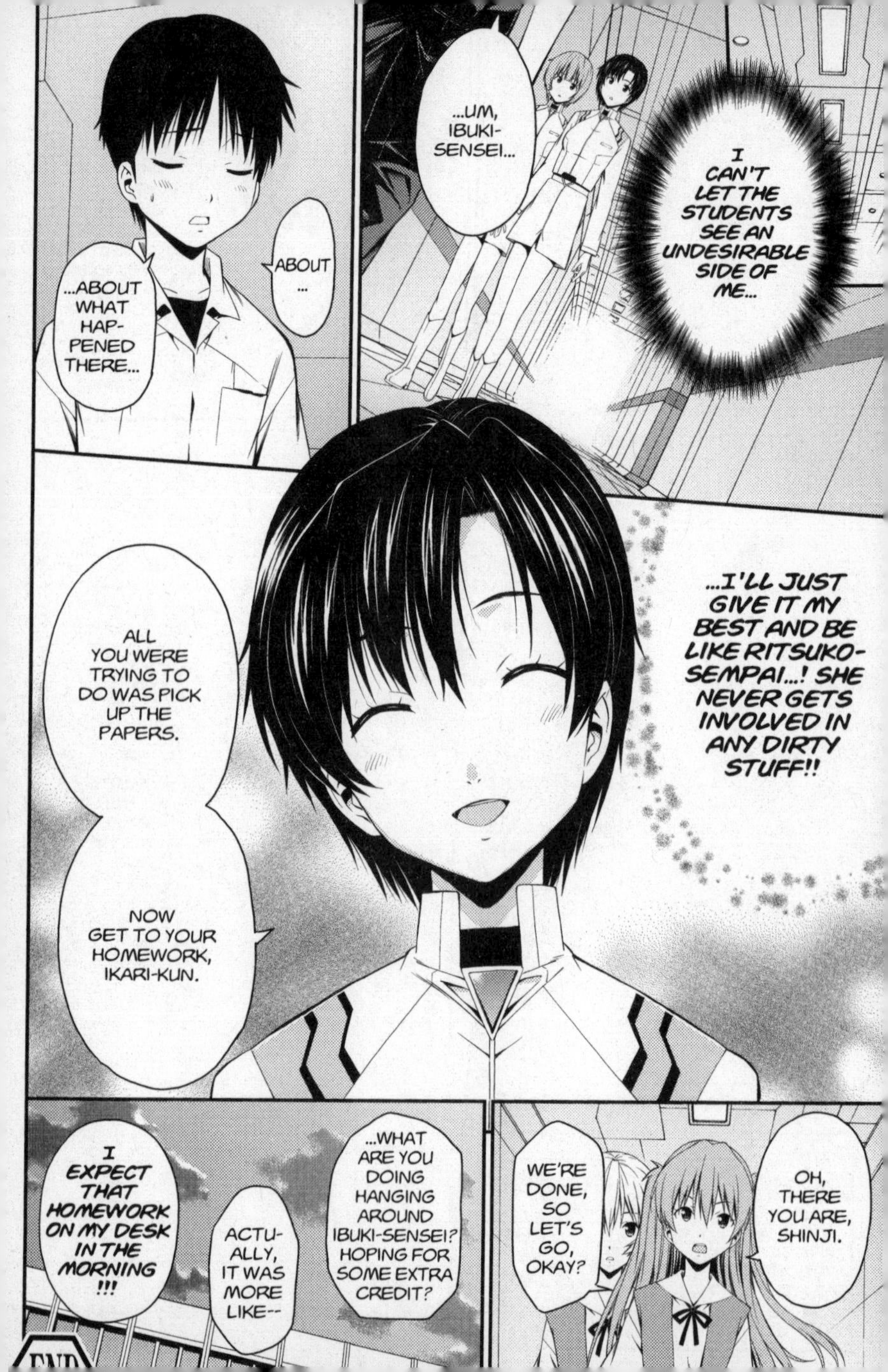
I CAN'T LET THE STUDENTS SEE AN UNDESIRABLE SIDE OF ME...
...UM, IBUKI-SENSEI...
ABOUT...
...ABOUT WHAT HAP-PENED THERE...
...I'LL JUST GIVE IT MY BEST AND BE LIKE RITSUKO-SEMPAI...! SHE NEVER GETS INVOLVED IN ANY DIRTY STUFF!!
ALL YOU WERE TRYING TO DO WAS PICK UP THE PAPERS.
NOW GET TO YOUR HOMEWORK, IKARI-KUN.
OH, THERE YOU ARE, SHINJI.
WE'RE DONE, SO LET'S GO, OKAY?
...WHAT ARE YOU DOING HANGING AROUND IBUKI-SENSEI? HOPING FOR SOME EXTRA CREDIT?
ACTU-ALLY, IT WAS MORE LIKE--
I EXPECT THAT HOMEWORK ON MY DESK IN THE MORNING!!!
END

AFTERWORD

In this particular volume (compared to previous ones) it's come to be that the so-called "supporting roles" tend to have the spotlight upon them. I guess this stuff just happens, sometimes, doesn't it.

-Osamu Takahashi

~STAFF~

Miki

Atsuhito Sakurai

and many others

COVER DESIGN

Seki Shindo

see you in vol. 16...

EDITOR
CARL GUSTAV HORN

DESIGNER
KAT LARSON

PUBLISHER
MIKE RICHARDSON

English-language version produced by Dark Horse Comics

Neon Genesis Evangelion: The Shinji Ikari Raising Project Vol. 15

st published in Japan as NEON GENESIS EVANGELION IKARI-SHINJI IKUSEI KEIKAKU Volume 15. © khara. Edited by KADOKAWA SHOTEN. First blished in Japan in 2013 by KADOKAWA CORPORATION, Tokyo. English translation rights arranged with KADOKAWA CORPORATION, Tokyo, through HAN CORPORATION, Tokyo. This English-language edition © 2014 by Dark Horse Comics, Inc. All other material © 2014 by Dark Horse Comics, Inc.

Published by
Dark Horse Manga
A division of Dark Horse Comics, Inc.
10956 SE Main Street
Milwaukie, OR 97222

DarkHorse.com

To find a comics shop in your area, call the Comic Shop Locator Service toll-free at 1-888-266-4226

First edition: December 2014
ISBN 978-1-61655-607-5

1 3 5 7 9 10 8 6 4 2
Printed in the United States of America

MiSATO'S FAN SERVICE CENTER

c/o Dark Horse Comics • 10956 SE Main Street • Milwaukie, OR 97222 • evangelion@darkhorse.com

DID YOU GET THE CHANCE TO SEE DARK HORSE AT ANIME EXPO LAST JULY? I'm guessing there's a good chance you did, because 80,000 people showed up at the con, and there must have been at least 300 of them at our *Neon Genesis Evangelion* panel! I have to thank everyone who attended, and also Aaron Clark of EvaGeeks.org, who arranged for our guest hosts on the panel, Rocco and Garrett of Mega64.

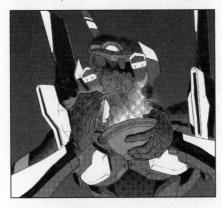

And, oh yeah! We announced that we're going to release a new *Evangelion* manga! You know the writer and artist: Tony Takezaki, from the stories he did in *Neon Genesis Evangelion: Comic Tribute* (Sgt. Frog as Kaworu, Shinji discovers the Reiquarium, etc.). Now we're going to publish an entire book of **all-new** *Eva* parody stories by Tony Takezaki, entitled, as you might guess, ***Tony Takezaki's Neon Genesis Evangelion***. SEE! The opening credits of *Evangelion* redone as a cooking show! SEE! Shinji and Kaworu's stand-up comedy routine! SEE! Ritsuko's student-intern days at NERV! SEE! A physical act George Carlin once discussed, yet I have

never seen depicted in a manga . . . UNTIL NOW! Look for ***Tony Takezaki's Neon Genesis Evangelion*** **in stores May 20, 2015!**

But enough about us (for a moment ^_^). Let's get to one of your letters:

Dear MFSC,

I'm a huge *Neon Genesis Evangelion* fan, and I'm especially a fan of the *Shinji Ikari Raising Project* manga that Dark Horse has been putting out. It's been a very enjoyable read from volume to volume. I just recently finished volume 14 and I already can't wait to read volume 15 whenever it becomes available.

But what I'm really writing to you about today is what my fandom has caused me and a few colleagues to do. See, I help moderate an *Evangelion*-centric website and forum that a few of us fans started. It's called RebuildOfEvangelion.org. We are still in our infancy, having only started a few months prior to this letter, but we are gaining ground every day. We have devoted ourselves to discussing all the wonderful anime, merchandise, and of course, manga that *Evangelion* has given us. In addition to that, a few of our members, including me, have recently started an *Evangelion* podcast. It's called *The Dummy Plug Podcast* and it is (to our knowledge) the first and only *Evangelion*- based podcast in North America. We recently put our episodes on the RebuildOfEvangelion. org website and even got on iTunes. Fans can subscribe to the podcast or download episodes absolutely FREE! Hopefully, this letter will make it into the next Misato Fan Service Center so that all the great *Evangelio* out about it, and come and chat about it with us. Heck, perhaps someday we'll get to interview some of your editing staff and talk about *The Shinji Ikari Raising Project* on a future podcast!

Sincerely,
George Gaynor, a.k.a. Gaynor79
Co-Host of *The Dummy Plug Podcast*

Thank you for your letter, George! By the way, one person who definitely was there at Anime Expo–we have photographic proof—is Major Katsuragi (we'll go by TV show ranks here). And who could be a more appropriate person to hang out in Misato's Fan Service Center than Misato herself? This fan was nice enough to come by Dark Horse's booth, and, as you can see, she's even holding up an MFSC card. She's reminding you all to write in!

—CGH

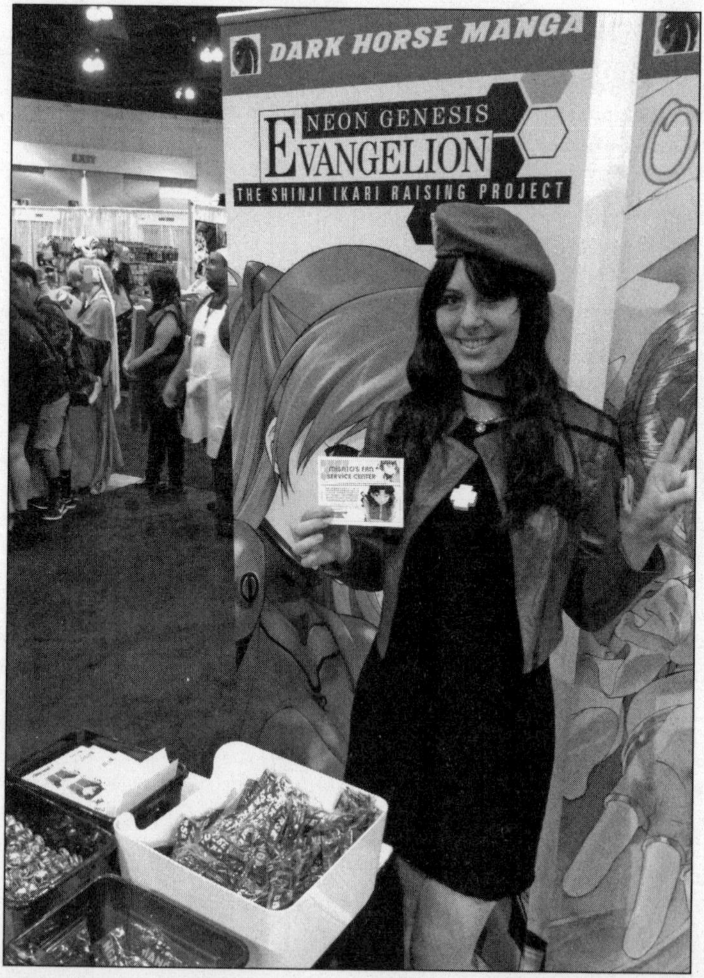
DARK HORSE MANGA
NEON GENESIS
EVANGELION
THE SHINJI IKARI RAISING PROJECT

NEON GENESIS EVANGELION

Dark Horse Manga is proud to present new original series based on the wildly popular *Neon Genesis Evangelion* manga and anime! Continuing the rich story lines and complex characters, these new visions of *Neon Genesis Evangelion* provide extra dimensions for understanding one of the greatest series ever made!

NEON GENESIS EVANGELION Campus Apocalypse

STORY AND ART BY MINGMING

VOLUME 1
ISBN 978-1-59582-530-8 | $10.99

VOLUME 2
ISBN 978-1-59582-661-9 | $10.99

VOLUME 3
ISBN 978-1-59582-680-0 | $10.99

VOLUME 4
ISBN 978-1-59582-689-3 | $10.99

NEON GENESIS EVANGELION COMIC TRIBUTE

STORY AND ART BY VARIOUS CREATORS

ISBN 978-1-61655-114-8 | $10.99

NEON GENESIS EVANGELION THE Shinji Ikari Detective Diary

STORY AND ART BY TAKUMI YOSHIMURA

VOLUME 1
ISBN 978-1-61655-225-1 | $9.99

VOLUME 2
ISBN 978-1-61655-418-7 | $9.99

NEON GENESIS EVANGELION THE SHINJI IKARI RAISING PROJECT

STORY AND ART BY OSAMU TAKAHASHI

VOLUME 1
ISBN 978-1-59582-321-2 | $9.99

VOLUME 2
ISBN 978-1-59582-377-9 | $9.99

VOLUME 3
ISBN 978-1-59582-447-9 | $9.99

VOLUME 4
ISBN 978-1-59582-454-7 | $9.99

VOLUME 5
ISBN 978-1-59582-520-9 | $9.99

VOLUME 6
ISBN 978-1-59582-580-3 | $9.99

VOLUME 7
ISBN 978-1-59582-595-7 | $9.99

VOLUME 8
ISBN 978-1-59582-694-7 | $9.99

VOLUME 9
ISBN 978-1-59582-800-2 | $9.99

VOLUME 10
ISBN 978-1-59582-879-8 | $9.99

VOLUME 11
ISBN 978-1-59582-932-0 | $9.99

VOLUME 12
ISBN 978-1-61655-033-2 | $9.99

VOLUME 13
ISBN 978-1-61655-315-9 | $9.99

VOLUME 14
ISBN 978-1-61655-432-3 | $9.99

Each volume of *Neon Genesis Evangelion* features bonus color pages, your *Evangelion* fan art and letters, and special reader giveaways!

DARK HORSE MANGA

DarkHorse.com

AVAILABLE AT YOUR LOCAL COMICS SHOP OR BOOKSTORE
To find a comics shop in your area, call 1-888-266-4226 • For more information or to order direct: • On the web: darkhorse.com
E-mail: mailorder@darkhorse.com • Phone: 1-800-862-0052 Mon.–Fri. 9 AM to 5 PM Pacific Time.

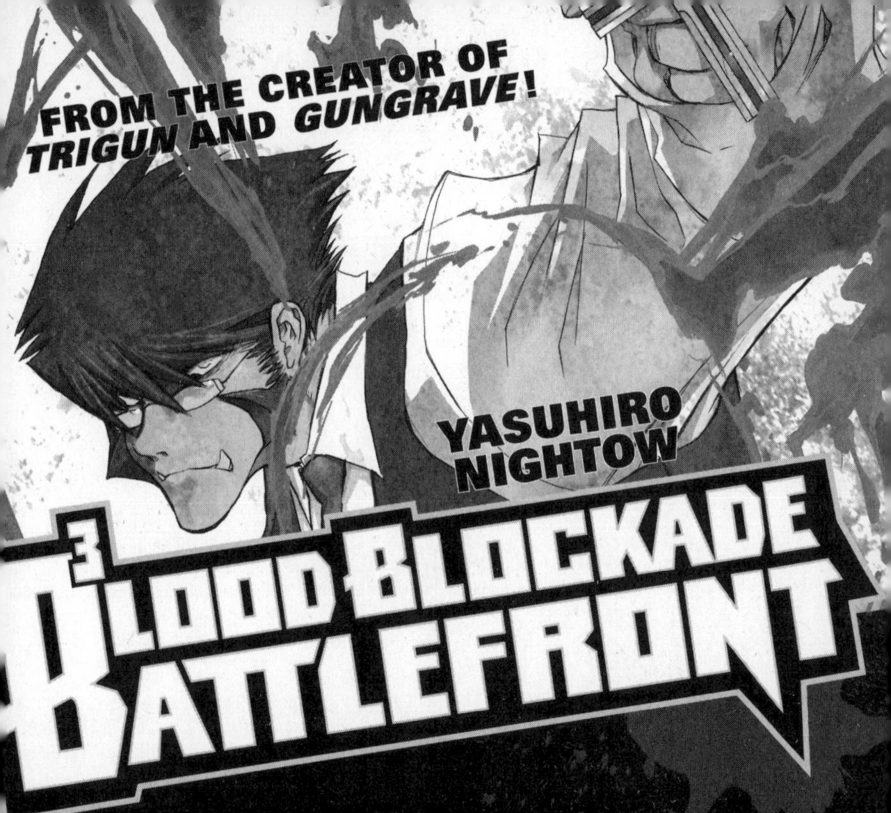
FROM THE CREATOR OF TRIGUN AND GUNGRAVE!
YASUHIRO NIGHTOW
3
BLOOD BLOCKADE BATTLEFRONT

Three years ago, a gateway between Earth and the Beyond opened over New York City. In one terrible night, New York was destroyed and rebuilt, trapping New Yorkers and extradimensional creatures alike in an impenetrable bubble. New York is now Jerusalem's Lot, a paranormal melting pot where magic and madness dwell alongside the mundane, where human vermin gather to exploit otherworldly assets for earthly profit. Now someone is threatening to breach the bubble and release New Jerusalem's horrors, but the mysterious superagents of Libra fight to prevent the unthinkable.

Trigun creator Yasuhiro Nightow returns with *Blood Blockade Battlefront*, an action-packed supernatural science-fiction steamroller as only Nightow can conjure.

VOLUME ONE
ISBN 978-1-59582-718-0 | $10.99

VOLUME TWO
ISBN 978-1-59582-912-2 | $10.99

VOLUME THREE
ISBN 978-1-59582-913-9 | $10.99

VOLUME FOUR
ISBN 978-1-61655-223-7 | $12.99

VOLUME FIVE
ISBN 978-1-61655-224-4 | $12.99

VOLUME SIX
ISBN 978-1-61655-557-3 | $12.99

AVAILABLE AT YOUR LOCAL COMICS SHOP OR BOOKSTORE To find a comics shop in your area, call 1-888-266-4226 For more information or to order direct: • On the web: DarkHorse.com
E-mail: mailorder@darkhorse.com • Phone: 1-800-862-0052 Mon.–Fri. 9 AM to 5 PM Pacific Time.

DRIFTERS

KOHTA HIRANO

Heroes from Earth's history are deposited in an enchanted land where humans subjugate the nonhuman races. This wild, action-packed series features historical characters such as Joan of Arc, Hannibal, and Rasputin being used as chess pieces in a bloody, endless battle!

From Kohta Hirano, creator of the smash-hit *Hellsing*, *Drifters* is an all-out fantasy slugfest of epic proportion!

VOLUME ONE	**VOLUME TWO**	**VOLUME THREE**
978-1-59582-769-2	978-1-59582-933-7	978-1-61655-339-5

$12.99 each

**AVAILABLE AT YOUR LOCAL COMICS SHOP OR BOOKSTORE
TO FIND A COMICS SHOP IN YOUR AREA, CALL 1-888-266-4226**

For more information or to order direct: On the web: DarkHorse.com · E-mail: mailorder@darkhorse.com
· Phone: 1-800-862-0052 Mon.–Fri. 9 AM to 5 PM Pacific Time.

**DARK
HORSE
MANGA**

STOP!

止 ま れ

THIS IS THE BACK OF THE BOOK!

This manga collection is translated into English, but arranged in right-to-left reading format to maintain the artwork's visual orientation as originally drawn and published in Japan. If you've never read comics this way before, take a look at the diagram below to give yourself an idea of how to go about it. Basically, you'll be starting in the upper-right-hand corner, and will read each word balloon and panel moving right to left. It may take a little getting used to, but you should get the hang of it very quickly. Have fun! If this is the millionth manga you've read this way, never mind.

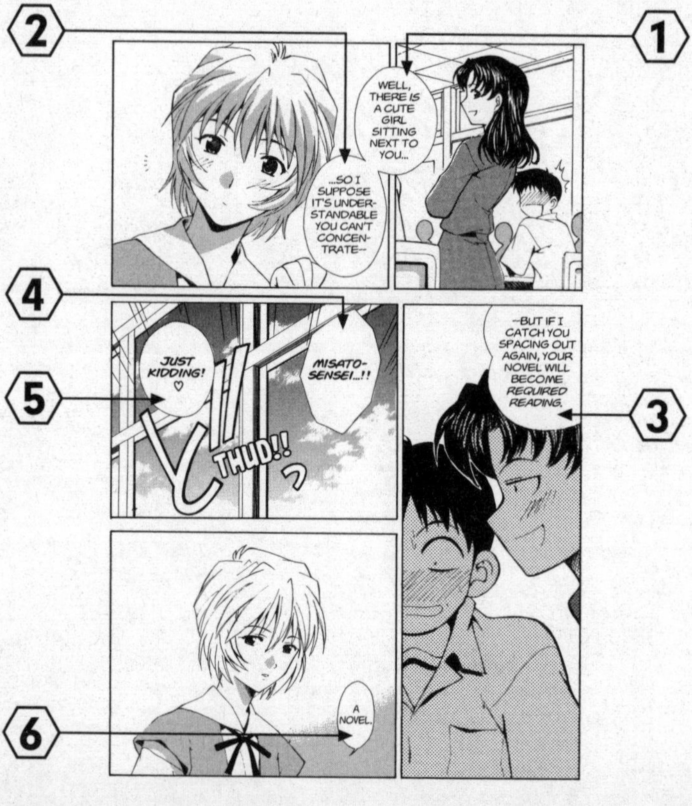
1
WELL, THERE IS A CUTE GIRL SITTING NEXT TO YOU...
2
...SO I SUPPOSE IT'S UNDER-STANDABLE YOU CAN'T CONCEN-TRATE--
3
--BUT IF I CATCH YOU SPACING OUT AGAIN, YOUR NOVEL WILL BECOME REQUIRED READING.
4
MISATO-SENSEI...!!
5
JUST KIDDING! ♡
THUD!!
6
A NOVEL.